AMERICA: THE NEW IMPERIALISM

In memory of Bertha Macintosh and for her family

Other Books by V.G. Kiernan

British Diplomacy in China, 1880 to 1885 (1939)

Metcalfe's Mission to Lahore, 1808–1809 (1943)

Poems from Iqbal (1947)

Poems by Faiz Ahmed Faiz (1958)

The Revolution of 1854 in Spanish History (1970)

The Lords of Human Kind: European Attitudes to the Outside World (1969)

Marxism and Imperialism (1974)

AMERICA: THE NEW IMPERIALISM

FROM WHITE SETTLEMENT TO WORLD HEGEMONY

◆

V.G. KIERNAN

V E R S O

London · New York

This edition first published by Verso 2005
Original edition published by Zed Press 1978

© V.G. Kiernan 2005
Preface © Eric Hobsbawm 2005
Epilogue © John Trumpbour 2005

1 3 5 7 9 10 8 6 4 2

Verso
UK: 6 Meard Street, London W1F 0EG
USA: 180 Varick Street, New York, NY 10014-4606
www.versobooks.com

Verso is the imprint of New Left Books

ISBN 1-84467-522-X

British Library Cataloguing in Publication Data
Kiernan, V. G. (Victor Gordon), 1913–
    America: the new imperialism: from white settlement to world hege-
mony
    1. Imperialism 2. United States–Territorial expansion–History
3. United States–Foreign relations.
    I. Title.
        325.3′2′0973

ISBN 184467522X

Library of Congress Cataloging-in-Publication Data
A catalog record for this book is available from the Library of Congress

Typeset in Garamond and Swiss by YHT Ltd, London
Printed in the USA by R.R. Donnelley & Sons

Contents

Preface *by Eric Hobsbawm*   vii

Foreword   xv

PART ONE: THE WINNING OF THE NATIONAL TERRITORY

1. The Birth of a Nation   3
2. The Pursuit of Happiness   15
3. White Man and Red Man   29

PART TWO: MIDDLE DECADES

1. The Literary Mirror   49
2. From West Indies to Far East   57
3. Civil War and After   71
4. The Last Indian Wars   79

PART THREE: OVERSEAS EXPANSION AND THE WAR WITH SPAIN

1. The Red Man in Custody   97
2. New Visions of Empire   105
3. Latin America and Further Asia   117

4. Anglo-Saxons and their Wars   127

PART FOUR: IMPERIAL CHOICES FOR A NEW CENTURY
1. The Progressivist Era   147
2. The Philippines Experiment, and Direct or Indirect Rule   153
3. Dollar Diplomacy in Central America   165
4. Old World Frustrations, and Ideas of a New World Order   177

PART FIVE: TWO STRIDES TO WORLD POWER
1. Great War and not so great Peace   197
2. Victory and After: the Mirror of Science Fiction   209
3. America, the World's Banker   217
4. Slump Years, and a New Look at the Red Indian   233
5. From Isolationism to Conquest   239

PART SIX: THE AMERICAN HEGEMONY
1. Capitalism, Militarism and the Cold War   265
2. The Old Empires and Neo-Colonialism   283
3. War in Vietnam and its Repercussions   295
4. The Middle East and Africa   309
5. Latin America   319
6. Retrospect and Prospect   333

Epilogue *by John Trumpbour*   363

Bibliography   405

Index   421

Preface
Eric Hobsbawm

Probably no historian has published on a wider range of subjects and periods than Victor Kiernan. Who else has written with comparable expert knowledge about the ancient Roman poet Horace, 20th-century Urdu poets (whom he translated) and Wordsworth, on early modern Europe and England in the era of the French Revolution, together with books about Shakespeare, duelling, tobacco and the Spanish Revolution of 1854? In the *Dictionary of Marxist Thought*, which he co-edited, he was personally responsible for the articles on Agnosticism, Christianity, Empires in Marx's day, Hinduism, Historiography, Intellectuals, Paul Lafargue, Ferdinand Lassalle, Nation, Nationalism, Religion, Revolution, M.N. Roy, Stages of Development and War. And this in addition to the work on imperialism and empires by which he is probably best known: notably *European Empires from Conquest to Collapse* and – my personal favourite – the marvellous *The Lords of Human Kind: Black Man, Yellow Man and White Man in the Age of Empire*. But even in this field he writes as a man of universal knowledge, and drawing on his lifetime study of empires and imperialism.

For Kiernan it began in the Cambridge of the 1930s, with a brilliant career in history (a double starred first, a Fellowship at Trinity, a book on *British Diplomacy in China 1880–1885*) and, from 1934, membership of the Communist Party. All Communists were strongly anti-imperialist, but even then Victor specialized in this field, for he looked after the 'colonial group' of students from what was then the British Empire – who were not technically in the British C.P. For some reason this group was led by a succession of historians whose work was to do much to making history less eurocentric. Victor's four-year Fellowship provided for a year of travel, and, given his friendship with the comrades from the Indian subcontinent, who provided most of the members of the 'colonial group', it was natural that he should go to India, 'with some schemes of historical study', and carrying with him a lengthy document from the Comintern for the Indian C.P., whose headquarters were then in Bombay (Mumbai) – a city which seems since then to have forgotten its left-wing traditions. The war caught him in India, and he was there throughout it, teaching and doing a great deal of radio work concerned with the war (at some risk of falling foul of his Party, until Russia became involved). He was living mainly in Lahore, now part of Pakistan; there he acquired a passion for its two great poets of that generation, Iqbal and Faiz, some of whose outstanding poems he translated.

He returned from India in 1946 – reading Thucydides on the Peloponnesian War on the boat, and being seasick – towards an unknown future. It turned out to be in Scotland. The university of Edinburgh opened its doors to him, and that is where, from 1948 on, he passed the rest of his academic career. In the meantime, in 1946, he had become part of a group of historians and history teachers, mostly young – though old enough to have gone through the Second World War – who formed a Historians Group of the (British) Communist Party, eager to enlarge their understanding of history, and put it at the service of the cause they believed in. Only a handful had found posts as (rather junior) university teachers before the Cold War closed this option for ten years or so. A few more had gone into the Adult Education movement. The activities of this group of friends in the course of the next ten years of debate, writing and collective self-education, were to have a substantial effect on the shape of subsequent historiography. Even today, a search for 'Communist Party Historians Group' on Google yields a considerable number of immediate references.

It has not been widely recognized how central Victor Kiernan's contribution to the formation of the British school of Marxist history was, not least by insisting on reading Marx and Engels critically and his persistent but always courteous determination to think out problems of class and culture for himself, whatever the orthodox view. To the discussions within the group he contributed chiefly original thoughts on the absolutist monarchies, the development of the nation-state and military organization. As usual his writings ranged far and wide beyond this through culture, religion and the 19th-century history of at least three continents – from Central Asia to Paraguay, the South American 'War of the Pacific', and the massively researched study of the Spanish Revolution of 1854. Yet it was not until the 1960s, the decade of Cuba, Vietnam and the liquidation of British and French colonialism, that he turned his major attention to the problems of imperial conquest, imperial ideology and imperial rule.

America: The New Imperialism: From White Settlement to World Hegemony (1978) belongs to this phase of Victor's writing. It is a book written during the Cold War, and inevitably dated by the passage of time since its publication. Written before the Nicaraguan revolution and Washington's activities in favour of the Contras, and before the fall of the regimes of South American torturers threw new light on the role of the U.S. in their period, its brief account of Latin American affairs in the 1960s and 1970s is plainly out of date. It predates the 1980s, when the U.S. created its enemies by mobilizing and arming Islamic *jihadis* (among them Osama bin Laden) against communism in Afghanistan and building up Saddam Hussein (poison gas, terror and all) as a counterweight to the revolution of the Ayatollahs in Iran. It long predates the fall of the U.S.S.R., the Gulf and Balkan wars of the 1990s, the impact on U.S. policy of the triumph of the ultra-right in Israel. More than twenty years separate the publication of this book from the fall of the two towers of the World Trade Center on 11 September 2001.

And yet, three continuities link the global U.S. of the Cold War era with the attempt to assert single-handed world supremacy since 2001. The *first* is its position of international domination, outside the sphere of influence of communist regimes during the Cold War, globally since the collapse of the U.S.S.R. This hegemony no longer rests on the sheer size of the U.S. economy. Large though this is, it has declined from its post-1945 position of dominance, though it still represents one-third of the global G.D.P. and, rapidly diminishing, of internet users, but only about one quarter of global manufacturing output. In 2000 the U.S. motor industry (not counting the assembly of foreign models) produced no more than 14 per cent of the world output of automobiles. The centre of the industrialized world is rapidly shifting to the eastern half of Asia. Unlike older imperialist countries, and unlike most other developed industrial countries, the U.S. has ceased to be a net exporter of capital, or indeed the largest player in the international game of buying up or establishing firms in other countries, and the financial strength of the state rests on the continued willingness of others, mostly Asians, to maintain an otherwise intolerable fiscal deficit.

The influence of the American economy today rests largely on the heritage of the Cold War: the role of the U.S. dollar as the world currency, the international linkages of US firms established during that era (notably in defence-related industries), the restructuring of international economic transactions and business practices – accountancy, credit-rating, consultancy, etc. – along American lines, often under the auspices of American firms, and executives with M.B.A.s from American or US-inspired business schools, etc. These are powerful assets, likely to diminish only slowly. On the other hand, as the Iraq war showed, the enormous political influence of the U.S. abroad, based as it was on a genuine 'coalition of the willing' against the U.S.S.R., has no similarly stable foundation since the fall of the Berlin Wall. Only the relatively and absolutely enormous military-technological power of the U.S. is well beyond foreseeable challenge by any potential state or coalition. It makes the U.S. today the only power capable of effective military intervention at short notice in any part on the world, and it has twice demonstrated its capacity to win small conventional wars with great rapidity and effectiveness. In case of need it could unquestionably do so against very much stronger opponents than Saddam Hussein's Iraq. And yet, as the Iraq war shows, even this unparalleled capacity to destroy is not enough to impose effective control on a resistant country, and even less on the globe.

Nevertheless, U.S. dominance is real. Confined, before the fall of the communist regimes, to the greater part of the globe, the disintegration of the U.S.S.R. has made it truly global. Who, even in 1989, would have expected to see U.S. military bases in ex-Soviet Central Asia?

The *second* element of continuity is the peculiar house-style of U.S. empire, which has always preferred satellite states or protectorates to formal colonies. The expansionism implicit in the name chosen for the thirteen independent colonies on the east coast of the Atlantic (United States of America) was continental not colonial: it envisaged, and achieved, the occupation of all land in North America 'from sea to shining sea' (failing in its objective only in Canada) and the assimilation of new territory into the political system of the United States. The expansionism of 'manifest destiny' was both hemispheric and aimed towards East

Asia, as well as (certainly for Secretary of State William H. Seward) modelled on the global trading and maritime supremacy of the British Empire. One might even say that in its assertion of total U.S. supremacy over the Western hemisphere it was too ambitious to be confined to colonial administration over bits of it. The brief plunge into European-style colonialism after the Spanish War of 1898 did not last, though it provided the U.S. with naval bases in the British manner in the Caribbean and the Pacific.

The American empire thus consisted of technically independent states essentially doing Washington's bidding, but, given their independence, this required continuous and substantial readiness to exert direct and indirect pressure on their governments and, where feasible (as in the mini-republics of the Caribbean zone), periodic unilateral U.S. armed intervention. As Kiernan's observations on Woodrow Wilson's Mexican policy in 1913–16 shows, 'regime change' when it suited the U.S. was a regular part of Washington's policy in Latin America, long before it was extended to the old world.

The *third* thread of continuity links the neo-conservatives of George W. Bush with the Puritan colonists' certainty of being God's instrument on earth and with the American Revolution – which, like all major revolutions, developed world-missionary convictions, limited only by the wish to shield the new perfection of the society of potentially universal freedom from the corruptions of the unreconstructed old world. The most effective way of finessing this conflict between isolationism and globalism in a democratic society was to be systematically exploited in the 20th century and still serves Washington well in the 21st. It was to discover an alien enemy outside who posed a threat to the American way of life and the lives of citizens of the U.S. that could be presented not only as real but as *immediate* and *mortal*. The end of the U.S.S.R. removed the most obvious candidate, but an academic ideologist soon (1993) found a way to detect another in a 'clash of cultures' between the West and other cultures reluctant to accept it, notably Islam. Hence the enormous political potential of the al-Qaeda terrorist outrages of September 11 was immediately recognized and exploited by the Washington world-dominators.

The First World War, which made the U.S. into a global power, saw the first attempt to translate these world-converting visions into reality, but Woodrow Wilson's failure was spectacular; perhaps it should be a lesson to the current world-supremacist ideologists in Washington, who, rightly, recognize Wilson as a predecessor. Until the end of the Cold War the existence of another superpower imposed limits on them, but the fall of the U.S.S.R. removed these. Francis Fukuyama prematurely proclaimed 'the end of history', that is to say the universal and permanent triumph of what amounted to the U.S. version of the political and economic *modus operandi* of capitalist society. At the same time the apparently overwhelming single-handed military superiority of the U.S., and its post-Soviet freedom of action, encouraged a disproportionate ambition in a state large and powerful enough to believe itself capable of world supremacy, as the British Empire in its time never did. And indeed, as the 21st century began, the U.S. occupied a historically unique and unprecedented position of global power and influence. For the time being it is, by the traditional criteria of international politics, the only great power; and certainly the only one whose power and interests span the globe. It towers over all others. All the great powers and empires of history knew that they were not the only ones, and none was in a position to aim at genuinely global domination. None believed themselves to be invulnerable. All knew enough history to be aware of impermanence. Even the Chinese Empire at its peak knew that it could be conquered, disintegrate for a while, and its dynasties could fall. Perhaps it is not surprising that politicians in the U.S. are tempted by the illusion of omnipotence.

Nevertheless this does not quite explain the evident megalomania of U.S. policy since a group of Washington insiders decided that September 11 gave them the ideal opportunity for declaring its single-handed domination of the world. This is more than could be expected from a simple extrapolation of past trends. For one thing, it lacked the support of the traditional pillars of the post-1945 U.S. empire, the State Department, armed services and intelligence establishment, and of the statesmen and ideologists of Cold War supremacy – men like Kissinger and Brzezinski. These were men and women who were prepared to be as ruthless as the Rumsfelds and Wolfowitzes. (After all, it was in their time that something like a genocide of Mayas, measured in six figures, took place in Guatemala in the early 1980s, unwatched on television screens.) But they had devised and managed a policy of imperial hegemony over the greater part of the globe for two generations, and were perfectly ready to extend it to the entire globe, once the collapse of the U.S.S.R., and the sudden end of even non-communist Russia as an international power, made this feasible. The 'new world order' of the post-Cold War world would be an enlarged U.S. hegemony, even if its details were not yet clear. They were and are critical of the Pentagon planners and neo-conservative world supremacists because these patently have had no concrete ideas about it at all, except imposing their supremacy single-handed by military force, incidentally jettisoning all the accumulated experience of U.S. diplomacy and military planning. No doubt the predictable and predicted debacle of Iraq will confirm them in their scepticism.

Even those who do not share the views of the old generals and proconsuls of the U.S. world empire (which were those of Democratic as well as Republican administrations) will agree that there can be no rational justification of current Washington policy in terms of the interests of America's imperial ambitions or, for that matter, the global interests of U.S. capitalism. It may be that it makes sense only in terms of the calculations, electoral or otherwise, of American domestic policy. It may be a symptom of a more profound crisis within U.S. society. It may be that it represents the – one hopes short-lived – colonization of Washington power by a group of quasi-revolutionary doctrinaires. (At least one passionate ex-Marxist supporter of Bush has told me, only half in jest: 'After all, this is the only chance of supporting world revolution that looks like coming my way.') At present such questions cannot yet be answered. It is reasonably certain that the project will fail. However, while it continues, it will go on making the world an intolerable place for those directly exposed to U.S. armed occupation and an unsafer place for the rest of us.

Foreword

'The history of the New World is peculiarly rich in lessons of imperialism', an American wrote a generation ago. '. . . And in this history the United States has played a central role'. He went on to refer to the opening chapters, the advance across the continent and the Indian wars which kindled 'some of the sharpest anti-imperialist sentiment ever developed in any country'.[1] Their contrary effect may have been to inject into the national psychology a streak of ruthlessness, puzzlingly at odds with a generally amicable disposition. This has shown itself most startlingly in America's wars in Asia, in which it has seemed to be compulsively fighting over again on a grander scale the Indian campaigns of its nonage.

What imperialism is has always been hard to define. In protean forms the thing has existed throughout history; modern capitalism has lent it special new forms. American capitalism has been the chief exponent of the oblique mode which has come to be known as neo-colonialism. This contrasts very markedly with the earlier stage, a necessary preliminary to it, represented by the European empires, annexing and occupying and subjecting peoples to direct rule. In spite of all differences, a common substratum none the less underlies the two. Very broadly, and whatever the relation between economic and other forces among the causes at work, imperialism today may be said to display itself in coercion exerted abroad, by one means or another, to extort profits above what simple commercial exchange can procure. In this light it may be seen as a continuation or recrudescence within the capitalist era of the 'extra-economic compulsion' which is the hallmark of any feudal dominion.

America's evolution as a nation was different from and less organic than that of the European nations; it lacks even a national name. Its peoples were first colonists, then rebels, then a mixture of all the peoples of Europe. Such a country could not take itself for granted, but had need of ideas, convictions, speculations, to grow up round; also of a guiding power to put its trust in, a pillar of cloud or a pillar of fire. Its aspirations were never confined within its own elastic frontiers, but embraced all human destinies. To outsiders it has often seemed that Americans were, and are, more adept at interpreting the divine will than any astrologer of old reading the stars, or Karl Marx the dialectic. In 1850 one of their great writers called on them to realize that 'the van of the nations must, of right, belong to ourselves'. 'God has predestined, mankind expects, great things from our race; and great things we feel in our souls.'[2] In 1893 a German-American was shaking his head over such 'youthful optimism ... the idea that this Republic ... could transform any country, inhabited by any kind of population, into something like itself simply by extending over it the magic charm of its political institutions'.[3]

In other words, the rest of humanity was only passive raw material, clay to be moulded by the potter's hand. This assumption of superiority may be called a legacy of British insularity, magnified by America's size and wealth. It could make for a habit of viewing the rest of the world with tolerant or disdainful indifference. Maxim Gorky encountered it when he was in the U.S., writing *Mother*, after the defeat of the revolution of 1905 in Russia. He was a great reader of Fenimore Cooper's *Pathfinder* novels, which as he said were admired by Belinsky and inspired a line of Russian revolutionaries.[4] But he met with scanty success when he tried to collect money for the cause. Even among socialists, from Eugene Debs down, not one showed any comprehension of the events in Russia; he felt they were taken as simply the sort of thing that happened over there: in Russia, one lady with socialist leanings remarked, 'there was always cholera or a revolution or something'.[5]

An Englishman felt a half-reluctant admiration for the Americans he met in 1910 in the depths of Amazonia, who 'bore themselves with the easy assurance of the favoured heirs of Adam'; their successful work in that tropical jungle perhaps justified their 'assurance of a divine favour which was so completely bestowed that irresolution never shook the aplomb of its lucky inheritors'.[6] Whether their work was justified by any benefit to South America, or various other regions, the inhabitants have at times doubted. Bolivar the liberator wrote to a friend in 1829 about 'the United States which seem destined to plague and torment the continent in the name of freedom'.[7] In 1892 when the fourth centenary of the discovery of the New World was being celebrated (not by its autochthonous peoples) Spain found its former colonies less unfriendly, because of 'the rueful reflection that in exchanging political colonialism under Spain for economic colonialism under the United States all was not gain'.[8]

In general the vision of the U.S. and its place in the world has been a wavering one. During the First World War, H.G. Wells wrote that Europeans were turning 'with a surmise, with a doubt', towards a country where new ideas of a better future were beginning to take hold of 'the finer intelligentsia'. He hoped to see America take responsibility ultimately for a new settlement of the world; but he had regretfully to add: 'Nowhere in Europe now do people seem to be in love with the United States.'[9] Nearly ninety years later these last words sound equally true. In a novel of the 1930s he made an American president his mouthpiece of human sanity in a welter of crazed international hatreds; but also an example of 'that strange mixture of forward-reaching imagination, hardy enterprise, exalted aims, and apparently inseparable cynicism which makes the American character a wonder and perplexity for the rest of mankind . . .'.[10]

America itself, or its 'finer intelligentsia', has gone through moods of discouragement. There was a time of gloom in the 1890s, when the penalty to be paid for industrial wealth in class conflict was sinking into national consciousness. Woodrow Wilson was one who was visited by another such mood shortly before 1914. Despondency was common again in the slump years before 1941. In all these cases the country might be said to have fought its way sword in hand out of moral depression, sometimes out of economic as well. Up to this time it was always expanding in something like a vacuum, first the waste spaces of the North American continent, then the political desert of the wrangling Old World, with whose follies the U.S. stood in sober contrast. After 1945, when it was for the first time fully determined to confer or impose its own civilization on all and sundry, it met for the first time with a force, in communism, at least equally rational, modern, and dynamic, and better able to join hands with the youthful energies, outside Europe, of nationalism.

In the ensuing contest it has too often seemed as if the cult of freedom, narrowly identified with free enterprise, alias capitalism, was denaturing traditional American qualities. An American who troubles to listen to what the rest of the world has to say about him must sometimes feel protestingly like Cassius,

> all his faults
> Set in a notebook, learned and conned by rote
> To cast into his teeth.

But his country's well-wishers have lamented those morbid symptoms because America has been an essential part of the modern world's progress; and it is in a way the second homeland of all Europeans. It has more than once before revealed a faculty of rejuvenation. Its vital spark, its ability to find a way forward, cannot be exhausted yet.

References

1. E.M. Winslow, *The Pattern of Imperialism – A Study in the Theories of Power* (New York, 1948), p.38.
2. Herman Melville, *Whitejacket* (1850), Chap.36.
3. 'Manifest Destiny', in Carl Schurz, *Speeches, Correspondence and Political Papers*, ed. F. Bancroft, Vol. V (New York, 1913), p.191.
4. *Literature and Life – A Selection from the Writings of Maxim Gorky* (trans. E. Bone, London, 1946), pp.96–7.
5. *Letters, Reminiscences, Articles* of Lenin and Gorky (English edn., Moscow, 1973), p.259.
6. H.M. Tomlinson, *The Sea and the Jungle* (1912; Harmondsworth edn., 1953), pp.192–3.
7. R.B. Cunninghame Graham, *José Antonio Páez* (London, 1929), p.239.
8. W.C. Atkinson, *A History of Spain and Portugal* (Harmondsworth, 1960), p.308.
9. H.G. Wells, *War and the Future* (London, 1917), pp.273, 279.
10. H.G. Wells, *The Autocracy of Mr. Parham* (London, 1930), p.301.

PART ONE

THE WINNING OF THE NATIONAL TERRITORY

1

The Birth of a Nation

America's early settlers left an England astir with progressive impulses, and might have seemed to be building in the wilderness the better society that the Levellers tried in vain to build in England. But there was always in this new land a duality, a division of the soul as deep as the racial cleavage between black and white. Aspiration towards a new life was never to succumb entirely to what our ancestors called 'the world, the flesh and the devil'. Yet these latter temptations remained potent, and imperialist hankerings – running all through America's history and at last becoming its most obtrusive feature – have been one consequence. There have been a great many variant species of imperialism, besides the classic types represented by such empires as the Roman or the Mughal or the British. It may even be said that every society has its own distinctive mode, determined by its economic and psychological make-up, of turning outward against its neighbours; this may be manipulated by interests more or less narrow, or be chiefly a diversion from a clash of interests at home, or it may be an organic function of the community's whole life. America has recapitulated many forms of behaviour of the Old World, but giving all of them a stamp of its own, and even originating novel ones. It has never ceased to be an enigma to itself and to others, incalculable because so untried, so little ballasted by tradition: compared with any of the European countries a figure without a shadow, a young giant, childlike, at once heroic and destructive, an innocently-trampling Siegfried – for whose hundredth birthday in 1876 Wagner composed a march.

America began as a not very big or important country, but one precociously conscious of great destinies, because penetrated by a sense of its newness, its differentness from everything that had gone before. Britain was as yet only on the threshold of industrial revolution; and that it, as well as its offspring, was destined to marvellous new growth was not apparent. Adam Smith, and many others, may have been expecting to see the child outstrip the parent more quickly than was actually to happen. As a young fledgling, America was more open than conservative England to the prospects that science and technology were revealing – of endless enlargement of 'the power of man over matter', as Benjamin Franklin wrote to Joseph Priestley in 1780, of disease abolished, of even gravity some day nullified.[1] Beyond the Atlantic, moreover, this great promise could harmonize (better than in a Europe curdled by too long experience) with a simple faith in Providence, and together with it help to conjure up the vision of a new civilization that would be a model for all mankind. But to the part of mankind most exposed to it, all this came before long to seem a swollen version of the national vanity long familiar to Europe, which has been as much an element of all patriotism as oxygen of the atmosphere. Yankee conceit, Tocqueville wrote, 'is not only greedy, but restless and jealous ... ready to beg and to quarrel at the same time'.[2]

Franklin's letter to Priestley was prophetic of America's contradictory future when he added, with a sorrowful recognition of the power of material things over man: 'O that moral science were in as fair a way of improvement, that men would cease to be wolves to one another ...!' The colonies forged themselves into a nation by their War of Independence the more readily because the national state was already firmly established in Western Europe; and aggressiveness was as inseparable a part of it as self-love. Like Holland growing up within the Spanish world empire and breaking away from it to begin seeking colonies for itself, America could not but be infected by the fierce rivalries and ambitions of Europe. Hamilton's declaration in *The Federalist* that for a country to be weak was to be miserable was, in the world he knew, quite true; Europe was as he said trampling on all the other continents, and would keep the Western hemisphere poor and backward if it could. Calling on his countrymen to repel its pretensions, to build a formidable navy, to 'aim at an ascendant in the system of American affairs',[3] he was looking forward to President Monroe. But between protecting the Western hemisphere and dominating it, between messianism and megalomania, there was liable from the outset to be a confusion of ideas.

Born in the West Indies, son of a Scots merchant, Hamilton married into a wealthy New York family. Scotsmen and Protestant Irishmen were very much to the fore in the building and running of Britain's dominions, and it might be found that their kinsmen's contribution to American expansion was equally weighty. Theodore Roosevelt could claim both Scots and Irish ancestry. And colonial America hugged its share of glory and triumphs over the French. Never an Eden of primal innocence, it had been rearing a crop of rich merchants and shipowners, whose eyes were often turned towards overseas endeavour. These were men born with an imperial spoon in their mouth. Under the shelter of the British flag they imported molasses from the West Indies to be turned into rum wherewith to buy slaves on the African coast. This triangular relationship linked New as well as Old England with West Indian slavery from the 1640s; West Indians sometimes removed to the mainland colonies, and planters from Barbados had a large part in the founding and shaping of South Carolina.[4]

Many Americans spent long periods in England, often as businessmen engaged in dealings with British possessions like the West Indian islands.[5] It is little wonder that when the Revolution came, members of the nascent capitalist class were among those who came out as Loyalists. They were men who 'dreamed of expanding trade in a powerful world-spanning British Empire'.[6] Franklin himself and many others who worked for independence had long wanted the empire to turn itself into a federation,[7] like many Irish and some Indian nationalists in later days. Partnership in this would have drawn America further and further along the imperial road. There might even have evolved, most likely out of the Southern planting families, a genus of American Nabob; what it would have been like may be guessed at from the career of Sir David Ochterlony, another scion of Scotland, born at Boston, who in 1777 – his father a Loyalist emigré – found his way to India, and in 1803 became Resident at Delhi, where Bishop Heber ran across him twenty years later reigning in regal splendour.

Independence and expulsion of Loyalists were thus in a double measure a protest against empire, against involvement with it as well as subjection to it. Nevertheless many proclivities of colonial days persisted. America was still far from a state of complete equality and fraternity; to say nothing of the planters, there was still a class of big merchants and monied men, with an appetite sharpened by the War of Independence itself: privateering had laid the basis of a number of fortunes.[8] It was sharpened too by the native temper of a New England whose soil, a visitor observed, could not support its people, so that they took readily to trading, and shifting their quarters. 'They are the Scotchmen of the United States', with sterling qualities, but 'men who make gain the master spring of their actions', obnoxious by their over-astuteness to the 'plodding Dutch and Germans of New York and Pennsylvania'.[9] With this keen scent for opportunity they could not miss the openings offered by European colonial expansion, and, albeit in a looser, unofficial way, association with the rapidly growing British empire also continued. Not seldom it continued illicitly. 'The Americans', Nelson wrote, 'when colonists, possessed almost all the trade from America to our West India islands; and on the return of peace, they forgot ... they became foreigners.' Indeed Nelson made himself unpopular with them and the islanders, as commander of a ship on the Leeward Islands station in 1784–85, by seizing numerous vessels and sternly enforcing the Navigation Act.[10]

But America was still a good trading partner to Britain, and the long wars in Europe from 1792 to 1815 were a windfall for the fledgling state, as Europe's domestic broils always have been. It was this that enabled Americans to be for a time the world's carriers, as the Dutch had once been – 'les Hollandais des temps nouveaux'.[11] By the Jay Treaty of 1794 they secured the right to trade direct with India (and in small ships with the British West Indies), and this privilege they interpreted so liberally that they were soon taking a big hand in all Indian import and export trade. British shippers might grumble, but in the war years American vessels had a better chance of getting Indian goods into a French-controlled Europe; they were in addition economical, because their provisions were cheaper, their crews smaller, and their seamen less drunken.[12] They were entering as well into the China trade, still restricted to the single port of Canton. In the twenty years before 1815 the leading feature of this was a big growth in the American share; American shipping was linking China, as well as India, with Europe, where it disposed of most of the tea it loaded. America's own main export to the Far East was a quasi-colonial product, furs, gathered on the Pacific Coast, frequently by trespass on Spanish territory. About 1810 Elias Derby, pioneer of the China trade, seems to have been the richest man in New York.[13]

The Federalist Party which represented the commercial interests pressed for the creation of a navy to watch over them, and an Act of 1794, providing ships to guard Mediterranean trade against the Barbary Coast pirates, was the thin end of its wedge.[14] Warships were costly, and the expense irked the inland townships and farmers, between whom and the mercantile centres on the coast there was a familiar pattern of discord, much as in the old Netherlands, or in Argentina when it won independence. Victory in 1800 for Jefferson and the Republican Party signalled a shift of ascendancy from coast to interior; and the latter had an expansionist programme of its own, that of a westward, overland advance. This would not mean, as its more Arcadian supporters liked to fancy, that the canker of money-power would be left behind, the weeds of oligarchy in the democratic wheatfield shrivel away. Thirst for wealth had its part from the outset in the westward movement too, and like the oceanic undertakings this, if not precisely imperialistic, would have lurking in it many of the ingredients of imperialism.

Already under the British aegis a kind of subsidiary imperialism had been hatching, on land as well as on sea, somewhat as Australia a century later developed a juvenile spirit of annexation in the Pacific, which ministers in London like Gladstone sometimes tried to hold in check. Movement westward had been limited by the British to the line of the Allegheny mountains, and there was impatience among both the poorer people, in need of new homesteads (population was already pressing on available land in the old colonies[15]), and the affluent, seeking openings for speculation. Americans wanted their new flag to fly over much more than the thirteen colonies, and in the peace negotiations with Britain Franklin was particularly desirous of Canada, which might perhaps have been obtained by firmer insistence.[16] Under the 1783 Treaty terms, the boundary was shifted as far west as the Mississippi, roughly doubling the national area. Beyond lay the uncharted stretches of French 'Louisiana', which was later bought from Napoleon in 1803, when he was cut off from it by British seapower: again Europe's strife was America's advantage.

Into these new lands the surplus or restless farmers of the East were free to pour. It was a 'people's imperialism' of land-hungry settlers, like that of the Russian peasants who drifted eastward across Siberia, or, over many centuries, the Vietnamese peasants moving southward to the Mekong Delta, and displacing more primitive stocks in their path. But every society of any degree of complexity is subject to other motives and pressures than the elemental quest of the cultivator. Tsarist Russia and Vietnam were feudal-military states as well as migrating peoples; and America was nurturing a capitalism which fed on the opening up of the border-lands. To investors in the East Coast cities, trafficking in land, timber and fur yielded soaring profits to match the intoxicating hopes and ideals of the new civilization. In one field maritime and continental profit-seeking converged. It was under the spur of greed for furs for the overseas trade that, no sooner was the Mississippi barrier removed in 1803, American explorers reached at a single stride the Pacific Coast, where both Russians and British or Canadians had arrived ahead of them. In 1811 John Jacob Astor, the self-made immigrant from Germany who was to die the richest man in America, founded Astoria at the mouth of the Columbia River. He and his henchmen in the backwoods were very much a law unto themselves, treating government agents and Indians in the same cavalier fashion.

Thoughts of Canada went on haunting the minds of Americans along the moving frontier. It was not exactly a desire to annex Canada itself, though its incorporation would enlarge and strengthen the Union: it was rather a question of removing a hindrance to American expansion west and north-west. The geography of the Lakes ensured entanglements, and there were quite enough sources of friction for 'Western' politicians to play upon; for some of them at least it was the simplest way of working themselves up the political ladder. Governments in Europe were also often manipulated in the same style by journalists, businessmen, soldiers, officials in colonial outposts. Propaganda against Britain's alleged wish to keep America bottled up, now as before independence, was given a more bitter flavour by charges that Indians along the border were being instigated to oppose American settlement, and to massacre pioneers. 'The English talk much about their honour and national morality,' John Quincy Adams wrote sourly in his journal at St Petersburg after an encounter with one of them, 'sometimes without meaning, but generally with a mixture of hypocrisy and of self-delusion in about equal proportions.'[17] A thousand foreigners must have made similar entries in their diaries about Americans. But belief in a sinister conspiracy to stir up the 'Redskins' took hold easily, as in later days with plots concerning Reds of another sort. It gave Americans a better conscience both for dispossessing Indian tribes and for demanding Canada.

The South had its own form of expansionism, generated by greed for new soil needed for new slave plantations. It had the further stimulus of the country being cut off at first from the Gulf of Mexico and its river outlets by the Spanish possessions; and Spain like Britain could be suspected of designs to utilize hostile Indians. Sparse population and feeble Spanish control left the way open for a creeping occupation, and even a statesman as conscientious as Jefferson could favour the spilling over of American settlers into the border-lands, as a means of bringing these areas peacefully into the American fold. In 1803 the Louisiana Purchase gave America the vital Mississippi Delta, but still not the coastal strip of 'West Florida', eastward from it, or the peninsula of 'East Florida'. Desire to get hold of these was keen, and early in 1811 the government was persuaded that it was time to act. General Mathews, who was to handle things, assured it that there would be no difficulty about engineering a revolution in the peninsula. Many American governments have been given similar assurances by their agents since then, and often the revolutions have duly taken place. Mathews lost no time in mobilizing a faction of 'patriots', American squatters complete with plantations and slaves, to declare Spanish rule at an end. This was a little too brusque, and President Madison and his State Secretary Monroe had to disavow Mathews; all the same they found pretexts for keeping up a *de facto* American occupation.[18]

While North (or West) and South thus each had its own divergent aims, neither was desirous of seeing the other grow too much, for fear of the balance of influence between them in the Union being upset in the other's favour. Their mutual jealousy could be a brake on any expansion; but if an occasion offered for both to gain something at the same time, it could be an incentive instead, just as with European rivalries in Asia or Africa where there was room for one to obtain 'compensation' when another annexed something. When war with England loomed up in 1812, initially over the issue of British interference with American shipping in the course of the blockade against France, it could be welcomed alike by Northerners who wanted Canada and by Southerners who wanted Florida, because Spain was England's ally. Besides, Spain was in a weak condition, struggling at home with Napoleon's invading army, so weak indeed that it seemed practicable for America to 'revolutionize' Mexico as well. A fiery newspaper article called for liberation of 'celestial Mexico', with appeals to ideals of freedom, profits for farmer and financier, and glory for America,[19] as comprehensive a mixture as Pope Urban's summons to the First Crusade in 1095.

Maritime grievances represented another convergent thrust, that of the coastal trading centres. Henry Clay as leader of the war party in Congress focussed his speeches on them; in his speech in favour of the new Army Bill in January 1813 he put the impressment of American seamen by British warships in the forefront, as the one with most popular appeal. There was a strong flavour of *Civis Romanus* in his eloquence on this subject: 'wherever the sacred rights of an American freeman are assailed, all hearts ought to unite; and every arm should be braced to vindicate his cause'. He went on to advocate conquest of Canada as the lair where 'the tomahawk of the savage' was sharpened, and from which tribesmen were furnished with the means of committing their 'horrible excesses and murders'.[20] Allegations of atrocities have figured in all colonial wars.

But sea-borne commerce had more to gain at the time by keeping on good terms with the British and playing second fiddle to them in Asia. During the conflict it suffered severely from the blockade imposed by the British navy, past-master by this time in the art. New England showed little relish for the war, and during it may even have lent more money to the enemy than it subscribed to its own government loans.[21] It was almost like the old dissension of Patriot and Loyalist over again. To America's credit, there has been criticism and opposition at all times when the country has been in a fit of aggressiveness. It was another genuine aspect of the new civilization, albeit with some English antecedents, that neither a real navy nor a real army had been built up. This was partly due to the wholesome principle laid down by Congress in 1784 that standing armies are a menace to liberty. But not many recruits came forward now that the nation was at war, either as regulars or as temporary volunteers. There was the practical obstacle, as before and after the war, that most Americans were too comfortably off to want to be soldiers or sailors. Like middle-class Englishmen at the time of the Napoleonic or Crimean wars, they might periodically fall into a warlike fever, but without feeling any inclination to don uniform themselves; they preferred the fighting to be done by someone else. Andrew Jackson defended New Orleans against British attack with a hotchpotch of militiamen, Creoles, black men, and pirates. Indeed the privilege of fighting, as distinct from bawling for war, has very generally and generously been left to the poor – including, in Europe or Japan, the poorer aristocracy. Until scientific warfare by remote control evolved, this lack of military ardour meant that America's bark was usually worse than its bite.

Hopes of winning Canada dwindled with the failure of attempts at invasion. When peace negotiations started, State Secretary Monroe put forward, for the record if no more, a claim for its cession. 'Experience has shown', he wrote, 'that

Great Britain cannot participate in the domination and navigation of the Lakes, without incurring the danger of an early renewal of the War ... The inevitable consequence of another war, and even of the present, if persevered in by the British Government, must be to sever those provinces by force from Great Britain.'[22] But Canada was becoming a mirage, and this meant at the same time that northerners were less disposed to underwrite southern aspirations. As early as February 1813 the Senate quashed a project for a takeover of Eastern Florida, and the government was obliged to withdraw its troops; in April 1814 the decision was taken not to recognize the 'patriots' still holding their ground there and not to admit them and Florida to the Union. Southerners were correspondingly less inclined to back northern demands for Canada. Thus most of the steam went out of the war effort, and at the end of 1814 the peace treaty of Ghent left America no better off than it had been before. Henry Clay was one of the peace commissioners; he came to take more sober views in later life, and in old age was opposed to the Mexican War of 1846 in which, as if by way of retribution, his son was killed.

America speedily recovered its buoyancy. One exhilarating factor was the collapse of Spanish rule in Central and South America which speedily followed. All of a sudden the U.S. found itself with – instead of a world empire – a troop of weak, inexperienced republics at its elbow, pupils eager it might be expected to learn from it. It was evident, an American wrote in 1828, that 'the emancipation of Spanish America would form, in fact, a new era in our political existence, would elevate us from the rank of a secondary to that of a first-rate power, and would place us at the head of one of the great divisions into which the Christian world would be thrown by the effect of this immense revolution'. European statesmen, 'reasoning, as they habitually do, upon the Machiavellian principle', would do their utmost to poison America's relations with its new neighbours, and vigilance would be needed to foil them. The same writer counted on seeing his country fall heir sooner or later to the British empire, and replace England 'as the commercial and political centre ... in every part of the globe.'[23] A few years later the not unsympathetic Cobden was seeing America as a bigger incipient threat to Britain – commercial, instead of military – than Russia.[24] Meanwhile in 1823 the Monroe Doctrine laid claim to something like a hegemony of the whole continent. When it was being framed John Quincy Adams, State Secretary and soon afterwards President, took care that the United States, debarring European governments from acquisitions in the New World, should not tie its own hands from snapping up trifles like Texas or Cuba at some later date.[25] Brother Jonathan (as Englishmen called Uncle Sam when they could still regard him as a pushing junior instead of as head of the family) was the good shepherd, but shepherding the flock and fleecing it go together.

This was for the future, not the present, but a future which might seem as distant as the moon was to American eyes already close at hand. Destiny, Providence, Nature, all provided symbolic expression for a conviction that this new nation's today was only the swelling prologue to an imperial theme. 'The waters of the St Lawrence and the Mississippi interlock in a number of places, and the great Disposer of Human Events intended these two rivers should belong to the same people', a Congressman declared in the House in 1811.[26] To another it was equally clear that 'the Author of Nature has marked our limits in the south, by the Gulf of Mexico; and on the north by the regions of eternal frost'.[27] Venerable habits of poring over the Bible to extract meaning from its dark sayings made it easier to decipher other oracles, and find religious warrant for what revolutionary France called 'natural frontiers'. In ordinary life good men still interpreted day-by-day happenings in terms of an overriding Will. An emulous young nation was bound to see Providence beckoning it like a stage prompter. The freedom movements in Latin America were an evident sign. It would be pusillanimous of the United States, a patriot wrote in 1828, not to recognize a duty to aid them, and so accept 'the high and responsible position in which the course of events, or, in other words, the will of Providence, had placed us'.[28] Heavenly trumpets were sounding in the West as well as the South, and during the Mexican War a Maryland Congressman was to hear them calling his countrymen to press on to the Pacific and fulfil 'the destiny of the Anglo-Saxon race', mindful of 'that high position which Providence, in his mighty government, has assigned them'.[29]

All this thinking was haunted by old Calvinist notions of a man's 'election' showing forth in his virtues, and these virtues in turn in his prosperity. By marching forward America would prove itself worthy of the divine favour. Put into secular terms this became a rude theory of historical determinism. In 1847 Vice-President Dallas had no doubt that the country was fully equal to 'the vast task which may be assigned to it by the resistless force of events – the guardianship of a crowded and confederated continent'.[30] Events thus took on a life of their own. In the beginning was the deed, not as in effete Europe the word. But this American pragmatism had no wish to shake off its higher sanction: heavenly command and earthly happening coincided, the bread was buttered on both sides. 'Events, the arguments of God,' said the imperialist Senator Beveridge during another war half a century later, 'are stronger than words, the arguments of men.'[31] *Vox historiae, vox Dei.* It was not Americans alone who read high omens in the stars (and stripes), or saw America and the Almighty walking arm in arm in a spirit of mutual confidence. Englishmen of the Evangelical era were well aware that they themselves stood first in responsibility to the world, and must make their country great enough to fulfil its charge; but the more enlightened among them were ready to recognize a partner, or apprentice. 'England and the United States of America,' a zealous young member of the Bengal Civil Service wrote in 1834 (in the course of an official report on local revenue policy), 'let who will gainsay it, are the favoured instruments of God's providence in the establishment of his kingdom of peace and love.'[32] His words sound like an invitation to America, long before Kipling's siren-song, to share the white man's burden.

2

The Pursuit of Happiness

Whatever messianic gleams shot across their thoughts, Americans were preparing for greatness in a strictly businesslike way, by getting rich. Tocqueville might well be struck by the spectacle of an entire nation in the grip of a frenetic pursuit of wealth. It was the first time that a purely bourgeois, money-making society had ever existed, and it took for granted that the way it found itself behaving was the natural way of human beings freed from feudal fetters, just as Europeans of Rousseau's day thought of Red Indians, untainted by civilization, as the archetype of natural man. To visitors like the leisurely Irish tourist who kept a journal in 1836, Americans appeared anything but normal. On the contrary the hotels he stayed in struck him as 'vast menageries containing some very extraordinary animals, rare specimens of the human species'. One of their traits was abbreviation of mealtimes, to let them get back sooner to the counting-houses – 'The first morning at breakfast I was absolutely astounded at the rapidity of their jaws.'[33] How Oliver Wendell Holmes's breakfast-table orators managed to hold their audience is hard to guess.

From this orgy of money-making, the outbreaks of freakish religiosity which likewise astonished foreigners were a periodical recoil. Religion might also be a consolation-prize, for not everyone could be lucky in the race for wealth, and poor immigrants were multiplying. Many of these were Catholics, entering a land of ingrained Protestantism, where the current of feeling against them in the 1830s had a marked anti-Catholic tinge, certain to affect feeling towards the rest of an overwhelmingly Catholic continent. Other tensions, those of class, had never been absent, but were coming more into the open as industrialism got into its stride. A radical denounced 'the rapid and powerful constitution of a new Aristocracy, of a commercial and financial Feudality, which is taking the place of the ancient aristocracy of nobles and warriors'.[34] Economic change was modifying political life more immediately than in a Europe where the bulkheads between them were much thicker. During Andrew Jackson's presidency, from 1828 to 1837, the spoils system was being thoroughly organized, and a moral anarchy was showing itself, a spirit of mob violence which Woodrow Wilson was to deplore in his History. Some Britons may have recalled that this was what Adam Smith predicted for an America cut adrift from the Mother country's benign influence.[35]

Internal distempers encouraged aggressiveness against outsiders, as a means of reconciling divisions. Cries for annexations might be as convenient to the American plutocrats who were coming under criticism as to unpopular rulers or ruling classes in Europe. Seizure of foreign territory could be made a panacea for all ills: it does not appear that Adam Smith's demonstration of the futility of colony-holding for national enrichment made much impression on America. There would be profits at any rate for the rich, and in the new climate of politics they had ready means of urging their views on the government. President Polk complained of expensive schemes 'pressed on Congress by a lobby influence, consisting of leading men out of Congress whose special business it was to induce members of Congress to vote for and support them'.[36] Rich men would find it just as easy now, a radical workman feared, to enroll soldiers for forays abroad, paupers compelled by misery to serve the banner of conquest, which once unfurled must spread fearfully far. He called for a levelling of property instead.[37] To this its owners made in effect the classic reply that the nation as a whole should seek more property, in other words territory. It was a persuasive argument in a world, and above all in an America, where the new gospel of Progress was commonly understood in terms of material growth and size – of cities, armies, population, bank balances. H.G. Wells's fantasy, *Men Like Gods*, of human beings whose only godlike feature is that they are growing taller and taller, might be called an unintended reduction to absurdity of this simple faith. In the land of opportunity where every individual could aspire to the godlike rank of millionaire, men filled with this noble passion would be ready to applaud any plans to make their country large enough to hold them, and would gaze at its bulging outline on the map even more rapturously than Britons gazing at the map of their empire. Even the poor could share in this sense of magnification, and patriotic excitement would do more than any studious perusal of the Constitution to educate poor immigrants into good citizens.

Some foreigners were expecting to see the United States take a hand in world affairs, and hoping to find a useful counterpoise against their rivals. As early as 1775, while the French were preparing to aid America to win independence, Vergennes the Foreign Minister felt misgivings about the irresistible naval strength which such a nation might speedily develop, sufficient to dominate the New World and swallow up French and British possessions alike in the West Indies.[38] With the decay of Spain and Portugal, the British and Russian were the only two world empires, though France was before long striving to rejoin them. Alexander I of Russia was quite willing to humour republican Yankees who might be serviceable against Britain; Canning countered by getting Monroe to endorse his defiance of the Holy Alliance and its designs of restoring Spanish authority beyond the Atlantic. A year later a Briton home from long years in India, where already was heard with foreboding the distant tread of Russian armies, speculated about American intervention there some day, arresting what might otherwise become Russia's 'universal sway over Asia ... It is most likely that Russia and America are destined to perform great parts on the stage of the world, and that the plains of Hindostan will be the scene of mighty struggles for empire.' Tocqueville too saw America and Russia as the coming giants.[39]

However, in the first half of the 19th century the naval strength necessary for power politics far away from home was being built up only very hesitantly. So full was the country of the sense of limitless reserves of power that it scarcely felt the need to transform them into actual weapons. An inventive spirit, such as America might be expected to display, was suffocated by a professional conservatism stiffer even than in Europe, which disliked all such new-fangled things as steam. In 1837 America built the first true steam-warship of any navy, and soon afterwards tried the first screw-propeller, but neither experiment was followed up, and while European navies rapidly put on armour America went on to the Civil War building wooden ships. Even these were few enough. But small squadrons were gradually being established on permanent foreign stations, beginning in 1815 with a Mediterranean flotilla and a renewal from a few years earlier of fighting with the corsairs of the North African coast. British precedent showed what temptations any far-flung naval activity brought with it, even if America's was so far on a very modest scale.

It could afford to be, because after 1814 American enterprise was going back to its tactics of following in the wake of the British whale, or skirmishing on its flanks. A convention of 1815 renewed the right of American shipping to trade direct between home ports and India. Trade with the British West Indies was before long fully reopened. In the Far East there were further inroads into the Canton trade, with the help of illicit dealings which irritated the mandarins both of the Celestial Empire and of the East India Company, but were welcomed by British manufacturers whose goods American ships sometimes conveyed. It was the clamour of these manufacturers for an opening up of the China market, with opium as the battering-ram, that in 1840 was to bring about the Opium War – by which America like other countries benefited without having to share the stigma. During these years the American market was adding a fourth component to the vast trade triangle constituted by Britain supplying policemen to India, India supplying opium to China (illegally, by armed smuggling), and China supplying tea and silk to Britain. Failing to get into the very competitive business of carrying opium from India (which the Company was too high-minded to do itself) American shipowners found an alternative source of supply in the Middle East.[40] This traffic grew markedly after 1815; in 1816 the keen-nosed Astor joined in it.

There were symptoms of weakness, nevertheless. With the ending of the Napoleonic Wars, America lost its privileged position in the carrying trade. Its independent opium supply was relatively small and inferior. Its own staple commodity was falling off. Apart from competition of Canadian and Russian fur-dealers on the Pacific coast, stocks of beaver and of seal were being reduced by wasteful and destructive hunting. For a short time fur sales to China were replaced by a large trade in sandalwood, accompanied by American operations in Fiji and still more, after 1817, in Hawaii, where traders acted as advisers to the monarch and as island governors and collectors of taxes payable in sandalwood, a royal monopoly. Missionaries helped to consolidate the position, and Hawaii was embarked on the long course that would end with it an American dependency.

All this maritime enterprise was secondary to the main thrust of American expansion, westward and overland, and taking on fresh vigour after about 1820. As before, it was a chaotic and headlong process, private appropriation of natural resources unchecked by any thought of public interest. F.J. Turner was to contrast this freebooting with 'the European system of scientific administration';[41] he was giving Europe rather too much credit, but in America the few enlightened men who preached rational ideas of conservation were indeed voices crying in the wilderness. For another decade or two, on the other hand, it seemed that the American appetite would content itself with something less than the whole breadth of the continent. When Congress debated the matter in 1824 the consensus was that the Rocky Mountains were the country's natural limit. As late as the 1840s there were fears of population coming to be spread out too thin, and it was only then beginning to spill over into the 'Oregon' region along the Pacific. Another point of view, appearing quite early with Jefferson and others, and as late as 1848 with Daniel Webster, was that American settlers could and should spread out to the Pacific, but that the lands beyond the mountains should form a separate nation. In 1825 a writer argued that to attempt to keep so remote an area within the Union would overstrain the democratic mode of government and render it unworkable.[42]

There was something here like the philosophy of Victorian England, wanting colonies of settlement for its surplus population but expecting them to stand on their own feet and go their own way as they grew up, while remaining good customers and friends. What was to turn the scales against such thinking in America was the convergence during the 1840s of the colonizing movement with a heightened desire among Eastern shipping magnates for Pacific ports, each requiring government backing against foreign rivals. Of increasing weight was the financial ascendancy of New York. As Chevalier wrote in 1835, the State of New York had earned the title of 'Empire-State' by its qualities of 'grandeur, unity, and centralisation', including firm supervision of banks and schools. He noted that this close neighbour of New England was free from 'the spirit of extreme division that is characteristic of the Yankees'.[43] As in various other countries, like Germany, a border province was taking the lead, and New York City as financial centre of a world-wide hegemony would one day justify the 'imperial reputation' in another way too.

An agreement of 1818 extended the boundary with Canada along the 49th parallel to the Rockies, leaving the wilderness beyond open to pioneers from both sides. But old animosities, and resentment at Canada being still in British hands, were far from extinct after 1814, even if official relations improved. There was an outburst of excitement in 1837–38 when rebellions took place in Upper and Lower Canada. Early in 1838 Lord Malmesbury, in London, commented in his journal on the clamour stirred up by one incident. 'The American radical papers are in a state of the greatest fury with this country, and are doing all they can to incite their countrymen to a war ... threatening vengeance, and writing the most absurd tirades.' To his relief both President and Congress were far more restrained.[44] America's lead in democracy meant among other things a lead in inflammatory newspaper rhetoric such as young Democrat expansionists like J.L. O'Sullivan were indulging in. Tocqueville was finding the press 'a singular power', strangely compounded of good and evil, with immense influence but addicted to 'open and coarse appeal to the passions of the populace.'[45]

Earlier boundary disputes dragged on and supplied fuel for journalistic fires until the Ashburton-Webster Treaty in 1842, and by that time fresh ones were arising over Oregon. Suspicion was fanned that the British would end by monopolizing the northern stretch of the coast. It was darkly hinted also that Britain, never weary of ill-doing, was intriguing with Mexico and scheming to get hold of California, which would complete America's exclusion from the Pacific. In short, while America picked up imperial manners from Britain beyond the seas, beyond the mountains it was hurried by fear of them into imitation of them. Meanwhile expansionism still had a second pacemaker, in the shape of the southern states, and here too imperial Britain had an accelerating influence. It renounced slavery in its own colonies in 1834, but helped to perpetuate it in the American South by providing the biggest market for its cotton, largely for the purpose of flooding India with machine-made cloth and thus adding industrial to political conquest.

Southern society was of a kind usually produced only by conquest at its most brutal, but with a black population that had been bought, not conquered. It was in harmony with the businesslike mentality of America as a whole that so large a part of its national territory was acquired by cash payments to foreign govern-ments or Indian tribes. For Brother Jonathan the dollar performed what lucky marriages so often did for European dynasties. Either way, there was no pretence of consulting the wishes of any local inhabitants there might be, any more than when provinces changed hands by conquest. In 1819 Spain was persuaded to cede what it still possessed of Florida, and this was camouflaged under a form of purchase. Next year a compromise over Missouri limited the spread of slavery northward; westward the way was blocked by the northern bulge of Mexico, which had scarcely achieved its independence before America was trying to buy Texas from it. This only resulted in Mexico becoming as suspicious of America as the latter was of Britain. There were still memories of the abortive attempt to seize Texas or all Mexico in 1806 by Aaron Burr, shortly after his term as Vice-President under Jefferson.

Texas was soon being won, in a fashion typical of the epoch America was now entering, by private enterprise. Settlers were filtering into the sparsely inhabited region, as into Florida earlier, men of spirit and determination, largely from the southern states. They agitated and aired their grievances very much like the Uitlanders or British settlers two generations later in the Transvaal. 'The province of Texas is still part of the Mexican dominions', commented Tocqueville, 'but it will soon contain no Mexicans'.[46] Events, those divine arguments, speedily overtook his prophecy. In 1836 the settlers repulsed an effort by President Santa Anna to bring them under control. Their leader, Sam Houston, was a personification of the American medley of opposite qualities. In early life he passed three years among Indians, learned their language, derived from contact with them it was surmised his charm and dignity. He believed in fair play for Cherokees, and short shrift for Mexicans. Texan independence was given prompt recognition by President Jackson. It was recognized also by European countries, including Britain which was known to want Texas to remain a separate state and was suspected as always of sinister motives. Many Americans on the contrary wished to welcome Texas into the Union, especially Southerners who looked on it as an enlargement of their own sphere. Land-jobbers and speculators worked up propaganda, extolling the Texans as 'heroic champions of liberty'.[47] Government agents were at work behind the scenes to persuade them to opt for joining America, partly by dint of fomenting strife between them and Mexico.[48] A convention duly voted for joining the Union. In 1845 President Tyler was enabled by public support to do what the Senate had prevented him from doing a year before, and admit Texas to the Union. Northern sentiment was against this, as an extension of the slave-system; Tyler was a Virginian, and – unlike Houston – died a Confederate. It is instructive to read Woodrow Wilson the historian on this affair, and on President Tyler, in the light of President Wilson's subsequent dealings with Mexico.

The public opinion, or noise, which enabled Tyler to get his way manifested itself in the 1844 presidential election, in which his successor Polk declared strongly in favour of Texas being admitted. Polk took a stiff line also on the Oregon dispute with Britain, now approaching flash-point. As in 1812 the competing sectional ambitions stimulated each other. 'Texas and Oregon were coupled upon the same principle as Florida and Canada in 1812.'[49] Together they stood for what first began in 1845 to be called 'manifest destiny'. A New York paper wrote of people 'puzzling their brains to find out new countries to annex'.[50] It was no very extravagant fancy of Jules Verne to make his Yankee space travellers think it ought to be a *casus belli* if Mexico refused them the mountain-top they wanted to fire their projectile from.

Polk may never seriously have intended to go to war with Britain, but his maxim was that 'the only way to treat John Bull was to look him straight in the eye'.[51] Brinkmanship has always appealed to the gambling streak in Americans, though Polk was also, as befitted his Scottish-Irish descent, a strict Sabbatarian. It may be doubted whether many ordinary people really wanted war either. 'You may sing to them the song of Canada Conquest in all its variety, but they will not be charmed', Daniel Webster had said in a debate on conscription near the end of the last conflict.[52] In our own day the 1960s song of Asia Conquest would have been far less beguiling if it had been known beforehand that the price would be massive conscription. Like some of his successors in later days Polk was partly the prisoner of a war party with whose backing he had come to power. But early in 1846, in face of British preparations to send naval reinforcements, he decided to draw in his horns. A reasonable adjustment of the north-western dispute was then soon reached.

Having in the eyes of his more intransigent critics climbed down there, he had the more incentive to prove himself a man of his word and his sword in another quarter, where it could be done with less risk. The aggressive mood that had been worked up was to be given vent at the expense of Mexico. California was the prize in view. There too the ubiquitous American settler was to be found, a small but vociferous colony; and visions of a great new Far Eastern trade, now that China was being opened up, added value to its harbours. It was largely as a base for commercial penetration of China that California, like the Philippines later, was to be taken. Texas while independent, truly American in its soaring aspirations, had its own gaze turned to the west, and men like Houston talked grandiloquently of an empire of their own, stretching to the Pacific. America took over with it these ambitions, and the further quarrel they had provoked with Mexico. Starting as usual by putting its cash on the table, the government was prepared to pay up to twenty-five million dollars for Upper California and New Mexico, or smaller sums for smaller bargains. Mexican refusal to sell was the effective cause of the war that broke out in May 1846.

In 1814 an anti-war radical in Scotland wrote to the press in ironical surprise at the Americans 'having the presumption to go to war with us, – with us, Sir, who have all along treated them with so much lenity and forbearance'.[53] Americans were now unaffectedly surprised at the audacity of the Mexicans in defying them. Annexationist ideas swelled into proposals to take over the whole of Mexico. Why make two bites at the cherry, as Europeans often said when giving way to similar temptations? Mexico seemed derelict, certain to collapse before long. Rumours of its mineral wealth painted it as a new Eldorado, and the Californian gold-rush was soon to justify some of these pipe-dreams. A canal through the Isthmus was already being talked of.

At the outset of hostilities Buchanan, the Secretary of State, found himself alone in a ministerial meeting when he urged that America should disclaim any annexationist aims: otherwise 'he thought it almost certain that both England and France would join with Mexico in the war'. Polk was 'much astonished' at this 'unnecessary and improper' idea. He maintained that Mexico and Oregon were quite separate questions; America was not going to war for territory, but territory would make an acceptable indemnity; if England and France did intervene he would defy them both 'or all the Powers of Christendom', and 'fight until the last man among us fell in the conflict'.[54]

Part of the war's purpose indeed was to forestall European meddling, and in particular to snuff out any English plot to get California. In point of fact there was no such scheme in the mind of the British government, despite promptings from some of its men on the spot; indeed, when Mexico offered California in return for British financial aid, Palmerston declined, rather than risk war with the U.S.[55] Polk was in the happy position of being able to win a triumphant race against an opponent who was not running at all. England's resources were taxed by the war of 1845–46 in the Panjab, quickly followed by the second, in 1848–49, which completed the conquest of India. When Bancroft went to London as American minister in September 1846, after being secretary for the

Navy, he assured Polk that there would be no objection there to all Mexico being seized.[56]

America was ready by this time to contemplate, like Europe, a civilizing mission, a duty to carry enlightenment to less favoured peoples; more unquestioningly in a way, because its institutions were more enlightened, and it was always taken for granted that they would be extended in full to the inhabitants of any lands under the American flag. Europeans sincerely believed that their rule made Asiatics or Africans less bad than they were when left to themselves; Americans were confident of being able to make all and sundry (except Red Indians and Negroes, perhaps) far better. Civil and religious freedom would work wonders – America was a moral Midas whose touch would turn the basest metal to gold. Some indeed doubted the wisdom of incorporating in the Union so large and unregenerate a population as Mexico's. One answer was that it would all be assimilated into the more vital American race, and cease to be a separate entity. Here was a heroic faith in the vitality of American genes as well as institutions, but the country was already busy assimilating millions of new arrivals from benighted Europe.

Estimates of the Mexicans were in any case jaundiced, and any civilizing mission presupposes that those who are to benefit by it are not yet civilized. They were racially a very mixed species, shading into Indian tribes on a par with those further north. Even about the higher strata, and the Latins of the New World at large, American feeling was akin to British, and must have derived a good deal from it. Paramount was a belief in their political incapacity and irresponsibility. 'When a Mexican has nothing else to busy him he gets up an insurrection.'[57] A more hostile spirit had been aroused by reports over many years of Mexican 'excesses and cruelties'.[58] Here was another example of how colonial wars have so often had an overture of atrocity charges against the intended victim.

One less boasted American institution was slavery, illegal in Mexico. During the 1830s the abolitionist campaign was getting under way, and making the South all the more anxious to enlarge its sphere of influence. Slavery issues were soon a complicating factor in debates about how much Mexican territory was to be annexed. Between spreading civilization and spreading slavery there was an all too visible discrepancy, and it was generally feared by the anti-slavery party that any more lands taken from Mexico would, like Texas, be fresh breeding grounds of the evil. Polk cared little about this; he was an anti-abolitionist, born in North

Carolina and settled in Tennessee, but he had to take account of the feeling in deciding how big his pound of flesh was to be. The West at large was annexationist: wherever in any decade the frontier lay, expansionism was rampant, very much as it was along Russia's moving frontiers in Asia, or Britain's in India. But New England, staunchly abolitionist, was suspicious of it and its motives. New York was all for annexing as much as possible, with a view to sharing in the spoils. It was widely supposed that the slave-owners' standpoint was the same; in reality it appears that they were divided, and many of their leading spokesmen were against going too far. They had Texas to digest; they may have feared that slavery would not be economically viable in other parts of Mexico, and that to try to introduce it would raise an abolitionist storm.

Slavery or no, the Mexicans showed little inclination to be civilized by their neighbours, or listen to the voice of Providence and History; they refused to consider any cessions of land at all, and the conflict proved long and stubborn. Here was another surprise for the Americans, who were expecting to come, see, and conquer – to scatter the degenerate descendants of the *conquistadores* as Cortes's men once scattered the Aztecs. When war was in the offing the crew of the *Portsmouth*, which took part in the seizure of California, were jubilant, 'boasting' – as one of them said – 'with all the vain glory of Yankees, that with our own good ship alone we could take the whole coast of Mexico, and even daring to assert that there were not natives enough in the whole of the Mexican provinces, to drive us off, or prevent our landing at our own good will and pleasure'.[59] The writer was a common seaman, with a rollicking devil-may-care philosophy much like that of the British seamen and private soldiers who have left records of their colonial campaigns; something of it must have reached the U.S. navy through its numerous English recruits. The navy was 'eager for the fray', its officers doubtless still more so than their men. 'They are all villains', the redoubtable Perry wrote of the Mexicans;[60] he wanted to annex a great many of them, with some lack of logic perhaps. He had been writing articles to rub into the nation how few warships it had: only two of the line in 1836, when France had 15 and Britain 23, with no steamships at all to Britain's 21.[61] War would have the added merit of bringing the navy and its wants before the public eye.

Mexico had no warships, but it had far more patriotic spirit than it was expected to show, and could hold out for two years because the war was clumsily planned and bunglingly fought by the invader.[62] All America's military operations of the nineteenth century had an amateurish character that helped to set bounds to its imperial career. It was standard practice to raise volunteer forces at the start of a campaign, on too short-term a basis to be properly trained, rather like the feudal vassals of the Middle Ages who only served for so many days in a year. On this occasion the government began by inviting 50,000 men to volunteer. Those who did proved of little use, and often behaved in such a fashion that the Mexicans might well fail to appreciate their civilizing mission. Worst of all were some cavalry regiments, turned loose on the population with complete disregard of discipline, of whose doings we learn from an army private who left an account. They were 'wild reckless young fellows', many of them 'duellists and desperados of the frontier . . .'. 'Looking upon the "greasers" as belonging to the same social class as their own Negro slaves, they plundered and ill-treated them, and outraged the women, and this sometimes in the presence of the fathers and husbands, who were tied up and flogged for daring to interfere in these amusements of the chivalry.'[63]

The small regular army had to be enlarged, but it was not until August 1847 that General Scott entered Mexico City. Surrender of any territory was still being refused, which made annexationists pitch their demands still higher. Perry wanted the Isthmus of Tehuantepec, if not the whole country and all Central America; an English company was surveying a canal route there, he reported to Washington, and this ought to be in the hands of the United States, to which Destiny had 'doubtless decided' that all northern America should one day belong.[64] Still there was enough dislike of such ideas in various quarters to force some moderation on the government; and the dogged Mexican resistance made it obvious how difficult and costly a permanent occupation would be. Temperamentally America has always wanted its adventures – as the rake in *The Vicar of Wakefield* wanted his amours – to end in swift, dramatic success, and has been disgusted by slow, dragging combats, where its favourite role of liberator wilted. And there was always so much going on at home that the tonic of foreign strife was only needed now and then, not chronically as in Europe. Opposition Whigs and anti-slavery men were denouncing 'Mr Polk's War', and the election of November 1846 resulted in a Whig majority in Congress.[65]

In February 1848 Polk decided to accept the treaty which his insubordinate agent Trist at last obtained. It gave him New Mexico and Upper California, and there was now an unbroken American belt – mostly desert, it is true – from the

Gulf of Mexico to the Pacific. Congress too accepted the treaty, though the Whig House of Representatives managed to combine principle with profit by passing a resolution that the war had been 'unnecessarily and unconstitutionally begun by the President'; a charge to which Polk was not the last President to expose himself. One observer commented: 'The people . . . are seeing that they have been bamboozled, as O'Connell used to say.'[66] Whether he was right or not, it has been another saving grace of America to change its mind quickly after fits of jingoism. But the national territory had expanded since 1844 from 1.8 to 3.0 million square miles.[67]

3

White Man and Red Man

Half of the states of the American Union have Indian names, acquired as a savage warrior might appropriate that of a defeated foe. More pacific as a rule than Europe in its foreign relations, America was chronically engaged at home or on its borders with the old inhabitants of the land, for two centuries before and a century after independence. This left, it has been said, 'an invaluable legacy' of fighting experience, of the arts of cover, ambush, mobility, for American soldiers as late as the Korean War.[68] For the nation the legacy was a share of the colonialist mentality that Europeans acquired in Asia and Africa, along with an intermittent habit of protest against it; also perhaps some part of that proclivity to violence among themselves that Americans have often lamented.

Most Indians met with in the early days of settlement were not too unfriendly to welcome trade. On their side the newcomers varied very much in their attitudes, and goodwill was not lacking. When an expedition was felt to be necessary against some mischief-makers, says Winslow's *Relation*, 'it much grieved us to shed the blood of those whose good we ever intended and aimed at, as a principal in all our proceedings'.[69] In numbers the two races were more evenly balanced than later on, and novelty helped to give the white man some degree of interest in his red neighbour, whom he found 'very ingenious and observative', and well worth bartering goods with.[70]

Amicable thinking reached its highest point with William Penn the Quaker.

He was agreeably impressed by the Indians' easy-going philosophy of life, floating on a willingness to share whatever they had. 'They care for little, because they want but little ... They are not disquieted with bills of lading and exchange, nor perplexed with Chancery suits and Exchequer reckonings.' He was struck too by the gravity and decorum of their council-meetings. 'I have never seen more natural sagacity ... and he will deserve the name of wise that outsits them in any treaty about a thing they understand.' Bad Christians, he held, were more responsible than Indians for trouble between the races.[71] He could not foresee that before very long his Pennsylvania would be offering bounties for Delaware scalps, women's included. It was a practice initiated in 1648 by Dutch colonists, from a country already hardened in Eastern Asia to the necessities of conquest.

Scottish and English pioneers had something not less brutalizing in their national background, in the form of the settlements in Celtic Scotland established by companies under license from the crown,[72] and of the long-drawn conquest of Ireland, with the Anglo-Scottish 'plantation' of Ulster in 1611 whose consequences we are still plagued with today. Seizure of soil beyond the Irish Sea and beyond the Atlantic belonged to the same book of empire. Few of the early settlers in America had any Quaker disposition; those who conned their Old Testaments most earnestly saw themselves as another chosen people taking possession of another Canaan. Engaged in a hard struggle to subdue the wilderness and its denizens, they had need of a hard religion to sustain them. They were often in danger of feuds among themselves, brought on by social divergences reflected in theological rifts: quarrels with pagan Indians could help better than anything else to keep them together and allow orderly communities to grow.

It was not lost on the Pilgrim Fathers that, just before their landing, the Indians in their neighbourhood had been thinned out by an epidemic and internecine strife. 'Thus God made way for his people, by removing the heathen'.[73] Sometimes the heathen might be put to good use, as by the enterprising leader who reported in 1622 how he captured an Indian 'king' and by holding him hostage 'forced his subjects to worke in chaines till I made all the country pay contribution; hauing little else whereon to liue'.[74] At other times it was settlers who were molested by Indians, and who could then retaliate with a good conscience. Some encounters took place as horrific, in their small obscure way, as any that mankind has waged; colonists behaved like another American tribe, as savage as the rest. In 1637 they surrounded and set fire to the Pequod stronghold in Connecticut, with four hundred people in it who were burned alive or killed as they tried to escape. 'It was a fearful sight to see them frying in the fire ... and horrible was the stink and scent thereof; but the victory seemed a sweet sacrifice, and they gave the praise thereof to God ...'.[75] Cromwell's sack of Drogheda twelve years later, and napalm raids in Vietnam over two centuries later, displayed the same confident righteousness.

Watching the spectacle joyfully were the Pequods' old enemies the Narragansets, whom they had vainly urged to join hands with them instead of with the English. In 1675 a Narraganset village was burned down by the colonists, with all those in it, mostly old men, women and children; some even of the assailants found it 'a most horrible and appalling scene'.[76] Next year took place the defeat and death of the chief of another tribe involved in the same war, 'King Philip', first of a succession of Indian leaders who tried to forge a united front against the intruders. 'Thus God ... has enlarged our borders', the latter piously reflected, 'by giving to us the heritage of the heathen, which they justly forfeited by their unreasonable rebellion.'[77] In Virginia all through the century Indians might be reduced to slavery; an Act of 1705 made this illegal, but it went on for decades longer.[78] One of Crèvecoeur's few criticisms of the Americans he sojourned among was that individuals were free to inflict injuries on Indians, of the sort that caused an attack on Virginia in 1774.[79]

In the north there took shape a strong permanent confederation, the 'Six Nations' of the Iroquois League, to whom L.H. Morgan was to pay tribute as 'a vigorous and intelligent people ... Eloquent in oratory, vindictive in war, and indomitable in perseverance ... they have illustrated some of the highest virtues of mankind in their relations with each other.'[80] Like many tribes of the eastern fringes they were no longer forest nomads, but lived in large and quite elaborate settlements; on the other hand their mode of living was only half a settled one, since agriculture was left to women, while the men followed the nobler avocations of hunting and fighting. It might otherwise be a mystery why, with their scanty numbers, they wanted to hold on to vast tracts of forest. In a sense it was this division between the sexes, far deeper than any between tribes, that was their undoing. Tribal enmities were however rendered more deadly by the white man's coming, through the spread of firearms and the jealousies stirred up by the fur trade. The Iroquois, as well as the Europeans, overran and despoiled their neighbours. In the South what was wanted was slaves rather than furs, and Indians were instigated to fight one another and capture prisoners for sale.[81] West Africa provided a ready model; slaves were bought from Africans in the same fashion.

Wars between British and French set Indians fighting one another on a grander scale. Their situation between the rival empires gave a special importance to the Iroquois League: the fact that they came to side with the British may have helped to turn the scales in their favour, and if so has left its mark on the whole history of the modern world. There was a recurrent idea of preserving an independent zone between the opponents, much as a hundred years later there were proposals to leave Afghanistan and the old kingdoms of Central Asia as buffers between British and Russians. At the end of the Seven Years War in 1763 the victorious British were confronted by another tribal alliance, headed by a chief named Pontiac who had been on the French side. It was a protest against encroachments on lands further west, and though it was defeated the government felt constrained to issue the proclamation of that year which forbade settlement beyond the mountains except by special sanction and with Indian consent.

Westward expansion was being planned by companies of speculators: in the forefront were Virginia's aristocratic landowners, among them George Washington who made light of the edict as no more than 'a temporary expedient to quiet the minds of the Indians'.[82] As with the revolt of Spanish America not much later, a leading motive of the breakaway from Britain was the desire for a free hand with the indigenous peoples, without interference from a government in Europe. History throws very long shadows, and the loss of America must have haunted, years later, the Liberal government in England, when it carefully refrained from any protection of the indigenous population in South Africa while handing over that country to the rule of its white minority in 1909.

During the Revolutionary War against Britain the Americans were the first to seek Indian auxiliaries, but after the failure of their attack on Canada in 1776 most of the tribes gravitated towards the British, who were the lesser because more distant evil as well as the better paymasters. Employment of red men by the enemy then became an American grievance, along with that of German troops; sometimes a charge was added that Britain wanted to stir up black slaves against their masters. A guilty anxiety about both coloured races was natural enough.

Reprisals against one of them followed in 1779 when Washington ordered 'destruction and devastation' of the Iroquois villages. Brutally carried out, it wrecked 'the North American Indian's finest civilization north of Mexico'.[83]

The United States inherited no British paramountcy over North America, and had to grope towards such a claim little by little. At the outset the tribes were recognized as 'domestic dependent nations', a vague title which might have pointed towards their becoming something like the 'Native States' of India under the British, as small republics instead of monarchies, and with Agents posted to them instead of Residents. Attitudes were, as before, diverse. The Revolution had invoked elevated principles, which some citizens took seriously. It had stimulated thinking, in a few minds at least, and it was from this date that Americans began to study Indians observantly and furnish reliable information about them to scholars in Europe.[84] On the other side, independence also stimulated thinking about race and racial inequality as the needful justification for slavery, something hitherto taken for granted, with the result that America now became 'a consciously racist society'.[85] Feelings about Indians could not be unaffected by feelings about Negroes.

The new nation's leaders were apt to be least realistic, on this front, when they sounded most benevolent. Washington expressed respect for Indian treaty rights, but his hope was that the red man would withdraw westward as the white man came on, without waiting to be driven away.[86] Jefferson could declare that 'the proofs of genius given by the Indians of North America, place them on a level with Whites in the same uncultivated state. I have seen thousands myself, and conversed much with them, and have found in them a male, sound understanding.'[87] All the same, he was a firm believer in American destinies, and trusted too readily that they could be harmonized with Indian well-being. He preached to clansmen the blessings of the white man's way of life, especially farming and private ownership. In all this was something of the obtuseness of Baillie Jarvie offering to take Rob Roy's sons away from their mountains to Glasgow as prentice weavers. Henry Knox too, Secretary of War from 1785, was strong for bringing civilization to the Indians, and optimistically fancied that only a small number of them would be averse to it. He regretted that so far Americans had been even more destructive than Spaniards: in their more populous areas the red man had almost disappeared.[88]

Unluckily it was only a small number of Americans who shared these sentiments. Having beaten King George and his red friends, most others were in a mood to give Indians short shrift. 'In my opinion,' John Jay wrote to Jefferson in 1786, 'our Indian affairs have been ill managed ... Indians have been murdered by our People in cold blood and no satisfaction given, nor are they pleased with the avidity with which we acquire their Lands.' He favoured a gradual, planned extension of the colonies instead of an indiscriminate rush.[89] But a hard-up government saw its best chance of raising money in sales of large blocks of land. In principle this was to be obtained by purchase, rather than seizure, but in practice tribes might be given very little choice whether to sell or not. New England was ready now to follow Virginia's lead and aspire to fresh territory westward. A fever of speculation in land seized everyone, much as stocks and shares have been the pastime and passion of latter-day America: the nation's unlimited, unexplored wealth made it a nursery of gamblers. Acres could only be turned into cash when there were cultivators to buy and work them. That a swelling multitude of settlers was pressing on the frontiers was in the first place the fault of a still aristocratic Europe which kept most of its people in abject poverty. But responsibility was shared by speculators who advertised their domains and puffed their attractions in Europe, to tempt more immigrants to come:[90] more hands were as necessary now for the plough as later on for the machine.

Meanwhile individual states, particularly in the South, had far less conscience than the federal authorities about Indian rights. They too had heavy debts to clear off, and huge properties were jobbed off to a few southern syndicates, like the Tennessee Company which got four million acres. One of the most avid grabbers was a Governor (from 1788) of Tennessee, John Sevier; he was also one of the local politicians who, to be rid of any restraints, were prepared to think or talk of secession.[91] If impatience to sweep red men out of the way had been a powerful motive for America to cut loose from Britain, it might well be a motive for Tennessee or Georgia to cut loose from America.

Further north the difference was more of words than of intentions. A federal ordinance of 1787 amounted to a programme of advance across Ohio, where a million and a half acres were sold to one company for a song, even though it was accompanied by assurances that 'The utmost good faith shall always be observed towards the Indians.'[92] Lack of official secrecy in democratic America has made for official duplicity, and a crop of phrases designed for the record. For the moment, with its army heavily run down, America would have found honesty the best policy; but the opposition to be expected was greatly underestimated, and the destruction of St Clair's ill-planned expedition in 1791 was the costliest defeat of any Indian war. Some building up of the army – or 'Legion', its appropriate empire-building title at this stage – became indispensable, and after refusal by the tribes in 1793 to give up the Ohio River boundary, a more successful campaign broke their resistance in 1795. Some Chickasaws from the south were employed in the north-western fighting,[93] but following the acquisition of Louisiana in 1803 there was fighting with southern tribes as well. In 1801–6 during his presidency Jefferson relieved his red friends of vast tracts. Yet the locust army of settlers was still spreading out, and intruding on the remaining Indian territories. From time to time the federal government ordered the eviction of trespassers, and sometimes its orders were carried out, but in the long run they could only be ineffective. With scarcely enough troops for grappling with Indians, it had far too few for policing its own turbulent subjects.

As another struggle with Britain loomed up, British agents felt their way towards new Indian alliances, as Americans so loudly accused them of doing. With this came a last chance of a coalition of tribes, from north to south, to halt the white advance. Its moving spirit, Tecumseh, represented a rejection of white civilization, while his brother the 'Prophet' was a revivalist of the old religion; but the standards of conduct of this remarkable leader seem to have been at least as 'civilized' as those of most of his opponents. He encouraged a further turn to agriculture, and discouraged alcohol, one of civilization's most potent allies; he wanted cessions of land to require the assent of all members of his league. This principle white leaders like Governor Harrison of Indiana, under pressure from their rude frontiersmen, were determined not to accept. Harrison invaded Shawnee territory, by one of those 'pre-emptive strikes' so much a part of American strategic thinking since 1945; Indian wars supplied plenty of precedents. In August 1812 Tecumseh captured the frontier fort of Detroit, which had baffled Pontiac; his following swelled to three thousand, an astonishing total for an Indian force, and it looked as if Indians with British aid might preserve their independence, as Americans with French aid had gained theirs. But he fell fighting in 1813, one of the most remarkable allies Britain has ever had, with the bizarre rank of brigadier-general, and his cause perished with him. To this triumph Harrison was to owe his elevation twenty-seven years later to the presidency.

His counterpart in the South was Andrew Jackson, who in 1813 led a punitive campaign against the Creek Indians in Georgia; they too had ventured to resent the white man's encroachments. At the end of it, friendly as well as hostile Creeks were deprived of most of their land. With Jackson, as with empire-builders like Cecil Rhodes, public duty and private interest went happily together, for he had early been engaged in speculative dealings in land, that quickest high road to fortune. In 1828 he rose to be president, another of those military politicians – not altogether unlike some of Latin America's – who came to the front by prowess against 'redskins' and by proving themselves vigorous land-clearers.

Baulked of Canada in 1814, the U.S. could fall back on further acquisitions from Indians. In the peace negotiations Britain had brought up again without avail the proposal of an Indian buffer-region. The American government continued to profess a scrupulous respect for treaties, but once more virtuous professions clashed with greed for the spoils. Land speculators were to the fore again, among them British investors, for whom the firm of Baring acted as broker; they helped to drum up emigrants at home, by advertising methods which Cobbett, who knew his America, called deceitful.[94] Furs remained another source of gain. Since 1796 the government had been empowered to open 'factories' or trading stations where they could be exchanged for trade goods at fair rates; but these were always obnoxious to private enterprise, whose tactics were to trap 'redskins' as they trapped animals. Indians were got into debt or fuddled with alcohol, and then overcharged and swindled.[95] Similar practices can be observed in the same epoch in some European possessions, as in Bengal where the Honourable Company and the indigo planters fastened the fetters of debt on weaver or peasant.

Organized fighting at this stage took place chiefly in the South, where tribes had been coalescing into a few large confederations like the Creek. The stiffest trial of strength was with the Seminoles, 'wild men', originally a mixture of Creek and other diehards. In 1817 the first Seminole War broke out over complaints that they were harbouring runaway Negro slaves. Forms of slavery had not been unknown among Indians, and some were now learning to make use of black bondsmen – one of the worst lessons they imbibed from their civilized neighbours, even if servitude among them was less onerous than on the white man's plantations. In pursuit of Seminoles and fugitives Jackson did not hesitate to invade Florida; after the cession of the province by Spain in 1819, the Seminoles were relegated to a reservation there.

In a book published in 1824 the British consul at New York found fault with the barbarity of some methods resorted to against the Indians in this war, and sought 'to excite a general sympathy in behalf of an oppressed and suffering people', condemned by almost all as a 'cruel, blood-thirsty, and treacherous race, incapable of civilization'.[96] Dislike of ungrateful Yankees might help a Briton to sympathize with Indians, and in Canada there was on the whole much less friction of races, because of smaller pressure of population. It might be said all the same that the Highland clearances which had just been taking place in the consul's native Scotland were not very different from the expulsion of Indians from their ancestral homes, and were swelling the tide of immigration into America which was responsible for it.

In 1826 *The Last of the Mohicans* came out. There is plenty of Indian cruelty and bloodthirstiness in this first great American novel, but also a real indignation at the crushing of the red man, when Fenimore Cooper is thinking imaginatively through his Indian characters; though when his mind returns to the workaday realm, he recognizes that the New World cannot, any more than the Old, be run by abstract justice, or he merely finds a hazy comfort in the spread of Christianity. Friendship between the races is possible only to a pair of individuals like the old Mohican chief and Hawk-eye, each isolated from his own kind; even then the white man is always conscious of a gulf between him and his companion.[97] In any case Cooper's Mohicans were symbolic of the whole Indian race, as many thought of it, in being a dying folk, which modern man might take leave of with a chivalrous tribute to its antique virtues. As time went on and fresh tribes came in sight, further and further west, the novel must have helped to inspire the more enlightened views that easterners could afford to indulge in when the noise of battle had rolled far away.

As yet there were few people to draw any useful moral from it. Tocqueville's America was growing very fast, but an authentic intelligentsia, and with it the spirit of enquiry kindled by the Revolution, grew very slowly. Europeans themselves, whose curiosity about pre-industrial societies began far earlier, embarked only quite late in the 19th century on systematic field studies, and until then the new science of 'anthropology' was largely a pseudo-science, infected with racialism.[98] In America, Morgan pointed out in 1877 in his *Ancient*

Society how little scrutiny his countrymen had yet made of Indian clan structures, archaic survivals of a social organization shared by their own forefathers.[99]

An America which felt itself to represent mankind's present and future, and to be so far ahead of Europe, not to speak of Asia, was indeed less likely than any country to appreciate the qualities of a prehistoric society. Collective ownership of land, which went with these tribal forms, was anathema to Americans, as it and other kinds of collective ownership have been in our day. 'Common property and civilization cannot co-exist', a Commissioner for Indian Affairs laid down succinctly in 1838: only separate holdings could breathe enterprise, morality, progress into Indians.[100] Here again Europe was no more open-minded; in England, in Spain, and elsewhere common lands were being confiscated from common people, and to make estates for the rich instead of homesteads for the poor.

Under the 'Intercourse Acts' a small annual sum was allocated to looms, ploughs and other equipment for Indians desirous of civilization. Among what were coming to be known as the 'Five Civilized Tribes' of the South, with a growing tincture of foreign blood as well as ideas, these novelties were making surprising headway, though white prejudices remained unsoftened. Mission bodies were taking the field and supplying further help, but often with the effect of undermining tribal solidarity, whether for armed defence or for peaceful survival. Not seldom it was the missionary who, as in many other corners of the colonial world, persuaded a people to accept an inequitable treaty.[101] His work might also lead to red men being enrolled to fight for their new masters against other Indians, whether or not they had any quarrel of their own with them. In a war in southern Oregon, characterized by Dunn as one of the least justifiable that Americans ever fought, use was made of a party of sixty Indian scouts, converts whose leader had been baptized as Donald McKay. 'They proved invaluable assistants, the only objection to them being that they absolutely refused to do anything on Sundays.'[102] Evidently they took their Scripture lessons too literally.

Soon after American Independence a luminary of Yale preached a sermon proving that Indians were descendants of Canaanites expelled from their homeland by Joshua, and therefore could be legitimately expelled from America.[103] By now this sort of logic was old-fashioned, except in the South with its slave economy, but something very like it was being woven into secular thinking, and producing a version of Social Darwinism before Darwin. 'Lower' races must give place to 'higher': this conviction was firm enough to outweigh a series of Supreme Court decisions upholding the sovereign rights of the tribes. The government still took action now and then against interlopers who infringed them, but it had too little public opinion with it, and too little determination to live up to its professed intentions.

President Monroe, who wanted to keep Europeans out of the New World, had no great desire to keep Americans out of the Indian part of it; on the contrary he proposed in 1825 that Indians instead of interlopers be removed, by a transfer of tribes to the unopened West. Congress failed to agree on this, in spite of the argument of Monroe and others, some of them sincere, that to leave tribesmen surrounded by 'civilization' and its infections must lead to degeneracy, from which the untainted wilderness would rescue them. It was very contradictory that the 'Civilized Tribes', which were assimilating modernity so rapidly, should be invited to go back to the wilds and learn to be 'Noble Savages' again; while their ejection to make room for more slave plantations would mean positive regression instead of progress. But the wish to combine the rewards of conscience and pocket was making equivocation a habit more ingrained in public life in America than anywhere else. What Gissing says of the typical Englishman, never doubtful of his country's moral superiority, might have been written at least as appositely about the American. 'To call him hypocrite, is simply not to know the man ... He is a monument of self-righteousness ... not personal but national.'[104]

Jackson, president from 1828, was not a man to boggle at any quibbles of logic. As Woodrow Wilson was to say, his notion of Indians was 'frankly that of the frontier soldier. They had no right, in his eyes, to stand in the way of the white man.'[105] Against loud protest from missionaries among the 'Civilized Tribes', and other humanitarians, in 1830 he pushed through the Removal Bill which authorized him to transport any Indians to beyond the Mississippi. This opened 'one of the blackest chapters in American history',[106] marked by sufferings akin to those of the 'Middle Passage'. In 1832 there was a war in Illinois and Wisconsin against tribesmen resisting this treatment under a chief named Black Hawk, in which Abraham Lincoln served as a militiaman and Jefferson Davis, his adversary in a bigger contest of days to come, as a regular officer. In the same year the government resolved on uprooting the Seminoles a second time. Some chiefs were got to agree to a treaty of banishment, but most of their people rejected it, and in 1835 the second Seminole War broke out. It dragged on among the swamps of Florida until 1841, after 30,000 troops had been put into the field and more than twenty million dollars spent.

A lieutenant on the staff, who published an account of the opening phase of this war, felt that the treaty had been illegitimate; also that Indians had been harried since the beginnings of America with warfare 'mercenary and very often wanton', and treated insultingly, as if no better than beasts. 'The rights of the Indian ... have been trampled under foot, and his feelings have been as little respected ...'.[107] At last about four thousand survivors were rounded up and despatched westward. Another participant in the wars of this period, who commonly thought Indians more sinning than sinned against, could not help commiserating with them when he watched them being driven off into exile, sometimes in long chain-gangs. 'It was a melancholy spectacle', he wrote of one such occasion, 'as these proud monarchs of the soil were marched off from their native land to a distant country, which to their anticipations presented all the horrors of the infernal regions. There were several who committed suicide rather than endure the sorrow of leaving the spot where rested the bones of their ancestors.'[108]

Of all the evictions, the most conspicuous was that of the Cherokees. Their language was now a written one, and in 1827 they adopted a constitution on the U.S. model and claimed sovereign status; but a legal judgement in Georgia in 1831 denied recognition to the 'Cherokee Nation'. In 1838 they were deported to Oklahoma, the abode assigned to the 'Five Tribes'. Before his retirement in 1836 Jackson had sent them some cold comfort in the form of a letter exhorting them to see that it was all for the best. 'Circumstances that cannot be controlled and which are beyond the reach of human laws render it impossible that you can flourish in the midst of a civilized community.'[109] In plainer English it was the white squatters and voters who could not be controlled. But appeals to historical necessity, so frequent in American annals, were in the spirit of a tumultuous society amid whose chaotic advance the individual might well feel that he was swept along by ungovernable forces, and could disclaim responsibility for what they or he were doing.

In 1834 Congress was busy overhauling the machinery for Indian affairs and the legislation on 'intercourse'. It rejected a proposed regular government for a permanent Indian homeland, with a governor and a council of tribal representatives, which would send a delegate to Congress and might ultimately become a State of the Union. Here was an intriguing possibility which, however, found many opponents, including no doubt some who did not want Indians to be left with so much land for very long. In Oklahoma the Five Tribes were for a while secure enough, and the Cherokees in particular recovered and again made remarkable progress. But tribes pushed out on to the plains might be trespassers on the hunting-grounds of formidable antagonists like the Sioux. What the legal relationship of any Indians to the United States might now be, neither lawyers nor anyone else could say.[110]

References

1. Quoted by W. Sullivan, *We Are Not Alone* (Harmondsworth edn., 1970), p.267.
2. A. de Tocqueville, *Democracy in America* (1835, 1840; World's Classics edn., London, 1946), Chap. XXXI.
3. *The Federalist*, No.11. See generally M. Savelle, *The Origins of American Diplomacy* (New York, 1967), Chap. XX, especially Part 2, 'Enticements to Imperialism . . .'.
4. R.S. Dunn, *Sugar and Slaves – The Rise of the Planter Class in the English West Indies, 1624–1713* (1972; London edn., 1973), pp.111–12, 336.
5. See W.L. Sachse, *The Colonial American in Britain* (Madison, 1956).
6. J. Hardy, *The First American Revolution* (London, 1937), p.94.
7. G. Lichtheim, *Imperialism* (London edn., 1971), pp.56–8.
8. J.B. Perkins, *France in the American Revolution* (London & New York, 1911), Chap. VIII.
9. Lt. F. Hall, *Travels in Canada and the United States in 1816 and 1817* (London, 1818), pp.443–5.
10. O. Warner, *A Portrait of Lord Nelson* (Pelican edn., London, 1963), pp.57–8.
11. L. Dermigny, *La Chine et l'Occident – Le commerce à Canton au XVIIIe siècle 1719–1833* (Paris, 1964), p.1168.
12. 'Papers respecting the Negociation . . . for a Renewal of the East-India Company's exclusive Privileges . . .', printed by the Directors (London, 1813), No. LXXXIII.
13. Dermigny, *op. cit.*, p.1171; and see generally on this trade Part 3, Chap. III, 'Yankees et fourrures'.

14. See H. & M. Sprout, *The Rise of American Naval Power 1776–1918* (Princeton, 1946), p.28 ff.

15. See K. Lockridge, 'Land, Population and the Evolution of New England Society 1630–1790', in *Past and Present*, No. 39, 1968, p.62 ff.

16. Perkins, *op. cit.*, p.471.

17. Entry for 6 September 1812, in *Memoirs of John Quincy Adams*, ed. C.F. Adams, Vol.II (Philadelphia, 1874).

18. See J.W. Pratt, *Expansionists of 1812* (New York, 1949), Chap. II.

19. *Ibid.*, pp. 124–5.

20. Text in *The Papers of Henry Clay*, ed. J.F. Hopkins (Univ. of Kentucky Press, Vol. 1, 1959), pp.765–73.

21. Pratt, *op. cit.*, pp.163–4.

22. *The Papers of Henry Clay, op. cit.*, p.859.

23. *America: or a General Survey ... of the Western Continent*, by 'A Citizen of the United States' (London, 1828), pp.268–9, 261, 248.

24. See W.H. Dawson, *Richard Cobden and Foreign Policy* (London, 1926), Chap. XI: 'The Friend of America'.

25. Scott Nearing and J. Freeman, *Dollar Diplomacy* (1925; New York edn., 1969), pp.236–7.

26. Pratt, *op. cit.*, p.52.

27. *Ibid.*

28. *America* (see n.23), p.269.

29. J.D.P. Fuller, *The Movement for the Acquisition of all Mexico 1846–1848* (Baltimore, 1936), p.45.

30. *Ibid.*, p.127.

31. Text in *Problems of American History*, ed. R.W. Leopold and A.S. Link (2nd edn., Englewood Cliffs, N.J., 1957), p.493.

32. C.E. Trevelyan, *Report upon the Inland Customs and Town-duties of the Bengal Presidency* (Calcutta, 1834), p.196.

33. *Thomas Cather's Journal of a Voyage to America in 1836* (London, 1955), pp.18–19.

34. Parke Godwin, 1844; see *American Issues:* Vol. 1, *The Social Record*, ed. W. Thorp *et al.* (2nd edn., Chicago, 1944), p.414.

35. A. Smith, *The Wealth of Nations* (1776), pp.623–4 (World's Classics edn., O.U.P.).

36. *Polk – The Diary of a President 1845–1849*, ed. A. Nevin (London & New York, 1952), under date 30 Jan. 1849.
37. Thomas Skidmore, 1829; see *American Issues*, Vol. 1, pp.237–8.
38. R.W. Van Alstyne, *The Rising American Empire* (Oxford, 1960), pp.36–7. Every student of the subject must be indebted to this work.
39. R.G. Wallace, *Memoirs of India* (London, 1824), p.219; Tocqueville, *op. cit.*, Chap. XIX. Cf. R.R. Palmer: 'It was common for Europeans to predict that the infant born in 1776 would become a giant' (in Library of Congress symposium, *The Impact of the American Revolution Abroad*, Washington, 1976, p.8).
40. See M.M. Greenberg, *British Trade and the Opening of China 1800–1842* (Cambridge, 1951), pp.108–9.
41. *The Early Writings of Frederick Jackson Turner*, ed. F. Mood (Univ. of Wisconsin Press, 1938), p.215.
42. Quoted by J.P. Dunn, *Massacres of the Mountains* (1886; London edn., 1963), p.54. Cf. H. Kohn, *American Nationalism. An Interpretative Essay* (New York, 1957), pp.103–5.
43. Michael Chevalier, *Society Manners and Politics in the United States* (1839; New York edn., 1966), Letter XXIX.
44. Earl of Malmesbury, *Memoirs of an ex-Minister* (Leipzig edn., 1885), Vol. 1, pp.91–2.
45. Tocqueville, *op. cit.*, Chap. X.
46. *Ibid.*, Chap. XIX.
47. *Thomas Cather's Journal, op. cit.*, p.44.
48. Van Alstyne, *op. cit.*, pp.105, 138.
49. Pratt, *op. cit.*, p.274.
50. Fuller, *op. cit.*, p.26.
51. *Dictionary of American Biography.*
52. See *American Issues*, Vol. 1, p.156.
53. George Kinloch, letter of 1 September 1814. I was shown the original by Mr Charles Tennant, who has written a biography of Kinloch.
54. See H.C. Allen, *Great Britain and the United States – A History of Anglo-American Relations (1783–1952)* (London, 1954), pp.407–8.
55. Fuller, *op. cit.*, p.95.
56. *Ibid.*, p.50.

57. Dunn, *op. cit.*, p.65.

58. O.A. Singletary, *The Mexican War* (Univ. of Chicago, 1960), p.14–15.

59. J.T. Downey, *The Cruise of the Portsmouth, 1845–1847*, ed. H. Lamar (New Haven, 1963), p.103.

60. S.E. Morison, *'Old Bruin' – Commodore Matthew C. Perry 1794–1858* (London, 1968), p.180.

61. *Ibid.*, p.127.

62. See Col. W.A. Ganoe, *The History of the United States Army* (revised edn., New York, 1943), p.207 ff.

63. S.E. Chamberlain, *Recollections of a Rogue*, ed. R. Butterfield (London, 1957), pp.89–90. Cf. p.87: 'The cave was full of our volunteers yelling like fiends, while on the rocky floor lay over twenty Mexicans, dead and dying in pools of blood. Women and children were clinging to the knees of the murderers and shrieking for mercy.' The whole narrative reeks of such things.

64. Morison, *op. cit.*, p.228.

65. R.S. Henry, *The Story of the Mexican War* (1950; new edn., New York, 1961), pp.186, 240. He regards the criticism of the war as factious, and denies American responsibility for the war (pp.32–3).

66. Louis Tappan; cited by O.D. Edwards, 'The American Image of Ireland: a Study of its Early Phases', in *Perspectives in American History*, Vol. IV (1970), p.264.

67. Allen, *op. cit.*, p.404.

68. F. Downey, *Indian Wars of the U.S. Army (1776–1865)* (1962; Derby, Connecticut edn., 1964), p.24.

69. *Chronicles of the Pilgrim Fathers* (Everyman edn., London, 1910), p.319.

70. *Ibid.*, pp.350, 354.

71. *Description of Pennsylvania* (1683).

72. W.C. Macleod, *The American Indian Frontier* (London, 1928), Chap. XIII, 'Celt and Indian'.

73. *Chronicles, op. cit.*, p.36.

74. *Ibid.*, p.256.

75. *Ibid.*, p.129.

76. Macleod, *op. cit.*, p.239.

77. *Chronicles, op. cit.*, p.226.

78. J.D. MacLeod, *Slavery, Race and the American Revolution* (Cambridge, 1974), pp.110–11.
79. Cited in H.S. Commager, *America in Perspective* (New York, 1948), p.33.
80. L.H. Morgan, *Ancient Society* (1877), Chap. V.
81. A.M. Josephy, *The Indian Heritage of America* (1968; Harmondsworth edn., 1975), p.322.
82. A.M. Sakolski, *The Great American Land Bubble* (New York, 1932), p.5.
83. Downey, *op. cit.*, pp.41 ff.
84. R.L. Meek, *Social Science and the Ignoble Savage* (Cambridge, 1976), p.218.
85. D.J. MacLeod, *op. cit.*, pp.8, 12.
86. R. Horsman, *Expansion and American Indian Policy 1783–1812* (Michigan Univ. Press, 1967), p.6.
87. *The Papers of Thomas Jefferson* (Vol. 8, Princeton, 1953), p.185.
88. Horsman, *op. cit.*, pp.57–8, 64, 85.
89. *The Papers of Thomas Jefferson* (Vol. 10, Princeton, 1954), p.599.
90. Sakolski, *op. cit.*, pp.31, 48 ff.
91. *Ibid.*, pp.126–7; W.C. Macleod, *op. cit.*, p.462.
92. Horsman, *op. cit.*, p.37 ff.
93. *Ibid.*, p.75.
94. Sakolski, *op. cit.*, pp.183–7.
95. F.J. Turner, *op. cit.*, 'The Character and Influence of the Indian Trade in Wisconsin'; e.g. p.160: 'The importance of this credit system can hardly be overestimated ... The system left the Indians at the mercy of the trader when one nation monopolized the field'.
96. J. Buchanan, *Sketches of the History, Manners, and Customs of the North American Indians* (London, 1824), pp.vii, xi.
97. Cf. Cooper's *The Pathfinder* (1840), Chap. II.
98. See Christine Bolt, *Victorian Attitudes to Race* (London, 1971).
99. Morgan, *op. cit.*, Chap. V.
100. J.E. Chamberlin, *The Harrowing of Eden – White Attitudes towards Native Americans* (New York, 1975), p.19.
101. D.R. Wrone, 'The Ground of American Indian Reform Policy', in *Cohesion* (Delhi), Vol. II, No. 1 (1971), pp.49–50.
102. Dunn, *op. cit.*, p.484.
103. H. Kohn, *The Idea of Nationalism* (New York, 1945), pp.668–9.

104. George Gissing, *The Private papers of Henry Ryecroft* (London, 1903), Part 4, No. 20.

105. Woodrow Wilson, *A History of the American People* (New York, 1901–2), Vol. IV, pp.16–17.

106. Josephy, *op. cit.*, p.325.

107. W. Potter, *The War in Florida* (1836; Ann Arbor edn., 1966), pp.38–9.

108. J.R. Motte, *Journey into Wilderness – An Army Surgeon's Account of . . . the Creek and Seminole Wars 1836–1838*, ed. J.F. Sunderman (Univ. of Florida Press, 1953), p.19.

109. Fritz, *op. cit.*, pp.123–4.

110. W.C. Macleod, *op. cit.*, p.207.

PART TWO

MIDDLE DECADES

1

The Literary Mirror

Melville and Whitman, America's two most original writers, belonged with many lesser ones to the middle years of the 19th century when the dewy sheen of a new civilization was fading into the light of common day. Accompanying this change were expansionist impulses, oscillating between the ideal and the sordid. 'Democratic nationalism' in America owed much to the stimulus of the French Revolution;[1] the Revolution had quickly turned imperialistic, and all the West European countries with which America had its closest intimacies were owners or seekers of empires. In Britain a thousand ties, gross or subtle, of family or interest or sentiment, linked novelists and poets with colonialism. In the U.S. something analogous can be found. A bustling Main Street environment might be wholesome, but held little inspiration for the Muses; men of letters, like the restless westward trekkers, might find further-off horizons more enthralling, and the onward march of destiny a more congenial theme than the humdrum daily life around them. In terms of literary earnings too, they were apt to be fish out of water, and to gravitate, like their counterparts in earlier Europe or in Asia at all times, towards official employment: often overseas, where they would breathe empire-germs floating in the contemporary air, even if some, like Mark Twain, might vigorously sneeze them out again.

Thus Hawthorne took wing in 1853 to a consulate in England – a lofty sphere which eluded his friend Melville, as if Shakespeare should have aspired in vain to be town clerk of Stratford. Bret Harte attained the same dignity, and finally settled in England; long before this, as a boy, he settled in California, in time to welcome the arrival of the Stars and Stripes. Lowell soared to the more eminent status of minister at Madrid and then London. Irving was minister at Madrid before him, after years in Spain collecting materials for works like his *Conquest of Granada*, a depiction of events of days gone by not without resemblances to some in his own day. It came out in 1829, when the French conquest of Algeria was about to start, and reads like a narrative by an imaginative Frenchman or Englishman of some recent colonial campaign, a dashing affair full of romance and adventure. In 1836 appeared his *Astoria*, a collection of stories and records of the American pioneers in Oregon, a tribute to their struggles with Nature and with savage Indians. 'In their more prosperous days,' Irving writes of some of these Indians, with an irony that could as easily have been directed against the nation which was taking their place, 'the Omahas looked upon themselves as the most powerful and perfect of human beings, and considered all created things as made for their peculiar use and benefit.'[2] His book was in part a polemic against the British who were trying to hog the fur trade, at a time when war with Britain over the Far West was on the cards. George Bancroft's term in the administration and then as minister at London during the Mexican War, later at Berlin, is another reminder that there were many links in that age between history-writing and empire-building, on both sides of the Atlantic. He had been much in Europe in youth. J.L. Motley wrote of the rise of the Netherlands to independence and power in the world, and was minister at Vienna and London.

Oliver Wendell Holmes was studying medicine at Paris in 1833–35 when the conquest of Algeria was getting under way. His 'Little Gentleman' of Boston declaims at the breakfast-table, with only a divinity student faintly demurring, about the Indians or 'original bipeds' of the country being a mere 'red-crayon sketch of humanity laid on the canvas before the colours for the real manhood were ready ... Irreclaimable, Sir, — irreclaimable! ... A provisional race, Sir, – nothing more ... passing away, according to the programme', to make room for a healthy new race 'with Lake Superior and Huron and all the rest of 'em for washbasins! A new race, and a whole new world for the new-born human soul to work in!'[3] America's soul was not really of quite such pristine freshness, but had migrated from an Old World, not in entire forgetfulness of ancestral sin; and the Great Lakes were to cleanse the new race far less than it was to pollute them.

Hawthorne too saw the red men as actors soon to quit the stage, even if he was less ready to hiss them off it. They built no monuments that could perpetuate their memory: 'when they have disappeared from the earth their history will appear a fable, and they misty phantoms'.[4] Longfellow raised an attractive if soon-crumbling monument for them in 1855 with his Song of *Hiawatha*, whose hero was partly a historical Iroquois character. He had always a sympathetic regard for the Indians, in some degree as colourful material for the American 'national' literature that he wanted to see growing up, though he was not advocating that 'every page be rife with scalps, tomahawks and wampum.'[5] He deplored his country's philistine materialism, and in old age its financial scandals and corruption. Forest and Indian memories were a relief from all this, like mountains and Highlanders for Scottish writers. He disliked Andrew Jackson, condemned the Mexican War, and disapproved of slavery. Thoreau, whose *Walden, or Life in the Woods* came out a year before *Hiawatha*, was a more militant anti-slavery man, while he too respected Indians as a people close to Nature and mother earth.

Herman Melville concerned himself with the psychology of frontier hatred of Indians.[6] In his own psychology a longing for the natural, simple, unspoiled, for a new dispensation, could take the form either of fervent American patriotism or of championship of primitive man, of any colour, and could set up insoluble contradictions which drove his genius into more uncharted waters than any his Captain Ahab sailed. His extraordinarily crowded harvest years began, with *Typee*, at the same time as the Mexican War. In the South Seas in his wander-years he encountered European civilization, French in particular, and his novel dwelt eloquently on its harmful effects on pre-industrial peoples; also on the bad effects of such intercourse on white men. He had a great deal to say to the discredit of missionary effort, forerunner – like a John the Baptist in the wilderness – or companion of so much European and then American expansionism. His warnings might have gone home more if allowed to reach the public in full; but the public's self-appointed guardians allowed *Typee* to circulate for many years only in heavily expurgated form.[7]

Whitejacket, in 1850, looked back to Melville's year of naval service in 1843–44, which may have commenced at Honolulu. At that time, aged twenty-four, he could feel a youthful optimism about both his own future and his country's, the two naturally blending in his mind. He could still hold fast to the vision or mirage of a new civilization rising upon the world, a beneficent luminary, which in days soon to come would be vulgarized into the stock-in-trade of earth-bound demagogues. But already Melville's warship the *Neversink* made a good symbol of the America which sent such a man to sea to dream dreams of his country in such a floating purgatory, where men poured out thought and fancy to one another up aloft in the crow's nest while every degradation reigned below deck.

On one of its evils *Whitejacket* had something like the impact of *Uncle Tom's Cabin*, and got flogging abolished with American promptness, in the teeth of conservative disciplinarians like Old Bruin, or Commodore Perry. Melville could achieve far less towards reforming the social composition of the navy, and the bellicosity that flowed naturally from this; it was too true-born a descendant of the British navy to pay heed to his complaint that 'such a thing as a common seaman rising to the rank of a commissioned officer in our navy is nowadays almost unheard of'.[8] Identifying himself emotionally with America, cultivating an 'extreme cultural nationalism' in his rejection of any European tutelage of American literature,[9] this democrat might be in danger of getting mixed up with the very abuses and ambitions which he challenged, in the repulsive person of Captain Claret, on the quarterdeck of the *Neversink*. He was part of the long tradition of an American radicalism always akin to the youth movements of today, both in hopeful ardour and inventiveness and in innocence of any theory, any intellectual chart or guide.

Republican contempt like Melville's for a bedizened emperor of Brazil[10] could easily turn into lordly contempt for the poor foreigners who truckled to such potentates; his grandfather John Bull was wont to despise as well as pity the Frenchman, ignorant of freedom. The United States could not help seeing its Latin American neighbours, and all other retarded peoples, as children to be protected against themselves as well as against wicked European uncles; just as today it cannot help being reluctant to admit that they are growing up. A creed of free competition, besides, of the career open to talent and the best man coming to the top, was readily translated into international terms. Melville's confident assumption that what was good for America must be good for the world[11] breathed the spirit of all messianic nationalism; it would be leadenly echoed a century later by the announcement that what is good for General Motors must be good for America.

Between the philosophy of *Typee*, where Melville was a human being on his own amid the flux of earth's peoples, and that of *Whitejacket*, where he was after all a retainer of Mars, a servitor though an astonishing one of the might of an ambitious nation, there were fundamental antitheses. They can be felt working obscurely in *Moby Dick* (1815), America's most towering work of imagination and one of the most colossal of all the 19th century. Here, exalted into vast Wagnerian cloud-shadows of myth and tragedy, is the theme, so much a part of that century's experience, of the conflict of warped civilization and elemental savagery. His doom-laden vessel, Melville does not neglect to remind us, takes its name from the Pequods, 'a celebrated tribe of Massachusetts Indians, now extinct as the ancient Medes'[12] – extinct because the American steamroller passed over it. When he invokes his 'great democratic God', raiser up of 'selected champions from the kingly commons', he sets among them, beside Bunyan and Cervantes, Andrew Jackson.

Heroic and grotesque are seldom far apart when men go out, like Captain Ahab, to conquer. Much like the hero-worshipping Carlyle, Melville was tempted to admire power in any shape, democratic or not, and Ahab's autocratic rule of his ship leads him to thoughts of that strapping mediocrity Nicholas I, Autocrat of all the Russias and policeman of Europe, as a monarch of 'imperial brain' under whose throne 'the plebeian herds crouch abased before the tremendous centralization' – the union of character and authority. He was not the only American to be awed by the huge, if half illusory, force concentrated in the Tsarist government: it was too far away for its crimes and feeblenesses to be as discernible as they were from Europe, and to admire Russia was an oblique mode of resenting the common rival, England. If all *terra firma* from Warsaw to Vladivostok belongs to the Tsar, ocean and its shores belong equally of right to their true native denizen, the Nantucket whaler, and America should proceed to take possession of Mexico – so Melville exclaims, early in the *Pequod's* long voyage from the real to the visionary world.

In the same flight of rhetoric he is carried on to an image as superb as empire has ever inspired in any language, and one that reveals how closely joined in his and his country's mind was the imperial course that Britain was running and that which America in turn must run: – 'Let the English overswarm all India, and hang out their blazing banner from the sun ...'. There is a bizarre symbolism of the Orient and its thrones and dominations in Ahab's boat-crew of mysterious easterners, who would be more at home in *Vathek*, a dramatic dressing-up of the exotic vagrants often to be met with in whaling crews. They are led (very unexpectedly) by a Parsee, with the (very incongruous) name of Fedallah, an emanation of the 'insulted, immemorial, unalterable countries' of the East. It was precisely in these terms that Englishmen visualized the East they were setting out to master, compelling the unalterable to obey the law of change. Kinglake's *Eothen*, published in 1844, overflows with the same transcendental orientalism. But underlying this in *Moby Dick* is the tragic sensation of conflict alike inexplicable and inescapable. Everything in the book is saturated with predestination, Melville's transposition into the key of tragedy of the manifest destiny of stump oratory. It haunts his ship down to the last fatal moments when the fated monster, 'strangely vibrating his predestinating head', makes the final onset.[13]

With all his national spirit Melville was one of those un-American writers, strangers to their country's facile optimism, like Poe, Hawthorne, and later Faulkner, who seem as Kohn says 'haunted by the malevolence and horror of existence ... obsessed with the ancestral curse coming down to the Americans from the recesses of their history.'[14] Their curse was a fusion of Puritan morbidity with a racial guilt which Calvinism had served to justify, but which now, when theology was rusting, forced its way back into consciousness. Freest from all this, or perhaps the one who talked loudest and most hopefully in order to feel free, was Whitman. Poetic feeling in him, like popular feeling in America, was compounded from a wide range of associations. The westward sweep that fired his imagination might be that of freedom, or of men with white skins, or of profiteering, or dominion. He was kindled to a burst of eloquence by the arrival of the first Japanese envoy, seeing in it an omen of the American eagle winging its way across the Pacific.[15]

Another was called forth by the fight with the Sioux in 1876 where General Custer and nearly all his force perished. An enterprising artist named Mulvaney, now long forgotten, spent two years sketching on the frontier, and then produced a massive painting of the battle, forerunner of a legion of illustrations for novels and film tableaux, with 'swarms upon swarms of savage Sioux, in their warbonnets, frantic ... like a hurricane of demons', Custer in the centre 'with dilated eye and extended arm, aiming a huge cavalry pistol'. So Whitman rhapsodically described it after a whole rapt hour of gazing, beholding in it 'a western, autochthonic phase of America, the frontiers, culminating, typical, deadly, heroic to the uttermost – nothing in the books like it, nothing in Homer, nothing in

Shakespeare; more grim and sublime than either, all native, all our own, and all a fact.' He rejoiced that it was free from 'the stock traits of European war pictures'.[16] In reality America was never less far or free from Europe than when seized by this exultant spirit of the white man militant and triumphant. But a new country is impatient for a history of its own, and the quickest way to accumulate either this or capital is with the sword.

In later years and gloomier moments, as he like Longfellow contemplated what his country was turning into, Whitman's accents suggest thoughts of the American eagle, or the new civilization, as the eagle nailed to the sinking masthead at the close of *Moby Dick* – 'the bird of heaven, with archangelic shrieks', drawn down with the doomed ship into the dark waters of the past. The grand Republican experiment would be a failure, he wrote, if America went on like Europe multiplying 'crops of poor, desperate, dissatisfied, nomadic, miserably-waged populations', swollen by more and more immigrants.[17] Such anxieties could prompt a turning back to expansionism and adventure – across the North American plains, or further yet – in search of relief and reassurance. If the dream of human happiness, perfectability even, were to fade away from America, it would be a dead end worse than the eventual closing of the western frontier.

2

From West Indies to Far East

When Robert Louis Stevenson visited California he found its old capital, Monterey, still a very Spanish town, but all the surrounding lands belonged to Americans who had somehow got them from their former old-fashioned owners, and who also held all the chief posts.[18] California's induction into the American family was romanticized in a novelette where one of the James Brothers turned up and helped a gallant young fellow, nephew of the first American governor, and in love with a bewitching *señorita*, to rescue her from a villainous Mexican gambler and a lynch mob.[19] Dual impulses of conquest and liberation have often found expression in stereotypes of the defeated males as degenerate riff-raff, the young females as pathetically charming and appealing. But very soon all thoughts about California were submerged in the discovery in 1848 of gold, and the gold-rush which Marx was to see as luring the country away from the road of progress into the swamp of get-rich-quick capitalism. It came at the right moment to perform this service, in the year of Europe's revolutions which brought over a fresh multitude of exiles, this time sturdy radicals or even socialists. In the gold-rush the double character of American expansionism was exhibited in intensified form. It was a popular stampede, with fortunes open to all; but capitalism was its stealthy camp-follower, ready to skim the profits like the merchant who, all through history, accompanied armies and relieved the fighting-man of his plunder.

Looked at in another light the winning of the Pacific provinces put the U.S. temporarily in a position more akin than ever before to that of the European empires. 'From the standpoint of national defense, California and Oregon were distant overseas colonies.'[20] Direct overland communication would be difficult for years to come. Routes by way of Central America might be blocked by the old enemy Britain, with its Caribbean bases, much as Britain was always in dread of its route to India by way of Suez being blocked by the Russians. To sail all the way round Cape Horn was on a par with British ships having to get to India by sailing round the Cape of Good Hope. This new situation was bound to fan interest both in the Isthmus and in the oceans. With the heightened confidence induced by military victory, it was quite enough to start America on a fresh fit of outward-turning restlessness. Polk and his government, not content with their Mexican laurels or spoils, were eager to push on southward and take Cuba. A series of filibustering raids failed to achieve this; but President Pierce, a north-erner brought into the White House in 1853 by southern backing, shared the same creed. Underlying it was the thought of safeguarding America's unstable unity by pushing national claims abroad. He had his eye on Hawaii as well as Cuba, and also on Nicaragua.

The Clayton-Bulwer Agreement of 1850 with England, designed to allay tension over the Isthmus, was dismally failing to do so. London could be accused of using the Spaniards to impede America's advance southward, now as in earlier days, or as formerly of using the Indians to impede it westward. In fact British policy was already wavering in the fifties, partly because of Spain's unsatisfactory behaviour. Cuba was chronically in disorder, and was still smuggling slaves in spite of all pledges at Madrid. Spain moreover was trying indiscreetly to rebuild some part of its lost position in the New World, to make up for its insignificance in Europe. After securing treaties with Costa Rica and Nicaragua in 1850 it had to be restrained by its British mentor in 1856 and 1858 from picking a quarrel with Mexico, and in 1861 occupied San Domingo, a move disliked in London if only as connected with Spain's desire to keep the slave trade going.[21]

American expansionism still had for a mouthpiece the 'Young America' wing of Democrats, with ideas a truly American medley of new-fangled and old-fashioned. They wanted their country to use its strength to spread free institutions abroad, and also to snatch at more trade and more territory: here the Southern greed for slave-plantations further afield played a prominent part. The

U.S. was far too big and heterogeneous ever to have a single, simple attitude to the rest of the world. With westward enlargement now facing more obstacles – California was enrolled as a no-slavery state in 1850 – the slave-owning South had to fear a steady dwindling of its relative weight in the Union. Its own expansionist motives, economic and political, were complex. There was need of new soil to replace what was exhausted at home by cotton-cropping. For the slave-breeding areas there was a need of fresh markets for their product. Governor Smith of Virginia declared in 1847 that territory to be taken from Mexico would provide a natural outlet for Negroes raised in his state. Slavery he remarked grew less profitable as population grew more dense, and therefore must have room to expand. 'The South never can consent to be confined to prescribed limits.'[22] In other words the 'natural frontier' demanded by the South was an absence of any frontier. But the acquisition of Texas made land more plentiful than labour, and any further expansion would injure certain planters by raising the price of slaves and lowering that of cotton, while seizure of Cuba would mean fresh competition for sugar-growers. But if the South continued to aspire to a Caribbean empire, political incentives were outstripping economic, and were strong enough to keep all Southern interests banded together.[23] Defence of slavery, now under stronger and stronger attack, must come first with them all.

Here then was a classic case of a country's internal divisions making it a menace to its neighbours. Politically the South formed a single bloc, wielding much influence in Union affairs. Psychologically it felt a compulsive wish to break out from moral isolation and ostracism. Socially it had a gentry class something like the English, and disposed to ape it, with a similar superfluity of younger sons. It had too its mass of 'poor whites', making up according to Cairnes seven-tenths of the white population.[24] These supplied recruits for the filibustering expeditions; and if they fought devotedly in the Civil War, they must have been defending not only slavery or state rights, but a dream of empire in which they would have a share and come into their own. It was another version of a 'people's imperialism'. In the Italy that reached unification soon after this date and at once began sniffing for colonies in Africa, the lead was taken by southern politicians like Crispi, offering the desperately poor population of the south, since they had nothing better to offer it, dreams of farmlands to settle on in colonies under the Italian flag.

To protect slavery, the racialist thinking stirred up by the American

Revolution had gone on hardening. It was necessary to believe that black men were less than human; one proof satisfactory to the Southern intellect was the curse incurred by Noah's son Ham, progenitor of all Africans – a second fall of man, but only of black men. In the South, with buttressing like this, simple Scriptural faith knew no decline. Of more practical significance was the need to quash any emancipation of Negroes in the vicinity, such as might take place in Cuba at some date; still more any spread of self-government for them. Negro revolt and independence in San Domingo had been an appalling spectacle, and free blacks from the French West Indies were barred from entry, as 'potential agitators'.[25] Participation in the Panama Congress of free American nations in 1826 was opposed by Southern politicians, as little able as South African politicians later to bear the thought of having free black neighbours. In such matters the North could be got to fall in as a rule with Southern wishes for fear of a breakaway from the Union, the same fear that made the East fall in with Western transgressions.

Against all this, an anti-slavery stalwart like Orestes Augustus Brownson would argue, when the split finally came, that Southern influence was a menace to democracy, to white as well as black freedom. It would turn the Union into something like an oligarchical Rome, 'prepared for future conquest'. Mexico and Central America would be overrun, their coloured inhabitants Americanized by being enslaved. Cuba and the West Indies would come next. 'It could then extend its power over the whole continent of South America, and threaten an advance on Eastern Asia . . .'. These words sound prophetic, though they have been fulfilled by a northern money-ocracy instead of a southern plantocracy. To Brownson it seemed that secession would mean the South, with its European markets and connections, growing richer than the North, and what was left of the Union disintegrating.[26]

But there was always a lingering, indistinct misgiving that the Union could only be healthy and firm while it expanded. There were, besides, economic links and mutual interests between North and South, which could find political expression through the Democrat Party. At many points in American history, sectional pressures could converge in favour of a bigger navy; though it was a chronic difficulty that, as Melville realized on board the *Neversink*, free-born Americans were reluctant to submit to the servitude of naval as well as military life. The Navy Secretary who proposed a big increase in 1841, after a wrangle with Britain, and who also proposed a naval base in Hawaii, was 'an aristocratic

Virginia planter', A.P. Upshur.[27] Fourteen years later during a quarrel with
Spain another Virginian, T.S. Bocock, chairman of a Naval Affairs Committee,
pressed for a navy big enough to secure Cuba and push the British out of Central
America. Again in 1858, when an imbroglio arose out of British interference
with American vessels illegally engaged in African slave trading, the South
wanted more warships, while the North was reluctant; there was however an
abrupt Southern change of front when it appeared that more warships would
mean stiffer measures against slave running.[28]

Here was another of those contradictions which helped to throw American
empire-building out of gear, or postpone it to a later day. With all the blustering
and filibustering, the real policy both of the Pierce administration and that of
Buchanan, its successor, was 'basically one of inaction'.[29] Repeatedly Washington
seemed to be on the brink of a decisive step, only to draw back; and this in spite
of the opening afforded by the Crimean War and its locking up of British and
French resources during 1854–56. There was no very obvious reason for the
failure to act; but – to say nothing of an American conscience, which there
fortunately has always been – the near-empty spaces lately annexed suited the
national digestion better than the crowded Caribbean. Allowance must also be
made for the weak, ramshackle machinery of a government not designed for such
work, as all big European governments had been, and strikingly deficient in
diplomatic apparatus. This often had the result of leaving more room for private
enterprise. In 1859 Lord John Russell at the Foreign Office was indignant over a
General Hamey taking it on himself to occupy the island of San Juan, off the
Pacific coast. 'It is of the nature of the U.S. citizens', he commented acidly, 'to
push themselves where they have no right to go, and it is of the nature of the U.S.
Government not to venture to disavow acts they cannot have the face to
approve.'[30] But private initiative required a more coherently organized state to
follow it up. Just at this juncture it turned out that President Buchanan was
eager for a visit from the Prince of Wales, due to tour Canada the following
year,[31] to shed glory on his reign at the White House. This made it easier to
patch things up, and the visit duly took place; another evidence of the
ambivalence of American impulses.

Lack of direction, as well as lack of armed force, hampered attempts at self-
assertion even more when these were directed further away, towards Europe or
Asia. Some of America's ideals and ambitions alike required for their

accomplishment a challenge in one shape or another to Europe. There was an early fit of interventionism, aimed at Asia's empire in Europe, during the Greek war of independence. This struggle helped to turn the thoughts of European radicals to the new power in the West; it helped to inspire 'the theme common in Shelley's poetry from *The Revolt of Islam* to *Hellas*, of the American republic as the beacon of revolutionary hope in the world'.[32] To lend the Greeks a helping hand against the Turks would be a logical enough progression from the sparring with the Barbary Coast with which America's Mediterranean career began; and might be the means of securing an established position in the Mediterranean. Feeling for and against action ran very high in 1823. Daniel Webster argued that it was the duty of Americans 'to let mankind know that we are not tired of our institutions'. An opponent, Alexander Smyth, retorted in words again with a prophetic ring: 'If there be a mode of destroying civil liberty it is by leading this Government into unnecessary wars.'[33] Washington had set his face against any venturing into the European quicksand, and his warnings must have been in many minds.

On the eve of the revolutions of 1848 Western Europe was heatedly divided between antipathy towards America, and sympathy. In 1846 the American minister to Piedmont, Robert Wickliffe, reported great interest there and else-where in Europe in the Oregon dispute, with emphatic right-wing support for England and for 'the doctrine of Mr Guizot, that there should be a balance of power in America'. There was always 'in certain circles' dislike of the United States, but now it was much more positive. 'Since the annexation of Texas it ... cannot otherwise be described, than as a general alarm. The moral power of the country displayed to the whole world by that annexation, has struck the people on this side of the water with wonder and the governments with fear ... The liberals exclaim "Look, England bullies all Europe, but she cannot bully the United States...".' Conservatives were declaring that if the U.S. were allowed to grow any stronger, Europe might face a peril not merely of revolutions but of actual invasion.[34] Things had changed indeed since the time of President Monroe, when England was glad to enlist America as an auxiliary against the Holy Alliance: now England was being hailed as reactionary Europe's champion against democratic America. Next year when Mr Wickliffe went out to pay his respects to the king during a royal procession at Turin he found himself unwittingly the centre of attraction. 'As soon as I was seen the immense assemblage rent the air with cries of "Evviva gli Stati!" "Evviva L'America!" "Evviva il Ministro della grande repubblica!" '[35]

Unluckily for European democracy, the great Republic it was looking towards was really behaving, as it carried fire and sword into Mexico, just like the old regimes of Europe at their worst; like the Hapsburg monarchy, for instance, subduing Hungary with sword and gallows in 1849. After the collapse of the revolutions, America gave shelter to refugees from all over Europe, and heroes like Kossuth (one of whose hosts was Longfellow) received a clamorous welcome. 'Young America' wanted to give this excitement a more practical expression. It had a footing in the diplomatic service; it could count on men like O'Sullivan at Lisbon, or Consul Sanders at London from 1853, a warm friend of exiles there; and while the ministers at London and Paris, Buchanan and Mason, were more discreet, the former's secretary, Sickles, was all for audacity.[36] His aim was to promote a republican rising in Spain, with the twofold object of freeing Spain from despotic rule and enabling America to get possession of Cuba and its slave-plantations. The incongruity of these two aims typified the hybrid complexion of all American policy, not to say of the American soul.

In the ground-swell left behind by the revolutions, Europe was drifting towards that awkward, irrational conflict, the Crimean War, and as always conflict in Europe spelled opportunity for America. During 1853 the most distinguished figure in the long roll of America's political columnists, Karl Marx, was writing in the *New York Tribune* about rumours widespread in Europe of the U.S. meaning to take a hand. 'American intervention is expected everywhere, and is even looked upon with favour by portions of the English public', he wrote in July; and next month: 'The great event of the day is the appearance of American policy on the European horizon. Saluted by one party, detested by the other, the fact is admitted by all.' Aid to a fresh Italian revolt against Austria could be given by the navy, which might be looking for a Mediterranean base.[37] In fact American meddlings were to be more modest; the chief episode was the brief but histrionic one of Pierre Soulé, of Louisiana. By origin a political exile from France, he was still a fiery republican, welcomed Kossuth to New Orleans, and called on him and Mazzini in London in 1853 on his way to take up his post as minister at Madrid. He was at the same time a fanatical advocate of an American Cuba. In April 1854 he was authorized to offer Spain a large sum for the island, and, if this was rejected, to resort to other methods.[38]

A ready and congenial method was to lend support to the revolutionary movement already smouldering in Spain, just as earlier Americans thought of revolutionizing Mexico in order to secure Texas. Soulé was already in touch with the leaders of the small Democrat faction, which was of course pro-American, and he thought they would be prepared to sell Cuba if they came to power, though the public he admitted was unlikely to acquiesce.[39] After an upheaval in July brought a mildly Liberal government into office, Soulé was accused of complicity in left-wing riots, and had to run away from Spain in haste. His coloured servant or slave took the occasion to run away from *him*. Spaniards alleged that secret agents were tampering with troops about to embark for service in the colonies;[40] also that while America was caressing the Democrats with one hand, with the other it was offering money to the emigré Carlist chief Cabrera in London to induce him to launch a fresh rising on behalf of his ultra-reactionary movement[41] – a rising which did before long break out. In October the 'Ostend Conference' took place, with Soulé, Mason (a Virginian) and Buchanan present, and ways and means of getting Cuba as its theme. It was sanctioned by President Pierce 'at the solicitation of southern men',[42] and its Manifesto breathed their annexationist spirit. Disorders in Cuba were asserted to be threatening the tranquillity of the United States, and would justify the latter in taking control.[43] In Europe the partitions of Poland had been justified by this identical doctrine.

Spain could count on some support from Britain and France, which were trying to persuade it to enter the Crimean War on their side: they were not prepared to offer a full guarantee of the Spanish colonies, but France hinted at a possible joint protectorate over San Domingo, to prevent the U.S. from making it a stepping-stone towards Cuba.[44] Both allies urged restraint over the case of the ship the *Black Warrior*, the subject of a prolonged dispute between Madrid and Washington;[45] they had no wish to make America any more friendly to Russia – the keystone of European reaction – than it already was. In August 1855 a Spanish offer of an indemnity was accepted. Marcy, the Secretary of State, was not pleased with his ill-disciplined representatives, and Pierce decided on prudence. As always, American counsels were divided. Northerners were disinclined to underwrite Southern buccaneering, conservatives to consort with a European left wing which had displayed in 1848 ideas more extreme than any dreamed of in American philosophy. One such conservative was Commodore Perry, who was striking a note often heard in our day when he talked scathingly of the public enthusiasm over Kossuth and 'the cause of Hungarian liberty (alias socialism & Red republicanism)'.[46]

America kept out of the Crimean War, sensibly content to snap up the commercial openings that it offered; and instead of challenging Europe on its own ground, threw out a challenge to its hegemony in Asia. Perry's expedition to Japan was being lengthily planned at the same time that the Spanish experiment was being tried. American enterprise in Asian waters and the South Seas was growing and finding new forms. Among these, the least reputable was a share in the 'coolie trade', or export from China of indentured labourers to countries like Peru, under conditions not many degrees less barbarous than the African slave trade.[47] Britain banned participation in 1855, America not till 1862. Most closely interested in the mission to Japan was the whaling business, which wanted to obtain necessaries for its crews at Japanese ports, rum and women heading the list. In this industry New England (and various shipowners of Quaker family) held sway, keeping up the ferocious pursuit of profit which Melville ennobled into Ahab's pursuit of *Moby Dick*, and the harsh temper that went with it – 'a certain implacable effrontery', as Veblen calls it; a spirit nurtured in the past by New England's leading place in the slave trade, where 'American business enterprise learned how not to let its right hand know what its left hand was doing.'[48]

Whaling ships were ruled by their captains with a more than naval brutality, which must have owed something to the economical custom of employing sailors local to the area. Half the crews of the ships operating round the Azores came to be recruited from the islanders.[49] R.L. Stevenson met a Pacific islander whom one skipper, from New Bedford, left marooned on a cannibal island to save paying his wages – an act 'simply murder'.[50] When government backing was wanted, these hardened men of affairs could weep tears as warm as any crocodile's, and they made much ado about the plight of crews shipwrecked on the inhospitable coasts of Japan. There has always had to be some victim to be rescued, whatever more material objectives may be in view, to galvanize America into action. Late in 1851 Perry was assuring a big whaling shipowner of his willingness to head an expedition for the purpose of securing a treaty 'and the emancipation of the unfortunates of which you speak, now suffering in cruel and hopeless captivity'.[51]

America liked to think it could open Asian doors without battering rudely at them as Europeans did; in practice it had been waiting for them to do this and then following behind. Now that it was feeling strong enough to take a line of its own in Asia, it would immediately begin copying European methods. Since moreover its armed forces were still in fact very limited, it would also very soon move towards collaboration with Europeans. Naval men like Perry, and other Americans, might be resentful of Britain's ever-growing power, but face to face with Asian peoples they became conscious of the white man's common interests and feelings[52] – much as conservative Europeans resented British power but had a fellow-feeling with Britain as against the United States. Dislike of Britain's empire could then easily turn into envy of it, and make some Americans want to emulate it.

Perry's record showed him very much a man of action, and an exponent of the peremptory mode of dealing with weak countries – for their own good – which in course of time was to become habitual to America. He was chosen for the mission on the strength of a varied experience of other races: of dealing with pirates in the Caribbean, taking part in a naval demonstration at Naples, and patrolling the Slave Coast of Africa. Here his conduct is variously depicted; he is described as protecting well-disposed tribes from marauders, and assuring their chiefs that 'he had not been sent to Africa to oppress or ill-treat the natives',[53] – but we also read that one of these palavers 'ended in a fight with bloodshed and in the burning of several towns. His "ball-and-powder policy" was long remembered by the natives.'[54] Mexicans were the next to have cause to remember him. It was now the turn of the Japanese. His instructions for the mission seem to have been drafted by himself. 'It is manifest from past experience', they lay down, 'that arguments or persuasion addressed to this people, unless they be seconded by some imposing manifestation of power, will be utterly unavailing.'[55] He was debarred from resorting to force except in self-defence; how he would choose to interpret this might be an open question.

Nearing Japan he paused at the Bonin Islands, bought a tract of land from one of the few settlers for a coaling-station, and thought his government ought to lay claim to them. In Japan he and his men found, or believed they found (as Europeans in Asia regularly did), the common people as friendly and welcoming as their rulers were unfriendly; women were offered on liberal terms. Dealing with the 'very sagacious and deceitful' officials, Perry congratulated himself on his familiarity with other strange lands.[56] He was accordingly more truculent than his government wished him to be, and was given a less free hand during his second visit to Japan to receive the answer to his demand for a treaty.[57] He got one without having to fire his guns; it was of slender value, but he had stolen a march on Europe. After his return he urged on public opinion the need for bigger commercial openings in Asia, and proposed that the port of Kelung in Formosa should be occupied, in deference to 'an over-ruling Providence' and the nation's 'ultimate destiny'.[58]

Perry had set sail for Japan with far bigger things in mind than a mere trade agreement: 'he conceived of it as the opening move of an eventual struggle between the United States and Great Britain for control of the Pacific.'[59] With him at the helm the fleet was to act as imperial path-finder. But he came back with some changed views, having found the British everywhere amicable, and seeing the Russians instead as the grand Pacific antagonist of the future. Townsend Harris, chosen to go out as first consul-general and first resident diplomat from the West in Japan, was prepared from the start for good relations with the British; or, more exactly, for a two-barrelled tactic of profiting by British and French moves in Asia while criticizing them behind the scenes in order to win local esteem. This failed businessman had knocked about a good deal in the East, and had many acquaintances in British colonies, particularly Sir John Bowring, Governor of Hongkong, who had lately negotiated a treaty with Siam and gave Harris helpful advice about Japan: he was ahead of his times in readiness to welcome Anglo-American co-operation.[60]

On his way Harris had to stop at Bangkok and get a treaty, and his instructions from Secretary Marcy were to impress on the Siamese the contrast between peace-loving America and bullying Britain, which had just swallowed Lower Burma.[61] Harris duly made use of this point to argue that Siam ought to give more liberal terms to his country than to Britain; the Siamese, more wide-awake than he guessed, made use of it to argue that America ought to be satisfied with less greedy demands than Britain. In Japan he, like Perry, set down the negotiators he had to deal with as inveterate liars. Americans had no C.I.A. as yet to conduct their affairs, and prided themselves on their frank and open approach. To them, as to Victorian Englishmen, commerce was sacred because it brought the nations together not only for exchange of wares but, ideally at least, for meeting of minds. Exclusion policies were 'anti-commercial and therefore immoral', John Quincy Adams had declared.[62] Harris was convinced, as he told the officials, that the ordinary folk of Japan would welcome intercourse with the

outside world, and that obstruction was confined to the aristocracy and the
military – 'two classes of people that in all countries were opposed to any
improvement in the condition of the great body of the people'.[63] A hundred years
later his own country would be controlling a good part of the world through
these two classes.

He also assured his hosts, the British learned with indignation, that England
and France were robbers, the U.S. alone could be trusted.[64] He procured a
reception at Yedo, or Tokyo, the capital, and there induced the government to
sign the new treaty he wanted, by dropping hints that if Japan did not come
peacefully to terms with him, the robbers would soon arrive and extort treaties by
force.[65] This was perfectly true; but without the bombardments of Japanese ports
by European warships in the next few years it may be doubted whether the
American foothold would have survived. As things were, Harris could afford to
be amiable; he left Japan in 1861 in an aura of popularity. As opener of Japanese
windows to the light of modernity and reason, America could bask in its
favourite role of liberator, all the more properly when it liberated its own slaves a
few years later. American teachers and missionaries were soon thronging into
Japan, and helping their country to make an 'enormous impression' on the
Japanese.[66]

During Harris's residence, China was stealing the limelight. In the Second
Opium War, from 1856 to 1860, Britain was joined by France, and at the same
time the climax of the immense Taiping Rebellion against the decrepit Manchu
dynasty was approaching. America had obtained its first treaty with China in
1844, in the wake of the First Opium War: here too Europeans often grudged the
way that America found fault with their rough proceedings but did not hesitate
to benefit by them. It was negotiated by Caleb Cushing, a lawyer of imperialist
temper who insisted firmly on extra-territorial rights. When a Chinese was killed
in rioting at Canton, he pronounced firmly: 'I shall refuse at once all applications
for the surrender of the party who-killed Hsu A-man'.[67] He went home to throw
himself heart and soul into the Mexican War, where he paid for the equipping of
a regiment.

In the next conflict the U.S. attitude was one of ambiguous neutrality, really
leaning towards the allies, who were anxious for moral support from both
America and Russia to convince China of Western solidarity. In 1856 Parker,
quondam medical missionary and now U.S. Commissioner, wrote to assure the

British Superintendent of Trade of his 'earnest desire to pursue that harmony of purpose and unity of action on the part of the Treaty Powers in all matters of common right and interest' and his 'deep concern' in British success for the sake of all foreigners in China. Parker went a little too far for his government's taste, but a year later his successor W.B. Reed had pleasure in notifying Lord Elgin, the British representative: 'I am instructed by the President to communicate frankly with you and the French Minister upon all points of common interest, so that it may be distinctly understood that the three nations are equally influenced by a determination to attain justice....'.[68]

All four Western envoys moved up to the north, as the allied forces gathered to assault Peking. In the attack on the forts at the mouth of the Peiho River, the American naval commander Tattnall gave some quiet assistance to the British, on the maxim that 'Blood is thicker than water'. In 1859, when new treaties were signed at Tientsin, the new American minister J.E. Ward insisted on being received at Peking to exchange ratifications. His European colleagues clearly wished him to think he was ill used there. As representative, wrote the Frenchman, Alphonse de Bourboulon, of 'a nation of which an excessive national self-respect is the distinctive characteristic, he must have, I am convinced, profoundly resented all the humiliations which they made him undergo.'[69] As it was, the Anglo-French sack of Peking the following year was not likely to evoke much American censure.

The United States could not radicalise Europe, but it could have found an easier field in China by lending encouragement to the Taipings, about whom Western opinion was for long divided. If Europe's commoners looked up to America as the land of the free, there were hints of a similar disposition among China's disinherited. Hung Jen-kan at any rate, a kinsman of the Taiping leader who joined him at his capital Nanking after studying Christianity at Hongkong, portrayed America – the 'Flowery Flag nation' – very favourably in his sketches of foreign lands. 'In politeness, justice, and wealth, she is unequalled. Though powerful, she does not invade neighbouring kingdoms ... There are no beggars in the United States.'[70] Among American missionaries W.A.P. Martin was one of those who were impressed by the Christian infusion in Taiping ideology, and recommended recognition of Nanking on the same footing with Peking. With the double-track thinking that came instinctively to so many of his countrymen, he argued that this would be good for American prospects as well as for

Christianity, because the two regimes could be played off against each other. 'Divide and conquer is the stratagem to be employed in storming the citadels of oriental exclusiveness ... should our envoy appear in the Yangtze with a squadron of our own lordly steamers flying the banners of liberty ... the Taiping chief ... would not be likely to refuse the utmost of our demands.'[71]

On the whole, America and Europe moved in the same direction of rejecting the Taipings and favouring the bad old feudal government, just as a century later when the Chinese Revolution entered its communist phase. State Secretary Cass's directions, a Japanese historian comments, 'indicated an opportunistic and almost cynical indifference to the development of the insurrection'.[72] But by 1860 when the Taipings threatened Shanghai and Europeans turned to active support of Peking, Americans were too much preoccupied with the approach of their own civil war and possible foreign meddling in it, to take China's seriously. It was left to private American adventurers to take a hand in the final suppression of the rebellion. A good many such soldiers of fortune were knocking about in the East, as well as trailing pikes in the Caribbean, advance-skirmishers of empire. One American mercenary, Josiah Harlan, turned up in the Panjab before its conquest by the British, took service with the Maharaja Ranjit Singh, and was promptly made governor of a town, destitute though he was of any qualifications for the position.[73] F.T. Ward was an ex-soldier who came to China in 1859 and organized a small foreign legion for the government, which before long blossomed into the 'Ever-victorious Army'. He was commonly believed to have hopes of carving out a principality for himself.[74] When he was killed in 1862 America still had enough interest in Chinese events to compete with Britain over the choice of his successor. With official backing Henry A. Burgevine, son of an officer of Napoleon who settled in the U.S., got the command. He was soon dismissed for insubordination, and came to a bad end, after apparently scheming like Ward to set up as a petty sovereign. Fears of this kind of thing happening were a serious preoccupation to the British;[75] it had happened in India in the dissolution of the Mughal empire.

3

Civil War and After

So far as the essays at a spirited foreign policy over the past dozen years had been designed to pull the country together and overcome regional and social divisions, they were proving a failure. The Civil War collision was not one that could be averted by the time-honoured European device of a turning outward, a gold-rush of excitements far away. As a last resort, a challenge to the old enemy like that of 1812 could be contemplated; and the British minister, Lord Lyons, thought he saw many tokens early in 1860 of Americans looking to war with Britain as the means of averting war at home.[76] When hostilities broke out there was a faction within the Federal camp, headed by Seward, which seemed to hope that they could be cut short by a foreign war, reviving the patriotism of the South and bringing it back into the fold. By the time this hope too faded, divisions within the Federal ranks were so acute that Lyons could suspect men like Seward of still wanting a foreign war, or the utmost friction short of war, to reunite their own followers.[77] Many of his letters to the Foreign Secretary, Russell, reveal how far such tactics were pursued. Upper-class Britain's unconcealed sympathy with the South offered plenty of provocation.

A true civil war – there have not been many – cannot be fought without a leaven of moral earnestness, and this was supplied on one side by anti-slavery feeling, on the other by defence of local autonomy against centralization – the same cause that made Basques and Catalans fight so doggedly on the wrong side in the Carlist War of 1833–39 in Spain. For the North at large, however, the conflict was only very half-heartedly against slavery, as the Second World War was for the democracies only very half-heartedly a crusade against fascism. To preserve the Union without abolishing slavery, as most Northerners were prepared to do, could have no point except to keep the Union strong, and it was already clear that its strength might be turned to aggression. No doubt an independent South, entering into European alliances, could be a menace to the republic. There was, all the same, an overtone of imperialism in the determination of the North to conquer the South, itself so firmly bent on conquering the Caribbean. A sermon like one of 1861 on the sinful delays of the Israelites in occupying the promised land,[78] was meant as censure of Northern hesitation to end Southern slavery; but the image of Canaan, always haunting the American mind, could be applied to manifold situations.

Lincoln had condemned the Mexican War. But Northerners made things too simple when they blamed all American transgressions on the South and its long ascendancy in national policies, and made it responsible – as a New York lady writing to the British abolitionist J.E. Cairnes did – for 'the Indian Wars, the annexation of Texas, the Mexican war, all of them heartily disapproved by the North, which have no part in them, but the expense incurred and that under the strongest protest'. In reply Cairnes confessed that the tone of the New York press made him uneasy about future American intentions. 'A very general apprehension prevails here that the ruling motive of the North in the war is ambition purely ... I wish I could believe that there was no foundation for this impression.'[79]

Seward's anti-British tactics could indeed be seen as expansionism persisting through the civil broils, with Canada once more among its goals. 'Canada is, as you know, looked upon here as our weak point', Lyons wrote in May 1861 to the governor-general, recommending a strengthening of defences. 'Some ministers believe there is a strong pro-American feeling there.'[80] They were not altogether mistaken. A respectable Englishman lately visiting the country was distressed to find that 'a radical, nasty sympathy was growing up between the English-born colonists and the United States ...'.[81] Later that year, after the Federal removal of Confederate envoys from the British ship *Trent*, a special envoy from Washington was reported to be saying in Paris that the possibility of war with Britain had been foreseen: if it came, he was to seek a French alliance, offering Quebec as prize. Palmerston assured the Queen that the French government had more sympathy with the South, and was 'probably thinking more about cotton than about Canada'.[82] If the offer was really contemplated at Washington, it was a striking deviation from the Monroe Doctrine, and if Napoleon III was not thinking about Canada he was soon thinking about Mexico.

Had the suggested bargain been struck, doubtless the rest of Canada would have been intended for the U.S. But in 1862 a Scottish-Canadian progressive editor, George Brown of Toronto, expressed dissent from the clamour of the London *Times* for precautions against alleged American designs; he maintained that desire for war was far livelier in British government circles, which always had numerous relatives in the army.[83] Canadian feelings were of course mixed. Brown himself, though very anti-Tory and during the Civil War a staunch friend of the North, was no admirer of American-style democracy, and had no wish to see Canada in the Union. Nor had Canadian businessmen, except briefly about 1850 after Britain adopted free trade and thus deprived them of a privileged market: since then Britain had regained their loyalty by investing in their railways and other enterprises, and by negotiating on their behalf a reciprocity treaty with the U.S.

Still, among ordinary Canadians there were undeniable symptoms of the same nasty democratical turn of mind that common people in Europe showed so much of in 1848; and there was now far better reason for goodwill towards America than when it was engaged in robbing Mexico. All the workers of Europe were as instinctively on the side of the North as their rulers on that of the South, declared the International Workingmen's Association in its address (drafted by Marx) congratulating Lincoln on his re-election in 1864 – 'even before the fanatic partisanship of the upper classes for the Confederate gentry had given its dismal warning, that the slaveholders' rebellion was to sound the tocsin for a general holy crusade of property against labour . . .'.

Just as conflict in Europe offered chances to the U.S., conflict in the U.S. was a temptation now to Europeans. In 1861 the Anglo-French partnership, lately so active against China and Japan after being formed to fight Russia, began putting the screw on Mexico in much the same style, this time with Spain making a third, for the benefit of their bondholders. They were acting against a revolutionary regime headed by an Indian leader, Juárez, and may have counted on this to disarm American objections. In 1862 the others dropped out: Napoleon, always impelled like his uncle by the need to *chauffer la gloire*, was drawn on into his most hare-brained adventure, and in 1864 installed a Hapsburg emperor. Spain was launching out on an equally foolish attempt to restore its standing in South America by chastizing Chile. At the end of the Civil War, Confederate soldiers were welcomed in Mexico by Maximilian, and it is not impossible to imagine enough of them going there to become his chief prop, and to console themselves for defeat at home by accomplishing in a new guise the old Southern dream of taking over Mexico. As for the French, they were soon compelled to withdraw by difficulties in Europe, worsened by fear of complications with Washington. A military demonstration on the border by Sheridan, and moral support and arms given to the patriots, ended any prospect of Maximilian being able to keep going with the aid of ex-Confederate forces. His downfall in 1867 gave the U.S. another easy scalp.

Whitman rejoiced to find demonstration in the Civil War that 'We have undoubtedly in the United States the greatest military power ... in the world', though he admitted that it was being very woodenly and wastefully used by its commanders. He felt just as intensely the 'fear and hatred' for America of all the governments of Europe, 'the united wish of all the nations of the world ... that she should be compelled to descend to the level of kingdoms and empires ordinarily great.' He continued to think that Canada ought to be in the Union, but he came to expect this through the quiet influence of a *Zollverein*; and looking back on the Civil War in a cooler mood he saw 'Two great spectacles, immortal proofs of democracy' – the Federal mobilization, and 'the peaceful and harmonious disbanding of the armies in the summer of 1865'.[84] Of these, the first looked less impressive to outsiders: the armies were built up awkwardly and painfully; but it could not be gainsaid that America had displayed a giant's strength, and it really was remarkable that instead of going on to use this elsewhere – to overrun Canada, for instance, as Lyons had feared[85] – the country was at once laying its panoply aside.

As on earlier occasions there was a quick recoil from warlike moods, and it was hastened now by the immense cost of the war, especially among the ordinary people who had to pay for it while the profiteers flourished. The country's readiest recruiting ground, the poor white population of the South, was disarmed. Liberal feeling against standing armies was still alive, and businessmen could agree with it because it fitted in with their philosophy of cheap government and individualism: army and navy were after all a species of nationalized industry. They could agree with it also as taxpayers, as could the inland front-iersmen who so often seemed to be spoiling for a fight with England, but who always baulked at buying ships. Only when actually at war did Americans appear willing to think seriously about a fleet, which could not then be improvised. Naval statistics continued to provide a barometer of the national mood, and they showed stagnation, not progress. In a generation of public indifference and professional conservatism the lessons of the Civil War were ignored; wooden ships went on being built instead of ironclads; in 1880 the United States did not possess a single first-class modern warship.[86]

The great fact was that industrial capitalism, now firmly installed as arbiter of the national destinies, had a rapidly growing market and a spacious field of enterprise at home, without needing to look for colonies outside. Before the Civil War there was little leisure to digest the spoils won from Mexico, and it was only now that they and Oregon and then the great plains were being effectively occupied and converted into dollars and dividends. In 1869 came the first railway link-up between East and West, and as the transcontinental lines closed the gap the Pacific provinces ceased to be remote dependencies and became part of the homeland; preoccupation with the Isthmus diminished, national security could be thought about more coolly. As before, the pushing of the frontier westward was a species of imperialism, even if to Americans it felt quite different from the empire-building of the Europeans; and the headlong growth of a capitalism which it helped to cram with profits was nourishing an appetite for further imperial projects in the future. For the time being, ambitions beyond the wide frontiers already obtained lacked appeal, and politicians trying to gather votes from them were failures. Most prominent among these was Seward, 'the central figure of nineteenth-century American imperialism', whose purchase of Alaska from Russia in 1867 was intended as a move towards north-east Asia.[87] Once more America was growing by paying, instead of by stealing in the European fashion, even if Alaska was at present poor compensation for the failure to buy Cuba. Seward himself was as avid as any of his predecessors for Cuba as one stride in a march into Latin America.

Before the Civil War, that threatened march had been spreading alarm. 'Latin America could hear only manifest destiny at work.'[88] During the fighting, Mexicans must have experienced pleasure at the sight of their late invaders tearing one another to pieces. But they had new invaders now, in resisting whom they benefited by the triumph of the North. In general the feeling of Latin America was of renewed hope and faith in the United States. This did not last long. It soon appeared that the policy of aggression had been scotched, not killed, by the South's defeat. It is true that attempts in America to push the government into intervention in Cuban troubles in 1868 petered out, and in 1869 President Grant failed to get the Senate to ratify his scheme to annex San Domingo in collusion with the local boss. Though they came to nothing at the time, these plottings were perturbing to all in the vicinity of the republic. They obscured the underlying fact that a millocracy was in the saddle now instead of a plantocracy, and would seek financial suzerainty rather than outright annexations. Already the new drift was revealing itself, with American capitalists busy building railways in Mexico. This might be all well and good, but foreign railways in backward lands were often to carry foreign tutelage with them, besides other cargo.

It was to be so in the Far East, though there America's role would for a long time be only a secondary one. At present it was satisfied to leave Europeans to go on licking China and Japan into shape (even if Seward made a point of having a token share in the naval action against Japan in 1864), and to enjoy the luxury of thinking – and saying – how much higher its own standards of conduct were. In 1868 the liberal Burlingame Treaty with China provided for reciprocal immigration rights. In 1869 there followed the two days in San Francisco that Bret Harte wrote of in his story *Wan Lee, the Pagan*, 'two days when a mob of her citizens set upon and killed unarmed, defenceless foreigners, because they were foreigners, and of another race, religion and colour'. (Ten years later R.L. Stevenson heard a mob orator there bawling for the people to liberate itself from the 'dirty Mongolians' as Lincoln liberated the slaves.[89]) In the Far East Britain continued in the lead, but there and elsewhere against stiffening competition, which inclined it towards curtailing its commitments beyond the Atlantic. This in turn helped to reduce American pugnacity, always most easily called out by a scuffle with John Bull.

Even before the Civil War, there was a willingness among some conservative Englishmen to look indulgently at Southern expansionism,[90] despite their dislike of U.S. expansionism in the same region. As in many other contexts then and later, Tory attitudes (like present-day American attitudes) were conditioned as much by sentiment as by calculation. Pro-Southern feeling expressed the nostalgia of an old ruling class that was being deprived of its freedom to do as it chose, as well as desire to see the Union weakened by division. But the Civil War was a display of energy of which the whole British empire was obliged to take account, as Disraeli pointed out in 1872. 'Such a unique, world-wide organization could not help being in some degree sensitive to the emergence of a new great power on the international scene.'[91] Conversely Spain was a weaker and weaker prop to lean on, and there was a gradual disengagement from the Palmerstonian line of buttressing its position in the Caribbean as a bulwark against the United States.[92] Its colonial possessions were so mismanaged that the prospect of America taking them over could begin to seem a lesser evil, while the abolition of slavery in the United States removed one objection to it as a colonizing power. When Spain and America came to the brink of war in 1874 over the affair of the ship *Virginius*, Madrid received a warning from London not to expect British help in defending Cuba.[93]

From 1868, following the federation of Canada in the previous year, there were no troops there under British command to act as red rags to the American bull. For some years longer there were fears north of the border that the U.S. would grab the still scarcely occupied expanses of the Canadian West, but on this side, more definitely than in Latin America, the U.S. was turning its thoughts from annexation to penetration. British opinion could move beyond disengagement towards the idea of a positive community of interests, and the notion of a manifest destiny in store for both branches of the 'Anglo-Saxon' family was beginning to stir. For its part America too was taking a fresh look at world alignments, as Perry did during his Pacific voyagings. Russia had often been looked upon complacently, as Britain's foe; now it was coming to be seen in the light of America's great rival exporter of grain and raw materials. When Continental Europeans looked complacently at America, it was often as Britain's foe; and there was point in the warning to American labour, drawn up by Marx and approved by the International Workingmen's Association in May 1869, to be on guard against a conflagration which would be damaging both to it and to labour in Europe. 'We need hardly tell you that there are European powers anxiously engaged in fomenting a war between the United States and England.'

4

The Last Indian Wars

In 1849 Indian affairs were transferred from the army to the new Department of the Interior. By now the resistance of the old race in those parts of the country long penetrated by the new settlers was at an end, and a treaty with some of the Indians, at Detroit in 1855, put an end to their tribal organization, much as the Highland clan system was swept away after the rebellion of 1745. Further west, however, relations were oftener than not military for another generation. War with Mexico had brought fighting with Pueblo Indians, whose walled townships only cannon could breach, and whose strange culture has proved equally resistant. With the annexed areas of Northern Mexico the U.S. inherited their long-standing predators, the desert tribes. Among these the Apache and Comanche seem to have fitted closely enough the stereotype of Indian ferocity, as if sharing the cruelty of their harsh environment. Mormons colonizing Utah to the north were accused of arming and inciting raiders. Like Penn and others they were inclined to regard Indians as descendants of the lost tribes of Israel, a lineage sometimes reckoned creditable, sometimes the reverse.

In California the Indians were far less warlike, and the savages were the white men flocking in, above all the gold-rush diggers. These men rivalled any Apaches in brutality, an illustration of how little the antithesis of civilization and barbarism, so much a part of 19th-century thinking, coincided with lines of race. Indians who could be made useful were reduced to bondage. Here the U.S. fell heir to some elements of Spanish feudalism, and one man who acquired an estate, where gold was discovered, had more than six hundred serf labourers.[94] Miners burned the Indian villages, killed or enslaved their men, raped the women; the same treatment was extended to blacks, and later Chinese. Here was the darker side of a 'people's imperialism'; colonists turned loose, without restraint of law, have too often behaved in this fashion. In Oregon, too, a good many of the tribal societies were surprisingly – to the bellicose white man – unwarlike, and suffered accordingly. American occupation required their wholesale removal, and a prompt start was made at this 'spring-cleaning' in 1853, when treaties were hastily forced on some clans by which they surrendered most of their land. Since their economy was principally based on salmon fishing, soil meant less to them than fishing rights along the rivers, and their stubborn clinging to these rights has bred trouble between them and the authorities down to our own day.[95]

Fighting was necessary to enforce some of these 'treaties'. It was spreading on the great plains east of the Rockies too; in 1854 a Sioux War was provoked by a rash young officer. These contests gave the army what Roon, War Minister of Prussia in those days, called 'healthy exercise'; it trained many of the commanders of the Civil War which broke out in 1861, a conflict for whose very different requirements Indian warfare was, however, poor preparation.[96] In 1914 the British and French armies were to pay the same penalty for having too many strategists from remote colonial frontiers. Indians in North America suffered also, by being dragged into the Civil War struggle and pitted against one another as they had been in the Anglo-French and Anglo-American wars. There was fratricidal division now even within tribes. The 'Five Civilized Tribes' had gone on making progress, but too much under the lead of an elite of slave owners of mixed blood, ready partisans of the Confederates who entered their territory early on; the majority leaned more to the Federal camp.

Regiments were raised on both sides, but were poorly equipped and not much used for combat purposes, except by the Confederates in the battle of Pea Ridge in March 1862. There the victorious Northern troops were as much outraged at the rebels, like the British in former days, using Indians against them, as the rebels were to be at Federal enrollment of Negro units. All Indians captured were killed out of hand, a Federal officer recorded, with the exception of eleven who fell into the hands of 'mild-tempered' soldiers. These were sent north to be exhibited as an advertisement of Southern villainy, but were all murdered on the way by their guards, or killed trying to escape; but it was the Southern rebels' propaganda that gained, and many more Indians joined them.[97] After the war the Five Tribes were punished by being deprived of the western part of Oklahoma, though this was to be kept as a limbo where other groups swept up from far and wide could be located and forgotten.

Various other Indians took advantage of the Civil War to try to turn the tables. There were hostilities in the south-west in 1863: the Navajos were quelled with the help of their Ute enemies, and then removed *en masse* from Arizona to New Mexico, a desolating experience like the removal of the south-eastern peoples earlier. In 1864 war broke out again with the Sioux of the northern plains. Reception from the Spaniards of the horse, and from the English of the gun, instead of transforming life there may have retarded evolution towards agriculture, and perpetuated a hunting stage of existence.[98] This meant also a feuding stage, with war as the great game to which all energies and skills superfluous to a simple economy were devoted. It prolonged the dilemma that a very scanty population needed a very large area to maintain it. Land itself was nothing; Plains Indians lived on the buffalo, as those of coastal Oregon lived on the salmon.

Hitherto they and their buffaloes had not been too much interfered with, because the plains were not wanted for cultivation; it was only the routes across them to the Far West that mattered, though the opening and guarding of these routes often stirred strife. After the Homestead Act of 1863 the tide of settlement began to submerge the plains too, and it was time for their nomad inhabitants to be dislodged. Next year's war was prefaced by a summons to the Sioux to abandon a good part of their hunting-grounds, and we have an eyewitness account of a formal palaver between American officers and Indian chiefs; where each made long speeches and boasted of incredible numbers of braves ready to take the field. General Mitchell resorted to a plea of equal human rights, with some ingenuity and, it must be admitted, not without some plausibility. 'He told them that the good Manitou, who put us all on earth, intended that each one should have his share of the earth'; it was unfair for white people to be cooped up while Indians had ten times as much as they were entitled to.[99]

To the officer who reported the conference, the Indians seemed an effeminate-looking lot, very unlike the red warriors so often admiringly described; he concluded they must be enfeebled by 'revolting and beastly habits and vices'.[100]

Any opponents of America must be depraved wretches: there is a glimpse here of the same moralizing conviction that was to identify communists with homosexuals. It might have occurred to this indignant observer that one of the white man's chief gifts to the red man was venereal disease.

In the years following the Civil War, with their revulsion against bloodshed, there was a chance for more sympathetic views to prevail. 'America developed what might be called a conscience – or perhaps only a weariness of these dark-skinned people who persisted in fighting the inevitable.'[101] Longfellow's influence counted. George Catlin, who in youth had fallen in love with the 'Noble Savage' and gone out west to make paintings of him and gather objects for a museum (the Senate in 1849 declined to buy his collection), was writing in defence of the Indian character and pleading for fairer dealings.[102] H.B. Whipple, Bishop of Minnesota from 1859, was doing the same, helped after the war by Quakers formerly preoccupied with the Negro cause.[103] Reconstruction in the South was enough to keep the government busy, and must have spread a feeling that if black men were going to be treated at last as human beings, red men had some claim too. Shielding Mexico from Napoleon and Maximilian, the U.S. was, willy-nilly, taking sides with the Indian patriot Juárez and his largely Indian following against his white assailants. Pressures of population and capital made the westward movement inevitable, but at least treatment of the aborigines ought to be as orderly and humane as possible. For the benefit of the more practical, this could be put in business terms. One calculation was that killing Indians cost the government an average of a million dollars a head; more accurately, the direct cost of a campaign against the Modocs in Oregon was put at $355,000, when their claim for a reasonable allotment of land could have been met for a twentieth of the sum.[104]

Hence what came to be known under President Grant as the 'peace policy', marked in 1867 by the setting up of a Board of Indian Commissioners, civilians and often idealists lending their services without pay. Grant was giving Agency posts to army officers, until Congress objected; there was then an opposite turn, and much of the management of settled or re-settled tribes was handed over to the churches, fifteen of which were allocated zones to work in. Whipple was among those who were trying to smooth the way for peoples like the Sioux into a new life. America itself was trying to turn over a new leaf and start a new life; and its efforts compare not badly with anything done or attempted by humanitarians in any colonizing countries of Europe, the Aborigines' Rights Protection Society in Britain for instance, after the long anti-slavery movement was over. Indian policy was at least being recognized as a problem, and publicly debated. However limited in conception or warped in outcome, this was one of the serious debates of imperial history, which has not been rich in them. It might be compared with the controversy in 16th-century Spain between Las Casas and his opponents over conduct towards Indians in South America. No such discussion took place, either in their own country or in Britain, over the fate of the Australian 'blackfellows'; or in Argentina, where a war of extermination was being waged against other wild Indian horsemen, who were only crushed at last in the campaigns of 1878–79.

Individuals in contact with western realities took the initiative, but it was only in the East that they could hope for backing. This maturer region of the U.S. could cultivate more detached views of a problem which no longer affected it directly, and exercise some restraint over the brutal temper of the frontier. East and West developed attitudes to the red man as incompatible as those of North and South to the black man. At the same time the East was undertaking a 'civilizing mission' in the West for the benefit of the rude white population, even more than for that of the Indians. Churches took the lead in education, missionaries went forth, 'an intellectual stream from New England fertilised the West.'[105]

What weakened the progressive cause was that while the West was always vociferous against it, Eastern opinion could only be widely aroused on special occasions. Good intentions, however sincere, were not easily translated into workaday programmes; they were apt to partake of the grand simplicity, and the indistinctness, of much American goodwill since then. Oregon was not very much less remote from New York than Sind from London, even if the absence of salt water between them made a psychological difference. And the East was, like London, the homeland of businessmen and bankers and their clients who might be perturbed about the way lands far off were being acquired, but could not wish to forego the portion of profit which accrued to them from those lands. Conversely, but for similar reasons, they could not think of confiscating Southern plantations from their white owners and giving the soil to the Negroes – even if America did, to the consternation of conservative Europe, give the Negroes votes, which for a while they were allowed to use. Without a new agrarian order, reconstruction in the South was doomed to disillusion; and fading of enlightened hopes there, and backsliding towards more summary methods in the West, went together.

This flagging of healthier views was exploited by Democrats for factional purposes, while the opposite kind of thinking was worsened by the advent of railways with their cargo of land-hungry settlers. A treaty of 1865 which secured spacious hunting-grounds to the tribes in Dakota and Southern Montana was now, like many others, only a scrap of paper. On the frontiers there was never any pretence of respect for peace policies, and a ruffianly type abounded which, as on many other outskirts of a changing world, clung to self-respect by pride of race, and was often responsible for stirring up violence. In the 1870s the Wild West experienced by a young newcomer like Frank Harris was 'a land of pioneers, adventurers, and desperados ... reservation boundaries were continually broken and Indians ... went stoically to their death in bloody battles....'.[106]

As for many of the world's small simple peoples in that epoch, it was not easy for Indians to steer a course between being too fierce, or too tame. If they were pugnacious their courage made the invader all the more determined to draw their teeth; if pacific, they were despised, as in Australia, and this might be equally perilous. One of the innumerable wars narrated by J.P. Dunn, the young man who went out west in 1879 to seek his fortune, arose in 1868 from a white man wantonly killing the chief of a clan 'looked upon with the contempt that frontiersmen commonly feel for the peaceable Indians'.[107] Dunn himself could not always help sharing this contempt, akin to that of a Spanish crowd for a bull reluctant to fight. Trappers would shoot a harmless Indian for amusement.

With all this, it was easy for ideas of an inevitable passing of the red man to reassert themselves. A Congress committee set up in 1865 saw it as part of destiny that a lower race in contact with a higher should fade away, like a ghost at cock-crow, and could foresee no future for the Plains Indians now that railways were coming and game disappearing. Men of action were prepared to expedite their departure; and since undeniably many Indians when not at war with the white man were given to robbing and killing one another, it could be felt by 'realists' that whether they were knocked on the head by one another or by an invader could matter very little. Here again Dunn, at times so vehement against acts of injustice, could wax impatient at some of the criticism emanating from the Eastern states and their 'Indian worshippers', and he reminded them of how *their* Indian nations had been dealt with in their time.[108] Meanwhile white hunters greedy for hides were rapidly wiping out the buffaloes, sometimes with encouragement from higher up because, without their herds, the Indians would be compelled to give up their old life and depend on whatever provision might be made for them on reservations.

To some military men 'Darwinian' ideas had a professional appeal.[109] At the very time when the Commissioners were trying to open a new era, the 'extermination policy' was pressing on in Arizona. A general given charge in 1869, 'an enthusiastic exterminator', told his men to hunt down Apaches 'as they would wild animals'.[110] Women and children were excluded from the hunt in principle, less strictly in practice. Apaches, it was agreed, carried off the palm for savagery; even so, among a minority of Americans there was at least as much searching of conscience as in Europe over the question of what punitive methods were admissible. It was an epoch when rules of 'civilized warfare' were being formulated, but were usually regarded as only binding between civilized enemies. Frontiersmen argued that Indians had to be beaten at their own game, Dunn observed, and he himself was sometimes ready to condone very robust tactics. 'There is not a bit of doubt that killing women and children has a very dampening effect on the ardour of the Indian', he could write.[111] Where Apaches were concerned he could approve a treacherous killing of tribesmen gathered for a parley, on the score that they themselves often indulged in treachery.[112]

Yet he felt as much horror as any easterner at a bloody and unprovoked onslaught on an Indian camp by a combined force of Americans, Indian auxiliaries, and Mexicans. 'Even conservative people who had not been inclined to Indian-worship recoiled at this atrocity'; Arizona applauded the 'monstrous crime'.[113] And he was ready to admit that some Indians showed unsurpassed heroism in defending their ancestral homelands, and that if rebel Irishmen, Greeks, Poles deserved admiration, so did they. 'There was never an exile of any other race to whom the American heart did not warm.'[114] His inconsistencies faithfully reflected the eddies of public feeling.

It was against the bloodshed still going on that Helen Jackson, a Massachusetts woman living in Colorado, wife of a Quaker banker, spent her last years in protest. Her book *A Century of Dishonor*, in 1881, led quickly to the setting up of an Indian Rights Association. The best that philanthropists could hope to do was to ameliorate the reservation system, which had been part of the 'peace policy' since 1873, but often proved irreconcilable with it. A tribe was either left with some part of its territory, or was carried off to another area, less attractive to white settlers. Miscellaneous groups were being planted, or penned up, in Western Oklahoma, often before any real preparations had been made for their reception. In 1867 Cheyennes, Comanches and others were scheduled for removal there, force had to be used, and resistance continued until 1875. It was a decision to relegate the Sioux to small reservations, depriving them of most of the territory assured to them by treaty, that brought on in 1876 the most dramatic of all Indian campaigns, ending in the battle painted by Mulvaney and rhapsodized by Whitman.

During the winter of 1875–76 preparations were made to enforce the decision. G.A. Custer, the officer put in command, was a Civil War hero, a flamboyant figure, still only thirty-six, but with presidential ambitions and hoping for a dashing frontier action to win him the nomination and sweep him into office like Andrew Jackson before him. He was one of sundry army men accused of making free with Indian women when in charge of bands of captives, and there is said to have been a half-breed son of his in the Sioux tents.[115] With him were a number of Indian scouts and auxiliaries, but the Sioux had several allies, among them the northern Cheyennes, and a bigger force assembled in Little Big Horn valley than red men had ever mustered since the days of Tecumseh's league.

Attempting a surprise attack on the encampment, Custer was beaten in fair fight, and his column nearly wiped out; but all white men in that age were reluctant to believe that they could be fairly beaten by men of any other colour. In the popular record the battle went down as the 'massacre' of a gallant band of daredevils; in patriotic mythology it swelled into a moral victory, a symbol of American courage. 'No other single event in American history ever captured the public imagination more completely than "Custer's Last Stand".'[116] Little Big Horn might have been another Roncevalles, and Charlemagne with all his peerage have fallen once again. For a while the country was in a mood of vindictive revengefulness, a mood oftener aroused by stories of isolated settlers and their women being butchered. Extermination was loudly talked of. It was not carried out; but overwhelming force was concentrated against the Sioux, and by the end of the year they were shut up in the districts marked out for them, with the promise of a subsidy. Chief Sitting Bull and some other intransigents took refuge in Canada, where they were given a cold and grudging reception. There was no more liking for Indian defiance now on one side of the border than on the other.

In 1877 it was the turn of the Nez Percés of Oregon, who had been on amicable terms with the white men until they were at last goaded into revolt by settlers and prospectors, for whose benefit the government resolved to coop them up in narrow limits. Under their Chief Joseph they fought a long-running struggle to escape their fate; they too tried to reach Canada, but in the end were surrounded and compelled to surrender. Next year took place the flight of a few hundred northern Cheyennes from their Oklahoma reservation, where they were neglected and half-starved. It was one of history's long marches; they fought their way, incredibly, across Kansas, Nebraska and Montana, back to their native hills in Wyoming. Even in that time of embitterment, the Cheyenne cause found some champions, including one frontier editor who wrote: 'The whole Cheyenne business is in keeping with the rest of the Indian Bureau management. It is a disgrace to the U.S.A.'[117] In the south-west the last rebel leader, 'Geronimo', was worn down in 1886; after capture he was put on show in exhibitions, and in 1905 in the cortege at the presidential inauguration, 'like a Gaul in a Roman procession'.[118] Imperial instincts have been tenacious, and Theodore Roosevelt was an imperialist with strong views on the proper way to deal with Indian savages.

Similar sporadic encounters, of course, were going on in various European colonies. In 1890 British troops were still 'pacifying' Upper Burma, annexed five years before, and new conquests were still going on, as in the fringes of Dutch Indonesia and many regions of Africa. Custer's defeat and death were no more severe a shock to the American people than the Zulu triumph at Isandhlwana three years later, or General Gordon's death at Khartoum nine years later, were to the British. Parallels between European operations and Red Indian wars were drawn a little later by a British authority on the tactics of minor campaigns. 'The United States troops used to retaliate upon the Red Indians in similar fashion', he remarked after describing how the French in Algeria and whites elsewhere in Africa raided tribes and swept off their livestock and other property. Red Indians on the warpath, and the Mutiny in India, came to his mind as examples of the 'treachery' to be expected from such opponents: 'in civilized warfare such a thing is almost unknown'.[119]

Other analogies are not hard to recognize between the subjugation of indigenous peoples in the U.S. and abroad, both among the 'men on the spot' and in the counting-houses far away where other men pulled the strings. In 1847 the murder of some missionaries in Oregon, in a situation complicated by Canadian-American and Catholic-Protestant rivalries, furnished the warrant for an attack on Indians;[120] in 1897 the murder of some missionaries in China provided Germany with a pretext to begin carving out a sphere of influence in Shantung. Even isolated incidents might duplicate themselves. After the death of a hostile Seminole chief his head was sawn off and used as a paperweight by an American officer;[121] after the British conquest of the Sudan the Mahdi's skull was used by General Kitchener as an inkpot.[122]

With so many little wars America had enough excitement to season the monotony of daily life, without much need to disturb the rest of the world. They had a nation-building value as well. Indian tribes might be incapable of growing together into a nation, but their presence unwittingly helped their white antagonists to do so. It must have helped to re-unite North and South; they could feel at one against the demons of the West. It helped to preserve a common spirit and purpose in this republic which like Jehovah called its sons from far and its daughters from the ends of the earth. Most of them arrived in America poor and hungry. Indians on reservations might be hungry and poor, but their sacrifice was salvation to the fugitives from Europe. Philanthropists were organizing emigration to the West for pauper children from the slums of cities like New York. 'In every American community', one of them wrote, 'especially in a Western one, there are many spare places at the table of life. There is no harassing "struggle for existence". They have enough for themselves and the stranger too.'[123]

References

1.   H. Kohn, *The Idea of Nationalism* (New York, 1945), pp.296–7.
2.   Washington Irving, *Astoria* (London, 1836), Vol. 1, p.271.
3.   O.W. Holmes, *The Professor at the Breakfast-table* (1859), Section 18.
4.   Nathaniel Hawthorne, *Collected Works*, Vol. IX, *Passages from the American Notebooks* (London, 1883), p.109.
5.   E. Wagenknecht, *Longfellow: a Full-length Portrait* (New York, 1955), pp.192–3.
6.   See W.E. Hollon, *Frontier Violence – Another Look* (New York, 1974), p.127.
7.   J. Freeman, *Herman Melville* (London, 1926), pp.42–3.
8.   Herman Melville, *Whitejacket* (1850), Chap. XXVII. Cf. C. Crow, *Harris of*

Japan (London, 1939), p.112, on 'the contempt in which the American naval officer of that period held all civilians'.

9. H. Kohn, *American Nationalism – An interpretative essay* (New York, 1957), p.65.
10. Herman Melville, *op. cit.*, Chap. LVI.
11. *Ibid.*, Chap. XXXVI.
12. Herman Melville, *Moby Dick* (1851), Chap. XVI.
13. *Ibid.*, Chaps XIV, XXVII, XXXIII, L, CXXXIV.
14. Kohn, *American Nationalism, op. cit.*, p.152.
15. See his poem *A Broadway Pageant*.
16. Walt Whitman, *Specimen Days in America* (revised edn., London, 1871), pp.288–90.
17. Walt Whitman, *Democratic Vistas* (London edn., 1888), pp.161–2.
18. R.L. Stevenson, *Across the Plains, with other Memories and Essays* (London edn., 1913), pp.62–3.
19. D.W. Stevens, *The James Boys in California* (reprint, Derby, Connecticut, n.d.).
20. H. & M. Sprout, *The Rise of American Naval Power 1776–1918* (Princeton, 1946), p.136.
21. Suzanne Doyle, *The Significance of British Policy towards Spain, 1859–68* (M.A. thesis, London Univ., 1949), pp.128, 148–9.
22. J.D.P. Fuller, *The Movement for the Acquisition of all Mexico 1846–1848* (Baltimore, 1936), p.87.
23. J.E. Cairnes, *The Slave Power* (London, 1863), pp.202, 293–4.
24. *Ibid.*, p.82.
25. Scott Nearing and J. Freeman, *Dollar Diplomacy* (1925; new edn., New York, 1969), p.236.
26. *Brownson on the Rebellion* (1861), in F. Freidel, ed., *Union Pamphlets of the Civil War* (Harvard, 1967), Vol. 1, pp.131 ff.
27. Sprout, *op. cit.*, pp.118–9.
28. *Ibid.*, pp.142–3, 146–8.
29. R.W. van Alstyne, *The Rising American Empire* (Oxford, 1960), p.161.
30. Lord Newton, *Lord Lyons – A Record of British Diplomacy* (London, 1913), Chap. II.

31. *The Letters of Queen Victoria*, ed. A.C. Benson and Lord Esher (London, 1908), Vol. III, pp.373, 380.
32. K.N. Cameron, *The Young Shelley – Genesis of a Radical* (London, 1951), p.235.
33. See *Problems of American History*, ed. R.W. Leopold and A.S. Link (2nd edn., New Jersey, 1957), pp.181, 186.
34. H.R. Marraro, ed., *L'Unificazione Italiana vista dai diplomatici Statunitensi*, Vol. 1 (Rome, 1963), pp.245–7.
35. *Ibid.*, pp.332–3.
36. A.A. Ettinger, *The Mission to Spain of Pierre Soulé (1853–1855)* (Yale, 1932), pp.294–6, 316–18.
37. Karl Marx, *The Eastern Question* (collected articles, London, 1897), pp.74, 80–1.
38. Ettinger, *op. cit.*, pp.339–40.
39. *Ibid.*, pp.298–9; see also V.G. Kiernan, *The Revolution of 1854 in Spanish History* (Oxford, 1966), Chap. VI.
40. M. Torrente, *Política ultramarina* (Madrid, 1854), pp.422–3.
41. J. Becker y González, *Historia de las relaciones exteriores de España durante el siglo XIX* (Madrid, 1924), Vol. II, p.312.
42. Woodrow Wilson, *A History of the American People* (New York & London, 1901–2), Vol. IV, p.172.
43. Ettinger, *op. cit.*, pp.363–4.
44. Becker, *op. cit.*, Vol. II, pp.287–9.
45. Ettinger, *op. cit.*, p.262.
46. S.E. Morison, *'Old Bruin' – Commodore Matthew C. Perry 1794–1858* (O.U.P., 1968), p.273.
47. See Persia Campbell, *Chinese Coolie Emigration to Countries within the British Empire* (London, 1923); Watt Stewart, *Chinese Bondage in Peru* (Duke Univ., 1951).
48. Thorstein Veblen, *Absentee Ownership* (London, 1924), pp.170–1.
49. F.T. Bullen, *The Cruise of the 'Cachelot'* (London, 1898), Chap. III.
50. R.L. Stevenson, *In the South Seas* (Edinburgh, 1896), pp.30–1.
51. Morison, *op. cit.*, p.273.
52. T. Crow, *Harris of Japan* (London, 1939), pp.71–2.
53. Morison, *op. cit.*, pp.172–3.

54. *Dictionary of American Biography.*
55. Morison, *op. cit.*, p.283.
56. *Ibid.*, p.361.
57. Crow, *op. cit.*, p.123.
58. Morison, *op. cit.*, pp.425–7.
59. *Ibid.*, p.429.
60. Crow, *op. cit.*, p.163.
61. *Ibid.*, p.95.
62. Van Alstyne, *op. cit.*, pp.171–2.
63. *The Complete Journal of Townsend Harris, First American Consul and Minister to Japan*, ed. M.E. Cosenza (revised edn., Rutland, Vermont, 1959), p.508.
64. S. Lane Poole and F.V. Dickens, *The Life of Sir Harry Parkes* (London, 1894), Vol. 2, p.21.
65. Crow, *op. cit.*, pp.211, 247.
66. Akira Iriya, *Across the Pacific. An Inner History of American–East Asian Relations* (New York, 1967), pp.37, 45.
67. W.L. Tung, *China and the Foreign Powers* (New York, 1970), pp.22–3; text of treaty in App.C.
68. D. Bonner-Smith and E.W.R. Lumby, eds., *The Second China War, 1858–1860* (London, 1954), pp.112–15, 242.
69. Masataka Banno, *China and the West 1858–1861* (Harvard, 1964), p.126.
70. S.Y. Teng, *The Taiping Rebellion and the Western Powers* (London, 1971), p.159.
71. Tung, *op. cit.*, p.190.
72. Banno, *op. cit.*, p.44.
73. Khushwant Singh, *Maharaja Ranjit Singh* (London, 1962), pp.147–8.
74. R.K. Douglas, *Li Hung-chang* (London, 1892), pp.30–1.
75. D.C. Boulger, *A History of China*, Vol. 3 (London, 1884), p.581.
76. Newton, *op. cit.*, Chap. II.
77. *Ibid.*, Chaps. III–IV.
78. E.E. Hale, in Freidel, *op. cit.*, pp.504–6.
79. Adelaide Weinberg, *John Elliot Cairnes and the American Civil War* (London, 1968), pp.131–6.
80. Newton, *op. cit.*, Chap. III.
81. Sir E. Hornby, *Autobiography* (London, 1928), p.64.

82. *Letters of Queen Victoria*, Vol. III, p.469.

83. *The Globe*, Toronto, 5 March 1862, cited in H.S. Ferns, *George Brown and Canadian-American Relations* (M.A. thesis, Queen's Univ., Kingston, 1936). I am indebted to Professor Ferns for further elucidation of Canadian attitudes.

84. Whitman, *Specimen Days in America, op. cit.*, pp. 35, 82, 100–1, 252.

85. Newton, *op. cit.*, Chap. III.

86. Sprout, *op. cit.*, pp.168-ff.

87. Van Alstyne, *op. cit.*, p.176.

88. H. Hyman, ed., *Heard Round the World – The Impact Abroad of the Civil War* (New York, 1969), p.308.

89. Stevenson, *op. cit.*, p.43.

90. Cairnes, *op. cit.*, p.105, cites a London *Times* article of 31 July 1861 recommending a 'Southern' annexation of Mexico.

91. Hyman, *op. cit.*, p.46.

92. C.J. Bartlett, *The Diplomatic Relations of England and Spain 1868–1880* (Ph.D. thesis, London Univ., 1956), p.223 ff.

93. *Ibid.*, p.254 ff.

94. Hollon, *op. cit.*, p.59.

95. P. Collier, 'Salmon Fishing in America', in *Ramparts* (Berkeley, California), April 1971, p.37 ff.

96. F. Downey, *Indian Wars of the U.S. Army (1776–1865)* (1962; Derby, Connecticut, edn., 1964), p.134.

97. Capt. E.F. Ware, *The Indian War of 1864* (1911; ed. C.C. Walton, New York, 1960), pp.3–5.

98. *The Early Writings of Frederick Jackson Turner*, ed. F. Mood (Univ. of Wisconsin, 1935), p.215.

99. Ware, *op. cit.*, p.113.

100. *Ibid.*, p.109.

101. Howard Fast, *The Last Frontier* (1948; Harmondsworth edn., 1953), Foreword.

102. See M.C. Roehm, *The Letters of George Catlin and his Family* (Berkeley, 1966).

103. H.E. Fritz, *The Movement for Indian Assimilation, 1860–1890* (Philadelphia, 1963), pp.38 ff., 50.

104. J.P. Dunn, *Massacres of the Mountains* (1886; London edn., 1963), p.15, 492.

105. Turner, *op. cit.*, pp.226–7.

106. V. Brome, *Frank Harris* (1959; London edn., 1962), p.35.

107. Dunn, *op. cit.*, p.339.

108. *Ibid.*, pp.354, 382.

109. A.M. Josephy, *The Indian Heritage of America* (1968; Harmondsworth edn., 1975), p.341.

110. Dunn, *op. cit.*, p.617; cf. p.310.

111. *Ibid.*, p.366.

112. *Ibid.*, p.333.

113. *Ibid.*, pp.623, 625.

114. *Ibid.*, pp.32–3.

115. D.H. Miller, *Custer's Fall – The Indian Side of the Story* (1957; London edn., 1965), pp.47–9.

116. *Ibid.*, p.vii.

117. Cited in Fast, *op. cit.*, (a novel about the flight of the Cheyennes), p.240.

118. J.M. White, *The Great American Desert* (1975; London edn., 1977) p.181.

119. Col. C.E. Callwell, *Small Wars – Their Principles and Practice* (War Office, 3rd edn., 1906), pp.40, 50.

120. Dunn, *op. cit.*, Chap. IV.

121. D.R. Wrone, 'The Growth of American Indian Reform Policy', in *Cohesion* (Delhi), Vol. II, No. 1 (1971), p.61.

122. W.S. Blunt, *My Diaries* (London edn., 1932), p.684.

123. C.L. Brace, *The Dangerous Classes of New York* (New York, 1872) p.232.

PART THREE

OVERSEAS EXPANSION AND THE WAR WITH SPAIN

1

The Red Man in Custody

Fighting between white man and red left a long, melancholy trail, heroic and murderous in about the same degree on each side. Bloodshed would have been far less if the moving frontiers had been properly policed, at the cost of a tax on the profits of land-speculators and others who were getting rich quickly. But the philosophy of free enterprise was against this. Now the echoes of combat were being turned to account in the Wild West novels which supplied a living to innumerable scribblers and entertainment for generations of schoolboys who grew up fighting over again in fancy the battles of the past. In quality it was a sad falling off from Fenimore Cooper to the '"yellow-backed novel", that generally condemned, and more generally read, school-book of American youth'.[1] It fed the nation's craving to dramatize itself, and gave it an epic record to look back on as the Greeks looked back, about as realistically, on their siege of Troy. Even much nearer our own day, ingenuous youth was given scant means of forming more rational ideas on the subject. 'Somehow, the American history textbooks I had studied in high school and college never seemed to ring true when it came to the Indian wars', writes a man who set out to study them for himself.[2]

Since the losers had been despoiled and were still in underhand ways being robbed by the victors, it was expedient that the latter should be depicted as heroes, the former as savages. The centuries of war between the races threw up some Indian leaders as dauntless and impressive as any that Cooper had drawn.

But these Kosciuskos or Toussaints found little place in the story-books. Here everything had to be black and white, or rather (as in latter-day tales of Americans battling with sinister emissaries of communism) red and white. Typical of the prevailing picture of Indian barbarity is the episode in one tale of the beautiful white girl in the clutches of an evilly disposed Sioux chief;[3] or of the Chinook braves (or 'bucks') in another forcing their white captives to draw lots for which shall be tortured to death first.[4]

A fiendish delight in torturing their prey was one of the strongest traits associated with red men. Francis Parkman, explorer and historian of Indian and Anglo-French wars, was once the guest of a warrior who could boast of fourteen enemies killed, and recalled with special relish 'a Utah, whom he took prisoner; and, with the other Sioux, scalped alive, cut the tendons of his wrist, and flung, still living, into a great fire'.[5] Americans could take pride in having left behind at an early stage, among themselves though not between them and black men, the judicial horrors of old Europe, and did not foresee a twentieth century when torture would be a *vade-mecum* of their world empire. They took legitimate pride also in the equality or privilege they accorded to women, again except black women, whereas Indians like many other untutored peoples could be accused of treating them as mere beasts of burden. In general Americans were content with ready-made stereotypes very similar to those that Europeans carried with them into Asia or Africa to classify the indigenous peoples by. Another was that of Indian cunning, a substitute for the white man's intellect, but as alien from it as the ant's instinct. 'Their low retreating foreheads and prominent brows', we read of an Apache war-band '... gave them a look of cunning and ferocity rather than of intelligence.'[6] Later in the same novelette the antithesis recurs. 'Of the cunning of the Indian there is no limit. Without appearing to possess great mental capacity, yet the race is a never-ending source of wonder to the palefaces.'[7]

Instead of any Indian patriots, the fables had for their protagonist Buffalo Bill, or W.F. Cody, army scout and scourge of all 'bad' Indians, whose apogee in frontier warfare was from 1867 to 1876. He came to epitomize all the qualities that Americans loved to admire in themselves. Unlike Cooper's Pathfinder he had no close Indian associates; but he was a chivalrous fighter, never guilty as so many white ruffians were of acts of treachery or cruelty. It was in harmony with his melodramatic exploits that he should turn them and himself into a circus-show; he lived to 1917, a legend in his own lifetime. For a while he had with him the old Sioux chief Sitting Bull, the man who defeated Custer and later was killed during the final defeat of his people in 1890. Though Cody seems really to have befriended him, only commercial America could have thought of turning such a man into a spectacle for crowds to gape at. But the whole Wild West pageant of cowboy and Indian, sheriff and bandit, stage-coach and train robbery, all jumbled up in a fine mixture of epochs and costumes, must have been doing much to weld into one the heterogeneous American stocks. It helped to infuse a common consciousness by conjuring up a common antagonist, without which no nation has come to feel its nationhood; a solidarity more romantic than the common antipathy of white man against black which served a similar function.

The Navajos were allowed to return home in 1868, after only four years of exile, but the uprooting must have been psychologically crippling. They came back ravaged by 'the diseases of despair: malnutrition, syphilis, tuberculosis', and alcoholism.[8] When R.L. Stevenson made his long overland journey in 1879 and watched his fellow-passengers jeering at the few tattered Indians to be seen hanging about the stations, he felt 'ashamed for the thing we call civilization', and sad at the thought of once-free tribesmen forced back and back and at last 'shut up into these hideous mountain deserts of the centre'.[9] Men brought so low could hope for salvation only through magic. Among the Sioux a strange new cult spread, one of many pagan and Christian hybrids which sprang up in the world's border-lands, from the Taiping rebel religion in China to the Watch-tower movement in Southern Africa. Unlike some of these, and unlike the revival of the old faith by Tecumseh's brother the Prophet long before, this cult put no trust in mortal weapons or courage. It taught 'ghost-dances' that would restore dead ancestors and cover the plains once more with bison, while the earth opened and swallowed up the white persecutor. Authority grew suspicious, and forces were sent to arrest the ringleaders. At the end of 1890, at Wounded Knee Creek, more than two hundred Indian men, women and children were killed, with the assistance of quick-firing shells. This, not the destruction of Custer's column fourteen years earlier, was the real Sioux massacre.

Consolidation of the homeland, in the late decades of the century, had among its tasks that of learning how to handle its interior colonies and its Amerindian subjects. There were also of course the Afro-Americans, whose fortunes were in these years at their lowest since emancipation. A Supreme Court judgement of 1896 legitimized segregation, and Apartheid was being firmly established.

White men often took action on their own, 'without tarrying for the magistrate': between 1880 and 1900 more than three thousand lynchings were recorded; many others doubtless were not. Wounded Knee might be called an official lynching. This was, happily, exceptional; but more peaceful approaches to the Indian problem were crowned with little success. Management of the reservations called for long, careful, patient effort, uncongenial to a volatile temper which found it easier to hand out money in fits of generosity than to keep an eye on what happened to it. A swelling proportion of the public consisted of new arrivals absorbed in their chances of sinking or swimming, who could not be expected to feel responsibility for races unknown to them.

But most other Americans were not much more concerned. Indians out of sight were Indians out of mind. That some modicum of land was being left to them, and some compensation paid them, was enough to satisfy the average conscience. The nation could take comfort in the thought that it was buying territory from the savages, as it did from kings and emperors, not stealing it as Europeans were wont to do; and the survivors were not in any obvious fashion being exploited, like the indigenous inhabitants of European colonies, so Americans could feel free from the taint of imperialism. But the price paid, supposed to support a tribe until it could accustom itself to a settled economy, might be woefully slender. So might the acres left for it to live on. All tribes in California were relegated to five locations, and those whose labour had built up the flourishing Catholic mission settlements were expropriated.

There was no organization qualified to deputize for a negligent public. In Latin America the methods of the Catholic Church had been successful enough on their own lines, but they belonged to another, older world, and could not be emulated by Protestants. America still had little in the way of a genuine civil service; the man who was campaigning for one was a German, the exile of 1848 Carl Schurz who rose to be a general in the Civil War and later Secretary of the Interior. For a good colonial service the country lacked suitable material, for much the same reason that it lacked a diplomatic service in the European sense. American society (very fortunately for itself on the whole) possessed no class corresponding to the English or Scottish gentry, so willing and over-willing and in some ways so competent to undertake the running of colonies; and this dearth was to play its part in limiting American experiments in direct rule overseas.

While the practice prevailed of governors of western states being entrusted with Indian affairs, injustice was inevitable because the obligations of the two offices were incompatible.[10] The agencies in local charge had at least their fair share of the inefficiency or venality common to so much of the government apparatus. In the twenty years after the Civil War legislation might take on a more benevolent look, but its effect was diminished by the absence of any proper means of enforcing it, exactly as with early factory legislation in Britain. Every enquiry into the conduct of Agents showed 'a shameful state of robbery and corruption', with money voted by a niggardly Congress seldom reaching the hands it was meant for.[11] When tribesmen took to the warpath again it was often because they were 'ill-treated and starved by the Indian agents and the stinginess in Washington'.[12] Except when there was an outbreak, and the army had to be called in, public opinion dozed; and while Congress might be disturbed by news of shootings, it did not mind letting its wards die slowly of malnutrition, or more quickly of famine as among the Piegans in 1884. It was about that date that prevention of famines in British India was belatedly acknowledged as a duty of government. American Army outposts 'made prostitutes of Indian squaws for the gratification of soldiers'[13] (as European armies did with local women in their colonies); when taxed with this they retorted the charge against the civilian Agencies. Demoralized Indian men could be induced to hire out their wives in exchange for liquor. 'The extent of the traffic was almost beyond imagination.'[14] Venereal disease followed in its train.

Once civilization had taken such a hold, things were very hard to change. In 1915 when an educated Sioux wrote a book about his people and their condition, nothing seemed to have altered, except that the agent was now called a superintendent. He had control of all welfare services, and anyone who found fault with his doings was set down as a malcontent. 'Too often he has been nothing more than a ward politician of the commonest stamp, whose main purpose is to get all that is coming to him. His salary is small, but there are endless opportunities for graft.'[15] In later days, aid donated by the careless or credulous taxpayer to client nations far away has often been embezzled on a much bigger scale by local politicians and military men and their business confederates. National habits persist, and the child is father to the man.

This hand-to-mouth system left open the longer-term issues of the Indians' future, on which even less thought was bestowed. What they were supposed to be receiving was everything from religious to technical instruction and aid that might be required to prepare them gradually for reception into American life. Peace policy planners saw education of children as the vital point of entry, and pressed for 'industrial boarding schools'. But this cost money, and Indians could at best contribute little to the labour force America was in want of, compared with the millions from Europe. These swarms had to be assimilated, but Americanizing an Indian was far harder; in European colonies there was no pretence of trying to turn more than minute elites of Africans or Asians into imitation Englishmen, Frenchmen, or Portuguese. It could not be undertaken without a great deal of interference with Indian inclination and tradition.

The Indian Defense Association was opposed to any over-hasty detribalizing and refashioning. It was another issue on which Dunn's hesitations were typical of the more thoughtful America. He could not help feeling qualms about the 'concentration policy' which cut Indians off suddenly from their old existence, offering no congenial substitute. Yet he agreed that they ought to be brought into the modern world, and also that this could not be done without compulsion; they must be 'born again into civilization'.[16] He was one of those who consoled themselves with the idea that the difficulty might disappear through the whole race being absorbed into the national stock. This was happening with so many other aliens, and Indians were so few, that it could not seem very unlikely; it has partially taken place. He expected it to be nearly complete by the end of the century: 'the Indian will be almost lost in the American.'[17]

Another expectation might be that their shrunken domain would compel all Indians to take to agriculture in earnest, as some had been doing while still free. Exponents of economic virtue considered that an extra squeeze should be applied to expedite this, much as in England they believed in cutting down poor-relief in order to cure the poor of laziness. An agent named Meeker, who 'greatly over-estimated his ability to civilize savages', endeavoured to train his charges into hard-working farmers by reducing their food rations to the hunger point.[18] Impatience at the slow progress of teacher and missionary was soon prompting resort to another, more potent stimulus, the sacred egoism of private property, as a magical short cut to progress. Individual energy must be set free from the swaddling bands of tribal collectivism. This was a tenet very generally adopted, even by idealists like Helen Jackson. Collective ownership of land was being discouraged or subverted likewise in colonies like India or Algeria.[19] It must have been an added motive with less idealistic champions of private ownership everywhere that it would help to put an end to resistance to white rule; and with some of them, that a cultivator on his own could be more conveniently cheated out of his holding than a clan.

In 1887 the General Allotment Act (somewhat fortuitously known as the Dawes Act) authorized the president to break up the land of any reservation into separate farms. Along with these, citizenship could be conferred. The Act was little operated in the south-west, where the fierce temper of the tribes could still inspire caution. Where it was implemented, its results were deplorable. Instead of turning Indians into self-reliant American individualists, it reduced them to degraded paupers. Enforced de-collectivizing was as doctrinaire a procedure as the too sudden collectivizing of the Russian peasantry by Stalin. It brought 'poverty, squalor, disease, and hopelessness'.[20] Land considered surplus was sold to white buyers, nominally for the benefit of the Indians, really more often of the Agents, and the area in Indian possession once more diminished rapidly. In the next half-century it fell by far more than half.

What was left of the reservations was only too likely to sink into a dull torpor, on a par with the life in store for Bantustans in South Africa today. One remedy proposed was that white settlers should be scattered among them, to set an example. Livingstone had the same rash plan for East Africa. In Oklahoma white men were not waiting for an invitation. Although its Indian communities were often willing to lease land to them at reasonable rates, there was a long history of unauthorized intrusion, and of the government trying to prevent it. As before, its efforts were in the long run ineffective. In 1889 a large tract was thrown open to homesteaders; subsequently further areas were bought from the tribes. While other Indians were failing to advance, the old Civilized Tribes were in danger of retrogression. In 1870 when a government for the Indian Territory was proposed, the Choctaws and Cherokees had been strongly against it because they suspected, not surprisingly, that it would be run by the same sort of politicians and speculators who shared with the Agents the plunder of the reservations. In 1906, as a logical sequel to the Dawes Act, their own tribal councils were dissolved.

By the time Busoni was turning his American student's collection of Red Indian tunes into an 'Indian Fantasy' for piano and orchestra, there might seem to be little left of the old race except a few such fragments of its culture. A frontier newspaper's prediction, in the confident American style of clairvoyance, seemed on its way to fulfilment: 'The same inscrutable Arbiter that decreed the downfall of Rome, has pronounced the doom of extinction upon the red men of America.'[21] It was left to the mystical Oswald Spengler to discover that the boot was really on the other leg: they were vanishing only to be reincarnated, because like all races, or plants, the white settlers were being metamorphosed by their environment. 'It has long been obvious that the soil of the Indians has made its mark upon them – generation by generation they become more and more like the people they eradicated.'[22]

2

New Visions of Empire

From the Civil War to the war with Spain in 1898 was just a generation, which seems to be about the time required after a big conflict for war to come back into fashion, the sword to glow again with a romantic lustre. America's armed strength remained meagre, at a time when Europe's was growing prodigiously and Japan's emulating it. This was the time of the 'molly coddle vote', the distaste for any warlike preparedness, that Theodore Roosevelt was to excoriate.[23] Manufacturers who might have been expected to clamour for armament orders could usually fill their books without them; and only a country with enemies close at hand, where taxpayers can be made to feel that they are in chronic danger, is easily got to pay for them. A recommendation in 1878 for a naval base in Hawaii went unheeded. When European trade was depressed in 1879 John Bright, the English Quaker and radical, thought that America was in a better position thanks to not having yet 'bred a Beaconsfield or a Salisbury to misdirect her policy and waste her resources' on imperial vagaries.[24] During the War of the Pacific, which broke out in that year, the Chileans, having bought a few new iron-clads from England, were able to defy Washington's clumsy efforts to save Peru from their seizure of its provinces. State Secretary Blaine's grandiloquent assertion in the course of this dispute, that U.S. military power was 'without limit, and in any conflict on the American continent altogether irresistible',[25] was ludicrously untrue in terms of available strength. In the following years

American officers cruising those waters resented a Chilean attitude which they felt to be insolent.[26]

American philosophy was already changing, or about to change. In the 1890s this was to grow apparent; latterly historians have been coming to view the 1880s as a prelude to them, 'a time of fumbling towards an international policy more in keeping with the country's new industrial strength'.[27] One symptom was a new naval programme adopted in 1881, even if its progress was not rapid, and there was much leeway to make up. Someone wrote a satirical prophecy of America provoking Britain to war and being easily defeated.[28] But in 1890 Captain Mahan's book on seapower came out, and immediately became 'the Bible of American, British, Japanese, and German rulers, politicians and admirals'.[29] Seapower is a branch of technology and in any such sphere the U.S. was ready now to come to the front. In the same years, if less impressively, the army too was trying to pull itself together, improve its officer training, and emerge from the 'dark ages' which followed the Civil War.[30]

One factor at work in a changing public mood was the reckless haste with which the resources of America's own domestic colonies were being used up. The story of the white man's advance was also 'the story of the looting and misuse of land'.[31] Oklahoma's light soil was quickly turned by its new farmers into a dustbowl.[32] Many of these farmers were loaded with debt, or forced to rent plots from speculative land-grabbers, or eke out a livelihood as sharecroppers. As very often in the West, 'homesteading' belonged to American democratic illusion as much as to reality. Veblen wrote the classic account of the spoliation of the timberlands, the American practice of 'converting all public wealth to private gain on a plan of legalised seizure'.[33] It was of course those with capital to deploy who got the profits; and the capitalists engaged in 'disemboweling the country's timber resources' were as a rule 'heartily approved and admired by their fellow citizens', and frequently elected as suitable guardians of the country's concerns.[34]

About all this, few misgivings were felt, but there was some alarm at the speed with which the process of appropriation was nearing completion. It was partly a psychological unease, the sense of a westward march of centuries coming to an end with no alternative in sight. 'The frontier has gone', Jackson Turner wrote in 1893, 'and with its going has closed the first period of American history', but American life had come to be imbued with an 'expansive character' which it could not now throw off: 'the American intellect will continually demand a wider field for its exercise'.[35] This restless intellect had lately pushed the country into a frenetic endeavour to overleap a ghostlier frontier: spiritualism, George Eliot learned from her friend Mrs Harriet Beecher Stowe, had made claims 'much more compulsory on serious attention' in America than in England.[36] There were other claims, all the same, more imperative still, those of Wall Street.

A stampede for wealth was nothing new, but by now it was on an unprecedented scale. Industrial growth had been accelerated by the Civil War, with its huge gains, more or less shady, for profiteers. A new order was being born from war and conquest. 'The South was the anvil upon which capitalism forged its political power.'[37] It then had the windfall of masses of readily exploited labour streaming in from Europe. The result was a headlong pace far outstripping the best that Europe could show. In 1888 Engels wrote from Montreal to a German-American friend about the sluggishness of life in Canada compared with the U.S. 'Here one sees how necessary the feverish speculative spirit of the Americans is for the rapid development of a new country ... the economic necessity of an infusion of Yankee blood will have its way and abolish this ridiculous boundary line.'[38] Many Americans thought the same, and French Canada at least might have been less stagnant as a member of the Union than as a backwater of British Canada. Numbers of French Canadians removed to New England. A future Canadian premier, Mackenzie King, was studying in the U.S. in 1896–1900, with the maelstrom of money-making all round him.[39]

Speculative fever brought with it, more exaggeratedly than in Europe, wild booms and sudden crises. There was a banking crash in 1883, another in 1893, followed by prolonged depression and heavy unemployment. In the same period America was achieving what economists call a favourable balance of trade, meaning that a country, by skill or luck, is managing to get rid of more than it receives. Large wheat exports began in 1879, exposing the farmer to the ups and downs of the world market. At the end of the century two-thirds of American exports were still foodstuffs and raw materials, and the export surplus partly went in paying dividends on foreign investment in America.[40] But now there was coming to be a surplus of manufactures as well, all the more formidable because of its novelty, and because it was being hastened by the depression at home. Bigger markets abroad came quickly to seem not merely desirable, but vital for survival.

There was of course no *rational* need of mountainous exports; hence an irrationality tingeing all the epoch of expansionism now starting. The U.S. was no longer dependent on Europe for capital goods, and not yet dependent on the rest of the world for many raw materials. But would-be exporters do not trouble their heads about the needs of the national economy; and America had long been the stamping-ground of the pressure-group, organized to propel the unwieldy waggon of state in one direction or another – grown-up relatives of O'Henry's 'Gentle Grafters' peddling their gold bricks and diamonds to credulous rustics. The country was producing both more manufactured goods and more food than it could consume, declared Senator A.J. Beveridge of Indiana, adding as an obvious deduction: 'Fate has written our policy for us; the trade of the world must and shall be ours.'[41] Here was both the curious logic of capitalism and the American obsession with destiny; a latter-day example also of how, as in the 17th century, Calvinist determinism could be fused with superabundant energy.

Vested interests clamouring for expansion could count on a more indulgent hearing because the country was in the grip of social and political tensions, which big industry would in any case have generated but mass immigration worsened. America suddenly found Europe and its maladies within its own gates; not only the economy but the social structure seemed to nervous eyes to be tottering. If the Southern oligarchy was still reestablishing its control over a society dislocated by the Civil War – on lines that compared with the old slavery much as neo-colonialism compares with direct imperial rule – the Northern bourgeoisie was struggling to keep control of a labour force swollen by not always grateful and docile immigrants. A huge mass of human misery was involved in the uprooting of millions of people and their transfer from Europe to America, only less painful than that of the millions from Africa. New York was a town very much like the Manchester described by Engels, with its horde of poor Irish immigrants, on a vaster scale. An Immigration Restriction League was making the most of the newcomers' deficiencies, which it often depicted as racial and inborn instead of as the outcome of social conditions.[42]

Fighting between workers and official or unofficial guardians of 'order' was breaking out before fighting between white men and red ended, and the habits bred by the older kind of warfare prepared the way for the new, especially on the side of the guardians. In New York, 1874 opened with a lurid episode of police firing on an unemployed procession; in 1877 a railway strike also led to loss of life. Workmen were learning that they needed quicker-acting weapons of defence than votes, and in 1893 disorders broke out serious enough to spread panic. 'The militia either would or could not quell these gigantic outbreaks. Mobs of the worst classes burned and looted cars.'[43] Economic distress partly provided its own antidote, by bringing a throng of unemployed recruits to the army. 'What Congress failed to create, Providence provided', writes the army's historian.[44] It was giving training in riot control to the local forces of order; and in 1903 came Federal recognition of the National Guard, as an elite militia with the same function as the National Guard set up in France in 1789 of arming the 'active citizens' or middle classes against the poor.

Capitalism had its own armed forces as well. 'In certain industrial regions of the United States', President Wilson was to tell the Paris Peace Conference, defending his proposals for the Saar, 'the great private companies maintain their own police, who operate in the factory or the coal basins, without any conflict with the local or federal authorities'.[45] There were, besides, reserves that any of them could call on. In his study of militarism Karl Liebknecht noted that 'in the armed Pinkerton detectives the American capitalists have a "black hundred" of first quality permanently at their disposal'.[46] Conan Doyle wrote a novel about a coal-mining valley in America, with a Pinkerton man for hero and a gang of murderous trade-union bosses for villains.[47] The time would come for C.I.A. men to liberate foreign countries from the sinister clutches of communism very much as their precursor liberated this Valley of Fear.

Socialism still spoke in mellifluous tones in Edward Bellamy's Utopian novel of 1888, which rapidly sold a million copies: a rosy forecast of Americans refusing to go on 'bowing down to a plutocracy like that of Carthage', and peacefully bringing the economy under public control. 'Public opinion had become fully ripe for it, and the whole mass of the people were behind it.'[48] But years of turmoil followed the financial crisis of 1893, and by the end of the decade the machine-gun, one of America's grand inventions, first seriously tried out in the Civil War, was in regular service in disputes of capital and labour.[49] The distance the country was traversing may be measured by that between Bellamy's novel and Jack London's *The Iron Heel*, published in 1907, which pictures an imminent future of ferocious class warfare, and prophesies fascism.

Social tension brought with it intellectual disquiet. A doctrine much in vogue as an answer to social protest was social Darwinism. Rockefeller was one distinguished exponent of the idea that the struggle for existence, by bringing men like himself to the top, was indispensable to progress. A drawback was that the theory could cut both ways: Marxists found in it an endorsement of class struggle. Similarly in the field of competition among nations or races, Darwinism might suggest depressing conclusions. Doubts were creeping in about the future of American and European civilization in the world, as well as about that of the plutocracy. Westernism in Japan might be a compliment to the U.S., but a yellow man furnished with the white man's guns, uniforms, and machinery might look even more alien than before; and popular hatred of Chinese labour at home was finding a parallel in businessmen's nervousness about industrial rivalry from an awakened Far East.[50] The English writer Charles Pearson's gloomy vision in 1893 of the white races submerged under a tide of colour made a strong impression on American readers.[51]

Brooks Adams' work *The Law of Civilization and Decay* was published in 1895 in London, and in revised form a year later in New York. It was a landmark in the history of American thinking, and has been seen as a striking anticipation of Spengler.[52] This member of one of America's most cultivated families, as much at home in Europe as on his own side of the Atlantic, was surveying history from Roman times, with something like a Marxian emphasis on economics, and finding it increasingly dominated by philistine business greeds and huge agglomerations of capital. He was pinioned between dislike of capitalist society and dread of socialism, a not unfamiliar condition of modern intellectuals. Of the two evils, for an Adams the second was of course the worse. He and his brother Henry were immensely relieved by the advent of Bernstein the revisionist, who they felt was depriving Marxism of its revolutionary teeth.[53] Brooks Adams was also an imperialist, an ally of Roosevelt in spite of the latter's impatience with his theories of decadence; he wanted America to join hands with Britain in a coming struggle for mastery in China. Many later philosophers of gloom were to find a like escape from their dilemma in fascism.

Abroad as at home Darwinism could be enlisted, in a positive aggressive version, on the conservative side, instead of being left to breed corrosive doubts. Moreover the nation's history allowed expansionism to be depicted as simply a logical sequel, a next chapter. One frontier had closed, others were opening; some inferior races had been quelled, the time had come for others to be disposed of. This line of argument was far more persuasive than any preaching of new, untried courses could be. Beveridge maintained that modern shipping and telegraphy made possession of overseas territories just as natural as landward expansion in the past.[54] Much of Theodore Roosevelt's skill lay in convincing Americans that this was not 'imperialism', but simply a natural continuation of the country's previous growth.[55]

In Roosevelt's own mind or emotional make-up, this was very much the case. A writer on the Wild West and the Indian wars, he took an 'authentically Western frontier attitude', and was quite prepared to explain the necessity of savage treatment of savages.[56] In this he resembled Sarmiento, president of Argentina, always preoccupied with the gulf between civilization and barbarism, and increasingly with the race problem in the New World.[57] For Roosevelt imperialism too had its evils, but they were the price that had to be paid for progress.[58] Conservatives have always found this a light price, because it is paid by others, whereas the price of socialist progress seems to them very exorbitant. With his friends Henry Cabot Lodge, Adams, Mahan, John Hay and others, Roosevelt belonged to a circle of expansionists, each of whom had his own special motive and made his own contribution. He himself suffered from physical weakness, and his efforts to overcome it may have helped to give him an admiration of force such as a withered arm inspired in the Kaiser.

Most successful of all as a propagandist may have been the Rev. Josiah Strong, whose widely sold book came out in 1885. One of his themes was the danger of over-population. Hitherto the older sections of the country had enjoyed the same safety-value of emigration to the West as Europe had in America. 'It seems to me', he wrote with this in mind, 'that God, with infinite wisdom and skill, is training the Anglo-Saxon race for an hour sure to come'. This was the hour of 'the final competition of races ... If I read not amiss, this powerful race will move down upon Mexico, down upon Central and South America, out upon the islands of the sea, over upon Africa and beyond ...'. It was not a 'war of extermination' he had in mind: the humbler races would simply shrivel away (also no doubt by Divine prompting): they were 'only precursors of a superior race'.[59] This was just what so many had said of the Red Indians, while others talked of wiping them out; and it was natural for Americans, surveying mankind now from China to Peru, to view all backward peoples as first cousins of their own aborigines.

Stirring calls like these must have done something to avert the social conflict so much feared by conservatives. It has been shown how 'nigger-baiting' in the South provided an outlet for the frustrations and discontents of poor whites;[60] in the industrial North jingo excitement could serve a similar purpose. It was the remedy Europe had been discovering, and an America infected by European ailments was very likely to light on the same cure. There was the added motive of turning newcomers into loyal Americans. One immigrant wrote an account, some years later, of how flag-waving worked, how a sense of inferiority among new arrivals made some of them feel or pretend to feel 'chauvinistically patriotic', and 'ready for almost any sort of shallow, ignorant nationalist or fascist movement....'.[61]

But many, with no wish for left-wing outbreaks, had no love of right-wing rabble-rousing either. In the critical year 1893, that staunch old radical Carl Schurz was moved to protest against the rising clamour; the more strenuously perhaps because his native Germany was in the grip of a similar mania. Manifest Destiny, he wrote, was always trumpeted to make any coveted extension of power look inevitable. After a lull following the Civil War when it excited only a few individuals like Seward, 'whose brain was constantly busy with schemes of annexation', it was being revived now in the form of demands for territory no longer contiguous with the U.S., but far away. It was encouraged by groups small but 'very demonstrative': nationalists, navy men, and businessmen with interests in foreign parts whose 'apparent patriotism ... should be received with due distrust'. Arguments of strategic security were being urged in its support: Cuba 'commands', or 'threatens', America's coasts, and in hostile hands would imperil them – but the same could be said of any number of other places. (A crystal ball would have shown him Greece and Taiwan among the number.) In reality, he contended, the U.S. was the only big country exposed to no serious risk of invasion, hence in no need of cumbrous armaments.[62]

Schurz's most deeply felt objection was that, given 'the spirit of our Constitutional system', any territory acquired would have to be admitted to the Union before long as a new state, and although Canada if willing could be incorporated readily enough, most other lands could not be included without peril to democracy. This thesis really ruled out any colonies, in the European sense, for the U.S. It was based on assumptions natural to the long epoch when the Stars and Stripes were multiplying across a continent occupied by no massive indigenous population. Strong's forecast, fortified by his blend of Calvinistic election with Darwinist selection, assumed that the same process would continue outside North America, and indefinitely; hence Schurz's dilemma would not arise. In reality densely inhabited lands would not empty themselves at the white man's destined approach. Nor was there any real prospect of America needing so much extra living-space. It was still groping, feeling its tentative way; but more room for settlers was not what it might want colonies for.

Strong's book was written to raise money for mission work. It might seem another illogicality to send out missionaries to races fated before long to disappear, but there has always been the anomaly of Calvinist thunders hurled at reprobates incapable of profiting by them. Religion was another force helping to direct aspirations outward, as well as to smooth over tensions at home; it was going on without a pause from its long task of carrying enlightenment into raw new corners of the Union, to the same undertaking in the world's backlands. As part of the old-fashioned hemisphere of its thinking America continued, as it still continues, to be a pious or church-going country; and its blossoming power in the world has always retained a missionary flavour, compounded from some genuine and many other ingredients. Europe has suspected it of cant or hypocrisy, very much as exasperated Frenchmen used to suspect their God-fearing neighbour John Bull; but it may be that any stirring, ambitious nation, bent on making the dust of history fly, requires a protective misunderstanding of itself and its motives, if action is not to be sicklied o'er with the pale cast of thought.

The U.S. began as a staunchly Protestant nation in an otherwise almost entirely Catholic or pagan New World, and this was bound to impose a sense of superiority, which might suggest a duty to rescue neighbours from their darkness. This was always present in feeling about Cuba, and could readily merge into the complex of impulses making for imperialism. Nearly all Protestant churches were to back the war with Catholic Spain. Some of them had been till not long before firm defenders of slavery, as some are today in South Africa of its successor, Apartheid. David Livingstone's brother Charles, who studied for some years at Ohio, wrote to him from there in 1847 of his reluctance to enlist with the American Missionary Society. 'A Society composed of slaveholders and of those who apologize for slavery is not the thing for me....'.[63]

Now that missionary effort was financed largely by capitalists, some of them with a not very dissimilar mentality, churches found it still more natural to defend free enterprise, and not hard to justify imperialism so long as this was garbed in respectable phraseology. There was 'a climate of opinion in which missions could be linked to more earthly considerations than becoming inebriated with the Holy Spirit ...'.[64] Mark Twain satirized the vindictive anger of missionaries in China after the Boxer Rebellion in 1900, and the jargon of the 'civilising mission'.[65] Church and state were converging; and if in the mission field Protestants held the lead, the Catholic minority in the U.S. was growing, and its missionary contribution helped to associate it with American prestige and thus establish it as truly American. In like fashion the French Catholic clergy were keeping their ground in the anti-clerical Third Republic partly by being useful auxiliaries in the occupation of Indochina. One day an American cardinal and chaplain-general would stand in Vietnam, on a Christmas Eve, breathing fire and slaughter against rebels.

Clearly the fondness of both Britons and Americans for regarding their conquests as 'liberations' of oppressed peoples had much in common with the missionary desire to set them free from the chains of sin and superstition (and later on of the ultimate bondage, communism) while inducting them into a new way of life, a rebirth that meant being made over into the image of their mentors. Long before Cardinal Spellman set foot in the Far East a medical missionary there, Peter Parker, who was made in 1855 American minister to China, showed himself an adherent of strong-arm methods of dealing with the Chinese; he would have liked his country to annex Taiwan.[66] At many other points too, the spiritual and financial capital America was investing abroad were to be found in close proximity. Missionary effort had its own accumulation of funds. To an Englishman in the Far East, its representatives appeared to be living in considerable comfort.[67] In Hawaii, where missionaries were very much in the lead in the establishment of American influence, some of them or their sons acquired land and set up as sugar-planters.[68]

'Most Americans involved in foreign operations are to some degree missionaries', one American, an ex-president of the World Bank, paused to remark.[69] The converse has been equally true: American missionaries (like those of other countries) have not forgotten their nationality, and have thought of the road to Heaven as an American-built highway. They have been less deaf than any others to the argument urged by many laymen that they ought to rise above divinity and show more concern for temporal progress – which in business terms meant the progress of profits. 'Immense services ... might be rendered to our commercial interests', as a spokesman of British commerce put it, 'if only the members of the various missions in China would cooperate with our consuls in the exploitation of the country, and the introduction of commercial as well as of purely theological ideas to the Chinese intelligence.'[70]

Trade, or capitalism, was part of a divine plan for regenerating the pagan world. In another light this concern for temporalities was part of a wholesome shift towards welfare work, medical aid, education. This suited America's practical bent, and could serve a dual purpose of expressing genuine philanthropy and winning customers for American goods, whether America aimed at colonial territory of its own or at gaining footholds and opportunities more indirectly. It was natural for its missionaries sometimes to feel the same desire for fields where they could work under their own flag, labour in their own vineyards, which made German mission bodies fervid supporters of colonialism. But in the British empire all higher education was in their own language, and the colleges they set up in China helped to make English the medium of modern thinking there as well. America's missionaries, like its businessmen, had funds, energy, and the rising name of their country to aid them; they brought a fresh organizing talent to bear on their task. Yankee hustle might breed burlesque schemes of mass production of converts, baptism more or less at sight, as in the mission in China encountered by that redoubtable Englishman Canon Tyndale-Biscoe, where conversions had to be forthcoming all the time to keep the dollars flowing in.[71] In more sober guise the effort put into education was valuable both for the recipients, who really had much to learn, and for America, which had so much to sell. Beirut's celebrated university began as a mission college as long ago as 1866, and has done much good; though there is no missing the significance of the fact that half its budget came to be paid by the State Department, and that the Lebanon is a country where America found it proper a few years ago to carry out an armed intervention.

3

Latin America and Further Asia

In the expansionist drive sugar, or the dollars it could be turned into, led the way. If America was in most ways a more strictly modern or bourgeois country than any in Europe, its plantations, at home or overseas, represented a type of enterprise only separated by a few years from ages of slavery. To these must be added the big sugar refineries. Taken together they represented a more primitive capitalism than the new manufacturing industries; they could be called a pro-longation of the old Southern drive for more land and cheap labour. Cuba was still the juiciest carrot dangling before the American nose. When rebellion was raging there in 1871 the British minister at Madrid, Sir Austen Henry Layard, was able to assure his government with some truth that it was not really a struggle for emancipation of the slaves, but an independence movement 'encouraged by a powerful party in the United States'.[72]

This party, like all others with an axe to grind in the Caribbean region, could as Schurz saw play on nervousness about national security. This gained a fresh irritant when Lesseps came forward in 1879 with his Isthmian canal plan, and stirred fears of a European stranglehold on an American lifeline. In January 1880 President Hayes (one of whose Christmas presents had been a 'very fine' Navajo blanket from General Atkinson at Santa Fe) sent a warship to each of two ports, on the Gulf and on the Pacific, adjacent to a proposed route across Nicaragua: for warrant, there were grants of land there, said to have been made to a U.S. citizen.

'With due regard to the rights and wishes of our sister republics in the Isthmus', he reflected a few weeks later in his diary, the passageway must be under U.S. control. On 10 February he gave his views – 'matured, distinct, and decisive' – to his cabinet, and secured (even with Schurz a member) unanimous assent.[73] To bolster this view of what Washington was entitled to insist on, the Monroe Doctrine was paraded; this use of it was 'a distinct novelty'.[74] It was the more anomalous because Frelinghuysen, at the State Department from 1881 to 1885, while working to extend U.S. influence in Latin America was prepared to take a hand in Europe too, in a style 'completely counter to the principle of disengagement from European affairs'.[75]

However deep its roots in an older epoch might be, sugar by now was caught up in the machinations of the newest high finance. An extraordinarily complex series of rivalries was in train, with refiners on the West and East Coasts as protagonists. The former looked to Hawaii and to the mostly American planters there for much of their raw sugar; a reciprocity treaty of 1875 was their sheet-anchor. Their leader was Claus Spreckels, another German by origin like Carl Schurz but of opposite outlook; he returned to Germany for long spells, and was doubtless reinvigorated by renewal of contact with a fatherland now on the march towards empire. His hated competitor on the East Coast was Henry Havemeyer, a money-maker no less uninhibited, who drew on Cuba's richer output, and who got the upper hand by forming in 1887 the Sugar Trust, one of America's early corporate juggernauts.[76] Louisiana cane growers were a rival, though only capable of meeting a limited part of the huge demand; growers of beet sugar were coming in to make a fourth. Tariffs and differentials on raw or refined imports were of vital concern to them all. Import duties mattered to many other industries; and if the Republican Party, now unmistakably the party of big business, was in the saddle through most of the period from 1860 to 1912, this was in good measure the result of its shrewdness in garnering campaign funds from companies which did not believe in leaving things to chance.[77] The Tariff Bill of 1894 was accompanied by unusually active lobbying, and sweetening of senators with sugar shares or other titbits.[78]

Hawaii, feebly independent, might be easier to get hold of than Cuba, and this ocean pearl far to the west had long been an enticement. In 1887 American planters, who could pass themselves off as republican reformers, forced the monarchy to introduce a parliamentary system, in which of course they held the whip hand. In 1893 they replied to Queen Liliokalani's attempts to regain ground by overthrowing her, and applying for union with America. It was all very much like the American settlers taking possession of Texas half a century before, and there was a further precedent in the old fears of America being forestalled in California by the wily British, now supposedly fishing for Hawaii. Cleveland, the Democrat president restored to office in 1892, felt obliged to reject annexation, but granted recognition to the bogus republic. Argument went on about the islands. Sugar interests were divided. Among politicians, advocates of a forward policy favoured annexation; one of them was Blaine. Schurz argued that Hawaii would be an 'Achilles' heel', weakening instead of strengthening American security; also that its mongrel population of a few indigenous inhabitants and a cosmopolitan mob of adventurers was as little qualified as any could be for inclusion in the Union.[79]

South America, by comparison with Central America and its outliers, was another continent, most of it remoter from the U.S. than from Western Europe. Roving individuals were blazing the trail there more independently, though government aid would be sought when wanted. An early episode started in 1845, a year of expansionist moods, when a semi-official spokesman, E.A. Hopkins, arrived in self-isolated Paraguay. He was bursting with free-enterprise principles, and lectured on them to the dictator C.A. López, who ruled with moderate discretion an economy based on the communal landowning of the Guaraní Indian population. It was a primitive version of the socialism that Washington is so determined to veto in South America today. One is reminded of Pizarro's chaplain haranguing the captive Inca emperor on the Book of Genesis and the fall of man; but Hopkins went home with sanguine hopefulness to organize a grand syndicate, and was very indignant when it was not allowed to set to work. He did manage to make things harder for Europeans, whose commercial designs he deemed it part of his republican duty to thwart.[80] In 1858–59 his government stepped in on behalf of an American company allegedly ill-treated, but gave way when arbitration went against it:[81] half a century later it would have been less squeamish.

In some other regions the forerunners of empire had an easier time. The most striking illustration of this was the legendary career of Meiggs, who left home a fraudulent bankrupt to become the great railway-builder of Chile and Peru in the 1860s and 1870s. All that was required of such an entrepreneur was that he should be as free from scruple about handing out bribes as Peruvian landlord-politicians were about pocketing them; also about handling local labour in the same summary fashion in which they handled Indian, African and Chinese labour on their plantations. There are frequent allusions in Meiggs's papers to the *buying* of Chinese coolies from the middlemen who dealt in them.[82] But larger-scale, corporate enterprise was now coming to the fore. By 1880 there was large investment in Mexican railway-building. At home in the U.S., railway companies led the way in buying up state legislatures, and this gave them excellent training for buying influence with governments abroad. Loans began to be floated for ramshackle governments like Peru's by firms like Morgan, which had before them many alluring British and French examples of how such regimes could be enmeshed in debt and their countries kept paying through the nose.

By this time the Monroe Doctrine was taking on a commercial dimension,[83] and being thought of as a claim to a special economic as well as political status for the U.S. With this, sensitiveness to European meddlings, real or suspected, grew more acute. The time was passing when forcible meddling by Europe could hope to go unchallenged, even far beyond the Caribbean, as it did in 1866 when Spain picked quarrels with Ecuador, Peru and Chile, and a Spanish fleet was blundering about the Pacific Coast. Seward announced that the U.S. would not always feel bound to intervene in a South American war with Europe, but would not allow republican institutions to be overthrown from outside; in other words, would not allow annexations. A century later, this has come to mean refusal to allow capitalism (or feudalism, in Latin America its half-brother) to be subverted from within. There was a much sharper reaction when the War of the Pacific led to the defeat of Peru and Bolivia by Chile and the seizure of their nitrate and guano areas. James Blaine, the sturdily anti-British Secretary of State in 1881, was convinced that Chile's victory was really Europe's. Americans often thought of Europe far more as a single whole than it really was. In this case Britain and France were at odds, and so far as British diplomacy was concerned Blaine's suspicions were mistaken, if less so as regards British capital. There were Americans who wanted to counter it by something like a U.S. protectorate over Peru.[84]

Peru had many factions and feuds, no true parties. Where there was room in South America for any serious cleavage between a conservative and a liberal – a more and a less unprogressive – party, U.S. sympathies were likely to attach themselves to the second. They could thus express a democratic spirit, which grew more muddled and adulterated at every further hundred miles from Washington; and also a desire to outflank European competitors, who were as a rule more strongly entrenched and likely to side with the more reactionary local groups. In Chile there was a pattern off and on of England favouring the landed aristocracy, the U.S. the dissident left wing. When the Liberal chief Balmaceda was being ousted in 1891 by a conservative revolt Blaine, Secretary of State again, took his part strongly, and gave him some unavailing aid.[85] It was another reverse, which the U.S. revenged in 1892 by pressing a dispute over a drunken seamen's riot and extorting an apology, as its navy was now formidable enough to do.

There was a similar pattern in Brazil, where it was a standing complaint of English and other European diplomats, enjoying the elegancies of the New World's solitary royal court, that U.S. newspapers and other influences were always trying to undermine the monarchy, until it fell at last in 1889.[86] When the navy mutinied in favour of a restoration, President Cleveland under prompting from business interests interfered by stationing warships in a position to hamper the rebels.[87] He was seconded by private enterprise in the shape of that world-roving embodiment of it – and of the arms trade in particular – C.R. Flint, who bought ships, hired volunteers, and within three weeks put his 'Dynamite Fleet' at the service of the Brazilian government, which then unluckily failed to pay him.[88]

Out of such scrimmagings a hankering for hegemony over the entire hemisphere was being born. The public was not yet much interested in what Secretary Evarts had called the 'paramount position' of the U.S. in the New World, but with stocks and shares pushing and pulling it would in due course take the same view as its mentors. As usual, self-assertion sometimes really had, and oftener pretended to have, a protective purpose. Japanese imperialism, it has been said, arose from an impulse to give Eastern Asia leadership against intruding Europe,[89] and this was at least one of its emotional taproots. A Peruvian admirer of the U.S. made the most of this theme when he declared that, but for the U.S., Britain would have turned all Central America into a colony and would now be taking possession of the mouths of the Orinoco.[90]

This was an allusion to the long-drawn boundary dispute between British Guiana and Venezuela, in which Washington took in 1895 a very stiff line against London. One Venezuelan device to ensure this – 'a most familiar, but extremely imprudent, expedient' – was bestowing large gold-mining rights in the disputed area on Americans.[91] Intermittently there was suspicion of other Powers, France and the newcomer Germany, having territorial aims in Central America. But hegemony could claim a further function, that of keeping the peace and preventing broils among the republics. An enlightened scholar, not without any misgivings about his government's policies, fell back on the plausible idea that in its own hemisphere it had to exert by itself the same kind of authority that the Concert of Europe wielded collectively.[92]

It was now, the same historian wrote in 1900, 'a well-established rule of American diplomacy' that affairs of the Americas must be settled by their own peoples.[93] In practice this formula would often mean dictation by Washington. Blaine asserted in 1881 that his country's actions in Latin America were always conducted 'with such fairness as to leave no room for imputing to our government any motive but the humane and disinterested one of saving the kindred states of the American continent from the burdens of war'.[94] Administrations at Washington have frequently paid themselves the fulsome tributes that in Europe are left to poet laureates or journalists to pay, and Blaine had been a journalist himself. A critic came nearer the mark when he said that the government's handling of the Pacific War had dissipated its prestige in South America and given ground for 'direct European interference'.[95] When in 1889 Blaine held the first regular Pan-American Congress, at Washington, doubts about U.S. motives were already well awake. Blaine wanted to push Europe out of South America, and therefore wanted U.S. manufactures to supplant Europe's in the market there, which they were not yet nearly robust enough to do. Political ambition was running ahead of economic appetite, as has not infrequently happened, but the appetite was growing quickly enough. Other Congresses followed in 1901, 1906, 1910. They were in a way a sketch for the League of Nations championed in 1919 by Wilson, and mixed motives were astir in them as in it. Between Pan-Americanism and U.S. paramountcy the distinction could only be elusive.

In some ways American attitudes in South America were reproduced in Eastern Asia. The U.S. resented there too Europe's, especially Britain's, lead and was inclined to express this by fraternizing with the indigenous peoples. But here it was less able to get a footing except by following behind the Europeans, as it had done in earlier days. Hence a frequent discordance between its two voices, a louder one of fellow-feeling with Asia, a more muffled one of approval of the bullying European. Europeans continued to complain of the duplicity of Americans who took full advantage of their 'Concessions', or extraterritorial settlements, while unctuously boasting of having seized none themselves.[96] American envoys often viewed with distrust their scheming colleagues, who in turn laughed at them in their sleeves as hempen homespuns. In 1868 Anson Burlingame, after being the first resident U.S. minister in China, took charge of a Chinese mission abroad, and tried to convince Lord Clarendon at the Foreign Office that China did not want to stand still, but only not to be hustled forward too roughly.[97] A decade later an American envoy could still contemplate China with something of the admiration that Europeans felt for it a century earlier: he doubtless had in mind a resemblance between it and his own country when he praised its moderation in respecting the rights of the little nations all round it.[98]

By this time a period of only languid commercial interest in Eastern Asia was ending. A fresh impetus came with the completion in 1869 of the transcontinental railway; there was some irony, which did not go unnoticed, in Chinese navvies building the line that would launch American aspirations across the ocean towards China. From the 1880s producers were being exhorted more and more insistently to seek markets in the Far East, though in fact trade with both China and Japan grew less rapidly than U.S. exports as a whole.[99] A suitable overture was provided by the long Asian tour in 1879 (just ten years after the 'shoddy episode' of his failure to grab San Domingo[100]) of ex-president Grant, presciently baptized Ulysses. It was intended to alert his countrymen to opportunities they were neglecting. Everywhere he preached modernization and progress; at Bangkok he found symptoms of the country being already on the way towards its later position as a U.S. satellite, for the father of one of the two kings was called George Washington, and was warmly pro-American. When Grant and his wife visited Peking a prodigious cloud of dust was stirred up by the throng of officials who welcomed them at the gate;[101] a good deal more than was stirred up by President Nixon's arrival a century later. In Japan too he was given a rousing reception, and he had several talks with the Mikado: his message was that Japan ought not to quarrel with China, because this would only strengthen the baleful ascendancy of Europe.[102]

In Japan, whose markets were for long relatively trivial, the idealistic side of the American outlook had more scope. It was well represented for many years by

John Armor Bingham, who won a certain status as Japan's friend and adviser, while some of the foreigners employed by the Japanese government were his countrymen. 'The object of the Americans is of course transparent', wrote the irate British minister Harry Parkes in 1878 – to get the Japanese to view Europeans, Britons above all, as their enemies.[103] Bingham combined with much sincerity something of the wisdom of the serpent, for he felt that Europe was blocking American trade in Asia, and was always impressing on the State Department, with many allusions to Justice, that Japan ought to be well treated because it was a natural gateway for American commerce.[104] Other countries feared that America would let them down over the long-vexed issue of Japanese demands for revision of the 'unequal treaties'; as indeed happened in 1878 when Bingham persuaded his government to make concessions to Japan, selfishly in the sense that tariff freedom for Japan would do more harm to Britain than to America.[105] A Liberal party was pressing for parliamentary rule, while the oligarchs in power insisted on an authoritarian constitution. Europeans (as in South America) favoured the latter; a strong government was needed to protect foreign interests against popular ill-feeling. To this view America has now long since come round, all over the world, but men like Bingham were suspected of foolishly encouraging the Liberal agitation.

In China, where more was at stake, the contradictoriness of American attitudes was showing itself earlier. During the undeclared war between China and France in the early 1880s over the French seizure of Tonkin or Northern Vietnam, the American minister at Peking, J.R. Young, was anxious to mediate, though he got no chance.[106] It was an early instance, to be followed by a good many others, of America playing or trying to play peacemaker, from idealism and self-interest along with a faith in processes of rational adjustment not shared by Europe. But a Chinese sent to Washington on diplomatic duty had already expressed disillusionment with Americans. 'I am heartily tired of them. Their estimate of themselves soars beyond my appreciation . . .'.[107] Next year an American in China, Commodore Schufeldt, was voicing a keener disillusionment with the Celestials, who he felt must be treated with 'justice untainted by sentimentality'.[108] He was employed in 1881–82 in getting a trade treaty with the Chinese protectorate of Korea, still the unopened 'Hermit Kingdom', where all foreigners were starting from scratch. Korean conservatives, as if foreseeing what an American presence would mean to their country one day, sat in hundreds for a week, clad in mourning clothes, outside the palace.[109] Superficially the treaty might look fair enough, an American historian was to write, but it was 'the instrument which set Korea adrift on the ocean of intrigue which it was quite helpless to control'.[110]

It was followed by American manoeuvres to gain concessions in Korea, in competition with British interests.[111] Thoughts of vast profits to be made by building railways in China were tantalizing American as well as European minds, and the Charles Denby who was minister at Peking from 1885 to 1898 was a railway lawyer and a subscriber to policies of pushing foreign interests in China by resolute methods. America was moving towards an active part in the 'Battle of the Concessions' waged in China during the 1890s, which seemed to be leading towards a partition of the country. By 1897 American business personnel in China numbered 1,564, a figure second only to the British total of 4,929.[112] (In number of firms America, with only 32, stood fourth to Britain's 374: evidently American firms tended to be larger, and would have louder voices to catch their government's ear.) In 1898 an American-China Development Company, with Rockefeller and Harriman participation, was working for a contract to build a railway from Hankow to Canton; there was a complicated struggle with opposing interests, and early in 1899 a partnership agreement with the British and Chinese Corporation,[113] a forerunner of many subsequent American initiatives towards international capitalist groupings.

Scouting round in 1899 on behalf of the British Chambers of Commerce, Admiral Lord Charles Beresford found that, though trade with China only stood at 8% of America's total, it was larger than appeared because many American goods were reaching China through English hands: at Shanghai this was the case with 60% of American piece-goods, nearly all of which came in British shipping, and some American firms there were partly British. American competition was certain to grow; Beresford heard of mills being erected in the States on purpose to supply the China market.[114] This was looked to more and more as the market of markets, the salvation from over-production. It was to prove mostly moonshine; but like the moon itself later on, it could do something to work off the American surplus, and far more to keep up American confidence.

All this moving out into the world was bringing with it a new awareness of the value of diplomatic skills. Hitherto most of the country's diplomacy had been as wooden as its warships, and as often at sea. During the War of the Pacific there was a remarkable record of bungling and cross-purposes on the part of the representatives at the three capitals concerned.[115] European professionals dealing with such amateurs had only to give them rope to entangle themselves in, and regarded them as scarcely superior to the envoys or politicians of Latin America itself. Corruption was often suspected. There was a scandal a little earlier connected with a General Schenk, minister at London, and a wildcat company he lent his name to.[116] On less irregular lines, however, helpful collaboration with private interests was what was required. It was burgeoning particularly in the Far East, where before the end of the century a new type of representative was emerging, more thrustful and realistic than the old sort. It was in the Far East too that, late in the century, efforts were started to train a body of career diplomats, secured against the hazards of the spoils system. Rich young idlers, too many of whom it was felt were joining simply with an eye to social distinction,[117] were not likely to be attracted to Peking or Tokyo. We have some entertaining memoirs by one of the new cadets, who says that instructions from Washington were so few and far between that one could only guess at one's government's views by reading six-weeks old newspapers.[118] At the State Department a close inner ring looked on the Secretary as an outsider, and on the diplomatic and consular services as 'public enemies'.[119]

4

Anglo-Saxons and their Wars

As always, it was with Britain that the U.S. had most points of contact, and therefore of friction, and Britain helped to draw the U.S. out into the whirlpool of *Weltpolitik* by both rivalry and example, repulsion and attraction. The two were having their very serious quarrel in 1895, over Venezuela, just before they came close together, while Britain and Germany in the same years seemed quite close just before they began quarrelling. Friction was partly a matter of incompatibility, as well as of conflicting aims. In 1895 Secretary Olney referred to British connections with the Americas as 'neither natural nor expedient'. In the same year Cabot Lodge was advocating annexation of Canada, as well as a Canal Zone, Samoa, and Hawaii.[120] Side by side with thoughts like these, there was still a lingering old radical feeling against British imperialism, nourished by republican antipathy to monarchy. Having no aristocracy of their own to resent (apart from the already defeated Southern planters) the dominant classes could find expression for their 'bourgeois' nature by disliking the British aristocracy and its ways. An industrial leader like Carnegie, of recent Scottish extraction and vigorously anti-war, associated war and imperialism with the decadent regimes of Europe. The U.S. moreover provided a home for some revolutionary movements or groups opposed to the British empire – Irish, and then Indian – as Britain had done for conspirators against Austrian or Tsarist despotism. Irishmen, through journals like the *Irish World* edited by Patrick Ford, denounced British rule not only in Ireland but in India and other colonies.[121] This stream of thought must have contributed to the resistance to imperialist policies when these got under way.

But jostling with it were other feelings, less clear-cut, about the British empire being at any rate not the worst of empires, and for America on the brink of a plunge into world politics a possible friend, even ally. In turning away from active expansionism after mid-century, America had moved on a parallel line with Britain, where there was a strong disposition to think of colonies as ana-chronisms. Now, with colonies all the rage once more, it was likely to feel some British influence again. If Irish immigrants brought hatred of Britannia and all her works, there were also multitudes of Englishmen and Scots arriving, with prepossessions in favour of empire. If some capitalists were sturdily mistrustful of John Bull, others were marrying their daughters to his aristocratic sons: less often, it may be conjectured, solid industrialists than financiers, Stock Exchange gamblers such as were to be found practising the same artful dodges in every capital; like the Leonard Jerome whose daughter Jennie married in 1874 Lord Randolph Churchill, soon to become Secretary of State for India, and afterwards rescued from penury by a lucrative speculation in South African gold shares.[122] 'All Americans took great interest in the career of Lord Randolph Churchill'.[123] This peculiar form of capital export by the American plutocracy helped to solder together aristocracy and millocracy in Britain into a combined plutocracy.

Bankers like J.P. Morgan took part in British flotations of capital abroad; the Venezuelan crisis caused a panic on Wall Street, and made money-bags on both sides realise how closely their fortunes were linked.[124] A good part of the massive British investment still aiding American growth came, in one way or another, out of the profits of empire. A good part of these profits came from the efficacy of American machine-guns in expanding the British empire, particularly in Africa.[125] Some of the American missionaries expelled from Lower Burma in 1839 made themselves useful in 1851 to the British, about to occupy the country.[126]

Buffalo Bill's show toured Europe, and helped to give British youth an idea of America as a land of swashbuckling daredevils, worthy partners in imperial adventure and the policing of turbulent frontiers. American tourists marched with mingled 'complacency and independence' through show-places like Gibraltar, where Mark Twian's 'Innocents' gazed upon Highland soldiers and cliff-hung batteries and 'uniforms of flaming red.'[127] Altogether there was more often than not a willingness to credit the British empire with a civilizing mission; from which it followed as the night the day that an America powerful in the world would be a more civilizing force still. Evarts' word *paramount* – an old term of feudal overlordship – might have been borrowed from the British usage, the claim of suzerainty over all India. In 1887 an American brought out a book to warn his countrymen against the growing power of Russia, and its menace to India. It seemed obvious to him that of the European countries only Britain and Russia shared with the U.S. 'unlimited facilities for growth', and only they had any future: the French had a brilliant past, but were now degenerate, thanks to 'the prevalent licentiousness which is ingrained in their literature as well as in their lives'.[128] Captain Mahan with his doctrine of seapower was calling on America to join Britannia as mistress of the seas.

Current use of the phrase 'Anglo-Saxon', in an epoch when racialist thinking was fed by many tributaries, implied a more general sense of falling heir to British tradition. It was being vigorously popularized on both sides of the Atlantic, each in the grip, Carlyle morosely told an American visitor, of a mania for 'blustering, vainglorious, hollow, far-sounding, unmeaning Talk'.[129] John Fiske, a leading American exponent, got an enthusiastic reception with his lectures to the Royal Institution in 1880, when he predicted an immense growth of the English-speaking peoples, which would soon form the great majority of the world's inhabitants.[130] Lady Randolph Churchill ran an *Anglo-Saxon Review*. Anglo-Saxon daydreams were dear to Americans of old stock, anxious to be able to feel that the nation was still what it had been, at a time when the vast influx of other peoples was in reality transforming its ethnic character. There was indeed an obvious streak of collective snobbery: to be 'English', or 'Saxon', was to belong to a privileged Ascendancy, an elite superior to any poor white trash from the rest of Europe. To these others, not Hibernians alone, all this was correspondingly distasteful, and might make England equally so; John Hay was lamenting in 1900 a widespread anti-British feeling.[131]

World power was the other implication. 'We are Anglo-Saxons', Beveridge proclaimed in 1898, 'and must obey our blood and occupy new markets, and, if necessary, new lands', civilization following the American colours to 'shores hitherto bloody and benighted'.[132] In another speech of that year he recommended 'Anglo-Saxon solidarity ... an English-speaking peoples' league of God for the permanent peace of this war-torn world . . .'.[133] This 'supreme orator of American imperialism'[134] came of Virginian slave-owning stock, with Scottish and Scottish-Irish forbears, a highly combustible compound; he rose in politics by patriotic rhetoric and a never-failing knowledge of the workings of the divine mind. A more academic voice, that of the New England literary historian Wendell, was declaring that the U.S. was now '– like England, at once democratic and imperial – inevitably confronted with world conflict . . . England and America are once more side by side'.[135] Side by side; but it was a favourite text of the Manifest Destiny men that the U.S., outstripping Britain in the Anglo-Saxon fold, must soon move to the front.

Annexation of Hawaii came in 1897, and was ratified by the Senate next year.[136] Whatever might be the reality, in form America was not destroying a nation, but welcoming a fellow-republic. It was to be a signal feature of its history that it never, in outward appearance at least, deprived any independent people of its national existence. The decision came under cover of strained relations with Spain. In 1895 the leaders of the latest Cuban rebellion had declared independence, and were recognized by Cleveland as belligerents. His Republican successor McKinley, elected in 1896, revived an old strategy by trying to buy Cuba. Spain was the one European country, not insignificant in size, that America was strong enough to challenge and defeat. By a three-day ultimatum impossible to accept, the war of April–August 1898 was forced on a Spain known to be looking for a mode of retreat; it was not unlike Austria-Hungary's attack on Serbia in 1914. Motives were very mixed, and are still hard to unravel. The humane pretext was a duty to rescue Cuba from the miseries of Spain's long-drawn efforts to hold the island down by force. Mahan found an analogy, and harped on it in an appeal to old emancipationist sentiment, between America defying international law to save Cuba, and good citizens before the Civil War breaking the law in order to help fugitive slaves to escape.[137] As always in Caribbean alarums, strategic security too could be made a great deal of.

Liberals could view the situation as one in which a reluctant president was pushed into war by a bellicose Congress and public opinion, or a jingo press.[138] Business opinion at large was hesitant. America could not be said to be shooting its way out of trouble, for economic depression had lifted lately, and there were fears that war might bring it back.[139] But it can be maintained that popular war hysteria was not really so overwhelming, and that McKinley was under at least as much pressure from particular business interests, and from his own conception of the country's needs.[140] Certainly he was very much a businessmen's president, and owed his place to energetic backing from conservatives frightened by the eloquently though mildly left-wing candidate Bryan, who took an anti-imperialist stand. Certainly also, McKinley and his entourage had a suspicious number of contacts with the Sugar Trust.

American growers of cane and beet, on the other hand, were opposed to a seizure of Cuba, and for the national economy the island could be no more than a very minor asset. If only for this reason the war needed an extra coat of emotional varnish, to prevent its rationale from being too closely scrutinized. Amid many competing currents, and shifts of government tactics, it may be necessary, as very often in the history of imperialism, to think in terms of an unstable general situation. Social unrest, conservative anxiety, foreign example, made an uneasy mixture: a few determined groups, including the sugar refiners, could provide a catalyst, and attain their aims in a way they could not have hoped for in other circumstances. American capitalism had no imperative need of the war and its spoils: certain American capitalists, however, required it.

Revolt against Spanish misrule was in progress on the other side of the world too, in the Philippines, a blend of upper-class desire for autonomy and a social-revolutionary movement of the masses. These islands offered a double attraction; they were another tropical region where sugar could be grown cheaply, and they were a Far Eastern outpost which might be turned into an American Hongkong. Their occupation represented twice as big an advance beyond Hawaii as Hawaii beyond the Pacific Coast, and brought the flag close to China, conveniently near for entry into the Chinese market and the struggle going on for shares in it. (Spain had conquered the Philippines three hundred years earlier, also with thoughts of using the islands as an imperial base in the Far East.) Men who stood for a forward policy like Admiral Dewey and the Assistant Secretary of the Navy, Roosevelt, were clearly determined, even before war broke out, not to miss the opportunity.[141] It seems that business opinion, deaf for years to their talk of colonies, was swung round quickly to support of their Philippine designs by the action of the European powers in 1898 in seizing points along the China coast as bases.[142] It was high time for America to find its own vantage-point, if it was not to be shut out.

Prospects of profit from war itself must have recommended it to many businessmen, and they made hay while the sun shone. 'The elements of gain are present in every war', a British trader in the Far East observed philosophically; even before its outbreak his compatriots were selling arms to the insurgents, with an American agent at Hongkong directing the traffic.[143] Inefficiency in the War Department left the army poorly equipped, corruption ensured that it was – as in the Civil War – expensively equipped. Ordinary citizens were invited to take a share, through the sale of government bonds in small denominations, which sold well; an American democratic device which caught European attention.[144] But the appeal to idealism had greater charms. Even now when the new civilization was succumbing to the most insidious of European habits, Providence with wonderful foresight arranged for it to be able to come forward as liberator instead of conqueror, bearing 'the flag that makes men free'. As a crusade on behalf of downtrodden peoples, the war came as a relief from the more squalid side of the American race for wealth which distressed Whitman in his later years. The trumpet-call of 1898 could sound as that of 1914 did to Rupert Brooke: Honour had come back, as a king, to earth.

In a patriotic war, moreover, the reunion of South and North, still far from perfect, could at last be sealed. Cuba had been the object of endless Southern filibusterings of earlier days, and many volunteers came from the South or South-West, even if in military terms these scratch recruits proved, as in the Mexican War, of little use. On one occasion in Cuba, the 'Rough Riders' had to be rescued by a regiment of Negro regulars.[145] Among the stalwarts of the Anti-Imperialist League formed late in 1898 was the T.W. Higginson who commanded one of the first Negro regiments on the Federal side in the Civil War, and all his life stood for racial equality.[146] Conversely, the second governor-general of the Philippines, L.E. Wright, was a Southerner who fought in the Civil War on the rebel side; he showed little liking for Filipinos, rebels or not.

Decrepit Spain was defeated without undue difficulty, and surrendered the remnants of its empire. Puerto Rico was annexed; besides sugar, it provided a strategic bastion a thousand miles off in the Atlantic from Florida, a counter-weight to Hawaii two thousand miles off in the Pacific. Further away still in the Pacific, Guam and Wake Island could be turned into fortified outposts. What was to be done with Cuba and the Philippines, the two most valuable prizes, remained to be determined. To some Americans these acquisitions would bring solid dividends; to the nation, its brisk little war gave the thrill of adventure. It satisfied a temperament now far removed from the Puritan gravity of older times, one ready to respond to an exhilarating spectacle, though it might tire of a protracted colonial contest as quickly as of visits to the moon. Norman Angell, the English liberal economist and anti-war writer, remarked that 'The Americans at that time were excited about war as, at other times, they become excited about baseball.'[147] Mahan and others had to take their countrymen to task for not comprehending the obstacles that made campaigning in the Philippines so sluggish.

At bottom it was America's saving grace to be comparatively free from that inveterate plague of the Old World, militarism. This has always made its temperament a puzzling one for Old World traditionalists. 'Among the national characteristics of the Americans', a Japanese general has written lately, in a manual for officers, 'we see that they are extremely quick-tempered and impulsive. Their guiding precepts appear to be an unqualified faith in their power, a desire to Americanise other countries, and an emphasis on the immediate rather than the long-range results of their actions.'[148] All this was to be seen in the Spanish War and its sequel, along with a love of the dramatic, even the histrionic. A nation still youthful, seeking a new identity, suddenly finding itself important in the world, was likely to be a self-dramatizing one. It was already so to speak viewing its world in glorious technicolor, instead of Europe's drab grey, long before Hollywood turned its visions into celluloid. A sense of imperial destiny, of America as a new Rome, peeped out in some of the names bestowed by parents on their young hopefuls. In the post of minister at Madrid a Romulus M. Saunders was followed within a few years by an Augustus Caesar Dodge. Nowhere but in America would an authority on asparagus bear the name of Homer Columbus Thompson.

A war anywhere is apt to make another more likely somewhere else, by force of contagion; the wars of modern times have come in clusters, and America's war with Spain was heralded by the Sino-Japanese war of 1894–95 and followed by the Boer War of 1899 and the Russo-Japanese of 1904–5. America seemed fully launched on *Weltpolitik*, with more than one prospective enemy in sight, Germany now as prominently as Russia. Admiral Tirpitz and the German navy had their eye on the Philippines when the U.S. snapped them up, and during the struggle with Spain it was Germany that took the lead in the European chorus of denunciation of America,[149] which at times sounded as threatening as the old

Holy Alliance talk of an intervention on the side of Spain against its New World rebels. Another breeding-ground of the many predictions of war between them was Samoa, two thousand miles south of Hawaii, which was drifting into the whale's maw of empire from the time of its submitting to a treaty in 1875. Foreign meddling worsened the feuds among the chiefs, and the outcome in 1899 was partition between America and Germany, with Britain as a sort of umpire.

In Britain the anti-imperialist aristocrat, Wilfred Scawen Blunt, wrote in his diary that, as between Spain and the U.S., he must sympathize with 'the older and more barbarous country. The Yankees as the coming race of the world would be even worse than ourselves'.[150] Tories privately agreed with him, but in public were guided by Britain's need of America as counterpoise to a hostile Europe. With many enemies and few if any friends, John Bull was remembering the 'American cousin' he had often slighted. In his speech at Birmingham on 13 May 1898, Joseph Chamberlain (whose third wife was the daughter of an American Secretary of the Navy) talked of the 'gigantic' China market and the necessity for Britain of an ally against Russia, and hinted that in return it might give America naval aid against Spain.[151] John Hay, anglophile ambassador in London until September and then Secretary of State, recorded that an alliance really was offered, but had to be declined because 'that unspeakable Senate of ours' was sure to reject it.[152] No naval aid proved necessary, but the British attitude must have helped to restrain Germany from interference. The Kaiser was querulous about this in a lunch-table talk with the British ambassador, saying he had 'information from a good source that the violent hostility of the American press was in a great measure due to English suggestion . . . .'[153]

When Chamberlain's war in South Africa started late in 1899, and all Europe was anti-British, with Germany again loudest, America was able to reciprocate the goodwill of the previous year. These two colonial wars had the same plausibly altruistic look, which allowed many progressives in America to approve of both, even though in South Africa a monarchy was attacking two small republics. Ostensibly Britain was fighting to protect its settlers from ill-usage by the Boers; harder-headed men in London had their thoughts fixed on gold and diamonds. The two contests resembled each other also in muddle and incompetence on the stronger side, and their opportunities for profiteering. But Britain had more prestige at stake, and the length of the struggle, protracted to 1902, made it feel uncomfortably isolated. John Bull's old maxim of *Oderint dum metuant*, let them hate so long as they fear, was out of date.

America's attitude was therefore a great relief. Convinced that the vital principle of American foreign policy must be 'a friendly understanding with England', Hay rejected a series of Boer requests for him to interpose, and showed a marked lack of sympathy, over the British use of concentration camps in particular.[154] In the U.S. an avid interest was taken in British heroes like Baden-Powell.[155] True, there was still an opposite current of feeling, and a number of American volunteers served with the Boers. One of them, surgeon-general with the force beleaguering Baden-Powell at Mafeking (which itself had some Americans in its composite population) wrote him a stiff letter of protest at the British employment of African soldiers, horror at 'the idea of arming black against white', and called on him to 'act the part of a white man in a white man's war'.[156] His letter is reminiscent of outcries by Americans in bygone days about the British employing Red Indians against them. They themselves had just been employing some Indians in Cuba against the Spaniards.[157]

Friendships between nations are most often, as Dr Johnson said of friendships between individuals, partnership in folly or confederacies in vice. Conservative Britain was always blind to the virtues that made America the hope of the 19th century, but was ready to encourage its worse proclivities; after looking with favour on the expansionist South, it was now looking with favour on Northern expansionism. The two countries encouraged each other in the work of suppressing their respective rebels, by what the British Liberal leader denounced in South Africa as 'methods of barbarism'. An America engaged in putting down colonial revolt could scarcely criticize Englishmen, or Frenchmen, or Dutchmen who were having to deal with nationalist movements in Asia, and could scarcely serve as a beacon to these movements. Senator Beveridge visited the Far East and was keen to learn about the British colonial system,[158] which various Americans were setting themselves to study as a model. America besides, as now a force in the Far East, might be useful not only to keep Russia in check, but to help in putting pressure on China. A British businessman with Japanese connections wrote in 1898: 'China will ... seek regeneration at the hands of Britain – whom she will trust when she once more fears her wrath – of America, soon to be an Asiatic power, and of Japan, best fitted of all to undertake the task.'[159]

Many other voices echoed this proffered partnership. 'It is always a joy to me to meet an American, Mr Moulton,' said Sherlock Holmes solemnly, 'for I am one of those who believe that the folly of a monarch and the blundering of a Minister in fargone years will not prevent our children from being some day citizens of the same world-wide country under a flag which shall be a quartering of the Union Jack with the Stars and Stripes.'[160] An admirer of the great detective must blush for the uses to which his blundering creator sometimes put him. A few years after this, an American actor was running a Sherlock Holmes play in the States, and Conan Doyle was writing a pamphlet to defend the Boer War and its methods of barbarism, which sold widely in the States as well as in Britain.[161] All that was needed to make the U.S. a friend and ally, Lord G. Hamilton said in 1903, was its entry into world politics.[162] Kipling, summoning Americans to 'take up the white man's burden', took it equally for granted that a U.S. with a taste for colonialism must automatically find itself at England's side. His influence was far from insignificant. 'It was in the day when high-school girls were poring over the "Barrack-Room Ballads" of Kipling with flaming cheeks in every nook and corner of the country ...'.[163] Another British exponent of empire-philosophy, while pointing out how much America had to learn from Britain about the management of 'natives', predicted that it would be 'the dominant factor in the mastery of the Pacific'. But neither nation must relax in its 'difficult and dangerous enterprises ... There can be no rest, no pause in the march of a great empire: it must advance or decay – history has made that plain.'[164]

References

1.   J.P. Dunn, *Massacres of the Mountains* (1886; London edn., 1963), p.435.

2.   D.H. Miller, *Custer's Fall – The Indian Side of the Story* (1957; London edn., 1965), p.viii.

3.   *Buffalo Bill's Tomahawk Duel, or Playing Redskins at their Own Game* ('The Buffalo Bill Stories', No. 234, New York, 1905; reprint, Derby, Connecticut, n.d.).

4.   *Buffalo Bill's Leap for Life* (same series), Chap. XVI.

5.   *The Journals of Francis Parkman*, ed. M. Wade (London, 1947), Vol. II, p.460.

6.   *Buffalo Bill's Featherweight* (same series), p.9.

7.   *Ibid.*, p.46.

8.   J.M. White, *The Great American Desert* (1975; London edn., 1977), p.163.

9. Robert Louis Stevenson, *Across the Plains* (1879; London edn., 1913), p.45.

10. H.E. Fritz, *The Movement for Indian Assimilation, 1860–1890* (Philadelphia, 1963), p.24.

11. Dunn, *op. cit.*, p.25.

12. Col. W.A. Ganoe, *The History of the United States Army* (revised edn., New York, 1943), p.349.

13. Fritz, *op. cit.*, pp.144–5.

14. *Ibid.*, pp.146–7; cf. p.31.

15. C.A. Eastman, *The Indian To-day* (1915), in *American Issues*, Vol. 1, ed. W. Thorp *et al.* (2nd edn., Chicago, 1944), p.657.

16. Dunn, *op. cit.*, pp.400, 626.

17. *Ibid.*, p.36.

18. *Ibid.*, p.592.

19. There is much on this subject in Rosa Luxemburg, *The Accumulation of Capital* (1913; trans. A. Schwarzschild, London, 1951).

20. A.M. Josephy, *The Indian Heritage of America* (1968; Harmondsworth edn., 1975), p.353.

21. W.T. Hagan, *American Indians* (Univ. of Chicago, 1961), p.117.

22. O. Spengler, *The Decline of the West* (trans. C.F. Atkinson, London, 1922), Vol. 2, p.119.

23. Theodore Roosevelt, *An Autobiography* (1913; New York edn., 1946), p.204 ff.

24. Speech of October 1879, cited in W. Page, ed., *Commerce and Industry* (London, 1919), p.277.

25. A.B. Hart, *The Monroe Doctrine* (Boston, 1916), p.173.

26. Admiral R.D. Evans, *A Sailor's Log* (New York, 1901). Cf. F.B. Pike, *Chile and the United States 1880–1962* (Notre Dame, 1963).

27. O.D. Edwards, 'American Diplomats and Irish Coercion, 1880–1883', in *Journal of American Studies* (Cambridge), Vol. 1, No. 2, (1967), p.213.

28. Anon., *The Great Naval War of 1887* (London, 1887).

29. G.L. Lichtheim, *Imperialism* (London, 1971), p.98, Note 1.

30. Ganoe, *op. cit.*, p.355.

31. W.R. Jacobs, *Dispossessing the American Indian – Indians and Whites on the Colonial Frontier* (New York, 1972), p.24.

32. See E. Hyams, *Soil and Civilization* (London, 1952), Chap. 10.

33. Thorstein Veblen, *Absentee Ownership and Business Enterprise in Recent Times – The Case of America* (1923; London edn., 1924) p.168.

34. *Ibid.*, pp.191–2.

35. *The Early Writings of Frederick Jackson Turner*, ed. F. Mood (Univ. of Wisconsin, 1938), pp.228–9.

36. Letter from George Eliot, 11 July 1869, in her *Life*, ed. J.W. Cross (New York, 1885), Vol. 3, p.67.

37. L. Corey, *The House of Morgan* (New York, 1930), p.79.

38. Engels to Sorge, 10 September 1888, in Marx and Engels, *Letters to Americans 1848–1895*, ed. A. Trachtenberg (New York, 1953), p.204.

39. H.S. Ferns, *The Age of Mackenzie King* (London, 1955), Chap. 2.

40. E. Varga, *20th Century Capitalism* (London edn., n.d.), p.13.

41. Akira Iriye, *Across the Pacific – An Inner History of American–East Asian Relations* (New York, 1967), p.77.

42. See B.M. Solomon, *Ancestors and Immigrants – A Changing New England Tradition* (New York, 1956), Chap. VII.

43. Ganoe, *op. cit.*, p.368.

44. *Ibid.*

45. P.M. Mantoux, ed., *Paris Peace Conference, 1919 – Proceedings of the Council of Four* (trans. J.B. Whitton, Geneva, 1964), p.152.

46. K. Liebknecht, *Militarism and Anti-Militarism* (1907; English edn., Cambridge, 1973), p.24.

47. *The Valley of Fear* (1915).

48. E. Bellamy, *Looking Backward 2000–1887* (1888; Cleveland edn., 1945), pp.61–2.

49. J. Ellis, *The Social History of the Machine Gun* (London, 1975), pp.21, 42.

50. Akira Iriye, *op. cit.*, p.62.

51. R. Hofstadter, *Social Darwinism in American Thought* (revised edn., New York, 1955), pp.185–6.

52. C.A. Beard, Introduction to 1943 (New York) edn. of B. Adams, *The Law of Civilization and Decay*, pp.3–4.

53. *Ibid.*, pp.38–9.

54. C.G. Bowers, *Beveridge and the Progressive Era* (New York, 1932), p.75.

55. M.B. Young, *The Rhetoric of Empire – American China Policy 1895–1901* (Harvard, 1968), pp.96–7.

56. D.H. Burton, *Theodore Roosevelt: Confident Imperialist* (Philadelphia, 1968), pp.22–3.

57. D.F. Sarmiento's last work was his *Conflicto y armonias de las razas en America* (Buenos Aires, 1883).

58. Burton, *op. cit.*, p.vii.

59. J. Strong, *Our Country* (1885), in *Readings in American History*, ed. O. Handlin (New York, 1957), pp.482–3.

60. See J. Silver, *Mississippi: the Closed Society* (London, 1965).

61. L. Adamic, *Thirty Million New Americans* (1934), in *American Issues*, Vol. 1, pp.787–8.

62. Article on 'Manifest Destiny' (1893), in Carl Schurz, *Speeches, Correspondence and Political Papers*, ed. F. Bancroft, Vol. V (New York, 1913), pp.191–5, 198.

63. *Livingstone's Missionary Correspondence 1841–1856*, ed. I. Schapera (London, 1961), p.116.

64. P.A. Varg, *Missionaries, Chinese and Diplomats. The American Protestant Missionary Movement in China, 1890–1952* (Princeton, 1958), p.56.

65. Mark Twain, 'To the Person Sitting in Darkness', *North American Review*, February 1901.

66. See J. Spence, *The China Helpers – Western Advisers in China 1620–1960* (London, 1969), p.52 ff.

67. A. Hamilton, *Korea* (London, 1904), p.263.

68. R.W. Van Alstyne, *The Rising American Empire* (Oxford, 1960), p.129.

69. E.R. Black, *Alternatives in Southeast Asia* (London, 1969), p.7.

70. A. Krausse, *China in Decay* (London, 1900), p.262.

71. *Tyndale-Biscoe of Kashmir – An Autobiography* (London, n.d.), pp.111–3.

72. A.F. Corwin, *Spain and the Abolition of Slavery in Cuba 1817–1886* (Univ. of Texas Press, 1967), p.266.

73. *Diary and Letters of Rutherford Birchard Hayes*, ed. C.R. Williams, Vol. III (Columbus, Ohio, 1924), pp.583, 586–8.

74. D. Perkins, *The Monroe Doctrine 1866–1907* (Baltimore, 1937), p.87.

75. O.D. Edwards, *op. cit.*, p.22.

76. See J. Fast, *Monopoly Capital and Empire: the Sugar Trust and American Imperialism, 1883–1909* (Ph.D. thesis, Univ. of London, 1976).

77. *Ibid.*, pp.51–2.

78. *Ibid.*, p.242 ff.

79. Schurz, *op. cit.*, p.198.

80. See H.F. Peterson, 'Edward A. Hopkins: a Pioneer Promoter in Paraguay', in *Hispanic American Historical Review* (1942); J.F. Cady, *Foreign Intervention in the Rio de la Plata, 1835–1850* (Philadelphia, 1929), p.174; C.A. Washburn, *The History of Paraguay* (Boston, 1871), Vol. 1, p.353 ff.

81. W.F. Johnson, *America's Foreign Relations* (New York, 1916), Vol. 2, p.192.

82. W. Stewart, *Henry Meiggs – Yankee Pizarro* (Duke Univ., 1946), pp.182–3.

83. Hart, *op. cit.*, pp.161–2.

84. V.G. Kiernan, 'Foreign Interests in the War of the Pacific', in *Hispanic American Historical Review* (1955), p.29.

85. Johnson, *op. cit.*, p.195 ff.

86. See V.G. Kiernan, *The Lords of Human Kind* (London, 1969), pp.295–6.

87. W.A. Williams, *The Tragedy of American Diplomacy* (new edn., New York, 1962), pp.22–3.

88. C.R. Flint, *Memories of an Active Life* (New York, 1928), p.89 ff.

89. W.J. Oudendyk, *Ways and By-ways in Diplomacy* (London, 1939), pp.42–3.

90. Alejandro Garland, *South American Conflicts and the United States* (Lima, 1900), Annex, p.5.

91. Perkins, *op. cit.*, p.44 ff.

92. J.H. Latane, *America as a World Power 1897–1907* (New York, 1907), pp.27–8.

93. J.H. Latane, *The Diplomatic Relations of the United States and Spanish America* (Baltimore, 1900), p.271.

94. Despatch of 29 November 1881; see H.S. Commager, *Documents of American History*, pp.108–9 (3rd edn., New York, 1946).

95. Perry Belmont, speech of 5 July 1882; see his *An American Democrat* (2nd edn., New York, 1941), p.221.

96. W.E. Soothill, *China and the West* (London, 1925), Chap. 5.

97. See *State Papers British and Foreign*, 1868–69.

98. M.F. Nelson, *Korea and the Old Orders in Eastern Asia* (Univ. of Louisiana, 1946), p.106.

99. Akira Iriye, *op. cit.*, pp.13–14.

100. Perkins, *op. cit.*, pp.15–16.

101. C.F. Gordon Cumming, *Wanderings in China* (London, 1887), Chap. 31.

102. On this part of Grant's tour see J.R. Young, *Around the World with General Grant* (New York, 1880,) Vol. 2.

103. Sir H. Parkes, letter of 24 November 1878, in S. Lane-Poole and F.V. Dickins, *The Life of Sir Harry Parkes* (London, 1894), Vol. 2, p.265.

104. See P.J. Treat, *Diplomatic Relations between the United States and Japan 1853–95* (Stanford Univ., 1932), Vol. 2.

105. *Ibid.*, p.53.

106. Lane-Poole and Dickins, *op. cit.*, Vol. 2, p.372.

107. D.C. Boulger, *Sir Halliday Macartney* (London, 1908), p.311.

108. V.G. Kiernan, *British Diplomacy in China 1880 to 1885* (Cambridge 1938), p.278; and see pp.274–8 generally on American attitudes.

109. W.E. Griffis, *Corea the Hermit Nation* (New York, 1882), p.431.

110. T. Dennett, *Americans in Eastern Asia* (New York, 1922), pp.461–2.

111. R. von Möllendorf, *P.G. von Möllendorf – Ein Lebensbild* (Leipzig, 1930), p.69.

112. Krausse, *op. cit.*, p.258.

113. P.H. Kent, *Railway Enterprise in China* (London, 1907), p.110 ff.; P. Joseph, *Foreign Diplomacy in China* (London, 1928), p.382.

114. Lord Charles Beresford, *The Break-up of China* (London, 1899), section on 'Shanghai'.

115. See Kiernan, 'Foreign Interests . . .'.

116. L.M. Sears, *A History of American Foreign Relations* (3rd edn., London, 1936), pp.363–4.

117. W.F. Sands, *Undiplomatic Memories* (New York, 1930), p.9.

118. *Ibid.*, p.56.

119. *Ibid.*, p.10.

120. Van Alstyne, *op. cit.*, p.165.

121. There is much of value on this in H.V. Brasted, *Irish Home Rule Politics and India 1873–1886* (Ph.D. thesis, Univ. of Edinburgh, 1974).

122. R.G. Martin, *Lady Randolph Churchill – A Biography 1854–1895* (London, 1969), Vol. 1, p.252. For details of some other marriages see Vol. 2, pp.318–19, 324, 327.

123. Chauncey M. Depew, *My Memories of Eighty Years* (New York, 1922), p.268.

124. E. Halévy, *A History of the English People in the Nineteenth Century*, Vol. IV (trans. E.I. Watkin, London, 1951), p.43.

125. Ellis, *op. cit.*, Chap. IV.

126. *The Dalhousie-Phayre Correspondence 1852–1856*, ed. D.G.E. Hall (Oxford, 1932), pp.399–400.

127. Mark Twain, *The Innocents Abroad* (1869), Chap. VII.

128. W.D. Foulke, *Slav or Saxon* (1887; 2nd edn., New York and London, 1899), pp.4, 7.

129. D.A. Wilson, *Carlyle to Threescore-and-Ten (1853–1865)* (London, 1929), p.389.

130. Hofstadter, *op. cit.*, pp.176–7.

131. *Ibid.*, p.183.

132. Speech of 27 April 1898; see *Problems of American History*, ed. R.W. Leopold and H.S. Link (2nd edn., Englewood Cliffs, 1957), p.492. On the rise of 'Anglo-Saxonism', cf. *New Cambridge Modern History*, Vol. XI (1962), pp.514–15.

133. Bowers, *op. cit.*, p.69.

134. *Ibid.*, p.93.

135. See J.H. Lawson, *The Hidden Heritage* (New York, 1950), pp.529–30.

136. See P. Renouvin, *La question d'Extrême-orient 1840–1940* (Paris, 1940), pp.178–9; O.J. Clinard, *Japan's Influence on American Naval Power 1897–1917* (Univ. of California, 1947), pp.8–9.

137. A.T. Mahan, *Lessons of the War with Spain* (1899; 2nd edn., London, 1899), p.227.

138. Latané, *America as a World Power, op. cit.*, p.22. Cf. E. May, *American Imperialism; a speculative essay* (New York, 1968), p.159: McKinley was a weak man who 'capitulated to the jingoes'.

139. See J.W. Pratt, *Expansionists of 1898; the acquisition of Hawaii and the Spanish islands* (1936; Gloucester, Massachusetts edn., 1959), Chap. VII.

140. Williams, *op. cit.*, pp.33–4. He stresses that it was not a mere conspiracy (pp.28–9).

141. G.F. Kennan, *American Diplomacy 1900–1950* (1951; New York edn., 1952), pp.18–19. His account tends to exculpate both president and businessmen.

142. This view is supported by Pratt, *op. cit.*

143. J.D. Ross, *Sixty Years in the Far East* (London, 1911), Vol. 2, pp.346, 348.

144. F.W. Hirst, *Political Economy of War* (London, 1915), p.228.

145. Ganoe, *op. cit.*, p.383.
146. See Introduction by H.N. Meyer to T.W. Higginson, *Army Life in a Black Regiment* (1870; New York edn., 1962).
147. Norman Angell, *The Great Illusion 1933* (London, 1933), p.304. The first version of this celebrated work belonged to 1908.
148. General Makoto Matsutani, *Guardian* (London), 14 May 1972.
149. See L.Y. Slezkin, *Ispano-Amerikanskaya voina 1898 goda* (Moscow, 1956), Chap. 3.
150. W.S. Blunt, *My Diaries* (London edn., 1932), p.290; cf. pp.295, 306.
151. Joseph, *op. cit.*, p.319 ff.
152. *Ibid.*, p.323.
153. *British Documents on the Origins of the War 1898–1914*, ed. G.P. Gooch and H. Temperley, Vol. 1 (London, 1927), p.101.
154. J.H. Ferguson, *American Diplomacy and the Boer War* (Philadelphia, 1939), pp.123, 131, 174–5.
155. B. Gardner, *Mafeking – A Victorian Legend* (1966; London edn., 1968), p.20.
156. *Ibid.*, pp.39, 80–1.
157. Latané, *America as a World Power*, p.46.
158. Bowers, *op. cit.*, p.109.
159. A. Diösy, *The New Far East* (London, 1898), p.367.
160. 'The Noble Bachelor', in *The Adventures of Sherlock Holmes* (1891).
161. H. Pearson, *Conan Doyle, his Life and Art* (London edn., 1946), pp.143, 172.
162. J.C. Bailey, *Letters and Diaries* (London, 1925), p.90.
163. Bowers, *op. cit.*, p.93.
164. A.R. Colquhoun, *The Mastery of the Pacific* (London, 1902), p.407.

PART FOUR

IMPERIAL CHOICES FOR A NEW CENTURY

1

The Progressivist Era

Class hatreds were far from vanishing overnight, under the spell of 1898 and its triumphs. 'In 1904 the Mine Owners' Association was breaking up mine unions with all the typical American strike-breaking weapons of vigilantes, deputies, company police, militia, federal troops and subservient courts.'[1] Pinkerton 'labour spies' regularly accused workers of plotting violence: this served to discredit socialism, and also of course alarmed employers into paying their agents more money.[2] A ferment of ideas accompanied this troubled atmosphere, and the years before 1914 could show quite a number of original thinkers,[3] among whom Thorstein Veblen was the most remarkable. In politics this was the era of 'Progressivism', a loose trend which did at least take account of the need for social improvement, and wanted government to promote class conciliation. Theodore Roosevelt, who stepped in to the presidency when McKinley was murdered in 1901, typified this approach. He was in his own estimation 'a very radical democrat', but desirous of combining 'orderly liberty' with 'efficiency'.[4] Everyone further right or left than himself, it has been remarked, he viewed as either 'dangerous reactionaries' or 'dangerous extremists', both of them menaces to social order.[5] Writing to Cabot Lodge he expressed warm agreement with his censure of both 'the lawless capitalist' and 'the Debsite type of anti-capitalist'.[6]

In the cabinets of this period, as until well after the Second World War, three-fifths of the members were businessmen.[7] There were millionaires, like Morgan, adamant against any concessions, but broadly the philosophy of rational accommodation, with room for both capital and labour in an expanding economy nourished by growing foreign markets, was gaining ground among both the industrial and the political elites. They were drawn from the same upper social level, and could understand one another well enough;[8] better than in most of Europe, where the social and mental gap between the two, though narrowing, was still real. All the Progressivist epoch down to 1914 was guided by the aim of fortifying a still very competitive capitalism by means of the kind of regulation that sensible employers might be willing to accept.[9]

Social legislation was in fact neither very original nor very effective; trying to curb the excesses of capitalism was like trying in earlier days to check the harrying of frontier Indians. Some real improvements were taking place, all the same. Prosperity continued after the Spanish War, owing something no doubt to the euphoria of victory and the nation's consciousness of its emergence as a power in the world. Agriculture was enjoying its golden age, and with this the Populist movement was slackening. The vast Steel Corporation formed in 1901 showed capitalism massing its portentous resources; but at the same time labour, or the skilled workers who were being organized by the A.F.L., acquired a better protected status, thanks to its own efforts and to some flexibility on the part of some employers. Real wages, which had flagged, were recovering in the years before 1914.

By that date a Socialist Party was growing, fast enough, as in Europe, to frighten the respectable. But ideas of fundamental change were not potent enough to leaven a very heterogeneous workforce, constantly diluted and divided by fresh hosts of immigrants. Some of these might carry unpleasant political germs in their rags, but this was counteracted by the incapacity of most of them for organized struggle. If the early settlers in North America were, as Antonio Gramsci called them, 'an intellectual, but more especially a moral, *elite*',[10] the same could not be said of most of the later ones, largely of peasant origin and under strong religious tutelage. In America they might learn quickly, but they would not be learning socialism. Their presence would, on the contrary, discourage radicalism among the older strata of workers, by making life easier for them, as well as for the middle classes. Since menial work, an English observer wrote, was 'increasingly felt to be beneath the dignity of the free white American', it was being largely left to Negroes, and to the 60% of female immigrants who went at once into domestic service. Hence 'the intelligent, highly-paid American is actually in the position of a ruling race, and is served and attended by negroes and alien immigrants very much as the ancient Athenian was served by a Thracian or an Asiatic'.[11] In other words the American was a colonialist at home, in the enjoyment of comforts that the ordinary European had to go to India or Africa in search of.

There would be no serious resistance from a labour aristocracy to the expansionist nostrums that were being so loudly advertised as the passport to prosperity for all. One of Jack London's forecasts in *The Iron Heel* was an outbreak of war in 1912 between an equally aggressive America and Germany, starting with a surprise attack on the U.S. navy at Honolulu.[12] He was as Utopian as Bellamy in imagining that this war would be promptly snuffed out by a general strike in both countries. He himself, moreover, was infected by Yellow Peril fever. Mixed feelings like his must have been common; and as in Britain, if labour was not enthusiastic, or only fitfully so, for aggressive courses abroad, it was not positively against them.

It has been pointed out lately, not much to the credit of history writers, that little study has been made of the links between internal political pressures and American foreign policies.[13] But it stands out that 'Progressivists' were also warm partisans of expansion. While annexation of any particular area would find many objectors, nearly all 'responsible' citizens were convincing themselves that the country's future depended essentially on growth of trade and investments abroad. This was turning into an article of faith, in very much the same way as Britons were once positive that they would be ruined if they lost the American colonies, and now were positive that they would be ruined if they lost India. America's obsession was as delusive as Britain's. But an economic system, like a nation or a religion, lives not by bread alone but by beliefs, visions, daydreams as well, and these may be no less vital to it for being erroneous. And there are always vested interests to keep them alive. Growth of the home market, through swelling population and rising standards of living, was much more genuinely important than anything that could be scraped out of the backward corners of the earth. But in the mood of the time it was necessary to believe that American enterprise must be free to overflow into them. By 1915 there was an impressive total of dollars invested abroad, but very few of these had travelled further afield than Canada, Central America and Europe.

As to what the dynamic policies in vogue really meant, or were expected to achieve, much remained obscure. A writer like Alleyne Ireland made short work of the question: the U.S. was simply obeying a universal law, that 'intellectual and physical vigor and territorial expansion' go together.[14] Before being commissioned by the University of Chicago in 1900 to report on colonial administrations in Asia, this expert had been overseer on a West Indian estate, and a defender of the traffic in indentured coolie labour.[15] Roosevelt could present America's mission as one of bringing order out of chaos, just as at home he wanted orderly relations in economic life. When the aged Carl Schurz wrote to him in 1905 to urge reduction of armaments, the president justified, as a necessary bridle on untutored humanity, the armed strength whose real cause was Great Power rivalry. 'The hopeless and hideous bloodshed and wickedness of Algiers and Turkestan' had only been put a stop to by French and Russian occupation.[16] Here were Beveridge's 'bloody and benighted shores' again, and the same appeal to an American sense of duty as had served the cause of intervention in Cuba.

In reality colonial order, under all flags, meant controlled violence, more intense than within the metropolitan society. A lurking element in colonialist thinking was the hope of reducing this factor at home by exporting it, as it were, to dependencies. There was a tacit bargain that capitalists would have a free hand in the backlands in return for submitting to some mild restraints at home. In a thoughtful commentary, P.S. Reinsch pointed out how jumbled was the prevailing 'intermixture of economic forces and idealistic moral impulses'. Everywhere the 'humanitarian optimism' of the French Revolution seemed to have revived; there was the sense of 'a new and universal forward movement of civilized society', and members of the human family who had fallen behind were to be 'led out into the light of freedom and reason'. Some of them, he warned his readers, might be as reluctant as in Napoleon's time, 'to accept the dispensations of a human providence'.[17]

Americans, he might have added, as new actors of the role of providence, or Prometheus bringing to mankind the flame of free enterprise, might be more easily captivated than Europeans by its romantic charm. But he was aware of a discordant note, a conviction that 'the Western races are to form a privileged caste'. There was 'an unavowed but powerful tendency to reduce a large part of mankind to a position of servitude'.[18] He was appealing in effect for an American imperialism more enlightened than Europe's. Against any probability of this was the fact of America itself possessing not only ethnic minorities of inferior status, only gradually being assimilated, but also a large coloured population kept in a position not much better than servitude. Contempt for the black man at home made it only too easy for the white man to think of all 'natives' abroad in a similar fashion.

Now that the first bites had been taken, others seemed very likely to follow. Many abroad, at the end of the Spanish War, were expecting to see Mexico and Nicaragua swallowed up in short order. A proclamation of April 1899 announced that America was taking complete possession of the Philippine islands, to ensure the well-being of the people 'and their elevation and advancement to a position among the most civilized peoples of the world'. Next year American troops were taking part, along with Europeans and Japanese, in the combined operation in China to suppress that vast popular protest against foreign meddling, the Boxer Rebellion; they took part also in the sack of Peking which was the climax of the campaign. An appeal to President McKinley by the Chinese government was of no avail.

General Chaffee, at the head of the American forces, favoured acquisitions: the navy wanted harbours, the two backed each other,[19] and Conger the minister at Peking made himself their mouthpiece. Very soon after his famous call for an Open Door in China, State Secretary Hay fell in with their views to the extent of instructing Conger to seek a naval base and its hinterland in Fukien Province.[20] This scheme fell through, partly because of Japanese objections, and for many years was kept as dark a secret as any in the secret diplomacy of Europe that Americans were wont to condemn. But it was rumoured that other powers were offering a slice of China, to gain American assent to its dismemberment, and it was later shrewdly surmised that Britain made a withdrawal in the New World, over the old Alaska boundary dispute, to make sure that such assent would not be given.[21] Early in 1906 a big impression was made by reports that the U.S. was prepared to send 40,000 troops to China, where the dynasty was on its last legs, in the event of renewed disturbances. Clearly, one Far Eastern observer commented, 'the curious altruism of yesterday is being rapidly replaced by ... common sense'.[22]

2

The Philippines Experiment, and Direct or Indirect Rule

No naval base was secured on the China Coast, but a big one was being created in the Philippines. That some parts of the islands would be kept as a platform for naval and commercial self-assertion in the Far East was a foregone conclusion when the Spanish War broke out in 1898; the decision to take the whole archipelago, and thus launch an American 'empire', came more slowly after Spain's defeat. One motive must have been reluctance to share the islands with Germany, which was likely to take anything left and was so awkward a neighbour in Samoa. A still more impelling one may have been a wish to prolong the patriotic excitement of 1898: an empire, whatever its utility or lack of it, would provide a further diversion from domestic broils. It was arguable that, with Germany and Japan in the offing, no part of the Philippines had any chance of building a national life except under guarantee by the U.S., which therefore might as well hoist its own flag. The decision to do this, reached by President McKinley at the end of his noted night of wrestling with the Lord in prayer, was not forced on him by any impossibility of establishing a less direct control. A local leader was to hand in Aguinaldo, elected president by his people in January 1899, through whom an adequate influence could readily be had. He was no very intransigent patriot, and he needed help, and might need protection. He was willing, it seems, to let the Americans have naval bases, and even customs control.[23]

His authority was virtually complete, army reports showed; yet no move was made towards an arrangement with him.[24] Instead the Americans waited until reinforcements arrived, and then in February 1899 carried out a sudden bombardment, very much as the French in 1946 broke off negotiations with Ho Chi Minh by bombarding Haiphong, and started the War of Vietnam. At home the collision was reported as a native revolt, and public opinion responded with true imperial logic: many 'now felt that the national honour was involved and that the country could not withdraw from the islands in the face of an uprising'.[25] So quickly does a novice pick up the mentality and the jargon of empire.

Educated Filipinos were indignant at being called 'niggers',[26] and at a song which became popular among the soldiers with the refrain 'Damn, damn, damn the Filipinos'.[27] Losses were heavier than in the fighting here with the Spaniards; during 1899 there were nearly four thousand casualties, and more troops had to be sent. Aguinaldo held out until April 1901. He and his lieutenants, who represented a modern-minded, still weak, national leadership of the kind that was emerging in India and elsewhere, were easier to deal with than the resistance down below in the villages. This was a continuation of the war against Spain, at bottom agrarian revolt against feudal landlordism, and guerrilla resistance went on for several years. Those engaged in putting it down could see it only as brigandage. It has been observed that Americans, with all their fellow-feeling for Ireland, were habitually unaware of its social problems;[28] they would be still more impervious to those of a remote colony, and this inability of a very new society to comprehend the mode of existence of very old ones has been typical of America's dealings with the pre-industrial world. Half a century later Owen Lattimore dwelt on this incomprehension of Asia's agrarian maladies, and the damage done by it in Korea.[29]

For a while the government had to make a show of conciliatory methods, in order to reconcile the Senate to the dubious novelty of colonial annexation. 'The half-civilized natives,' says the army's chronicler, 'as they invariably act under such treatment, ascribed our overtures to cowardice and weakness.'[30] This was a maxim that men of the 'realist' school had often drawn from the Red Indian wars, and Europeans from their colonial wars. Thoughts of setting Asians to fight Asians were not slow to appear; in 1901 Congress authorized recruitment of Filipino (and Puerto Rican) troops, to be commanded by American officers. This attempt to emulate the colonial armies of Britain or France did not get far. An

American scholar writing in 1905 in support of colonialism admitted that things were made worse by employment of the Macabebes, 'a most savage and cruel tribe, bitterly hated by the more peaceful natives upon whom they had long preyed'.[31] He was candid enough also to point out that, considering what conditions were in many American cities, not much could be expected of the colonial police system that was being set up, with local myrmidons.[32]

Another parallel with those cities could have been seen in the police practice of setting officers of one ethnic group to patrol working-class areas inhabited by other groups. But the most obvious affinity of the guerrilla struggle was with the Red Indian wars only lately concluded; it was a postscript to them on the other side of the world. Nearly all the commanders had done their first fighting against Indians.[33] Even to a liberal-minded American, the Filipinos appeared to be guilty of 'great cruelty, treachery, and ferocity', but he added the 'humiliating' admission that the civilized Americans were soon retaliating in kind. 'Murder, rape, torture and other crimes were too frequently committed by American soldiers and by the native scouts commanded by American officers.'[34] No empire has ever been built without some resort to such methods; their victims lie buried in the foundations like the human sacrifices anciently buried under the walls of Indian fortresses. There was indignation in America at the brutalities, as there has always been against the nation's misdemeanours abroad. No Bolshevik peril had yet been invented, and Filipinos were after all Christians of a sort, if a dubious sort. Army spokesmen complained of sentimental criticism at home exactly as they had complained of moralists in the Eastern states who sympathized with Red Indians.

Exposure of the sombre aspect of colonial warfare helped to deter America from wanting to repeat the ugly experience, and to turn it away towards more tactfully disguised forms of imperialism. At the time the task of conquest, light-heartedly undertaken, could not, with the world looking on, be relinquished. Violence in the Philippines must rather have had the effect of stimulating resort to violence at home, instead of providing a substitute for this, and then in turn was further inflamed by it. Strong-arm methods against Filipinos and trade unionists or anarchists or any others outside the pale went together. Attacks on African-Americans were multiplying. 'There have been terrible doings in America', W.S. Blunt wrote in his diary in 1906, 'Lynchings and massacres of negroes, acts of reprisal against the black community for isolated assaults ...'.

A year later he was writing: 'In America six hundred Hindoos have been set upon by a mob and beaten, an act of race fanaticism.'[35] Pogroms against Jews in Tsarist Russia provided another of many curious resemblances between the two opposite giants.

Administratively as well as militarily, America's domestic record did not augur well for the dominion over palm and pine that it was assuming now. Elihu Root, appointed Secretary of War in 1899, was a corporation lawyer who had done yeoman work for the Sugar Trust, and in politics a reactionary of the deepest dye.[36] Before the end of 1900 a civil commission was set up in the Philippines alongside the military authority, with powers enlarged a year later. Its head, and then first governor-general, was W.H. Taft, another staunch conservative, at home all for shooting down rioters or strikers. He exhibited, however, the flexibility of a man on his way to the White House. Privately he considered all Filipinos mere children, publicly he was amicable to the higher classes in order to win them round to acceptance of American rule.[37] In this he was successful enough; national freedom won by the armed peasants must mean also agrarian revolution, and the higher classes were mostly landowners. America was beginning to forge the alliance with the feudal upper classes against the masses that was to be the sheet-anchor of all its later positions in Asia – an exact reversal of what it stood for in its early years.

By 1907 the Philippines could safely be granted a National Assembly, as well as local government councils; though behind this facade all key administrative posts were kept firmly in American hands.[38] In effect the system meant leaving the countryside to be run in their own manner by the landlords, while America held political power and skimmed off the cream of the profits. Landlords of the old stamp were growing sugar now for American refineries; they represented 'that class rule which so identifies *cacique* oligarchy with government as to make a mockery of any pretensions to democracy'.[39] Habits of a feudal society infected more modern developments as well, including American-owned mills. 'Private industrial employers inherited the attitudes and to some extent the power of the great landowners of Spanish times.'[40] American mill-owners harassed by mutinous trade unions at home could bask in the same unfretted bliss as Europeans in their colonies, with docile, well-policed local labour instead.

In colonial policy benevolence and self-interest could blend happily, Mahan argued, on condition that the good of the 'native' was put first, as he believed

Britain had learned to put it. More than mere protection was owed to 'alien subjects, still in race-childhood' (a phrase he might have thanked Kipling for). Colonies could only be secure when ruled for their own advantage, even though 'The inhabitants may not return love for their benefits, – comprehension or gratitude may fail them ... '.[41] Whether he was thinking of benefits to landlords or to peasants he did not specify. All this was confused and confusing, and the muddle that the Philippine experiment was turning into was at least conveniently trouble-saving. To achieve such a situation, on the other hand, direct or permanent control might well seem unnecessary. Fully committed to empire-building as the U.S. in the first years of the century might appear to be, the annexations of 1898 proved before long a deviation from the main line of advance, a passing fantasy or a specific tonic for a spell of domestic sickness.

Whatever the country's kinship with Europe, there were important divergencies as well. Capitalism is inherently expansionist, but the European type of empire required political motivations and social conditions too, not all of which were present in America. In European history it was the landowning instinct – never concerned with income alone, but with social position and power also – that showed itself, magnified, first in the building of larger states, then in amassing colonies. An entire British or French nation could think of itself as a collective landlord, with a vast estate worked for it by the denizens. America had no such tradition of landed estates, apart from the plantations, but the wealth of its millionaires came largely from land-speculation, forest-grabbing, plundering of the public domain. Their colonizing impulse was not towards government of a far-off land and its people, but towards appropriation of its natural resources.

Absence of a gentry class meant a scarcity of 'natural' aspirants for a colonial civil service. Visiting the Philippines in 1904 Ireland found officials well-meaning but quite unversed in tropical administration and ignorant of methods worked out elsewhere. His own stereotyped predilection was for one-man rule; he endorsed the common European belief that 'tropical peoples' could only comprehend authority vested in a single person, and he disapproved of the 'corporate' system America was setting up. This might rather deserve commendation, as a move in a more modern direction, instead of being condemned as 'blindness to local conditions and contempt for universal experience'. He was on firmer ground in saying that a service of high quality, which required patient training from youth, could only be secured by better pay and stiffer entrance tests.[42] But

America had no monarchical tradition to lend dignity to state employment, and a man with the requisite qualities would be able to make more money and a bigger name without setting foot outside America, or by going out on a company payroll.

There was blunter criticism from the outset in some British quarters, not anti-imperialist alone. Englishmen were not sorry to have a chance of retorting American censures of their own colonial conduct by commenting on American behaviour during the subjugation of the Philippines; also on the treatment of coloured men in the States.[43] Feelings like these were to jostle together in John Bull's mind down to the last days of his empire. It was being said, a Hongkong newspaper wrote, that the islands were in for a poor time under the American spoils system, with ever new functionaries coming out to make fortunes.[44] Then, within a few years, America was running to the other extreme and talking of self-government for the Philippines, an imprudence which might have an unsettling effect on other Asian possessions.

Thus Mahan's vision of an American empire on the British model which he extolled, by contrast with the other grand precedent, that of Spain,[45] was scarcely being realized. And apart from questions of method, there was the simple fact that outside China not much of the world was left by this time for snapping up, as Germany though starting a dozen years earlier discovered. Any acquisitions the U.S. could hope to pick up without fighting stronger opponents than Spain would be too small to offer much in the way either of markets or of materials; too small also by contrast with its own vast bulk to have the psychological appeal that their colonies had to small countries like Holland or England. The single large field open to it was Latin America, which consisted, nominally at least, of civilized Christian states, instead of the unredeemed savagery that the Beveridges were in search of. U.S. predominance could be established there, in Central America for a start, without any actual seizures.

Altogether America felt more uncomfortable than exhilarated at finding itself for the first time proprietor of colonies, lands far away from home. There was real reluctance to face the fact, an inhibition against descending to the same level as the old empires. A Colonial Department was planned, but was not set up: the name had an illegitimate ring.[46] Samoa remained under the navy. Hawaii became in 1900 a Territory. Its population might be alien, with a large Japanese infusion, but it had a solidly American ruling class in the form of the planters. In

1917 the Puerto Ricans were rewarded for docility by the grant of citizenship. There was something here akin to the fiction by which Europe labelled some of its colonies provinces of the metropolitan territory: Algeria was theoretically part of France, Angola and Mozambique were technically provinces of Portugal, though with very restricted rights for the mass of their inhabitants.

But whereas cheap Algerian labour was wanted in France, and Portugal's Africans could easily be kept where they were, many of America's new subjects might if allowed pour into a country which was already raising barriers against immigrants, and where prejudice against any people of colour was ensured by agitation against Chinese and Japanese settlers. It was bolstered by a hotchpotch of pseudo-science. 'Modern science', according to Reinsch, 'is agreed that inherited psychological elements ... are the most persistent phenomena of which we have any knowledge.' This made true assimilation impracticable, except for a few favoured individuals like African-American graduates of American colleges. His more sensible conclusion was that indigenous peoples' cultures and social structures ought to be preserved; it was 'insensate folly and criminal cruelty' to sweep them away as mere rubbish.[47] Clearly this line of thinking was relevant to the Red Indian problem as well. But the practical effect of all racial speculation was only too likely to be retrograde. Bryan was putting the idealist case against imperialism when he said in 1899 that 'This nation cannot endure half republic and half colony – half free and half vassal.' In other words, there should be no first- and second-class citizens under the American flag. In fact there were already, inside the U.S, many millions of third-class citizens. It was unfortunate that anti-imperialists found it easiest to get a hearing by harping on the danger of American life being adulterated by alien stocks. To make this worse, most of the nearby island population was of African descent; and it was a time when a drift of Blacks from the South into the Northern states was spreading racial friction more widely.

There was heated argument about whether the flag carried with it automatically, or ought to carry with it, the benefits of the Constitution. Supreme Court decisions in the 'Insular Cases' of 1900 and 1901 ruled that it did not. America's history as an immigrant nation made it harder than for Europeans to envisage possession of lands whose people were not free to come and settle. But with things as they were now, colonial immigrants could scarcely be welcome. In itself, a fear of American civilization being swamped by too heavy a load of historically retarded aliens was perfectly rational, whether felt by 'Brahmin' upholders of the good old ways or by labour, threatened with cut-throat competition. Unfortunately they both resorted too often to denigration of 'inferior' or 'native' stocks as congenitally inferior. Samuel Gompers of the A.F.L. talked of Filipinos as savages.[48] Any opposition to imperialism by labour was diminished by the Exclusion Bill of 1902 which shut them out. Meanwhile its leaders' contemptuous talk about 'natives' was grist to the mill of imperialists like Roosevelt (who rejoiced at the outcome of the 'Insular Cases') and Cabot Lodge; they likewise depicted indigenous peoples as primitives and used this as justification for relegating them to colonial status. Filipinos were, declared Beveridge, a race unfit for self-government[49] – permanently, it might be assumed: after all, they had been under colonial rule already for three centuries without making much progress; though this *might* be evidence against foreign rule rather than against native blood.

Mixed up with the question of admitting 'natives' into America was that of admitting colonial products: one of great concern to more important interests, and much harder to solve without empire being reduced to an absurdity. America's own output was so vast and various that the range of products which could be allowed in without damage to some sectional interest was limited. Had Europe been a similar economic unity, it would have had a similar allergy against colonialism and its resulting intake of colonial goods, most of which could be produced somewhere at home. Today the European Common Market is beginning to demonstrate this. Division into a group of small competing states was what made European-style imperialism viable. In America's case sugar, the first big lure towards expansion, was also a stiff obstacle. Markets for sugar and other colonial commodities could be looked for elsewhere in the world, but their obvious market was the United States, where consumers, growers, and refiners all pulled in different directions. In the same way cheap wine produced in Algeria by big French planters competed painfully with home produce.

Feeling about sugar, as well as about coloured immigrants, could set the South against annexationism, in spite of its jingo temper. Such sectional factors did more to shape Philippine policies than any public enlightenment. In particular they helped to prevent, in spite of Taft and his officials, acquisition of large landed properties by Americans, which in 'independent' Cuba and Central America there was nothing to hinder. This did little good to the peasants, left (as in so many parts of the British empire) under the tyranny of their own feudal lords; but it did reduce American commitment to permanent political control of the islands. Where colonialism has established a large-scale landownership of its own, it has been more reluctant to withdraw than where its profits have been mainly industrial and financial. One may contrast British willingness to surrender direct control of India after the Second World War with French refusal to withdraw from Indochina or Algeria, or Dutch from Indonesia.

Only a single Filipino product could in fact be discovered whose admission was not resented in America – hemp, for rope-making,[50] scarcely a strong enough tie to bind the economies together. Altogether this colonial venture was not proving profitable. As a market for American manufactures it suffered from competition of cheaper foreign goods, notably British textiles.[51] If American rule was benefiting only a few Filipinos, it was also benefiting only a few Americans, chiefly the owners of sugar refineries in the islands, who secured preferential terms in the home market. Not many Americans would gain tangibly from the other, more oblique line of expansion that their country was turning to, but at least the costs to the taxpayer would be better hidden or disguised. Decisions need not be brought forward openly, but could be palmed off on the public by sleight of hand. Because of this, and because opposition to imperialism, though weightier than in any European country, was based too much on sectional self-regard instead of principles, it never arrived at being debated in full.

America's colonial flutter was running into insoluble contradictions: out of this, and out of the simpler tactics concurrently adopted in Cuba, was emerging a choice in favour of indirect control. A pointer to this could be found in the Open Door notes of 1899–1900, ostensibly concerned with the right of American traders not to be excluded from the China market. Looked at more broadly, they heralded 'a classic strategy of non-colonial imperial expansion', or as it has also been expressively called 'imperial anticolonialism'.[52] Inevitably the official title of the new policy was partly misleading or concealing. It meant that all doors must be open to America, and to anyone else strong enough to claim entry; where America was in a position to dictate, others would find the door only half or quarter open to them. Not only would no other power have a right to shut China's door against America, but no China, no Morocco, above all no Mexico, had any right to close its own door against foreign enterprise, least of all against American. Hence a good Bostonian could virtuously reject colonies, but endorse other kinds of interference with countries supposedly free, much as his Puritan ancestors were said to compound for sins they were inclined to by damning those they had no mind to.

Anti-imperialism in a man like Bryan might thus be sincere, but very restricted. His prescription for the Philippines was to work up a stable Filipino-run government, and then extend to it the same kind of 'protection' as to Cuba.[53] It would only very slowly and belatedly dawn on the American mind that 'stable' governments, in contexts like this, meant puppet governments composed of feudal landlords or racketeers and stabilized by marines. Other men, like Roosevelt and Hay, seduced for a while into British-style colonialism, moved away towards more indirect methods. They and the Bryan school thus met at a comfortable equator. By 1906 Roosevelt would have liked to find a way of getting rid of the Philippines altogether, without losing face. 'The Philippine Islands form our heel of Achilles', he wrote in 1907, the same words Schurz had used of Hawaii. 'They are all that makes the present situation with Japan dangerous.'[54] He kept a warm regard for the British empire, perhaps a kind of vicarious consolation, a nostalgia for a juvenile plaything that years of discretion obliged him to discard.

'Neo-colonialism' is a novel term for a quite old relationship, a morganatic imperialism, pioneered by Britain side by side with empire-building. It was first tried out inside Europe, where Portugal was from the early 18th century an economic colony and political semi-dependency, its harbours regularly at the disposal of the British navy. One day in 1847, a shrewd American observer at Oporto beheld an English fleet riding off shore, while a Spanish army acting in conjunction with it entered the town. John Bull was upholding his commercial rights against Portugal, and 'When popular institutions and free privileges come into conflict with port wine, John knows his cue.'[55] Latin America offered a field for similar arrangements. A Foreign Office memorandum of 1841 sketched a policy for remedying the chaotic conditions which were hampering trade there. 'By prudent management ... we might keep the Central Americans in complete check, as well as throw a vast amount of British trade into that section of America.' In general, meddling with other countries might be wrong, but 'there is a point at which it may become to a certain degree justifiable, if not imperative, upon each State to look to such interference on account of self-interest, and as a means of self-preservation'.[56] What Britain's over-stretched resources allowed it to attempt in the New World only on a limited scale was now to be made a consistent programme by the U.S.

Some of the arguments used by anti-imperialists played into the hands of the neo-colonialists. Carl Schurz, one of the many who took for granted that any territory brought under the flag must be incorporated in the Union, had urged in his polemic of 1893 that the Union would be denatured by addition of tropical regions like those of Central America, because their peoples, by contrast with the 'Germanic', had no comprehension of democracy. 'The so-called republics existing under the tropical sun constantly vibrate between anarchy and despotism.'[57] This kind of thinking might shelter them from annexation, but laid them very open to other forms of interference, for if their condition when left to themselves was really so deplorable it might well be a kindness, even a duty, on the part of the U.S. to take them in hand. A capitalist America which was putting its own house in order in those years, and prospering accordingly, was likely to feel all the better qualified to put other people's houses in order. Such was the conviction of the San Francisco millionaire in Joseph Conrad's novel, whose English, Scottish, German and miscellaneous derivation gave him 'the temperament of a Puritan and an insatiable imagination of conquest.' Dilating to his English visitors from the Latin-American republic of Costaguana on its rottenness, he wound up: 'Of course, some day we shall step in. We are bound to ... We shall run the world's business whether the world likes it or not. The world can't help it – and neither can we, I guess.'[58]

3

Dollar Diplomacy in Central America

There was really no word in America's political dictionary for the kind of relationship with weak countries it was setting out now to develop, but very soon the European term 'protectorate' was being, more loosely, used. It fitted Cuba snugly enough. Having been promised independence, the Cubans held elections in 1900 and drew up a constitution in 1901, but were obliged to tack on to it the celebrated Platt Amendment drawn up at Washington by Congress. This might be compared to the treaty imposed by Metternich on the kingdom of Naples at the end of the Napoleonic Wars, which gave Austria a right to suppress liberalism there; but America was acquiring a right of intervention that could in effect be exercised in favour of U.S. interests either political or commercial. With this for model, the U.S. would go on to assume similar rights, without benefit of treaty, all over Central America, and finally all over the world.

What was emerging might be called, in Veblen's phrase, a system of 'absentee ownership', or power without responsibility, in some ways more harmful than direct rule. For the capitalists preparing to take advantage of it, possession might be very direct. In 1901 the United Fruit Company – a more primitive contemporary of United Steel – bought a vast tract of land in Cuba, cleared it for sugar-cane, and built mills. The Sugar Trust was doing the same. A reciprocity treaty two years later gave preferential tariff terms to Cuban sugar (of which by 1914 a third came from American-owned mills) in the U.S. and to American goods in Cuba.[59] By contrast with the torpor of Spanish days American investment could stimulate change, and there was the inspiring example of American progress for Cubans to look to.[60] But with this went a built-in impossibility of emulating it, because the protectorate system, there and in Latin America generally, had the same result as direct rule in the Philippines, in that it fossilized social structures by preventing any free process of transformation.

Indirect rule was far from excluding direct action to keep it going, though this would be intermittent and chiefly directed to removing undesirable individuals or parties from power and making sure of governments congenial to American profit-making. Colony and protectorate differed, after all, only in degree. In either case local assistance had to be made use of; in one case foreign troops would be there all the time, in the other they would be ready round the corner. Most of the time the U.S. could keep itself out of sight; there were established regimes in Central America for it to work through, presiding over countries largely aboriginal (like the Philippine islands) in blood, but with 'white' or westernized upper layers tainted by centuries of Spanish rule and semi-feudal conditions, by Catholicism at its crudest, sometimes by slavery. It was in the most corrupt sections of the higher social layers that – as later in South-east Asia – America had to look for associates. The outcome was that American business interests flourished, while America at large was divided, like Britain contemplating China, between impatience at these countries not waking up and making progress, and alarm whenever they showed signs of wanting to do so after their own bent.

A likelihood of other countries being brought under the same yoke as Cuba was, at the end of the war with Spain, obvious enough. To the U.S. its triumph, and the expulsion of Spanish power, appeared to have sealed its old claim to the primacy of the New World. An occasional voice from southward echoed this view. 'The Spanish war has sanctioned her leadership on this continent', her championship of 'the noble principle of continental public right.' But this was a Peruvian, angling for U.S. support in the old feud with Chile, and he admitted that many Latin Americans were fearful of the U.S. seeking dominance over them.[61] Mahan himself was constrained to observe that 'In the matter of general policy our hands are by no means clean from aggression.'[62] After defeating decadent Spain the U.S. might logically enough set about bullying Spain's decadent offspring. It might be the more tempted to do so because, having stepped forward as a world power, it had little chance to play the part convincingly anywhere but in its own backyard. Bullying small countries round the Caribbean was one means of enjoying a sensation of authority commensurate with mounting wealth and population.

With the U.S. now firmly planted in both Atlantic and Pacific, the old desire for a linking canal under its own control became irresistible. In 1903 a bold *coup*, very much in the old filibustering style, brought about a revolt of the province of Panama from Colombia, followed by the lease of a Canal Zone to the U.S. A lump sum was paid, and later an annual rent; once more America was, formally at any rate, buying territory rather than stealing it. Roosevelt's message to Congress of January 1904 justified this piece of buccaneering in the name of treaty rights, national requirements, and the progress of civilization. They were a trio of claims often to be repeated later: America always loved to think that whatever it wanted was just what the human race needed. Once more could be seen a worship of the march of history as apotheosis of America's growth, and a commitment to ends irrespective of means.

Once more also America was, in form, acting to protect a small neighbour, while in reality manipulating a fifth column. Self-esteem still required it to be able to claim this protective function. And there was no denying the probability of further European intervention, on behalf of bond-holders or concession-hunters, if the U.S. were not pre-empting the ground; even if prospects of European intervention might easily and conveniently be exaggerated. Mahan warned that a big colony of Germans in Brazil might one day declare independence just as the American colony in Texas had done;[63] British settlers in the Transvaal were a more recent object-lesson. When British and German claims on Venezuela were being pressed in 1902 by force, the victim would undoubtedly have fared worse if Britain had not shrunk from giving offence to Washington. Its legation there reported in December 'a growing feeling of irritation in Congress', chiefly on account of the sinking of Venezuelan ships. 'The administration is not suspicious of us, but it is undoubtedly apprehensive as to German designs.' Sir Michael Herbert added that, in view of Berlin's persistent efforts to make trouble between Britain and the U.S., he was reading the press attacks on Germany 'with a certain feeling of complacency, if not of satisfaction'.[64] Alarm at the increasing German resort to coercion obliged London to seek a way out of the quarrel, and with America lending its good offices the dispute was referred to the Hague Court.

In 1905 Cabot Lodge told Roosevelt that he suspected the 'restless and tricky' Kaiser of scheming for a coaling station at St Thomas in Denmark's Virgin Islands in the Caribbean, which would be used for warships; Germany would try to block the sale of these islands to America, and he suggested a quiet attempt, to begin with, to buy Greenland from Denmark.[65] All this, like the Panama *coup*, belonged to the realm of strategic, not economic, imperialism; but the two advanced side by side, each encouraging the other. Mahan considered Puerto Rico no less essential to the defence of the Isthmus than Malta to Egypt;[66] every outpost secured seemed to make new ones necessary.

Roosevelt's message to Congress of December 1904 – the 'Roosevelt corollary' to the Monroe Doctrine – claimed in fact a right to intervene in order to forestall intervention by others. This meant, he explained, that nations must conduct themselves 'with reasonable efficiency and decency ... Chronic wrong-doing, or an impotence which results in a general loosening of the ties of civilized society', called for remedial measures, which in the Western hemisphere should come from the U.S. Clearly socialism, whenever it might sprout in any of the republics, would be a loosening of civilized society. Whether there was enough 'chronic wrong-doing' in Alabama or Mississippi to warrant foreign intervention, Roosevelt did not enquire. He might have been reminded that not very long since the London *Times*, complaining of repudiation of debts by sundry states of the Union, was denouncing the U.S. as 'one vast swindling shop'.[67] In practice his formula might well mean, as a senator alleged in 1906, that wherever weak peoples were attacked, 'we are to have a hand in the pillage'.[68]

One action sanctioned by Roosevelt's teaching was the taking over of the customs administration of San Domingo, where rival factions had piled up debts to voracious European lenders. In 1911 a proposal was submitted to the Senate for a similar arrangement for Honduras. It arose out of an application for financial aid, and could be made to look perfectly plausible. 'Honduras', it was stated, 'is bankrupt, famished, and discouraged.' There had been seven revolutions in the past fifteen years, and twice lately the U.S. had been compelled to send warships to protect American lives: this was perpetually happening in Central America, and might be costing the U.S. more than a million dollars a year. Honduras was deep in debt. A 'highly objectionable' plan was being hatched by the British on behalf of foreign bond-holders. The prime motive of all the factions was to get their hands on the customs revenue, the country's chief income: what was now proposed would put it out of their reach. Honduras would borrow money in the U.S., pledging this revenue as security, and instead of having a receiver imposed on it, like San Domingo, would be free to choose one from a list drawn up by Washington. It was a chance for America to indulge its 'purely altruistic motives': in addition, its southern ports would benefit from more orderly conditions in Central America.[69] To be able to think that merit and profit went together was always agreeable, and much, if not all, in this picture was quite correct. China was better off in those years through having its maritime customs collected under British direction. None the less, the proposal was negatived by a suspicious Senate.

By and large, however, an informal protectorate over all that region was becoming an accomplished fact. 'Whether rightfully or wrongfully,' the proponents of the Honduras plan pointed out, 'we are in the eyes of the world and because of the Monroe doctrine, held responsible for the order of Central America.' In altered guise, the old Southern dream of empire was on its way to fulfilment. Clearly also this was coming about so easily because Isthmian public life was so often deplorable; things would have gone differently if the U.S. had been neighboured by a set of virtuous little Denmarks and Belgiums. On the other hand, where American interests were taking root, pressure for action by their government was very apt to come from them, and they would care no more than European bond-holders about the morality of their demands.

From 1906 to 1909 Cuba was under military occupation. Not all Americans were prepared to believe that while such things were vicious when done by Europeans, they became virtuous when done by the U.S., and the State Department hesitated for a time because it feared public disapproval.[70] Vested interests concerned in such cases represented, after all, only marginal greeds of the national economy; though this also made it harder for their critics to decipher what was really happening. Later on, the communist bogy was to be invaluable in ensuring automatic support for them. Criticism did help to push the government towards a change at least of style, substitution of financial for military controls, silken bonds for handcuffs. In Taft's presidency (1909–13), this came to be known as 'Dollar Diplomacy', as distinct from what in the Far East was called 'gunboat diplomacy', or what Roosevelt called 'the big stick'.

It carried with it the need to find local bosses to do the rougher work, and save America from the opprobrium of having to do this itself. *Caciquismo* or boss rule was native to this quarter of the world: it was indeed from the Caribbean that the word *cacique* originally found its way to Spain. In making use of local dictators, as well as in helping bond-holders to cut off their pounds of flesh, America was once again following in Europe's footsteps. There was a shining example, until his overthrow in 1911, in Porfirio Díaz, for many years absolute ruler of Mexico. His regime admirably suited foreign profiteering, even if U.S. businessmen were resentful of their British rivals standing higher in his favour. A preference for 'stable' rule by dictators, mostly from the barracks, was to become habitual with the White House and Wall Street; in these obscure Caribbean operations a world-system for the American Century was being rehearsed.

The shift of method could not do away with the necessity of direct action from time to time – a capitalist equivalent of what anarchists called 'the propaganda of the deed'. Taft was a seasoned operator, having served as governor in Cuba as well as in the Philippines; he was to live to round this off by becoming professor of law, and finally Chief-Justice of the U.S. Supreme Court. In 1912 there was a fresh occupation of Cuba, on the pretext of race riots – too common an occurrence in the U.S. to call for much attention there. Bosses sometimes had to be propped up on their shaky pedestals. In Nicaragua a man named Estrada was being propped up, although feeling was so hostile that, the U.S. minister had to report in 1911, 'even with some members of Estrada's cabinet I find a decided suspicion, if not distrust, of our motive'. It is intriguing to notice that in this year one F.C. Harrison, late of that elite corps the Indian Civil Service, turned up in Nicaragua as financial expert for a group of American bankers.[71] A harsh loan arrangement forced on Nicaragua by the government was refused ratification by the Senate; it was not the only time when the Senate spoke for the better America, of the eagle instead of the vulture. Quite unabashed, Taft in 1912 sent a naval force and marines to put down a Liberal rising against Estrada's no less unpopular successor.

On these lines, U.S. intervention was very far from transforming San Domingo or Nicaragua into a Denmark or Belgium; rather it meant a symbiosis of local politics with American finance, likely to bring out the worse attributes of both. More grossly perhaps than any of its neighbours, Guatemala exhibited the blighting effects of the protectorate system. After a hopeful era of liberalism and progress the country fell under 'the bloody and tyrannical regime of Manuel Estrada Cabrera', who reigned from 1898 to 1920. Not fortuitously, it was in these years that the United Fruit Company got its stranglehold on Guatemala and turned it into the 'Banana Republic', with control of all railways and ownership of half a million fertile acres.[72] In Tudor England it was said that men were being destroyed by sheep; in Guatemala men were giving way to fruit.

There was always this other aspect of the American hegemony, the aim of a monopoly of profitable opportunity. An open door, a fair field and no favour, was all right for after-dinner speeches, but in the daytime businessmen thought on other lines. In the Philippines, discrimination against British goods could scarcely be practised openly, though the authorities were accused of putting quiet hindrances in the way of British banks;[73] in a protectorate, foreign competitors could be more conveniently squeezed out by manipulation behind the scenes. Thus the British interests headed by Lord Cowdray, which competed with American companies in Mexican oil, found themselves excluded from oil-prospecting contracts in Colombia, Costa Rica, and Ecuador, by American rivals backed by pressure from Washington on local governments.[74] Oil magnates, like railway tycoons, learned the arts of political skulduggery at home in the U.S. before they moved abroad.

U.S. investment in Central America, Mexico above all with Cuba a distant second, grew rapidly: by 1913 it was only slightly below the British figure, and by 1929 more than double it. In South America the time had still not come to realize Blaine's premature design of pushing Europe out commercially as well as keeping it out politically. U.S. investment up to 1913 was trivial, in 1929 still only half the British.[75] A preliminary skirmish started in 1907 with the Beef Trust (under sharp attack by muckrakers for its doings at home) breaking into the British-dominated field of meat-packing in Argentina. During the Great War these rivals and their governments joined forces, and workers on strike 'were driven back to work by detachments of Argentine marines'.[76]

There was quite enough meddling or talk of meddling in Southern America, a protester in the U.S. warned in 1913, to antagonize the bigger republics. His countrymen, he wrote, were 'still woefully ignorant' about them, and it was high time to understand that to those nations 'the very idea of the existence of the Monroe Doctrine is not only distasteful, but positively insulting'. They regarded as crude imperialism the new version of it which they believed the U.S. to be adopting, a right 'to chastise any of the American republics that do not behave'. One Argentinian patriot, Manuel Ugarte, was crusading for a federation of Latin

American peoples, to save them from being swallowed up one by one; a good part of his book consisted of 'quotations from the bombastic utterances of imperialistic politicians in the United States'.[77] Some of these utterances might not deserve to be taken very seriously, but much that was going on lent credibility to them. 'I spent most of my time', retired Major General Smedly D. Butler was to write, looking back on his life with the marines, 'being a high-class muscle-man for Big Business, for Wall Street, and for the bankers. In short, I was a racketeer for capitalism . . .'.[78]

This mode of conducting foreign relations, combined with the squalor underlying public life at home, required a more than usual dose of high-minded language to gloss over. As Kennan says, American diplomacy retained its penchant for big vague moralizing pronouncements, but 'whatever was urged in the name of moral or legal principle bore with it no specific responsibility . . .'.[79] Woodrow Wilson – whose brief reputation of 1919 as a great world statesman is as incomprehensible today as President Kennedy's – was an embodiment of the American duality, the peculiar blend of real though hazy goodwill and sordid profiteering. In his election programme in 1912 he condemned any 'policy of imperialism and colonial exploitation in the Philippines, or elsewhere', and talked as others before him had done of independence for the Philippines as soon as might be. He continued the Progressivist line of mild regulation at home, talking of overcoming troubles by 'economic efficiency and social justice',[80] and of official collaboration with business expansion abroad. He took a very personal hand in this, supervising representatives abroad closely and making decisions himself.[81]

Towards backward peoples his attitude would be, as towards labour at home, paternalistic, but with a marked assumption of racial superiority. He was by descent one more of those Scottish-Irish Calvinists who played such a part in manifesting American destinies to the world, and by upbringing a Southerner. It is significant that the picture he drew in his *History* of slavery in the old South was a very indulgent, very rose-coloured one, where philanthropic planters exerted themselves under many handicaps to provide for their big cheery feckless family of darkies.[82] Here was a native American version of the white man's burden, composed about the same time as Kipling's. His first Secretary of State, the erstwhile radical Bryan, was all admiration for his programme of throwing undeveloped countries open to 'an invasion of American capital and American enterprise'.[83] Despite the evidence piled up by the 'muckrakers' and others about shocking labour conditions inside the U.S., still only slowly being remedied, it was taken for granted that American capitalism abroad, subject to no rules or discipline, must be synonymous with enlightenment and progress.

Dollar Diplomacy, now part of established routine, went on, with some further turns of the Caribbean screw; there was even less need of disguise or apology now because Europe was engrossed in its slide into war. Whatever his election plat-form, a Democrat president could not afford to lag behind Republicans in guaranteeing 'national interests', any more than the Liberal Gladstone who occupied Egypt in 1882 could afford to lag behind his Tory opponents. In 1915 Haiti was forced to submit to American direction. Military occupation followed, and was charged with various brutalities; in a Black country like Haiti, these were only too likely to happen. Early in 1916 a treaty was imposed on Nicaragua, securing canal-building rights and establishing American ascendancy. Later that year there was armed action in San Domingo, on the plea of disorders there, and full control was maintained until 1924. In 1916 too America was once more acquiring territory by purchase: the Virgin Islands, coveted for some years, were bought from Denmark, to the detriment – as Danish liberals foresaw – of their Negro inhabitants.[84] Beyond the Atlantic a rumour spread that America intended to take over the Negro republic of Liberia.[85] American advisers were reorganizing the small army and empty treasury; a loan was advanced; 'the American cruiser *Birmingham* helped to stop a rising of the wilder coast natives'; in 1913 an American corporation was seeking large concessions. Liberia was alert enough to see the menace to its independence, and refused.[86] Not lying within the American sphere of influence, it could do so with impunity.

But Wilson's most important arena was Mexico, the country whose treatment by President Tyler long ago he censured in his *History*. Here too there were disorders, following the downfall of Porfirio Díaz in 1911; and it was the unruliness of these republics that always did most to palliate interventionism, to make an invasion of Haiti look quite different from an invasion of Belgium. In the 1860s the enlightened British observer Cairnes thought Mexico so chaotic that 'almost any change would be a change for the better', even its handing over to the Southern Confederacy.[87] So little did even socialists in America now grasp of the realities of imperialism that Eugene Debs dismissed the subject as irre-levant to the working class, and some others were arguing, much like Bryan, that

'The capitalists have their necessary work to do in developing the natural resources of Mexico.'[88]

By the time of Wilson's advent in 1913, the U.S. had a bigger stake in Mexico than all other foreigners together, with 75,000 resident planters, traders, engineers, and 1,200 million dollars of investment. 'Mexico was practically an economic colony of the United States.'[89] Naturally Americans watching the country fall into confusion felt it would benefit by the same treatment as Cuba; equally naturally they saw what was really an outworn feudal structure as a defect of 'race and national character': Mexico was not truly a white country, 'it was a great shambling Indian Republic.'[90] This was to ignore the fact that under the surface something serious was stirring, the agrarian revolution long damped down by Díaz. As always the U.S. was historically too remote, though geographically so close, to have much inkling of Mexico's tribulations, more akin to Asia's than to its own.

Wilson immediately fell foul of Britain, which was suspected of backing, for the benefit of its oil men, a usurping right-wing leader named Huerta. On its side London took for granted that Washington's opposition to him was dictated by Standard Oil; but, in moving towards intervention, America could once again hug the thought that it was protecting the New World against European meddling. Wilson came out with 'an entirely new principle for dealing with Latin-American republics', non-recognition of leaders who seized power by force:[91] practically this would mean usurpers not in the good books of Wall Street. About the planning of some of the flurry of risings that now broke out in Mexico, 'there can be little doubt that the United States Ambassador knew far more than was wise. He obviously associated himself with the rebel leaders and gave them substantial advice at the same time that his conduct was injuring, if not undermining, the president whom his government had recognized'.[92] This kind of activity was coming to be a basic part of the duties of American diplomats.

In April 1914 Wilson went further, by occupying the port of Vera Cruz, an action which grated on the national feeling of all Mexicans and tended to combine them against the old foe. He professed, wrote the censorious Blunt, to be fighting not Mexico but only Huerta, just as Gladstone professed to be entering Egypt only to rid it of an upstart Arabi Pasha. 'Rothstein ... attributes this to Wilson's naivety, which believes it possible to reconcile moral principles of government with the rascalities of financial politics.'[93] Naive or not, Wilson was very much addicted to clandestine methods, making use of secret agents to back one faction against another without letting his right hand know what his left hand was doing.[94] In June 1915 he issued an admonition that disorders might compel the U.S. to intervene, for the good (of course) of the Mexican people.[95]

In October he granted recognition to Carranza, the most progressive of the party chiefs, but he reacted sharply against a proposed nationalization of oil, and a noisy campaign of propaganda against Carranza was worked up by financial and Catholic quarters. In vain he protested that the U.S. was being misled by calumnies designed to frustrate his programme of reconstruction; any progress in Mexico was obnoxious to the reactionary Church there, and the way its denunciations of the Carranza government were taken up abroad might be called a rehearsal for the world-wide Catholic and fascist outcry against the Spanish Republic twenty years later. Early in 1916 border disturbances provided a pretext for a punitive expedition under General Pershing. Wilson resisted pressure for a large-scale operation only, it must be supposed, because the prospect of involvement in the European war was now looming up.

By this time interventionism, though it still had its critics, was an established philosophy, generating the same kind of moral fervour, the same certainty of the eagles being on the side of the angels, as Europe's empires had done, and with a similar perilous gap between illusion and reality. If Wilson's mind was an automatic translator of market cupidities into high-flown sentiments, it was his envoy W.H. Page who carried off the palm by his hunger and thirst after righteousness and its due dividends. He prosed and moralized at London about the new American gospel as Bingham used to do at Tokyo about the old one. He was perfectly convinced that what was being done in Cuba was a wonderful fresh substitute for Spanish misrule or indigenous anarchy, and – as his biographer calls it – 'one of the greatest triumphs of American statesmanship'.[96] Though an ardent anglophile, he discerned a wide gulf between this dedication to high aims and the uninspired routine of British colonial rule, and was indignant at British leaders, including the Foreign Secretary Sir Edward Grey, for preferring politics plain, with no virtuous seasoning of ideals. 'Nobody gives us credit for any moral purpose', he wrote querulously to Wilson. 'Nobody recalls our giving Cuba to the Cubans or our pledge to the Philippine Islands ... This illustrates the complete divorce of European politics from fundamental morals.' Grey cared nothing about 'the moral foundation of government or about the welfare of the Mexican people. These things are not in the European ruling vocabulary.'[97]

One day when Grey pressed him about Mexico, Page responded that if necessary Americans would stay there for two hundred years and ' "shoot men for that little space till they learn to vote and to rule themselves." I have never seen him laugh so heartily. Shooting them into self-government! Shooting them into orderliness – he comprehends that; and that's all right. But that's as far as his habit of mind goes.'[98] Grey might well laugh at this enthusiasm, this resolve to educate laggard peoples with bullets, which in reality could only mean shooting them until they learned to vote as Wall Street wanted them to. It was to be given a long trial in Vietnam, though not nearly long enough for Page's time scale. One can fancy his America exclaiming, like the celebrated headmaster Dr Grimstone, 'I'll have no mutineers in my camp! I'll establish a spirit of trustful happiness and unmurmuring content in this school, if I have to flog every boy in it as long as I can stand over him!'[99]

4

Old World Frustrations, and Ideas of a New World Order

While Americans consolidated their sphere of influence (to borrow the soulless European phrase) round the Caribbean, they were exploring possibilities in Asia, with much less success because there they came face to face with other countries, militarily stronger or more resolute, and intent on securing spheres of their own. In Persia this was being done by agreement, from 1907, between the Russians working in the north and the British in the south. W.M. Shuster was the head of a group of American experts employed by the Persian government to try to bring order into its chaotic finances. He was backed for the post by President Taft, as part of the policy of extending American influence to new realms.[100] He found himself in a situation something like the Yankee's at the court of King Arthur. Treasury guards had to be sent round to compel grandees to pay their taxes.[101] But his great lament was about the way Britain and Russia were 'strangling' the country. It would be interesting to know what he would have thought had he been working in Nicaragua or Guatemala. Not far away, in the decrepit Ottoman empire, State Department backing of a concession won by Admiral Chester, against German competition, gained its ratification by the government. It was for a railway line through Asia Minor with oil-prospecting rights along the route. Nothing came of it: American diplomacy and business enterprise alike still lacked experience on this kind of ground,[102] though the ghost of the concession survived to haunt international oil rivalries of the post-War years.

Meanwhile American surpluses and exports continued to pile up. By 1912–13 total exports were a shade larger than Germany's, and not far behind Britain's; yet imports were scarcely bigger than those of France, well below Germany's, little more than half Britain's.[103] For the mysterious ailment that made this export drive seem the key to salvation, China continued to be the longed-for cure. 'Always more a potential than an actual market, the myth of China's four hundred million customers was an American reality.'[104] China was to be the bottomless absorber of whatever America could produce. As in so many other ways, an old notion was being taken over from Europe and inflated: England had pipe-dreams in the 19th century, like America in the 20th, of a vast China market, a heaven-sent panacea for all ills of over-production.

Sentimentally, some older feeling of sympathy with China lingered, aided perhaps by a kind of fascination of the world's oldest nation for its newest. Boxer rebels chilled American as well as European goodwill, but there was some difference even then, and a generally milder attitude. Some reflections of this can be found in the letters of Mrs Conger, who as wife of the U.S. minister went through the siege of the Legations. 'How *dare* China touch the Legations?' she bursts out in one epistle; but amid her frequent appeals to the Almighty she clearly wished to be not as other diplomats' wives are, and she could also write: 'The foreigner often treats the Chinese as though they were dogs. My sympathy is with China. A very unpopular thing to say ....'.[105] Her husband, who had been taking a stiff line on missionary issues,[106] had more in common with the up-to-date, hardboiled school of Americans in the Far East, one of whom, Consul-general Jernigan at Shanghai, brought out a book in 1904 advocating determined methods, with no scruples about treading on China's toes.[107] Congress trod on them that year by passing a law to exclude Chinese immigrants; a boycott of American goods followed, and some missionaries were killed near Canton. It was the U.S., nevertheless, that led the way in turning over its share of the 'Boxer indemnity' extorted from China to education for Chinese students.

With Japan it was the other way round: there was mistrust on both sides, but a realistic readiness to do business. America was happy in 1904 to see Russia's advance in the Far East challenged and halted by Japan, but was soon wondering whether Japan might not prove still more troublesome, especially to the vulnerable Philippine outpost. This feeling was in evidence before the end of the Russo-Japanese War; at Tokyo the premier Count Taro Katsura, aware of a 'shade of solicitude about the future', talked reassuringly to an American clergyman of the spread of Christianity in Japan, and said his country was only fighting in self-defence like ancient Greece against Persia.[108] Later on, mistrust of Japan was to be romanticized into a legend of America as China's well-wisher and guardian. 'American-Asian contact from the beginning has been fraught with romantic images, distortions, wishful thinking, irrelevant generalizations, and logical inconsistencies.'[109] Only in a spiritual sense might America be said to be protecting China: by the 1920s there were thirteen American colleges and 2,500 missionaries there. Many of those in Korea hoped that their government would prevent the Japanese annexation: many Koreans had the same hope, and flocked to join their churches.[110] Even after it took place in 1910, a disapproving Briton blamed these missionaries for putting indigestible Western ideas into the heads of Koreans and making them pine for freedom.[111]

Few other Americans had any objection, for a long time, to Japanese expansion on the mainland, provided that no American interests seemed to be threatened. Some of their more thrusting representatives wanted to see their own country playing the same game. H.N. Allen, minister in Korea from 1897 to 1905, was working towards an American protectorate, before the Japanese takeover, though he had no orders to do so, and during the Russo-Japanese War he wished his government to take the opportunity to annex something. America's still very loose diplomatic arrangements allowed men of energy to hatch policies in a manner very seldom open to British diplomats. And the forceful methods America was employing in its own part of the world were bound to influence the attitudes of Americans elsewhere. Resorting to force in the Far East would, however, be a very different thing from resorting to it in Central America, and the U.S. was far from ready yet to face the risk of war with a Great Power and its allies, and the cost of preparedness for war.

America wanted an open door, a free field for competition everywhere in China, in which its commercial strength would give it advantages. But everyone else preferred spheres of influence, monopoly, with the exception of Britain, and even Britain doubtfully now because of its political commitments to Japan, France, and Russia. Hence the way forward seemed to lie in agreements and arrangements with others: in a rational co-operation, an international linking-up of capitalism which would be a valid extension of the great trusts and combines that were forming within the U.S. and other countries. If, at the end of the

Russo-Japanese War, many voices were raised in favour of a stand against Japan, within a few years the same voices often favoured partnership with it, as with anyone else within reach.[112] The Roosevelt government helped to set the tone, by the Taft-Katsura Agreement in 1905 which recognized Japan's possession of Korea in return for a promise to respect America's of the Philippines; and by the Root-Takahira Agreement of 1908 which gave recognition to Japan's special position in Manchuria.

Taft, who had visited China as Secretary of War in 1907, set out to be less self-effacing in the Far East. His State Secretary Knox, 'whose intimacy with Wall St', a Japanese wrote acidly, 'is well known, was ready to back a group of money kings.'[113] Manchuria was an area where American interests were trying hard to get a foothold. Conger was keen on this, and Willard Straight, as consul-general at Mukden and briefly head of the Far East section of the State Department before returning to China as a banking and railway agent, gave it a powerful impetus. He resented the 1908 Agreement, and tried to hold the Japanese in check in Manchuria by co-operation with the Russians. Taft supported him, actively helping to push American capital into Manchuria 'in order to check Japanese ambitions', as a British observer wrote, 'in a region which had much the same significance for Japan as the Caribbean for the United States'.[114] A sequence of grandiose schemes ended in failure; Manchuria was too remote, and collaboration proved easier, despite their recent conflict, between Russia and Japan. Straight was left 'hating the Japanese', he confessed, 'more than anything else in the world. It is due I presume to the constant strain of having to be polite and to seek favors from a yellow people ... Kipling was absolutely right ...'.[115]

Nor did wider American plans of getting into China fare much better. Manila was not growing into a second Hongkong. Hopes were refreshed by the Revolution of 1911;[116] the fall of the last imperial dynasty was welcomed like that of Díaz in Mexico in the same year. Significantly, however, it was a would-be Chinese Díaz, the army boss Yuan Shih-k'ai soon at work building a right-wing dictatorship, who attracted American favour, not the radical idealist Sun Yat-sen. Before long the young republic was tottering, and its weaknesses encouraged a too great concentration of American as of other foreign effort on the tempting business of offering loans on conditions that would tie it hand and foot. Too little study has been made of the divergent claims of this parasitic type of financial capitalism and those of industrial capital; but it appears that in most areas the latter took the lead, whereas in Asia 'the House of Morgan's pro-Japanese policy became the *de facto* policy of the government ... for the next two decades'.[117]

In 1911 the Taft government was positively urging hesitant bankers into taking part in a grand international consortium intended to float a big China loan, whereas Wilson on taking office in 1913 refused to approve American participation. He alleged that the proposed terms amounted to an encroachment on Chinese autonomy, that it was secured on unpopular taxes, that it could not be squared with American constitutional principles;[118] all perfectly true, but equally relevant to the Central American loans which Wilson like his predecessors was sending bailiffs, or marines, to enforce. As usual his real – or determining – motives were of another sort: he judged, it seems, that consortium tactics were not doing America much good, and that it would be better to strike out on a new path; he was with those 'who sought an aggressive, independent American role in the Far East'.[119]

In this region, therefore, America was showing impatience at a lack of success. Very little of its flood of foreign investment was finding its way into any part of Asia. Wilson came at the close of the Progressivist era, when the country was far stronger in many ways than a dozen years earlier, and correspondingly more aspiring: more secure at home, firmly in control of Central America, industrially ahead of the world. Yet in armaments it still lagged behind. One Secretary of State after another declared that there was no intention of going to war over the Far East;[120] and expansionism had a readier acceptance by the public because it wore the garb of sweet reasonableness, could even appear as a contribution to world peace. These were years of an energetic movement of support for Hague Conferences, arbitration treaties, an International Court, and all the other peace-keeping formulae that were in the air. Since 1898 the U.S. might be committed to its own version of imperialism, but it was strenuously shutting its eyes to any realization that involvement in world politics must compel it sooner or later to join in the world game of cannonballs. It clung to the illusion that technological skill would suffice by itself; that the other nations would come round to its own creed of peaceful competition, with the devil taking the hindmost.

It did not yet see, what it was to learn so thoroughly later on, and what young Winston Churchill understood very well in 1908 when he wrote that 'economic superiority ... has never been and never will be in the history of the world the final arbiter'.[121] The Old World had its own philosophy, with the sword ready to be thrown into the scales if they tipped too much the wrong way. To expect those dinosaur-states to turn vegetarian and let themselves be worsted by the higgling of the market was self-deception. By 1904 the army, after its spurt during the war with Spain, was in the doldrums once more, down to half its authorized strength. Army life was ill-attuned to the individualistic American temperament; though this benefited capitalism on balance by working still more strongly against socialism. Socialism and militarism, though opposites, have grown in the same Old World soil, closer to the tribal collectivism of the past. Like the civil service, the army was liable to be regarded as a refuge for those who failed to do better outside. Its historian has a pathetic passage on the devoted officer who, turning his back on worldly gear, 'enters his profession without hope of wealth or gain, much as does the clergyman', and is not rewarded even with honour.[122] On this point America and China thought alike, in striking contrast with Germany or Japan where the military were the lords of creation.

As to the rank and file, they were so much looked down on by a prosperous citizenry that in 1911 Congress had to legislate for their protection, for example against exclusion from places of public entertainment.[123] This contempt must have been all the deeper because, for want of other recruits, the army 'always enrolled large numbers of emigrants, often soon after their arrival in the United States', though there were some doubts about their reliability: during one crisis a Democrat said that under the test of war these newcomers as a species might turn out no better than 'hordes of modern Goths and Huns'.[124] Most of those from continental Europe would have been familiar at home with conscription; many emigrated to escape it, but it would be instructive to know how many had performed military service before leaving home. They were to the U.S. army what impoverished Irish and Highland peasants were to the British.

This unmilitary character led to America being underrated by Germany as an opponent before its entry into both World Wars. In the small Caribbean countries only minimal armed force was required against resistance not yet based (as in the Philippines) on mass insurgency; a fact which also reduced public awareness of what was happening there. Mexico was beginning to be different, and was also bigger, and there America's land forces were scarcely adequate to the task of coercion. In 1914 'All manner of materials for war were absent'; there were only twenty-one planes, little field artillery, scanty ammunition; and things were not much better when America entered the Great War in 1917,[125] with very few even of the machine-guns it had itself forged. As so often before, the nation, trusting to its genius for improvizing, was first going to war and then preparing for it. Only as ally of a war-hardened coalition, in a Europe already worn by two and a half years of slaughter, could this gamble be safely risked: for the U.S. to have taken on singlehanded any strong, fresh adversary would have been out of the question, at any rate away from its own borders.

Dislike of the drilling and uniform-wearing that were second nature to continental Europe helped, along with geography, to guide the thoughts of Americans who wanted their country strong in the world, even more than those of Britons, from army to navy. While Europeans turned themselves into machines, the new civilization wanted its work done for it by machinery. Not manpower, but warships, and later on planes, ultimately missiles, would be America's investment in the arms race it was irresistibly being sucked towards. This harmonized also with the strategy of indirect rule instead of colonial occupation, for which a regular army is indispensable. Whatever increase of armed strength was being made in these years was in naval construction, and was due primarily to suspicions of Japan. But even this went ahead in much more leisurely style than the Anglo-German naval race, partly because of Congress putting a brake on Roosevelt's programme. Had economic depression lasted longer it would have been another matter; as it was, now as earlier industrialists were astonishingly slow to tumble to the fact that the ideal, inexhaustible market is not in any far-off Cathay, but at home, in government orders for armaments: the kingdom of heaven is within us.

A more wholesome way was being found, fumblingly, in a nascent belief – inspired at bottom by a socially more egalitarian climate than Europe's or Asia's – in mass output for mass consumption; an ideal of efficient production of wealth instead of the primitive grabbing for wealth represented by war. Perhaps from psychological causes more than from economic necessity, American society remained divided by race, more obtrusively than by class. An American world would be like it, except that there would be less room higher up and far more lower down. The new device of arbitration or government mediation in industrial disputes was likely, it has been suggested, to reinforce similar trends in international contacts;[126] and America already had a long record of arbitral treaties with Britain. Individual attitudes varied widely. A Carnegie might be all for fighting it out with labour at home, while working for sensible relationships among states; Mahan, more predictably, was all against tying America's hands by any arbitration pacts, on the ground that this would 'vitally impair the moral freedom, and the consequent moral responsibilities, which are the distinguishing glory of the rational man, and of the sovereign state'.[127] It would also of course impair the navy's chances of glory.

Roosevelt tried to combine 'big stick' postures (a *stick* in America's homely imagery corresponded with Europe's rattling sabre) with promotion of Great Power harmony. His prime aim, he declared in his autobiography, was peace, but world order had to be upheld by governments both civilized and strong, and his sending the battle-fleet on an ostentatious cruise round the world was meant to advertise this fact.[128] With all his suspicions of the Germans, he was ready for an accord with them as well as with Japan or Britain, and was trying to play the same go-between or bringing-together role in world affairs as he did at times between capital and labour. He was active behind the scenes, before the Algeciras Conference in 1906, in helping to avert a European conflict over the barren sands of Morocco;[129] at the Conference he and Elihu Root, his State Secretary, came down more on the Anglo-French side than the German, but their main concern was to preach the Open Door, including, of course, progress for the poor Moroccans.[130] They could indulge the thought that here was a beneficent spread of civilization for the 'natives' and commercial opportunity for all the advanced countries. In reality, as in all such cases, the strong power on the spot (here France) would want to reward itself with the lion's share of the profits; and the indigenous inhabitants would have to be crushed by years of irregular war before anyone could set about civilizing them.

The more utopian blueprints for mankind's future that America was concocting suffered from the same kind of unrealism. In Bellamy's fantasy Europe and Australia, Mexico and parts of South America, evolve into 'industrial models', following the lead of the U.S., and forming with it a loose world federation charged with dealings with 'the more backward races, which are gradually being educated up to civilized institutions'.[131] Jane Adams, writing on peace and doing social work among poor immigrants about the turn of the century, viewed the United States as a hopeful exemplar, and the world as a family of peoples who ought to live together in harmony. A family is a hierarchy; and in Roosevelt's world-view a line was clearly drawn between countries civilized and strong (the two attributes were virtually identified) and the rest. To him Japanese expansion on the mainland appeared not merely a lesser evil than Japanese oceanic foraging would be, but positively useful as promoting conditions favourable to business activity.[132]

From this point of view there might be less unreality than Mahan found in 'the dream of some advanced thinkers, of an International Army, charged with imposing the decrees of an International Tribunal'.[133] There were progressives on both sides of the Atlantic who felt that big countries ought to be exerting more authority over backward ones; in Britain for instance Norman Angell, who thought no one should grudge Germany policing a region like Asia Minor, because it was for the common good that it should be policed; or Fabian Socialists such as the Webbs and Bernard Shaw. Considering what a nuisance small nationalities like those of the Balkans could be, there was some logic in this; but these Fabians were not uninfluenced by the Liberal Imperialists, and Shaw lived to approve of Mussolini's conquest of Abyssinia.

Behind utopian hopes, at any rate, lay the reality of an advanced group of countries capable, if they could come to terms, of jointly taking control of the world. Of such a future America was the standard-bearer. If in its salad days it spoke in the Far East with two voices, one of disinterested fellow-feeling, one of White solidarity, these two themes were now converging. Bryan's world tour left him talking in the strain of an 'avowed expansionist', and predicting the victory of 'progressive civilization'.[134] And within the advanced group, or upper class of nations, America would be increasingly disposed to claim a special place, as Wilson showed signs of doing even before the European War thrust greatness upon him. World peace would be a *pax Americana*, a revised edition of the *pax Britannica* dreamed of by the Victorians when British warships were preparing the way of the Lord by patrolling the seas, and Tennyson was writing with as much fervour about 'the parliament of man' as about the charge of the Light Brigade.

Thoughts of a rational consensus, if not brotherly love, among the rich and great had a less rosy side when it came to their joint relations with weaker peoples. Here too fiction ran ahead of history. The English Catholic novelist, Rolfe, conjured up an English pope dividing the earth among the five virile states capable of bearing sway – Britain, Germany, Italy, Japan, the U.S. – with German armies given the task of quelling anarchic France and Russia, and the U.S. placed in command of the entire New World south of Canada.[135] 'Thus the

Supreme Arbitrator provided the human race with scope and opportunity for energy.' Rolfe's first principle was the duty of obedience: 'rebellion was worse than the ... worst prince'. Equally this has been the first principle of all imperialism. Within forty years Hitler's 'New Order' in Europe and Japan's 'Co-Prosperity Sphere' in Asia would show how far Rolfe was guessing the currents of history aright, but also how far ugly fact differed from cosy dream.

Meanwhile there were tentative signs of an emergence of at least larger groupings of the big nations, with Bismarck's system of permanent coalitions leading the way. The Germany of the Kaiser had visions of a Continental bloc united under German leadership by antipathy to Britain, America and Japan. More concretely there was a drawing together of the three great colonial powers: Britain, France, Russia. As 1914 approached, American thinking about the grand coalition that would bring together all the big states and avert conflict among them – the fading Concert of Europe revived and magnified by America's moral leadership – took on a more urgent, purposeful note. Wilson threw out ideas in a speech of 1913 at Mobile which were eagerly taken up by Page in London and by House, Wilson's roving envoy, who two years earlier had written a novel with a similar scenario.[136] House wanted his government to smooth the antagonism between Britain and Germany, and soften British antipathy to the German desire for expansion.[137] In 1913 he held forth to a German representative about how much good a combination of America, Germany, Britain and Japan might do to preserve the Open Door, in China and everywhere else.

In London that year he was putting forward 'a co-operative policy of developing the waste places of the world'.[138] The phrase had a pleasantly constructive ring, though the policy if adopted might very well mean places laid waste by fresh Boxer expeditions. He wanted rich nations to lend money at 'reasonable rates': of course, he wrote to Wilson, it would be necessary to establish 'conditions by which such loans may be reasonably safe'.[139] How this might be done is elucidated in a memorandum by Page. 'It seems impossible to talk the Great Powers out of their fear of one another': hence 'sound psychology' dictated that 'some common and useful work', 'some great unselfish task', be found for the armies they refused to disband. 'Nobody can lead in such a new era but the United States.' Mexico might soon offer a field of action, where they could 'clean out bandits, yellow fever', etc., and 'make the country healthful, safe for life and investment'. Military power must come first in each case, but it would be

'conquest for the sole benefit of the conquered, worked out by a sanitary refor-
mation'. In Cuba and the Philippines the U.S. had demonstrated that 'there was
just one honourable way of dealing with the less fortunate and more primitive
races in all parts of the world'.[140]

Metaphors of hygiene and sickness, denoting civilization and barbarism, and of
sanitary elimination of bad men and germs unfriendly to profitable investment,
were to cluster thickly round the coming American hegemony. But these pipe-
dreams had to await a later and more oblique fulfilment, after two world wars.
House and Page were hankering for a return to direct colonial rule, though now
on a collective basis, which did not fit in with America's line of development; and
though collaboration with foreign troops might be all right in China, they would
scarcely be welcome in Mexico or anywhere else in the Western hemisphere. It
was a much lesser objection that under their plan weaker peoples, or their
independence at least, would have to be sacrificed to avert bloodshed among the
strong. They of course would not have put it, even to themselves, in these terms,
since the entire scheme was in line with traditionalist thinking about the rich
being trustees on behalf of the poor, and took as axiomatic that the proposed
relationship between rich and poor nations would be twice blessed, a boon to
both. This seemed the more self-evident now because what was in view was the
introduction of capital investment and free enterprise, a modern New Testament
added to Victorian England's gospel of the blessings of free trade.

House thought it would be a good thing, as a start, for Germany to be
admitted to a share in the 'development' of Persia,[141] then being virtually par-
titioned between Britain and Russia. With such ideas, he might hope for a
meeting of minds when he interviewed the Kaiser in 1914. It was a memorable
encounter between New World and Old, bourgeois and feudal capitalism,
Kentucky colonel (House's hosts, who took such things seriously, were puzzled
by his title) and Supreme Warlord. House outlined his scheme of a world
partnership of the advanced nations to 'develop' the backward regions,[142] in
other words to canalize rivalries into a super-imperialism such as Kautsky the
Marxist was predicting. It all fell on deaf ears. The colloquy was taking place at
Potsdam during an annual Prussian army festival, and the All-Highest was in an
exalted mood. Strong enough industrially to take the new road, unlike Russia or
Japan which had to rely on their swords to keep them in the ring, Germany was
fettered socially and psychologically to the same archaic past. The envoy left

Berlin with a gloomy sensation of 'militarism run mad'.[143] A few weeks later an archduke was murdered, and the Great War broke out.

References

1. E. Davies, *American Labour – The Story of the American Trade Union Movement* (London, 1943), p.23.
2. R. Jeffreys-Jones, 'Violence in American History: Plug Uglies in the Progressive Era', in *Perspectives in American History*, Vol. VIII (1974), pp.536–7.
3. R. Hofstadter, *Social Darwinism in American Thought* (revised edn., New York, 1955), p.168.
4. *The Letters of Theodore Roosevelt*, ed. E.E. Morrison (Harvard, 1954), Vol. 8, p.1253 (15 November 1898).
5. Jeffreys-Jones, *op. cit.*, p.564.
6. 8 October 1913; *Selections from the Correspondence of Theodore Roosevelt and Henry Cabot Lodge 1884–1918* (New York, 1929), Vol. II, pp.440–1.
7. R. Miliband, *The State in Capitalist Society* (1969; London edn., 1973), p.53.
8. G. Kolko, *The Triumph of Conservatism – A Reinterpretation of American History, 1900–1916* (1963; Chicago edn., 1967), p.284.
9. *Ibid.*, Introd. and Chap. 1.
10. *Selections from the Prison Notebooks of Antonio Gramsci*, ed. Q. Hoare and G.N. Smith (London, 1971), p.20.
11. F.W. Hirst *et al., Liberalism and the Empire* (London, 1900), pp.138–9.
12. Jack London, *The Iron Heel* (1907), Chap. XIII.
13. J. Israel, *Progressivism and the Open Door – America and China, 1905–1921* (Pittsburg, 1971), p.xvii.
14. Alleyne Ireland, *The Far Eastern Tropics – Studies in the Administration of Tropical Dependencies* (London, 1905), pp.186–7.
15. H. Tinker, *A New System of Slavery – The Export of Indian Labour Overseas 1830–1920* (London, 1974), p.310.
16. *Correspondence of Roosevelt and Lodge*, Vol. II, p.197 ff.
17. P.S. Reinsch, *Colonial Administration* (New York, 1905), pp.3–4, 6. Reinsch, an academic, was later minister to China (1913–19).
18. *Ibid.*, pp.12–13.
19. A. Vagts, *A History of Militarism* (revised edn., London, 1959), p.388.
20. See e.g. Sir J.T. Pratt, *War and Politics in China* (London, 1943), p.160.

21. P. Joseph, *Foreign Diplomacy in China* (London, 1928), p.410.
22. 'L. Putnam Weale', *The Truce in the East and its Aftermath* (London, 1907), p.414.
23. R.B. Sheridan, *The Filipino Martyrs* (London, 1900), pp.45–6, 50.
24. Ireland, *op. cit.*, p.196.
25. J.H. Latané, *America as a World Power 1897–1907* (New York, 1907), p.77.
26. Sheridan, *op. cit.*, p.153.
27. *American Issues*, Vol.1, ed. W. Thorp *et al.* (2nd edn., Chicago, 1944), p.890.
28. O.D. Edwards, 'The American Image of Ireland', in *Perspectives in American History*, Vol. IV, 1970, p.256.
29. O. Lattimore, *The Situation in Asia* (Boston, 1949), p.94.
30. W.A. Ganoe, *The History of the United States Army* (revised edn., New York, 1943), p.398.
31. Reinsch, *op. cit.*, p.407.
32. *Ibid.*, p.414.
33. W.J. Pomeroy, *American Neo-Colonialism* (New York, 1970), p.92.
34. Latané, *op. cit.*, pp.96–7.
35. W.S. Blunt, *My Diaries* (London edn., 1932), pp.568, 598.
36. J. Fast, *Monopoly Capital and Empire: the Sugar Trust and American Imperialism, 1883–1909* (Ph.D. thesis, Univ. of London, 1976), p.170 ff.
37. Pomeroy, *op. cit.*, p.238.
38. *Ibid.*, p.211.
39. B. Lasker, *Human Bondage in Southeast Asia* (Univ. of North Carolina, 1950), p.134; cf. E.H. Jacoby, *Agrarian Unrest in Southeast Asia* (New York, 1949), Chap. 6.
40. Lasker, *op. cit.*, p.231.
41. A.T. Mahan, *Lessons of the War with Spain* (1898; London edn., 1899), pp.247–50.
42. Ireland, *op. cit.*, pp.189, 210–11, 218–19.
43. R.H. Heindel, *The American Impact on Great Britain 1898–1914* (Univ. of Pennsylvania, 1940), p.69.
44. Sheridan, *op. cit.*, p.153.
45. Mahan, *op. cit.*, pp.244–5.
46. Pomeroy, *op. cit.*, p.132.
47. Reinsch, *op. cit.*, pp.20–1, 26, 29.

48. Pomeroy, *op. cit.*, p.107.
49. A.K. Weinberg, *Manifest Destiny – A Study of Nationalist Expansionism in American History* (Gloucester, Massachusetts, 1958), p.307; B.M. Solomon, *Ancestors and Immigrants – A changing New England tradition* (New York, 1956), p.120.
50. Pomeroy, *op. cit.*, p.175.
51. *Ibid.*, p.173.
52. W.A. Williams, *The Tragedy of American Diplomacy* (new edn., New York, 1962), p.43, and title of Chap. 1.
53. *Ibid.*, p.39.
54. Pratt, *op. cit.*, p.162.
55. S.T. Wallis, *Glimpses of Spain* (New York, 1849), pp.359–60.
56. Foreign Office memo of 1841, cited in V.G. Kiernan, 'Britain's First Contacts with Paraguay', in *Atlante* (London), Vol. 3 (1955), pp.176–7.
57. Carl Schurz, *Speeches, Correspondence and Political Papers*, ed. F. Bancroft, Vol. V (New York, 1913), p.199.
58. Joseph Conrad, *Nostromo* (1904; London edn., 1947), pp.76–7.
59. L. Huberman and P.M. Sweezy, 'Cuba, Anatomy of a Revolution', in *Monthly Review* (New York), Vol. 12, Nos. 3 & 4, 1960, p.21.
60. Williams, *op. cit.*, p.2.
61. A. Garland, *South American Conflicts and the United States* (Lima, 1900), pp.16–7 and Annex, p.4.
62. Mahan, *op. cit.*, p.283.
63. *Ibid.*, pp.294–5.
64. *British Documents on the Origins of the War 1898–1914*, ed. G.P. Gooch and H. Temperley, Vol. II (London, 1927), pp.162, 164.
65. *Correspondence of Roosevelt and Lodge*, Vol. II, pp.135–6.
66. Mahan, *op. cit.*, pp.28–9.
67. F.W. Hirst, *Political Economy of War* (London, 1915), p.229.
68. I. Raynor; see *Problems of American History*, ed. R.W. Leopold and H.S. Link (2nd edn., Englewood Cliffs, 1957), p.524.
69. J.W. Gantenbein, *The Evolution of our Latin-American Policy – A Documentary Record* (New York, 1950), p.73 ff.
70. See Scott Nearing and J. Freeman, *Dollar Diplomacy* (1925; New York edn., 1969), pp.178–9.

71. *Ibid.*, pp.157, 161.
72. A. Bauer Paiz, 'Imperialism in Guatemala', in *Science and Society* (New York), Vol. XXXIV, No.2 (1970), pp.146–7.
73. Pomeroy, *op. cit.*, p.188.
74. J.A. Spender, *Weetman Pearson, First Viscount Cowdray 1850–1927* (London, 1930), pp.210–11.
75. See tables in E. Varga and L. Mendelsohn, *New Data for V.I. Lenin's "Imperialism"* (London edn., n.d.), p.191.
76. H.S. Ferns, *The Argentine Republic* (Newton Abbot, 1973), pp.109–11.
77. H. Bingham, *The Monroe Doctrine – An obsolete shibboleth* (New Haven, 1913); pp.63–7.
78. Smedley D. Butler, "America's Armed Forces" (part 2), *Common Sense* 4 (11), November 1935, p.8. Also cited in L. Huberman, *Man's Worldly Goods* (London, 1937), pp.265–6. For milder criticism see D.G. Munroe, *Intervention and Dollar Diplomacy in the Caribbean 1900–1921* (Princeton, 1964).
79. G.F. Kennan, *American Diplomacy 1900–1950* (1951; New York edn., 1952), pp.49–50.
80. Israel, *op. cit.*, p.92.
81. See R.W. Child, *A Diplomat Looks at Europe* (New York, 1925), Chap.1.
82. See Woodrow Wilson, *A History of the American People*, Vol. IV (New York, 1901), pp.30 ff., 78 ff., 101 ff., 160, 194 ff., 250.
83. Williams, *op. cit.*, p.62.
84. Nearing and Freeman, *op. cit.*, p.212 ff.
85. Blunt, *op. cit.*, pp.729–30 (28 July 1910).
86. See E. Rosenthal, *Stars and Stripes in Africa* (London, 1938), pp.85–6.
87. J.E. Cairnes, *The Slave Power* (London, 1863), p.105.
88. H.B. Davis, *Nationalism and Socialism – Marxist and Labor Theories of Nationalism to 1917* (New York, 1967), p.177.
89. B.J. Hendrick, *The Life and Letters of Walter H. Page* (New York, 1922–25; London edn., 1930), Vol. 1, p.178.
90. *Ibid.*, p.177.
91. *Ibid.*, p.182.
92. W.H. Callcott, *The Caribbean Policy of the United States, 1890–1920* (New York, 1966), pp.301–2.
93. Blunt, *op. cit.*, p.838 (26 April 1914).

94. Information from Dr R. Jeffreys-Jones; see his *American Espionage – from Secret Service to C.I.A.* (London, 1978).

95. *Papers Relating to the Foreign Relations of the United States: 1915* (Washington, 1924), p.694 ff.

96. Hendrick, *op. cit.*, Vol. 1, p.178.

97. *Ibid.*, p.184 (25 October 1913).

98. *Ibid.*, p.188 (2 November 1913).

99. 'F. Anstey', *Vice Versa, or a Lesson to Fathers* (London, 1882), Chap. 4.

100. A. Yeselson, *United States–Persian Diplomatic Relations 1883–1921* (New Brunswick, 1956), p.112.

101. W.M. Shuster, *The Strangling of Persia* (London, 1912), p.158.

102. See J.A. De Novo, *American Interests and Policies in the Middle East 1900–1939* (Minneapolis, 1963), Chap. 3; C. Davies, *British Oil Policy in the Middle East 1919–1932* (Ph.D. thesis, Univ. of Edinburgh, 1973).

103. See figures in M. Baumont *et al.*, *L'Europe de 1900 à 1914* (Paris, 1966), p.396.

104. Israel, *op. cit.*, p.xi; cf. pp.xxii, 17.

105. Sarah Pike Conger, *Letters from China* (Chicago, 1909), pp.45, 100, and 176.

106. V.W. Purcell, *The Boxer Uprising* (Cambridge, 1963), p.203.

107. T.R. Jernigan, *China's Business Methods and Policy* (Shanghai & London, 1904).

108. *Japan Russia War* (Tokyo, 1904–5, monthly), No. 4.

109. Akira Iriye, *Across the Pacific – An Inner History of American–East Asian Relations* (New York, 1967), p.281.

110. K.K. Kawakami, *American–Japanese Relations* (New York, 1912), p.276.

111. J.O.P. Bland, *China, Japan and Korea* (London, 1921), Chap. 10. Cf. Younghill Kang, *The Grass Roof* (New York, 1931).

112. Israel, *op. cit.*, p.31.

113. Kawakami, *op. cit.*, p.89.

114. Pratt, *op. cit.*, p.163.

115. Akira Iriye, *op. cit.*, p.104; and see C. Vevier, *The United States and China 1906–1913 – A Study of Finance and Diplomacy* (New Brunswick, 1955), *passim*, and Chap. 9: 'Defeat in China'.

116. Israel, *op. cit.*, p.101.

117. W.A. Williams, 'The Large Corporation and American Foreign Policy 1890–1958', in *American Socialist* (September 1958), pp.15–16.

118. W.L. Tung, *China and the Foreign Powers* (New York, 1970), p.138, note 93.

119. See Williams, *The Tragedy of American Diplomacy*, pp.67 ff., 73–4; cf. Israel, *op. cit.*, pp.106–7.

120. Israel, *op. cit.*, p.84.

121. Winston Churchill, *My African Journey* (London, 1908), Chap. 3.

122. Ganoe, *op. cit.*, pp.460–1.

123. *Ibid.*, p.438.

124. Vagts, *op. cit.*, p.253.

125. Ganoe, *op. cit.*, p.473; cf. pp.429–30.

126. A suggestion of Dr R. Jeffreys-Jones, in a seminar at Edinburgh on 25 January 1971.

127. Mahan, *op. cit.*, p.209; cf. p.223.

128. T. Roosevelt, *An Autobiography* (1913; New York edn., 1946), Chap. XV.

129. *The Intimate Papers of Colonel House*, ed. C. Seymour (London, 1926), Vol. 1, p.242.

130. Williams, *op. cit.*, pp.58–9.

131. R. Bellamy, *Looking Backward 2000–1887* (1888; Cleveland edn., 1945), p.138.

132. Akira Iriye, *op. cit.*, pp.108, 110.

133. Mahan, *op. cit.*, pp.217–18.

134. Israel, *op. cit.*, p.63.

135. Fr. Rolfe ('Frederick Baron Corvo'), *Hadrian the Seventh* (London, 1904), Chap. XXI.

136. Israel, *op. cit.*, p.141.

137. *Papers of Colonel House*, Vol. 1, p.245.

138. *Ibid.*, pp.246, 248–9.

139. *Ibid.*, p.271.

140. Hendrick, *op. cit.*, Vol. 1, pp.272–3, 280.

141. *Papers of Colonel House*, Vol. 1, p.253.

142. *Ibid.*, p.261 ff.

143. *Ibid.*, p.255: House to Wilson, from Berlin, 29 May 1914.

PART FIVE

TWO STRIDES TO WORLD POWER

1

Great War and not so great Peace

In face of an intransigent Japan and a goose-stepping Germany, it had been natural for some Americans to think again of co-operation with Britain. No doubt there had been plenty of friction between the two countries since the wars of 1898–99 had – in Mahan's words – 'rent the veil . . . and revealed to each the face of a brother', and since another American had advocated a permanent confederal arrangement with the British empire.[1] Anglophobia still lingered, with the Hearst press to amplify it. Denouncing a decadent monarchy and aristocracy was another way of uniting Americans and hushing domestic discontents; thirty years later, Mayor Thompson was still building a career on a pledge to give King George a poke on the nose if he ever set foot in Chicago. But long before George V came to the throne, Britain had been displaying a carefully conciliatory spirit.

Like the America of the 1890s, perhaps like all nations in bouts of imperial fever, Britain wavered between aggressive optimism and nervous depression, gloomy forebodings of its empire following Rome's into decay. Morally as well as physically it was in need of reinforcement, and first of all it wanted fewer quarrels on its hands. The Anglo-French Entente began in 1904 as a simple settlement of colonial disputes; the Hay-Pauncefote Agreement with the U.S. three years earlier, which virtually left the U.S. a free hand in the Canal area and opened the way to its Panama *coup*, had a similar character, except that here Britain, still entangled in South Africa, was weaker, and the settlement more one-sided. But it did facilitate the policy soon adopted by the British navy of concentrating in home waters, ready for battle with Germany. For its part the American navy soon declared that national security was being 'greatly strengthened by strong ties of friendship' with Britain.[2] British anxiety not to disturb these ties was shown by the care taken in 1902 not to fall foul of Washington over Venezuela: the clash of 1895–96 there had been sufficient warning.

Care was all the more requisite because of the Anglo-Japanese alliance, another outcome of Britain's consciousness of isolation and over-extended strength. The Russians, at whom it was aimed, had an uneasy impression of 'Anglo-Japanese-American solidarity with respect to Manchuria',[3] and clearly with Japan on one arm and America on the other Britain would be comfortably able to squeeze Europe from each end. But this was too much to hope for. Roosevelt's mediation in the peace settlement of 1905 between Japan and Russia was inspired in part by unwillingness to see Japan getting too much. From the British point of view it could be welcomed as committing America to responsibilities in the Far East, helpful towards a new balance of power; even if there was some head-shaking over a supposed misguided idealism due to 'the responsive and enthusiastic American character'.[4]

A British empire, with Canada and other Dominions now autonomous, could look like part of the scaffolding of a new world order, all the more as American capital had a growing stake in it. Roosevelt continued after his presidency to award it certificates of merit. In 1910 he was invited by Lord Curzon, lately Viceroy of India and now chancellor of the university, to speak at Oxford; expectably enough, he declared that rule of one race over another must be organized for the good of the ruled.[5] He gave another address at Cairo university, eulogizing British rule as fully coming up to this virtuous maxim. 'He is a buffoon of the lowest American type,' W.S. Blunt exploded in his diary, 'and rouses the fury of young Egypt to boiling point.' And soon afterwards: 'That swine, Roosevelt, has made another speech, this time at the Mansion House, about Egypt, worse than before.'[6]

U.S. Ambassador Page was ardently in favour of America and Britain going forward together. If only his government would take a little more care to indulge the Englishman's foible for ceremonial courtesies, he confided to House, anything could be done with him. 'And you know what it would lead to – even in our lifetime – *to the leadership of the world*: and we should presently be considering how we may use the British fleet, the British Empire, and the English race for the betterment of mankind.'[7] In 1911 General von Bernhardi, the German fire-eater, wrote of Britain being forced to give ground to America, and of a collision between them being still on the cards: he found fault with Britain's 'unpardonable blunder, from her own point of view, of not supporting the Southern States in the American War of Secession'.[8] There was a good deal of wishful thinking here. Although no formal alliance took shape, a relationship was ripening; the two countries were in effect moving towards co-operation, as the British and French governments were doing in more headlong fashion. In the end Britain did have the U.S. for ally, drawn into the Great War, though slowly and circuitously, by a complex of unofficial connections and commitments as well as by national interests, as Britain was drawn in at once by its unavowed league with France.

Wilson's appeal to his countrymen at the outset of the war for moral, as well as diplomatic, neutrality was well received. Roosevelt, already indignant at Wilson's too mild handling of Mexico, was disgusted to find his Republican friends joining in praise of the president's 'noble and humanitarian peace policy'.[9] It surprised him less to see Wilson 'cordially supported by all the hyphenated Americans, by the solid flubdub and pacifist vote', and by every 'soft creature, every coward and weakling'.[10] But that there were millions of German-Americans, Irish-Americans, and so on, was a fact the government could not overlook. Apart from this, in condemning the war as an aberration Wilson was quite consistent with his view that the strong nations ought to stand together; war among Great Powers was worse than a crime, it was a blunder. America's manifest destiny, by now, was to lead the capitalist world, to shepherd the others, not join in senseless scrimmages among them. Early in 1916 House was sent back to Europe to try to rig up a negotiated peace. When Roosevelt had helped to end the Russo-Japanese War eleven years earlier, revolution had been breaking out in Russia; by now it was not hard to see that the same might happen again if war was allowed to drag on. But in spite of a half-promise that America would join them if Germany rejected a peace conference, the Allies refused.

Meanwhile there was the unpleasantness of Japan being free to make hay in the Far East. Race prejudice in the States had not yet given way to the logic of the market, and as 1914 approached, talk of the Yellow Peril, and of an inevitable conflict of races, was reaching a crescendo. Plans for a possible war with Japan were drawn up in 1913, and then periodically revised,[11] with a big programme of naval construction from 1915. But for the time being America's position was slippery, the more so because Britain was trying, though hesitantly and in vain, to bring Japan fully into the war.[12] In January 1915 came Japan's Twenty-one Demands on China, whose gravity the American minister Reinsch at Peking underlined; but despite China's appeals, Washington only felt able to respond with a repetition of its open door evangel,[13] now highly academic.

On the brink of entering the European war Wilson was still looking nervously over his shoulder across the Pacific. He told his cabinet that he feared the yellow race getting the better of the white;[14] exactly what the Kaiser told House at voluble length in 1914. America now, like Britain, had to seek Japanese support by further concessions, which took shape in the Lansing-Ishii conversations later in 1917.[15] They ended in something a good deal closer to a Japanese Monroe Doctrine for Eastern Asia than to an American open door. Between these two concepts a third might be discerned, that of Japan as policeman of the Far East. Lansing, a staunch conservative at the State Department, had little desire to prop up a decrepit, disorderly China. U.S. trade with and investments in Japan, faithful to their own instincts, were growing rapidly.

In April 1917 America entered the European war. It is never possible to reconstruct exactly the intricate combination of forces which carries any country into a big war: for this the past would have to be brought back to life, and the historian has only its relics, the things buried with it in the tomb. As in the war of 1812, maritime rights and wrongs were in the political forefront, with unrestricted submarine warfare by the Germans providing a *casus belli* for America just as the German invasion of Belgium had for Britain. On quite another plane was the industrial boom stimulated by Allied war orders, after two or three lean years. American loans were required to keep these orders flowing, and the loans, totalling more than two thousand million dollars by early 1917, were never likely to be repaid if the Allies were beaten, as with Russia crumbling they seemed quite likely to be. Wilson had given way often enough to demands for armed backing of financial interests in minor spheres. He himself, even before reaching the White House, was coming to see Germany as America's most threatening commercial rival, and Americans had not yet left behind altogether the European delusion of trade being a limited asset, to be won or lost. They were the nearest to outgrowing such archaisms. But if they were to impose their own more expansive philosophy on the world market, it could only be through taking part, at a certain stage, in the others' conflicts, and trying to see them suitably wound up.

There was of course an obbligato moral fanfare to go with this. As Mahan had summoned it to do years since, the U.S. was casting away the timidity and false ideas of peace which 'smother righteous indignation or noble ideals'.[16] 'We have no selfish ends to serve. We desire no conquest, no dominion', Wilson declared in his war message to Congress on 2nd April. '. . . We are but one of the champions of the rights of mankind.' Translated into terms of an American concept of progress, identical with a certain social and economic order – the most progressive yet known in history, unquestionably – this rhetoric was not without meaning. Civilization was a kind of Union, from which, for Wilson as for Lincoln, no state had a right to secede, as Germany was doing, and Russia, far more drastically, was about to do.

Bryan parted company with Wilson over the drift towards war, though he had reconciled himself cheerfully to Dollar Diplomacy, and was replaced by Lansing. As in Europe, the public fell into line readily enough. It was unattracted to war in 1914, rather than positively repelled, and could not withstand now an organized enthusiasm. Eugene Debs and the Socialist Party had been taking a strong line against Wilson's 'preparedness policy', as generating a bellicose atmosphere, as well as against intervention in Mexico. Because the U.S. was immune from attack, it was easier for socialists to make such a stand there than in any European country. Their handicap was the paucity of their links with union labour, which compared with Europe's was unpolitical, though over bread and butter issues it might be even more militant. As in Europe it was exceptionally militant just before the war. In 1912 a strike in railway repair shops was met with summary arrests, and violence and loss of life on both sides followed. From this point of view, war could hold out a promise of improved labour discipline, and Roosevelt's hankering for universal, compulsory military service had a family likeness to that of many pre-1914 conservatives in Britain.

War prosperity, doubling the gross national product between 1913 and 1918, was as welcome to labour as to capital. Labour leaders were eager to find common ground with the government, which in recent times had posed as umpire or honest broker between the two. Samuel Gompers of the A.F.L. pledged loyal support in advance to an entry into the war, and silenced objectors.[17] Once the sword was drawn he and his friends were boundlessly patriotic; they made

themselves useful also by sending delegations to spur the flagging zeal of workers
in the Allied countries. There was a big opportunity for mass indoctrination, all
the more needful after the Bolshevik Revolution. Educating labour and Americanizing recent immigrants went together, and stiff measures could be taken
against the unconvinced. 'To make the world safe for democracy, democratic ideals
had to be forgotten.'[18] In 1912 Debs as presidential candidate had been given an
alarming total of nearly a million votes; he repeated the feat in 1920, but from
inside prison. There were signs that Wilson, though never an advanced liberal,
was disquieted by the length repression was going to, and 'chafed under the
corporate and business interests that during the war had tightened their hold'.[19]

He may have found some consolation in sending a mission to preach liberal
principles to the Russians, who when he entered the fray had just overthrown
tsarism in the first of their 1917 revolutions, and to exhort them to persevere
with the war. His ambassador at Petrograd, David R. Francis, hoped to see
American influence supplanting French and British, and urged financial aid on
the ground that it would help to put American businessmen ahead of their
European rivals.[20] There was criticism of the choice of Elihu Root as leader of the
deputation. This die-hard conservative and former State Secretary had strongly
imperialist leanings, and might well be viewing Russia now as a business empire
for America. Two of the other deputation members were big business representatives, one with large interests in Russia. In addition there were two
spokesmen of Labour, now taking its place side by side with Capital in the
promotion of American expansion under the watchwords of democracy and
liberty. James H. Duncan was vice-president of the A.F.L., Charles Russell a
socialist of very right-wing affiliation.

The mission was inspired by an optimism prophetic of many later American
miscalculations about distant lands with deep-rooted problems, a technological
society's belief that they could all be solved by money and manipulation. That
Russia's urgent need was radical agrarian reform, Root and his companions had
scarcely any inkling. Like many of their long line of successors in other backward
regions, again, they blundered through Russia with very little tact. A Russian
officer compared them to a band of missionaries descending on benighted Pacific
islanders.[21] They could hardly avoid seeing these peasants as useful cannon-
fodder, in much the same way as the French looked on their African troops, or the
British on their Indian. They and the Allies were advising the Provisional

Government to have Lenin and Trotsky shot[22] – as these two must have known or guessed; once more, advice prophetic of much later American counsel to regimes faced with mass unrest.

With the Bolshevik seizure of power about to take place, Wilson was in the same kind of dilemma as Truman thirty years later with China, between a discredited conservatism and a tide of popular anger. His inactivity was blamed by Root's coterie in Congress for the Russian collapse, as Truman was to be blamed for not 'saving' China. Quite apart from the loss of a war ally, the idea of Russia as a vast semi-colony for American capital had a lively appeal, even if there was no organized 'Russia lobby'; it would be more than compensation for pre-war disappointments in the Far East. Root was encouraging businessmen to look forward to repayment of loans in the form of concessions to exploit Russia's resources.[23] These alluring gleams were part of what led the U.S. to take a share in the war of intervention in Russia after 1918; they faded with its grey disillusion.

Recent experience in Mexico might well have made Wilson hesitant about this new and far bigger gamble. The manner of his decision threw into relief what Kennan called 'The extraordinary workings of the American mind in matters of inter-Allied relations.'[24] It came in 'a single vague and cryptic declaration',[25] in July 1918, very irritating to partners who had been pressing vainly for six months for joint action in Siberia against the Bolsheviks. Wilson and Lansing were deeply mistrustful of the motives for this pressure, and they found a pretext for their own action in a desire to rescue the Czech ex-prisoners of war who seized Vladivostok. Lansing saw this as 'introducing a sentimental element into the question of our duty': helping the Czechs would be 'an entirely different thing from intervening on other grounds'.[26] To Europeans this kind of reasoning could only seem another piece of the American humbug that always aroused their ire. For America the affair had another awkward complication: it brought up the Japanese menace from a fresh angle. Japan was elbowing its way into Siberia, as well as into China, and would only too obviously want to stay in both and build a paramount position in the Far East.

Roosevelt was convinced that shortly before the German collapse Wilson was again scheming for a negotiated peace, followed by German membership of his projected League.[27] Such a denouement might well have suited him and the U.S. better than a too complete triumph of the Allies, to say nothing of the risk of social revolution spreading from Russia to a defeated Germany. He was weakened in another way by the elections of November 1918, which like the 'Khaki election' in Britain strengthened the right wing, so much so that Wilson himself could be charged with socialistic leanings. America was emerging from the war with the flush of success strongly tinged with reaction, and infected by contact with reactionary Allied governments, however much it might squabble with them. From now on anti-communism would be a permanent feature of the American advance in the world.

To the die-hards 'Moscow gold' was sufficient explanation of the rapid spread of Bolshevik ideas in Europe, and the proper way to counter them was by force; they wanted the intervention in the Russian Civil War to be pushed on. More sensible men saw that hunger was doing more to subvert society than gold, and Hoover, the future president, as Director-General of Relief, was arranging for food shipments to Europe. These, it was recognized, could also serve to win economic advantages, and 'speed the return of unfettered capitalism'.[28] Wilson called on Congress to expedite 'this means of stemming the tide of anarchism'; and industries with stocks to dispose of, as well as agriculture which had a large surplus on hand, were happy to combine business with philanthropy.[29] Lenin saw very clearly how food from America was being used to counter ideas from Russia. In 1921 he was realistic enough to try to get a share of it for famine relief in Russia, and asked his friend Gorky to ask Bernard Shaw and H.G. Wells to endorse an appeal.[30] Hoover imposed strict conditions, including payment in gold on the grounds that otherwise this gold would be utilized for subversion abroad.[31] In a hungry world American food surpluses have regularly played a double part, capitalist and humanitarian.

By then the war of intervention had petered out. It had opponents in the Senate like R.M. LaFollette and W.E. Borah; Wilson hoped that Bolshevism left to itself would collapse under its own weight of ineffectiveness, and he was also more and more nervous of Japan proving the chief beneficiary. His country was beginning to experience those complexities and perplexities of world-wide commitment which beset the British empire and in its final decades were gradually immobilizing it. Also, American as well as French and British soldiers were restless at being kept in the field after Germany's defeat, even if American labour was not capable of a 'Hands Off Russia' campaign.

This unlucky venture might well have had the effect in turn of cautioning Washington against any more entanglement in the devious doings of the old empires; in particular, against saddling itself with any of the colonial territories that were to come up for disposal. Nearly all of these would be embedded among possessions of other powers and their feudings and plottings, unlike America's existing island dependencies. Britain was playing once more the part of tempter. Its position in Asia was undermined, and needed fresh props, as it was realizing in the later stages of the war. A British cabinet paper of January 1918 asserted that German propaganda in the U.S., though furthered by the Irish, was failing to shift 'the stigma of Imperialism' from Germany to the Allies. But, it went on, the Middle East was now in a parlous state because Britain, having sacrificed its old friendship with Turkey and Islam in 1907 by joining hands with Russia, was now losing its Russian ally, and might find Bolshevism and Muslim nationalism both together on Germany's side. Britain lacked resources to confront such a combination. There was only one way out: 'To find a trustee for these countries acceptable to both parties. This could only be the United States.'[32]

Next year a similar suggestion came from a different quarter, in the form of a tentative proposal by some Turkish nationalists that America (which had not declared war on Turkey) should assume a mandate over their country, and rescue it from Anglo-French-Italian imperialism and Greek rapacity – 'the thousandfold methods of oppression that are practised on us by imperialistic Europe'. 'America', Halid Edib wrote to Kemal Pasha in August 1919, citing as proof the reorganization of the Philippines, 'is the only country that understands what the soul of a nation means and how a democratic regime is constituted ... It ... could create a new Turkey within the space of twenty years.' Kemal raised no objection in principle, but shrewdly enquired what the Americans would be expecting to get in return.[33] Not enough, it appears, for them to take the idea very seriously.

Clearly this unheroic wing of Turkish nationalism was taking a rosy view of America's colonial record, either from lack of information or from a belief that men like themselves would be able, as in the Philippines, to find a comfortable place as America's partners. This new model of colonialism which was being unveiled in 1919, the Mandate, might be described as a hybrid between the old type and the neo-colonial; and it might be said that the U.S. was already in the habit of conferring mandates on itself from time to time in Central America. There was some fear among men like Lansing that Wilson's exuberant talk of self-determination might unsettle the British empire; to call the captured

German and Ottoman possessions 'mandates', nominally at least under only temporary administration for their own good, instead of annexing them, offered a happy compromise.

Wilson wanted also to confer responsibilities on the League, which all the Allies agreed must be set up to satisfy public feeling, but to which he wanted to give a particular impress. Mandates could be put, again at least nominally, under its authority. Lansing, who remained sceptical, discovered that his chief was deeply impressed by a phrase coined by Smuts, about the proposed League as 'the heir of the Empires'.[34] It fitted quite well into the kind of ideas House had been canvassing just before the war. Smuts himself made a strong impression at Paris on Wilson, who was not without his own vein of racialism; while the South African was known to his countrymen as a very artful person. As we learn from his son's biography, he felt that it would not do to ask Wilson for leave to annex the German territory of South West Africa outright. 'He did the next best thing ... He saw to it that the Union took over South West Africa under a "C" Mandate, which was almost tantamount to annexation.'[35] Wilson was left to cherish the illusion that empire was fading into something new, a fresh era dawning.

Even so, America was not an applicant for any mandates. Wilson, it is true, could reckon that through his League he would be able to exercise a sort of supervision over them all; the mandate system might have developed differently had America, after all, joined the League. In the course of the peace conference, Britain gave a good deal of thought to bringing the U.S. into the colonial arena, partly in order to forestall any objections it might raise to British appropriations.[36] Now, as in 1898, it was being invited to take up its share of the white man's burden. Palestine was thought of as another suitable bait, but Lloyd George changed his mind about this: 'It would involve placing an absolutely new and crude Power in the middle of all our complicated interests in Egypt, Arabia, and Mesopotamia', he reflected.[37] German East Africa was brought up instead, and there was also talk of Armenia, a troublesome corner which nobody else wanted. Wilson personally would have been prepared to take Armenia on. His colonial adviser, G. L. Beer, was not at all reluctant;[38] and if something as attractive as the mandate of Iraq – rightly believed to be rich in oil – had been offered, Washington might perhaps have been pushed by the oil companies into accepting. If so, America could hardly have stayed out of the League, and history would have gone a different way. As it was, the net was spread in vain. It was remarkable testimony to America's ingrained aversion to old-style colonialism that, even now, all these blandishments were being rejected. This meant also, however, that American capitalism could feel so confident by this time in its overwhelming strength as to have no need of colonies, to be able to stride over all frontiers.

Wilson was aiming at something grander than any mere private sphere of influence: nothing less than a universal order, a world made safe for free enterprise by commonsense agreement among the governments that counted. In terms of capitalist evolution, such an ideal went with the trend towards international patent-sharings or price-fixings, harbingers of the 'multinational' corporations of the future. In political terms it went with the leaning America had already shown towards a sort of 'ultra-imperialism'. Many plans for regulating international relations were being bandied about, and here too Smuts was ready with a suggestion, for joint Great Power control or management of Eastern Europe, Western Asia and Asiatic Russia.[39]

Some such arrangement could appear all the more needful because the collapse of authority in Central and Eastern Europe had balkanized a great part of the continent. By welcoming the emergence of the new free countries, Wilson had helped to give the war a progressive complexion, but it went counter to the American preference for large agglomerations. A rabble of small nations in Europe could not be kept in order by the same simple methods as in Central America, and would be as much open to Bolshevik as to American influence. A League, however, would supply a framework. As the grand design took shape, painfully and imperfectly, it was not without a resemblance to the framework of the U.S. itself, with a General Assembly supplying like the Senate an equalitarian element, but also with a Council through which the bigger and richer countries could assert themselves.

Lansing objected on the score that it meant in reality 'the establishment of an international oligarchy of the Great Powers to direct and control world affairs'.[40] Possibly he perceived what Wilson did not, that the real weight would be with political and military strength, more than with financial. From Wilson's standpoint the defect lay in the 'oligarchs' being so slow to sink their trivial disagreements over anachronisms like frontiers. The other side of this was America's reluctance to supply leadership in a form, including armaments, which the Old World could recognize and respect. Spengler spoke for this Old World when he said that peoples concerned only with economic gain, like Carthaginians or Americans, are incapable of true political thinking.[41] There was some force in this, in the sense that bourgeois America was too rational for its thinking to be effective in a demented Europe. Conversely Europe, incapable of rising to the American level of rationality, was condemning itself to the futilities of the next twenty years, and another great war.

America refused to join the League, in spite of the campaign of persuasion on which Wilson spent his remaining strength. There was disgust at having been dragged into the European morass; there was impatience for the U.S. to be free to act by itself, for instance in its own sphere of influence, Central America. There was a fear too that League debates and disputes would have a divisive effect on multinational America. 'It will all tend to delay the Americanization of our great population', said Lodge, leading the anti-League phalanx in the Senate, and the need 'to make all these people good Americans' was far more important than any petty European wrangles.[42] Good Americans were, of course, devotees of free enterprise, admirers of big business, and Europeans too often were not.

In a speech in London, Wilson ascribed to ordinary soldiers he had talked with a resolve 'to do away with an old order and to establish a new one': to get rid of balance-of-power politics where 'the balance was determined by the sword . . . by the unstable equilibrium of competitive interests'.[43] It was no bad summing up of the old order, which the man in the street, or the trench, really did, however dimly, want to be delivered from. Addressing the peace conference, Wilson declared that 'The fortunes of mankind are now in the hands of the plain people of the whole world.'[44] There was too much in this of an American fancy or pretence that all men not belted earls or jackbooted generals are 'plain men', from millionaires down. For Wilson himself it must have had a psychological lure. 'President Wilson was silent, secretive and detached from the normal incidental contact of diplomacy',[45] or of anything else: to a man like him the idea of open diplomacy, public treaties, a plain man's era, would have a deceptive charm. His own practice, however, belonged far more to the secret labyrinth over which American hegemony would one day be reared. The truth of his situation was that during his presidency, especially during the war, he had isolated himself from the common man, or the nation's more progressive forces, whose backing he now wanted.

2

Victory and After: the Mirror of Science Fiction

On 10 July 1919, President Wilson gave the Senate his justification of the peace treaties and of the League of Nations and America's duty to lead the world. It was a compendium of a century of swelling augury and aspiration, ripe now for fulfilment. Tied to the tail of his kite were all the string of catchphrases, clichés, metaphors with which politicians had shepherded the country on its long march towards grandeur: vision, dream, spirit, truth, light ... 'The stage is set, the destiny disclosed. It has come about by no plan of our conceiving, but by the hand of God who led us into this way ...'. Cromwellian and Miltonic overtones are very audible; and as Cromwell said, no man goes further than he who does not know where he is going.

America turned its back on the League, but this did not mean renouncing the world; rather, confidence of ability to make its weight felt without need of any compromizing leagues or alliances. There was a real and jubilant sense of a new era opening, a new and American page of history being turned. Years before this time, Henry Adams, visiting the Pacific, met a Samoan chief who assured him with emotion 'that his only hope was in Christ and America'.[46] Now the U.S. was of age, a great force in the world, equal to all such hopes, ready to be the dispenser, arbiter, prophet of the age. It alone had ascended Mount Sinai, interviewed the Almighty, and brought back the tablets of the Law. 'The God of Israel', a clergyman exclaimed, 'has anointed us to champion the cause of the poor, the weak and the downtrodden. We also shall struggle for world power.'[47] Liberation and domination, as often in America's daydreams, went together.

In the literature of a nation learning to tower among the peoples, little was left of the soaring imagination that earlier, fresher moods kindled in Melville or Whitman. The best of their successors were not enthusiastic about the empire now a-building, as the earlier writers, seeing it rhapsodically from afar, had been. And if these earlier writers tended to drift away abroad, this went furthest with Henry James, who renounced his native land altogether and became an Englishman, of the Order of Merit. England was always the touchstone of American feelings about the world, and they can be seen polarized between James's savouring of an old, rich civilization, a London where everything was bathed in a mellow 'international' light,[48] and Mark Twain's skit on it as still an ancient Britain:[49] a side-splittingly funny picture, but a none the less devastating satire on Europe's atavistic class system, its brutal indifference to the common man, its senseless bellicosity.

This did nothing to abate the popularity of that ancient Briton, Kipling, whose vogue beyond the Atlantic was to last longer than at home; the U.S. would still be advancing when the trident was slipping from Britannia's hand. His gospel of *service* by the white man to the colony he administered, which could so easily sink into cant, rhymed with the businessman's own cant of service to the public. An American domiciled in England noted in 1936 that 'Kipling has little or no message for the youth of this country ... though I believe that in America he is still a best-seller'.[50] At the end of the Second World War a Navy Secretary, Forrestal, circulated copies of Kipling among his friends, as part of a crusade to keep America from disarming.[51]

Fiction of the Kipling school shaded away in one direction into the Western saga, whose Buffalo Bill had something of the gentlemanlike quality and sang-froid of a Kipling hero. Wild West yarns, still inexhaustibly pouring out, fitted in well with Dollar Diplomacy and the exploits of the marines, another sort of vigilantes stepping in to establish law and order and protect legitimate interests from Caribbean equivalents of outlaws or bad Indians, as men like 'Denver Dan and his Mystic Band' did at home. The American who read of these stirring deeds was a more dualistic creature than the European, because he, like his country, contained within him both a sober New Hampshire and a lawless Nevada, and could enjoy the sensation both of unfettered adventure and of vindicated virtue.

Into a tale of the Wild West a new mystery weapon might stray:[52] its mythology shaded in turn, as fantasy came under the sway of technology, into the fiction of space travel and exploration, another escape from the closed frontier. This branch of the novelist's art was opened up by French and English writers, Jules Verne and H.G. Wells, whose mortals or Martians voyaged through space, and cosmic battle loomed, while the French and British empires reached out and collided with strange races. It was then naturalized in America and reflected American expansionism in all its quirks and confusions. Its grand pioneer was Edgar Rice Burroughs, who served briefly in the cavalry, prospected for gold in Oregon, herded cattle in Idaho, donned a policeman's uniform in Salt Lake City: his life a good sample of American experience, except that he was a failure until he started the series of novels that sold in dozens of millions of copies.

How the moving frontier of the West turned into a more elastic frontier in space may be seen from the opening of his first story, and the first of his most remarkable set of romances, *A Princess of Mars*. Written in 1912, it starts with the hero in Arizona, pursued by a band of Apaches thirsting for 'the fiendish pleasure of the torture', but abruptly translated to Mars to continue his wanderings through Arizona-like deserts among four-armed green men still more addicted to the same pleasure. Captain Carter is a Virginian, late of the Confederate army, and very much a gentleman. In his person the Chicago-born Burroughs is literally regenerated into a new world, leaving his old body behind on earth and putting on a fresh one on Mars, where like the fortunate young peasant of folklore he marries a beautiful princess.

Tarzan of the Apes, his other archetypal creation, appeared in 1914 and had immediate, enormous success. Tarzan turns out to be an English nobleman, lost at birth in the jungle; he is indeed an idealized portrait of an athletic British aristocracy. Snobbery of race and class are happily blended in these two variations on the Nietzschean Superman, the 'blonde beast', who was coming into fashion by 1914 and whispering in the youthful ears of Mussolini and Hitler and thousands like them. (Tarzan is in fact spoken of as a 'super-man'.[53]) If Kipling invaded the U.S., Burroughs invaded Britain, where both his leading figures found the warmest of welcomes. His *Princess* was first published there in the year after the Great War, and ran through nine editions in eighteen months. It and its sequels have been reprinted in the past few years, proof of a remarkable buoyancy.

Tarzan can be traced to many sources.[54] There are, for instance, in the first novel of the series obvious echoes of *The Jungle Book*. Tarzan with his 'godlike exterior', and disposition to match, belongs to the genus Noble Savage, but he is also a true-blue white man; a solitary white man keeping at bay the wild creatures round him, including the Africans, by higher skill and invincible courage, very much as Kipling's district officers mastered their underlings. Kipling is said to have greatly enjoyed Tarzan, easily recognizing in him a likeness to Mowgli. He faces life with 'that self-confidence and resourcefulness which were the badges of his superior being';[55] he faces a gorilla in the spirit of one in whose veins 'flowed the blood of the best of a race of mighty fighters'.[56] When we hear Senator Lodge in 1919 denouncing the Bolsheviks as 'a band of anthropoid apes',[57] we may surmise that he too has been reading Tarzan.

Burroughs's Africans show American anti-colonialism and racialism side by side. Tarzan's black neighbours are fugitives from cruel oppression by the rubber-collectors of 'that arch hypocrite, Leopold II of Belgium'.[58] On the other hand they are such a beastly lot that, the reader must feel, scarcely any fate could be too bad for them. 'Their yellow teeth were filed to sharp points, and their great protruding lips added still further to the low and bestial brutishness of their appearance.'[59] They are cannibals (like the sophisticated black race on Mars), and torture their victims at the stake exactly like Red Indians painted black. Tarzan has no feeling of kinship with them, except that an obscure instinct warns him not to eat any of those he kills. A 'sleek and hideous thing of ebony' is his impression of the first he meets.[60] ('Hideous' is the stock epithet for them all.) Tired of ruling his ape tribe, he goes off in search of true fellow-men, white folk like himself. Before long he has found a white woman to fall in love with; she is an American, a Southerner attended by a conventionally ridiculous negress named Esmeralda. She is also laudably patriotic,[61] and the union constitutes an Anglo-American, or Anglo-Saxon romance.

On Mars, Burroughs's inventive gifts had a far more spacious field. Barsoom is a highly aristocratic world of jewelled nobles and ladies and their slaves, its sole form of government monarchy, though with a more than American technology – rifles with wireless range-finders firing radium bullets eighty miles, telescopes revealing every event on other planets, monster battleships of the artificial air. Life is so warlike that even clerks wear swords at their desks. Americans too are fond of owning weapons, but they have had sensibly little taste for massed armies and parade-grounds; and on Mars pitched battles, except in the air or among the green savages, are few: it is the duel, or the lone fighter against odds, that we watch, spellbound – as, once more, in the Wild West. Men fight hand to hand, by a chivalrous code, and John Carter, though called on in the course of his exploits to dispose of legions of opponents, and priding himself on his miraculous swordsmanship, has nothing of the juggernaut conqueror about him. Altogether it makes a bizarre but compelling spectacle, proof of how nostalgia for Old World glories and grandeurs, fanned by breezes from the Old South and West, jostled in the American mind with the glamour of dollars and cents, and progress.

Still, in this American mind moonshine and daylight have had a knack of keeping not too far apart, as they ought to when a nation is energetically pushing out into the world and into history. Burroughs knew a good deal of life, and he was writing other novels about drug addiction, lynch-law, prostitution, the big-business jungle. (He set out at first to write science fiction under the pseudonym 'Normal Bean', meaning normal head, or sound mind.[62]) Amid much that is absurd in the Martian epic, there runs a vein of Yankee modernity, rationality, contempt for outworn creed or superstition, not without a resemblance to Mark Twain's. Burroughs's hero stands, as an American should wherever he goes, for enlightenment. In the second of the three first and best novels of the series, he delivers Mars from the tyranny of a false faith kept up by cunning priestcraft, a distillation of the outlandish native cults from which the white man was freeing earth. There is an oddly moving speech by the green warrior whom his friend returns from earth to find battling with ferocious creatures in the mysterious valley whither the credulous are enticed. 'This is the valley of love and peace and rest to which every Barsoomian since time immemorial has longed to pilgrimage at the end of a life of hate and strife and bloodshed ... This, John Carter, is heaven.'[63]

Subsequently it falls to the hero, and then his descendants, to enfranchise gifted individuals among sundry strange races from thraldom to outworn custom, mental chains, beginning with the inhumanly rigid collectivism (in which we may detect a travesty of socialism) of the green hordes. Rationality is again at odds with superstition in the third novel of the series, where the archpriest of the false religion finally meets with a grim but well-deserved death. A newly discovered land of yellow men in the arctic north is ruled by a despot who venerates a species of monstrous white beasts, which the nephew who supplants him announces his sensible intention of wiping out. International relations, however, are this time the main theme. At the outset the arrogant black race has just been overthrown by a victorious coalition, and its country occupied. 'From the high pinnacle of their egotism the First Born had been plunged to the depths of humiliation' – as the Germans had just been, we may add. At the conclusion, we take leave of a planet welded into a 'sodality of nations'.[64]

Fighting his way to the Teutonic title of 'Warlord of Mars', the hero has nevertheless brought with him from his native soil the American instinct for rational, orderly arrangement. American leadership might be failing to bring the wrangling terrestrial powers together, but on Mars it was inaugurating a reign of peace, through a federation of the most powerful kingdoms under the guidance of Helium. Most civilized among the Barsoomian peoples are the red men, but leagued with them now are white, black, and yellow, and even the non-human green swarms. Civilization rises above colour or race. And just as there is no question of Mars being conquered by America, but only by American ideas, old imperialistic custom on Barsoom is jettisoned, and each people left under its own sovereign. The new ruler of the north, hitherto a forbidden land as impenetrable as old Japan or Tibet, proclaims an open door policy, extending a welcome to all comers.

Admired and loved as the hero is, he remains in a way very much alone. He narrates his adventures himself, and none of the other personages have any inwardness: they are seen exclusively through his eyes. There is an unconscious parable here of America in a world out of phase with it, which it was quickly having doubts about its ability to remould. It may be a symptom of the years when the euphoria of 1919 was wearing off that Burroughs was descending from the open skies of Mars (where only the blacks lived underground) into the ghostly interior of the earth or the moon. He was preoccupied now with the spectre of communism, or a mindless revolt of the masses. This pursued him on the moon and on Venus, as if the solar system was being exposed to a sort of domino process. With this went a lamentable falling off of quality, very obvious in the two lunar novels, written in 1923 and 1925 with a patently didactic purpose.

Across Burroughs's orbit the shadow of revolution had fallen, and instead of Martian magnificence everything on or in the moon is grey and dingy. Here is another polarity between civilization and barbarism, human and non-human, the latter this time a breed of centaurs, with a degraded religion and, once again, a close resemblance in temper to 'the savage Indians of the western plains' of bygone days[65] – resurrected far away to allow American explorers to pursue their time-honoured warfare. Here too is another princess to be rescued from the savages by an American hero, but a poor Cinderella by comparison. In the good old days power and wealth were unequally shared, but generously used; in contrast, mass education spawned a secret society of 'Thinkers', who spread discontent until the commoners rose in rebellion. 'The Thinkers would do no work, and the result was that both government and commerce fell into rapid decay.'[66] One remnant of the old culture survives, where 'people of highly refined sensibilities' are waited on by descendants of 'the faithful servitors who had remained loyal to the noble classes'[67] like darkies faithful to their white masters: older and new aberrations of American thinking run together. Even this last haven is crumbling now, with an ambitious demagogue stirring up a 'rabble' poor at fighting – 'one noble is worth ten of them' – but equipped by a renegade earthman.[68]

Meanwhile earth has been in good shape, half a century of conflict after 1914 having ended in 'the absolute domination of the Anglo-Saxon race'. But the time comes when it is enfeebled by an anti-scientific cult, and pacifists who cripple the combined armed forces of the U.S. and Britain, 'weaklings' like those excoriated by Roosevelt. It was only 'England's king who saved us from the full disaster of this mad policy'. In the year 2050 earth is invaded and overwhelmed by hordes from the moon, whose rabble are now 'seasoned warriors': a reflex of the West's double image of Soviet Russia as pathetically inept and formidably powerful. These invaders are joined by all 'the lazy, the inefficient, the defective, who ever place the blame for their failures upon the shoulders of the successful'.[69] Being collectivists as well as imperialists, the conquerors instead of forcing earth men to toil for them only permit them to work four hours a day, and life relapses into bleak drabness. Resistance is kept up by free Americans in Arizona, who have slaves to do their work for them, and wear feathers and follow tribal chiefs as if they had turned (as in Spengler's forecast) into Red Indians. In the end their dashing young leader defeats the moon men and becomes overlord of America.

3

America, the World's Banker

Whatever its dreams of grandeur after the Great War, on land America had no intention of keeping up its armaments. Once more disgruntled patriots saw their country throwing away the sword and succumbing to delusions of perpetual peace. 'Well-meaning idealists of a fatty nation propagated rapidly within certain sects and schools.'[70] A National Defense Act of 1920 fixed the limit of peacetime strength at 280,000 men, and in 1922 it was reduced to 175,000. But an imposing navy was being maintained, and its strength was advertised by the Washington Conference of 1921–22. This was summoned by way of a supplement to the peace conference, a demonstration of American ability to improve on it and its treaties. By the 5–5–3 ratio, parity was achieved with the British fleet, and the Japanese kept substantially smaller. At the same time these two were being separated. The war had put a strain on their partnership, and the U.S. wanted it ended. 'American opinion had developed a neurosis towards the Anglo-Japanese alliance', and blamed it for all miscarriages in the Far East.[71] Finding Washington and Tokyo 'apparently irreconcilable', as a Foreign Office paper in 1919 said, London could not hesitate for long.[72] The alliance was replaced by a harmless Four Power Treaty, by which these three and France undertook to respect, and very vaguely to guarantee, one another's Pacific possessions.

Economically America in the 1920s was going from strength to strength. Recovering after 1921 from post-war difficulties, industry had grown in 1929 by

45%, with only trivial recessions, while exports grew even more, and a big trade surplus encouraged investment abroad. This had doubled between 1913 and 1919, leaving the U.S. a net creditor by more than $3,000 million, instead of a debtor. In the next decade it furnished two thirds of all new long-term foreign investment, or nearly $9,000 million more.[73] Avaricious lenders in those years, it has been mildly observed, 'sometimes overlooked the pecuniary welfare of the recipients. The United States was particularly culpable in this respect'.[74] But nearly a third of its holdings in 1930 were in Europe, where its loans helped to bolster shaky capitalist economies, especially Germany's, as they were to do again on a bigger scale after 1945. At the same time America was earning the name of 'Uncle Shylock' by its insistence on repayment of war debts, while payment was made more difficult by its unwillingness to reduce tariffs. This contradiction between appetite for profits from abroad and lack of digestive organs to absorb them was to be a feature of America's foreign economic relations for a long time to come.

Relying primarily on economic strength to achieve its purposes, the State Department from early in 1922 called on companies to notify it of any proposed lending. 'After that date almost every foreign loan had the approval of the United States government.'[75] Politics and finance were converging, but not yet nearly so fully as they had done much earlier in Europe. Walter Lippmann was to complain that all through the first half of this century America had no foreign policy.[76] States crowded together in old Europe were always forced to think 'politically', to meditate on their ambitions and frame plans accordingly. Britain had been partly free from this compulsion; America was still more securely remote, though in a shrinking world it was coming to form a new 'Middle Kingdom', between Europe and the Far East. It was less in need of a deliberate programme, and the range and diversity of its burgeoning interests made it in any case an arduous task to design one. A writer on Pacific problems in 1921 remarked that they interested mainly the West Coast states, whereas the Eastern were preoccupied with European events. 'We think that America is a nation, but the utter ignorance of one section with regard to another ... is appalling.'[77]

Ethnic minorities were not the sole divisive factor. They were a diminishing factor now, because mass immigration had been interrupted by the war, and was ended in 1922 by the quota system. For Europe this was the closing of a frontier, and an addition to inter-war frustration and instability. For America it meant a more distinct identity and self-sufficiency. Isolation, so strenuously preached, went naturally with this. It implied no withdrawal from competition. Rather it meant that economic activity pushed out in advance of official calculations, and the less there was of regular policy, the more readily each interest could impose its wishes on the government. The flag was following trade. Far and wide American dealers were looking for open doors, or trying to push doors open.

With its strength on the oceans and its financial preponderance America could not but be suspected of angling for the mastery it was only to achieve after 1945. Emergent communism of course thought of it as the grand capitalist fortress. In his *Imperialism and World Economy*, written in 1915 (shortly before he left Europe for America) Bukharin spoke of 'the appearance on the world arena of one of the largest state capitalist trusts' – U.S. capitalism as a whole.[78] In a post-war preface to his 1916 tract on *Imperialism*, Lenin treated the U.S. as now fully committed to the same pattern of behaviour as Europe. In July 1921 the third congress of the new Communist International predicted that either England would have to sink into the background, or 'in the near future be forced to engage all the forces it has acquired in the past in a life-and-death struggle with the United States', using Japan as an auxiliary.[79] Next month, with the Washington Conference looming up, the executive committee reversed this forecast by saying that Britain, forced to choose between the United States and Japan, would choose the former, and the result would be 'the formation of an Anglo-Saxon capitalist trust', under American headship, at Japan's expense.[80] Future events were to show some truth in this prognostication, though they lay further away than its authors supposed. The same might be said of some words of Trotsky in the manifesto of the fifth congress: 'This American "pacifist" program of putting the whole world under her control is not at all a program of peace. On the contrary it is pregnant with wars and the greatest revolutionary convulsions ....'.[81]

Forebodings about Britain passing under American sway were far from being confined to Marxists. On 16 July 1921, the London cabinet discussed the matter in a gloomy vein which would greatly have amused any agent of Moscow at the keyhole. It was complained that 'the United States was continually suggesting that the American navy was available for the protection of civilization and the white races of the world'.[82] For many years Britannia had prided herself on 'policing the seas', now a stronger rival was getting ready to take over the task. The racialist note in American thinking was again clear. Private observers too in

Britain were aware of a gathering transatlantic cloud. 'The moment has come', D.H. Lawrence wrote in 1923 in what might be called his vorticist style, 'when America, that extremist in world assimilation and world-oneness, is reacting into violent egocentricity, a truly American egocentricity. As sure as fate we are on the brink of American empire.'[83] In 1929 Bernard Shaw's play *The Applecart* depicted a patriotic King Magnus endeavouring to escape promotion to Emperor of America, and to save Britain and its empire from being swallowed into the American maw. That same year when Ramsey Macdonald visited Washington, the first British premier to do so, President Hoover suggested that he might like to hand over Bermuda, British Honduras and Trinidad, in lieu of war debts. 'He did not rise to the idea at all', Hoover regretfully records.[84]

While Britain and Europe felt nervous of an American ascendancy, America still had a resentful feeling that Britain wanted to keep it under tutelage, or *in statu pupillari*. ('A Dominion gone wrong' was the summary verdict on the U.S. still being repeated after the Second World War by an authority on Common-wealth studies at Cambridge.) One of its representatives at the Lausanne con-ference in 1923, Child, thought that the Englishmen there were trying to work amicably with the Americans, but could not quite bring themselves to treat them as equals. He thought all the European participants old, dried up, useless; the Genoa conference in 1922 similarly struck him as a scene of intrigue, jealousy, futility, a total absence of any spirit of co-operation.[85] Americans were viewing Europe very much as Britain or France had always viewed the squabbling Balkans.

Child favoured a firm line with the brawlers and babblers. He professed 'infinite faith in the rightness and power in world affairs of a sensible and scientific rather than a sentimental America'.[86] Hoover likewise was confirmed by post-war experience of Europe in his belief that 'the American System ... was alone the promise of human progress and the force which had led our nation to greatness'.[87] 'Europe was infested with age-old hates and fears with their off-spring of military alliances and increasing armaments. Its rival imperialisms continued as smoldering fires ... I had no desire to see the United States involved.'[88] Powerful nations, like powerful classes, are quick to identify the light of reason with their own way of seeing things. Yet it must be confessed that, in judgements like these, there was a great deal of force. The contrast between the placid confederal politics of the American Union and the madhouse of inter-war Europe was startling, and revealed America as indeed a new and superior civilization. To look back on the statesmanship of the era when Mussolini was 'indulging his favourite pastime, sabre-rattling',[89] is like gazing into a nursery full of unruly children, spitefully busy tweaking each other's hair and kicking each other's shins.

Even Britain, which Washington wanted to stay on good terms with, was felt to have its share of transatlantic folly, particularly in its persistence in naval competition.[90] In H.G. Wells's fantasy novel of 1930, *The Autocracy of Mr Parham*, this notion was fully endorsed. A British dictator from Oxford, full of archaic infatuations, after attacking the Soviet Union blunders into war with America, and the two fleets sink each other in a great Atlantic battle. The American president then strikes a new note of sanity in world affairs by announcing a unilateral abandonment of the conflict. 'In America there is still an immense sentiment towards world peace', says Sir W. Atterbury, a pillar of the League.[91] And General Gerson, the Neanderthal soldier, laments that 'the business men and the bankers are rotten with pacifism. They get it out of the air. They get it from America. God knows how they get it! "Does war *pay?*" they ask....'.[92]

How limited on some sides was the New World's vision showed in one way in its refusal to see in the U.S.S.R. another, though very different, breakaway from the European madhouse. One administration after another withheld recognition. 'I often', Hoover recalls, 'likened the problem to having a wicked and disgraceful neighbour. We did not attack him, but we did not give him a certificate of character.'[93] There is a saving grace in one, negative clause; after America's half-hearted participation in the Intervention, to think of attacking Soviet Russia again was left to the wildest of the Europeans. On the other hand again, some of these enjoyed a fair measure of sympathy among some Americans. If Europe was such a bedlam, deaf to the voice of reason from across the Atlantic, or else dissolving into communism, an order of things loudly proclaiming itself both up-to-date and anti-communist, like Fascist Italy's, could count on a welcome.

With Mussolini, soon followed by Primo de Rivera in Spain and Salazar in Portugal, rule by caudillo was entering Western Europe, by its southern or Latin door. It was a mode of government the U.S. was already familiar with, and knew how to utilize, in Latin America. Morgan loans helped Mussolini to establish his position.[94] A diplomat like Child could admire him, as many of his tribe were to admire later dictators; so, more oddly, could a man like Lincoln Steffens, who was enthusiastic about the Soviet Union.[95] There has been in Americans, conscious of their country's vast potentialities, a streak of readiness to be dazzled by any display of power, any parade of will and purpose by Men of Action like the windbag *Duce*. Herman Melville admired Nicholas I, the policeman of Europe; Theodore Roosevelt admired all strong men until his animus against the Germans in the Great War left him uncertain 'whether most to admire their efficiency or to abhor their hideous moral degeneracy'.[96] Strength and civilization were not, after all, one and the same thing.

Open or sneaking approval of fascism (widespread in Britain too) was the more insidious because at home in America the Progressivist era and its culminating war had not in the end banished the atmosphere of class conflict. Like the Civil War, or any other big conflict, the Great War bred racketeers and profiteers as well as heroes, and the 'hard-faced businessmen' were as firmly in the saddle in America as in Britain. Labour was unable to defend itself effectively against the Red-baiting of the 1920s, American capitalism's domestic crusade against the socialist peril that Mussolini and his ilk were combating abroad. Legal or illegal pressures were employed, extending at times to violence, while big business played on the fears of timid citizens 'by dubbing every union man as a red and by associating all union activities with revolution, and union leaders with bolshevism'.[97] In short, the masses at home were being treated very much as those in America's economic dependencies have gone on being treated. But American labour, divided against itself by the War and then by the Russian Revolution, never learned to make common cause with the colonial peoples.

'United States capital is turning away more and more from the chaos in Europe', the Third International commented late in 1922, 'and is trying most successfully to build a large colonial empire in Central and South America and the Far East.'[98] 'Colonial empire' may sound a misnomer, but Leninist theory made little distinction between direct and indirect rule. Capitalist practice made a great deal. As Norman Angell pointed out, American businessmen wanted a 'stable' regime in Mexico, but they did not want the country annexed, because then they would be trammelled with U.S. labour laws and other impediments.[99]

A hopeful liberal writing in 1921 regretted that 'Few Americans have ever taken any interest in their insular possessions.'[100] In the Philippines he thought (mistakenly) his country had made the first effort in colonial history 'to treat its subject natives with any degree of equality, – legally, if not socially'. He did not want the islands kept as a strategic base against Japan. 'We need the Philippines more as a base for democratic experiment than as a fortified zone.' Successful production there of the democratic 'serum' could be used to inoculate Japan. 'Let the germs of democracy persist in the Philippines and be rushed to the island empire. And let America stand as a great moral force, impressing upon Japan that the rights of the people shall not be suppressed.'[101] Here was America's favourite medical imagery again, along with the concept of a moral, rather than military, hegemony; a hope of converting Japan by peaceful example, as Gandhi was trying to convert British imperialism. Here too was the besetting failure to be aware of the stultifying absence of anything like social equality or justice in the Philippines, or anywhere else under American (or European) sway, direct or indirect.

As early as 1902 Roosevelt had forecast eventual independence for the islands; in 1904 Root predicted that they would gain the same status as Cuba.[102] An obvious difference was that forces withdrawn from Cuba could quietly return there at any moment, whereas to send them back across the Pacific would make too much stir. Somehow, while Washington continued to talk of freedom for them one day, the stars and stripes continued to float over them. In 1916 the Jones Act transferred most internal affairs to reliable Filipino hands, but further concessions made after the war fell far short of what the national leadership was hoping for. Coolidge had to cope with feelings ruffled by governor-general L. Wood, who 'acted like a military martinet and as something of a racist', but did so by upholding him; he made some amends by designating as his successor in 1927 the far more tactful Stimson, later Secretary of State.[103] Angell found a fresh buttress for his grand thesis, that sensible capitalism had no need to quarrel over colonies, in 'an intense *capitalist* agitation (from the sugar, cotton and oil interests) for the independence of the Philippines', inspired by the wish to exclude their competing products.[104] This contradiction, little known to British colonialism, was raising its head again.

Hoover might want more Caribbean territories for strategic purposes – in that region a highly flexible concept – but otherwise he professed dislike for any permanent possessions. 'Our mission was to free people, not to dominate them.'[105] But he held that, without its present advantage of free trade with the U.S., the economy of the Philippines would collapse, so that independence for it would be precarious. He might have added that colonialism is always apt to produce or perpetuate a lopsided, limping economy. In December 1932 he vetoed an independence bill passed by a Democrat Congress. Filipinos already enjoyed, he declared, 'as great a substance of ordered liberty and human freedom as any people in the world'. He was forgetting the peasantry and their feudal bonds, as Americans have nearly always done. He may have been more correct in asserting that, in private, the upper-class Filipino leaders did not really want independence.[106]

By the later 1920s Cuba was supplying nearly half of American sugar consumption. Wartime boom conditions gave way to reviving competition from beet, and there was further strenuous jockeying over tariffs among the multiple interests concerned.[107] Whoever gained, it would not be the labourers. A wave of strikes, and fear of social upheaval, was a leading cause of the U.S. intervention in 1917. Another big strike in 1919 brought warships flocking to Havana. Next year saw deepening financial and political crisis. Wilson, who had a reputation to live up to now, shrank from sending more troops; instead he sent a General Crowder on special mission. By 1922 Crowder had worked out a 'moralization' programme, and began plying a reluctant President Zayas with his 'famous "Fifteen Memoranda" dealing with political and financial reform'.[108] *Reform* of course meant ensuring high profits for planters and bankers. Discontent found expression in nationalist complaints, to soothe which the U.S. had to make a number of concessions, including withdrawal of marines sent in 1917. Reassurance for vested interests came with the presidency, from 1925, of Machado, a businessman who earned the cordial support of American businessmen by pursuing policies agreeable to them while striking nationalist attitudes, and firmly silencing objectors. This worked well till the slump came, and few Americans cared to ask how ordinary Cubans were faring. 'In Cuba, as in other parts of Central America and the Caribbean, stability covered a multitude of sins.'[109]

In Mexico, because of political troubles, American investment fell off during the 1920s; elsewhere in the New World it expanded, in South America rapidly for the first time. It still largely took the form of usury capital, as with earlier practitioners, especially the French; it was to shift more and more towards direct investment, extractive or productive, but at present any effect of enlarging local economies was limited. Far more dollars went in loans, chiefly to governments and municipalities, and nearly all Latin American states were adding to their indebtedness. As before, protection of the New World from European intrusion was also a goal for U.S. monopoly. 'In practice it became a further stage in the successful efforts of American business to displace their European rivals, but it covered their efforts with the mantle of moral rectitude.'[110]

In the Isthmian region of Central America an adequate degree of supervision through local bosses continued to be the aim, but resort to more direct methods was still needed on occasion. It was 'primarily for benevolent reasons', we are assured, because of their disorderliness, that Haiti was occupied in 1915 and turned into a protectorate, and the Dominican Republic taken over in 1916.[111] But the end of the war brought mounting criticism, especially because management was left too much in military or naval hands, and in Haiti two thousand rebels had been killed, as against minute American losses. Some changes had to be introduced. A British diplomat in the Middle East felt it a little hard that his government's agreement of 1919 with Persia should be stigmatized by Washington as interference in Persian affairs, while American marines patrolled both these two countries and Nicaragua.[112]

At the end of 1926 another marine operation in Nicaragua was decided on. There were protests in the press and in Congress; Senator Borah, less one-sided in his isolationist principles than some others, was an objector. There was civil strife, but State Secretary Kellogg's clumsy attempt to depict it as due to communist influence was derided by critics.[113] It was good enough for labour leaders, and the A.F.L. gave its cordial blessing to the intervention against 'communist subversion'.[114] In later days labour was to come forward as promptly on behalf of bigger American actions abroad. Mexico was being watched all the more vigilantly because of rumours of communism there, which interested parties could easily set afloat. Yet even in Central America the other face of the U.S., so often obscured by the worse, could shine through here and there. Aldous Huxley stayed at Quirigua with Dr N.P. MacPhail, director of the United Fruit Company's hospital, and found him an admirable physician, 'the universal god-father of Guatemala', battling with the virulent malaria of the valley.[115]

On the official level there was a recurrent impulse towards showing the better face: administrations tended to have fits of deathbed repentance as they drew to a close. Disillusioned with the results of its Caribbean exercises, during 1920–21 Wilson's government set out 'to match more closely American deeds with its professed ideals in Latin America', and thereby, it has been maintained, 'contributed significantly to the progress of PanAmericanism'.[116] In 1921 a representative was being chosen for a goodwill tour of Latin America. General Pershing, the invader of Mexico, was proposed for the duty, but some envoys in Washington felt him to be 'not entirely suitable'.[117] Coolidge in turn tried to varnish things over by sending Stimson on a mission to Nicaragua, and by encouraging his successor-elect, Hoover, to tour Latin America. Hoover found a 'sinister notion' current, as he said in a speech in 1929, 'fear of an era of the mistakenly called dollar diplomacy': he disclaimed any right of the U.S. 'to intervene *by force*' for the benefit of business interests abroad, and wanted 'the moral rectitude of the United States' to be more fully displayed.[118] There are of course other, quieter ways of achieving the purposes of intervention. He laid down that there was to be no more resort to arms except to safeguard American lives; issued in 1930 a definition of the Monroe Doctrine shorn of Theodore Roosevelt's gloss, thus 'eliminating the idea that we were concerned with the domestic affairs of the other American Republics'; and admonished bankers against the sort of unscrupulous loans they had been floating.[119] Later on he began to remove marines from Nicaragua; withdrawal from Haiti was also started.

All this was very well, but Washington had an air of continually turning over the same new leaf: goodwill missions continued to be mechanical routines, Pan-American fraternity a will-o'-the-wisp. *Plus ça change*, critics south of the Río Grande could be excused for thinking. A gradual shift was in progress none the less from open meddling by Washington to self-help by business interests powerful enough to fend for themselves, with more discreet backing behind the scenes. An example could be found in Peru, where the big Cerro de Pasco mining company had been at work since the start of the century. A smelter installed in 1922 ruined an immense area of pasture by pollution from noxious gases: intentionally, Peruvians asserted, in order to compel farmers to join its labour force. Meanwhile the company bought up a great deal of pasture-land, restored it, brought in breeding experts, and became the country's biggest raiser of sheep.[120] U.S. technology was showing its versatility, and the contradictory consequences it could have. Relations with U.S. officialdom, if not with the Peruvian public, were smooth. It was a matter of course that the company's manager 'called the [U.S.] ambassador to his office for what amounted to instructions.'[121]

A circumstance that was making Washington more chary of visibly helping to squeeze British or other competition out of Latin America was that other gov-

ernments now, notably the British in the Middle East, were being more actively
pressed to accept open door policies. Hitherto for Americans a sandy wilderness
attractive to few but missionaries, the Middle East was abruptly transformed by
the collapse of the Ottoman empire and the gushing of oil, that liquid gold of the
20th century. American companies had been selling home-produced oil all over
the world; to keep their grip on world markets they now had to find additional
supplies abroad. Eager to extend their tentacles into these fruitful deserts, they
could play on fears, partly genuine, of an approaching dearth of oil reserves at
home.

Gloomy talk of shortages of raw materials already had a long history. Early in
the century there was controversy between Carnegie and Schwab about how long
iron ores would last.[122] Estimates about oil have fluctuated more widely than any
others, and after 1918 America was faced with schemes of British capitalists to
corner production; there were even rumours, exaggerated no doubt, of an
approaching oil war between the two countries. Persia's southern oilfields were in
British hands, and Iraq was a British mandate. U.S. corporations were determined not to be left out, and a maze of intrigue and counter-intrigue spread
among boardrooms and governments, amid hard bargains, share-swappings,
double-crossings. In London the Foreign Office was not seldom out of its depth
in these shifting sands: the State Department was naturally still more so, but in
the end the chief American contestants, represented in the consortium known as
the Turkish Petroleum Company, got shares in the concession granted to it in
1925 by Iraq.[123] They were now planted in the Middle East, and with them a
new main line of American expansion, economic and political.

There was little desire to dismantle the European empires: the area had to be
policed, and America did not wish to take on the task. Their services were
entitled to the same kind of appreciation as those of a regime like Mussolini's in
Europe. In this tacit arrangement there was something akin to the way the
industrial bourgeoisie in Britain had been content to leave the running of government, armed forces and colonies to the aristocracy and gentry. As before the
war, the British empire harmonized not badly with the American conception of a
world directed by a few responsible governments, all welcoming free commercial
competition even if each might keep a few cards up its sleeve. Capital was
flowing across imperial as well as national boundaries. In 1928 the colonial thesis
of the Third International called attention to both U.S. and British investment in

Dutch Indonesia. American money was pouring into the British empire: by 1930 long-term investment there was approaching $4,600 million, and 'Britain's position was seriously threatened by American investors who were often financially much stronger.'[124]

Their preference however was for the nearby British West Indies and, above all, Canada. It struck British visitors that Canadians often referred to the U.S. as 'our great neighbour to the south', with a touch of apprehension; there were fears of being swallowed up by it, in a different style from what had been threatened a century before. Mackenzie King, Liberal premier of Canada most of the time between 1921 and 1948, it may be permissible to think of as a highly superior counterpart to the caudillos on the other flank of the U.S. When he retired, a fairy godmother in the shape of J.D. Rockefeller, Jr., gave him a present of $100,000. He had earned it partly by halting moves to stem the inflow of American capital. 'Under Mackenzie King's leadership Canada moved with ever increasing momentum into the economic and political orbit of the United States.'[125]

Wilson's last speech before his collapse, on 25 September 1919, in his campaign to advocate the League, included a glowing tribute to the British empire, as fully entitled to the plurality of votes allotted to it; the seat for 'that fine little stout Republic down in the Pacific, New Zealand', or South Africa, so sagely represented at Paris; there too were Indian spokesmen, with 'an older wisdom than the rest of us', and 'for the first time in the history of the world, that great voiceless multitude, that throng hundreds of millions strong in India, has a voice ...'. He did not add that the voice would be that of a British ventriloquist. Before 1914 the British in India had been uneasily conscious of some American disapproval. Morley as Secretary of State felt it, and the authorities there could even suspect encouragement of sedition by Americans, chiefly Irish.[126] Ambassador Page in London drew a half-amused picture of the Englishman's passion for discipline. 'He has reduced a large part of the world to order', he wrote to House in 1913. 'He is the best policeman in creation', but with no higher ethics.[127] U.S. exertions in policing Central America made for fellow-feeling, and so more directly did the Philippines. A Scottish writer on Eastern Asia, a hard-boiled empire man, expatiated on how Americans were having to learn lessons long familiar to Britons in the handling of slippery natives;[128] and a retired governor of Malaya, Sir Andrew Clarke, had given helpful advice about the pacification of the islands. In 1915 the British were able to get an Indian revolutionary, Bhagwan Singh, expelled from the Philippines, because Filipino nationalists had been extradited at America's request from Hongkong.[129] In the chaos left by the war and the Bolshevik Revolution, a reputation for genius at keeping order might well entitle Englishmen to higher respect; while the creation of the Irish Free State put a damper on the old Irish and Irish-American habit of abusing the empire.

In India, besides, with the Act of 1919 and the inauguration of some limited self-government, Britain could profess to be setting out to train the country for nationhood. In other words it could appear to be following in America's wise footsteps, however tardily. Some notice was taken in the U.S. of the second civil disobedience movement started by Gandhi in 1930, but pro-British sentiment persisted in spite of it. When the philologist Sir Denison Ross, formerly in service in India, visited Chicago in 1931 he found everyone very well disposed.[130] Those he met may be supposed to have felt a vicarious satisfaction at the spectacle of a government standing firm against the froth of agitation, a government moreover of white men over coloured. Katherine Mayo – author of *Mother India*, which came out in 1927, had a big success, and gave umbrage to all Indian patriots – wrote to Lord Lothian at the India Office to express her esteem for British rule in the most glowing terms.[131] Among her other works were *True Stories of Heroes of Law and Order*. Hollywood was happy to utilize material supplied by the Indian government in making films with a marked bias; there were thirty-five of these from 'Hindoo Fakir' in 1902 to 'Gunga Din' in 1939.[132]

Fountains like these, more than any publicity about the U.S.'s own colonies, must have played upon Sinclair Lewis's young man at college in the 1920s, with his head full of the romance of empire, of a governor's life 'all palms and parrots and parades', who considered it part of his country's 'essential philosophy' that white nations should give up their folly of fighting one another, and combine to rule, 'tenderly but firmly', the yellow, brown and black.[133] Long before this, the American-born adventurer who gave his name to Yale rose to be a governor in British India, and dealt with a native butler who fell foul of him by having him hanged on a charge of piracy.[134] In 1932 Winston Churchill made a lucrative lecture tour of the States, preaching their duty to stand with Britain, and protect poor Europe, against communism. He came home to begin writing his *History of the English-Speaking Peoples*.[135] An Anglo-American was bringing 'Anglo-

Saxonism' up to date, with Bolshevism for a more tangible adversary than its parent, barbarism.

'Japan regards herself as infinitely superior to all mankind. So do we.'[136] An American was stating the problem of the post-war Pacific succinctly. Trade with the Japanese continued profitable, and there was no wish to meddle with them on what by now was their own ground, any more than with Europe's empires. Washington had nothing to say in 1919 when Korean patriots proclaimed their independence, only to be shot down. 'Woodrow Wilson and his points had caught the imagination of the 20,000,000 Koreans', one who escaped wrote.[137] On the other hand, at the 1922 Conference it obliged Japan to withdraw from the sphere it had taken over from Germany in Shantung, and to join in signing the Nine-Power Treaty which pledged respect for China's sovereignty and equal access to its markets for all. By now the Open Door had gathered public endorsement, as a grand American initiative.[138] But the treaty provided no enforcement machinery, and hence had less weight in terms of Old World policy than of New World ideology.

By 1925 it could appear to some that 'China has become an American sphere of influence'.[139] This could be no more than a mirage, given the country's anarchical condition. China was floundering through its Warlord period, while Sun Yat-sen and his radicals tried to create a new national focus at Canton. He was bitterly disappointed, as an old admirer of democratic America, when the U.S. took part in a hostile naval demonstration there in 1923, and declared that he might have looked for an American Lafayette to come to his aid instead.[140] Washington could not relish his attempt to rebuild the Kuomintang movement in partnership with a young Communist Party and with the Soviet Union. Americans often sighed for another strong man, more successful than Yuan Shih-k'ai, to pull the provinces together and nip social revolt in the bud, a Chinese Mussolini or Porfirio Díaz. A director of relief work during the 1920s thought this the only solution.[141]

There was a basic inconsistency here with another part of the American canon, faith in Education. To bring this to Asia would be to repeat in a fresh setting the programme of 19th-century social workers and reformers at home for enlightening and Americanizing the legions of benighted immigrants; it was being applied now to Puerto Rico. Just as Britain had inducted India into the modern schoolroom, America meant to do the same with China, and with too much of

the same resolve to transform the oriental into its own image. In 1905 Edward
Hume went out to join the 'Yale in China' project at Changsha. 'Get hold of the
students, of the educated men', was his maxim, 'and China will be won!'[142]
China might want to be taught, but it had no desire to be *won*, as this devoted
teacher through many uphill years came to realize. Anti-foreign riots in 1924
confirmed his misgivings about the depth of incomprehension on both sides; in
1927 all American workers had to be withdrawn.[143]

In that year Coolidge declined a British invitation to contribute troops for the
protection of foreigners in Shanghai. After sending thousands of marines into
Nicaragua he 'was probably leary of another military expedition'.[144] Next year he
recognized the regime of Chiang Kai-shek, who having broken with the communists and the Soviet Union appeared exactly the strong man for China and the
right man for the U.S. But peasant risings under communist leadership were soon
erupting, and a corrupt and tyrannical Kuomintang found them impossible to
crush. In this situation a previous willingness to see Japan assert itself on the
mainland could revive with more force. Hoover had come to the conclusion as
early as 1921 that Japan had no title to territory there, and no need of anything
except a stable market, but China seemed unable to put its house in order, and if
other countries did not band together to do this, 'Japan was likely to act'.[145] Ten
years later Japan did act, by occupying Manchuria.

There was much manoeuvering between Geneva and Washington as to which,
if either, ought to bell the cat. Neither was keen, but it appeared to Hoover that
his State Secretary Stimson 'was at times more a warrior than a diplomat', with an
excess of faith in the efficacy of economic sanctions as a 'magic wand of force by
which all peace could be summoned from the vasty deep'.[146] Such a faith might
flow naturally from his countrymen's conviction of the primacy of trade and
investment, the transatlantic version of historical materialism. But Hoover (with
no premonition of what would happen at Pearl Harbour when Japan was ten
years stronger) considered himself hard-headed in rejecting anything beyond
diplomatic expostulations. Japan might well argue, he wrote in a memorandum
for the cabinet in the autumn of 1931, that China was still in a state of chaos:
'Half her area is Bolshevist and co-operating with Russia'; and since America was
not prepared to join in measures to 'restore order', it could not object to Japan
doing so single-handedly.[147] 'Half her area' was a gross over-estimation, but it

effectively put an end to any chance of League sanctions against Japan with American participation.

Kennan in his survey of American foreign policy was to be frank about the calculations at work; he himself was very indulgent, if not to Japanese militarism, then to 'the Japanese soul',[148] which perhaps at that time came to much the same thing. J.C. Grew went out to Tokyo as ambassador in 1932 cherishing 'a great deal of sympathy with Japan's legitimate aspirations in Manchuria', if not with its methods.[149] As to these, there was a clinging to the belief that moderate elements were striving to hold the army back, and ought to be given every latitude. These moderates were supposed to include the Mikado, but undoubtedly the 'bankers, traders, and industrialists'.[150] Since 1917 capitalists could not afford to brand one another publicly as aggressors, as they had been artlessly fond of doing: all businessmen now had to be granted benefit of clergy, and treated as exemplary characters, while irresponsible demagogues or generals became the scapegoats.

4

Slump Years, and a New Look at the Red Indian

'There seems little question', Galbraith writes, 'that in 1929 . . . the economy was fundamentally unsound.' One root weakness was social imbalance: 30% of all personal income was going to 5% of recipients. A second was that American enterprise 'had opened its hospitable arms to an exceptional number of pro-moters, grafters, swindlers, impostors, and frauds'.[151] Links between both these factors and overseas investment would not be hard to find. Clearly, also, it was from the U.S. that the slump spread across the continents,[152] though the country's leaders were understandably unwilling to admit this. All was well, wrote Hoover, until 'the European economic hurricane swept over us'.[153] Englishmen and Frenchmen used to talk in much the same way of 'the French disease' or 'the English disease', with the same ailment in mind.

It was three years before Franklin Roosevelt came on the scene to put Humpty Dumpty together. Capitalism's health was only very imperfectly restored at any time in the 1930s. The potent stimulus of one major war had worn off, reju-venation would only come with a second. Meanwhile it was being nursed by New Deal methods highly distasteful to it after years of Republican pride. In Nazi Germany capitalism was being rescued by more drastic means, socialist or trade-union trouble-makers crushed underfoot. Thus set free from its alarms it seemed able to forge ahead boldly, while Wall Street brooded. Still, the 'American System' revealed all this time an immense strength of inertia; the long ordeal failed to push the country on to any radically new road, good or bad. There was labour militancy, partly of foreign derivation; the big sit-in strikes of the 1930s were known at first as 'Polish strikes', because textile workers from Poland led the way. But socialism, never strong and crippled by wartime and post-war harrying, failed to gain ground.

There was by this time a popular American culture which on its own level could express vividly, for the world as well as for its homeland, the moods of these years. It was a synthetic mass culture suited to modern urbanized populations increasingly separated from their own cultural heritage and traditions. Industrial capitalism had created a vacuum which in Europe it had no notion how to fill, except with beer and drums. America, a more democratic society, could fill it with the help of its technology, which got the cinema going, and of its black minority, whose music and dancing in a diluted form it took over. While American teachers and missionaries plodded on with mixed fortunes in the outlands, the new civilization was scoring a far bigger success by exporting entertainment. The flooding of first Britain, and then Europe and beyond, with American films and jazz was among the most remarkable events in the history of the arts. It brought in further dividends by spreading a taste for American goods or gadgets; but it was also in its way part of the emergence of a cosmopolitan human consciousness. In 1942 a war correspondent met a Japanese officer who had gone out of his mind amid the horrors of the jungle fighting in New Guinea, but who remembered with glee a film called 'The Gold Rush',[154] made by an English comedian who worked in Hollywood until the Cold War made things too hot for him, and died in Switzerland.

In some films of the slump years could be found 'a condoning and even glorification of violence which reflected the cynical state of mind of many Americans at this time'.[155] It could be found also, along with opposite qualities, in the science fiction which had become another American speciality. One of its practitioners in England recalls his first encounter with it, in days when 'branches of Woolworth's used to have a counter boldly labelled "Yank Mags" ', selling for threepence and full of 'glaring and fearful diseases of style', but none the less enthralling.[156] They were heralds of a new age, and their story-tellers frequently wrestled with social problems and transmuted things good or evil in their society into fantasies benign or horrific. One in 1926 visualized the whole Western hemisphere under the dominion of a single capitalist with a food monopoly, and a mechanized economy in which human beings were unwanted.[157]

Another, in England, drew a sombre picture in 1930 of European wars joined in by China and America, the one coming to dominate all Asia, the other, armed with frightful weapons, the rest of the globe; a final conflict between them ended in union, with America supreme.[158] In the U.S. a year or two later, S.G. Weinbaum struck a more hopeful note, in a tale about exploration of Mars which has been hailed as one of the masterpieces of the genre. Of his four comrades one came from a France under communism, a second from a Germany under dictatorship, and the others from a democratic U.S.: one of these two was a believer in anarchism, firmly opposed to any thought of a race war with the Martians, or of conquest. 'The Sahara desert is just as good a field for imperialism, and a lot closer to home.'[159]

In terms of race relations nearer home there was still a long way to go. In the last year of the Great War, while thousands of African-Americans served in France hundreds were lynched in the Southern states. Those in the army might be considered a species of colonial troops. They fought on the western front along with black troops from French Africa; it was one of history's cases of two branches of a long-divided people coming together, whether or not any members of either were conscious of it at the time. Film-makers vied with historians in denigrating the black man. D.W. Griffith, the first great director, was an apologist of the South, and his African-Americans were brutes or clowns. He was also, with a contrariness commoner in America than in Europe's more homogeneous countries, a genuine idealist and progressive.

Griffith made other uncomplimentary films about Red Indians. When the silver screen first dawned, the era of frontier warfare lay only a decade or two behind, closer than the old Highland forays to Walter Scott when he began writing novels about them. In the cinema as in the novelette, red men continued to embody unsubdued barbarism, the white man's perpetual foe, and more of them must have been despatched than ever existed in fact, as if Indians had been as numerous as bison or beavers. With feathered war-parties charging *en masse*, yelling like demons, whole clans could be polished off in a trice: America's image of the war of civilization against savagery was concentrated into its most vivid form.

Before long Indians were being enrolled for crowd scenes in these films, like Sitting Bull in the travelling circus. But some even of the earliest films were of a better sort. 'Heart of an Indian', in 1912, by Ince, was about motherhood, the most elemental symbol of common humanity.[160] There is an air of puzzlement about these aliens, or the white man's relation to them, in Ernest Hemingway's juvenile fantasy of 1926, *In Honour of the Passing of a Great Race*, with its preposterous characters and parodies of stereotyped phrases about everything Indian. When faith in the American revelation was shaken by the slump, doubts could be felt about the very idea of white superiority. Aldous Huxley found some Americans reading books about the Soviet Union, others recoiling from 'the horrors of industrial reality' and taking refuge in a pre-industrial twilight, which they could visit by crossing their southern border. They fell into 'extravagances of admiration for everything Mexican', and peasant arts and crafts.[161] In this light red men could be credited with a culture and a way of life still worth their place in the sun. A book about them in 1931 was entitled *Contributors to Civilization*.[162]

From a more practical point of view, Americans had long found their responsibility for the surviving Indian tribes an irksome one, the more so since their recovery from the brief infatuation with colonies. One question fumblingly settled was that of the Indian's civic status. In 1906 a twenty-five year probation term had been enacted for the citizenship held out by the Dawes Act; but in 1916 the Supreme Court decided that citizenship was compatible with tribal life; in 1919 it was conferred on Indians who had done war service, in 1924 on all. This still left voting rights, which might be conditional on literacy, uncertain. Economically tribes were having mixed fortunes because, while many lands were lost, some reservations were enlarged by the government; that of the Navajos, for instance, the biggest of all the tribes, whose numbers and those of its flocks were growing. Indians were *not* a race passing away, though much of their culture might be decaying. Navajo land was protected from white greed by its aridity, until discovery of oil put it in jeopardy. A Leasing Act of 1920 was injurious to Indian rights; in 1927 an Indian Oil Act gave these better protection.[163]

All this time it had been growing painfully evident that the idea of separate allotments and private ownership releasing imprisoned Indian energies like an Open Sesame was not being fulfilled. It was not the short cut to a quick and easy solution of the Indian problem which the nation was always hankering for. This was pointed out in the Meriam Report of 1928, which recognized virtues in the tribal spirit and found fault with attempts at hasty assimilation. With this current of thinking went criticism of the Bureau of Indian Affairs, always liable to be made the target, but really guilty of many shortcomings in matters like health and education.[164] A new, more positive programme came with the Roosevelt era, when Ickes as Secretary of the Interior chose for Commissioner the social worker John Collier, who had studied Indian life in New Mexico.

Opposed to any more private allotments, Collier could be denounced as regressive, even communistic; but his aim was neither to assimilate nor to segregate, but to preserve a minority culture in a plural society.[165] He would encourage entry into the present without sacrifice of all the past. New Deal programmes could supply material aid, for example to provide new employments for Navajos suffering from over-grazing of their pastures by too many sheep. Under the Indian Reorganization Act of 1934, framed by Collier, many though not all tribes were given the option of forming their own administrative bodies. Allotment legislation was repealed; in view of the plight of the white farmer, its merits looked more dubious than ever.[166] More provision was made for education, more land made available, more fertility ensured by irrigation. American skills and generosity were having a chance. Indian responses varied, but the setting up of some tribal authorities, together with the respect now being shown for traditional cultures, brought a new hopefulness and activity.

5

From Isolationism to Conquest

It is remarkable that in 1934, at a time when America might be supposed desperately in need of imperial expansion, not only was self-government offered to Indians but a Philippines Independence Act was passed. There was to be autonomy for the islands under a new constitution, and full independence within fourteen years. Thereafter there would be no obligation on the U.S. to defend them; nothing like a British family of free Dominions was contemplated. On 15 November 1935, the Commonwealth of the Philippines was inaugurated. That year British politicians were haggling over every jot and tittle of a very limited extension of self-government for India. But Congress was acting in deference to renewed opposition at home to Filipino imports, far more than to any growth of enlightened opinion or pressure of Filipino nationalism. Before long, doubts were being raised as to whether the Filipino economy could be readjusted within so short a time, and still be viable after the cutting off of the free trade relationship with the U.S. market which had moulded it ever since 1907.[167]

Puerto Rico, much closer at hand, was another matter. There U.S. rule and a policy of assimilation, with the gift of U.S. citizenship in 1917, were welcomed by many. But the soil was being Americanized as well as its inhabitants. U.S. companies owned most of the sugar estates, which ran up to 15,000 or 20,000 acres; when a limit of 500 acres was fixed for corporate holdings it proved easy to evade. Hoover came back from a visit dispirited. Improved administration had doubled the population. 'In consequence the people were more impoverished than before', he wrote. 'I did not know any answer except birth control, and that was impossible.'[168] More land growing sugar for export meant less land growing food for subsistence. Here were more contradictions of colonialism, and more reasons for preferring indirect rule. Hoover wished he could turn Puerto Rico loose, keeping only military bases. But this would not suit the plantation owners, and a nationalist movement set up in 1922 was stiffly resisted. It gathered strength in the 1930s, when the depressed economy bred a restless generation. In 1934 it headed a big strike of sugar workers; next year police action was launched against it; in 1937 there were a number of casualties.[169] The movement was curbed, and Puerto Rico in 1940 was a tropical colony much like any other. 'The wretchedness of the poorer classes beggars description'; company officials lived in 'beautiful houses and surroundings ... a truly foreign colony taking little or no interest in social conditions'.[170]

Roosevelt took office in 1933 with slight interest in most aspects of foreign affairs, and far more urgent tasks at home. Cordell Hull at the State Department did not stand very close to him, and had few definite views except a conviction that the way to peace on earth was removal of trade barriers. Within its own hemisphere a somewhat chastened U.S. was aware that more prudent courses were advisable. Hitherto its behaviour had not been such as to warrant any idea of the League of Nations being morally weakened by its absence. Now that lawlessness was coming out into the open in Europe as well as the Far East, it would be invidious for America to appear as a fellow-aggressor; and to do so might make Latin America more vulnerable to influences from beyond the Atlantic. To insulate the New World from the Old was a prime motive of the 'Good Neighbour policy' now being worked out.

It was a continuation of the shift already observable before Roosevelt, away from cruder forms of interference towards conciliation: a good understanding, that is, with circles through which U.S. interests could work. In 1934 the marines were at last called off from Haiti; in 1940 the treaty imposed on the Dominican Republic in 1925 was abrogated.[171] In Cuba Machado continued to give satisfaction until, with the slump, opposition made headway against him and in 1931 fighting broke out. Washington professed neutrality, but the bankers went on supporting their man. Sumner Welles was sent to investigate, with an unofficial tender of good offices between the two camps. American opinion, he told Machado, was being 'very frequently shocked by acts of terrorism' on the part of his opponents, but also by the 'cruelty and oppression' of his own forces.[172]

It is seldom that the U.S. has deplored such conduct by right-wing establishments, and then usually when they have been overthrown or are likely to be, as Machado was in August 1933. What took his place was a regime run in effect by the army, with the ex-sergeant Fulgencio Batista as chief of staff. Welles at first thought its ideas 'frankly communistic', and wanted intervention,[173] but like many Americans now as well as then he did not discriminate very clearly between communism and fascism. Batista speedily proved amenable, and 'became the guarantor of a Cuban government friendly to the United States and its interests'.[174] His rule was heavy-handedly repressive, but there was no danger of this being held against it at Washington. Three members of Roosevelt's 'Brain Trust', and three of his cabinet ministers, had business interests in Cuba.[175] Relations were to remain unruffled down to the Castro revolution in 1959.

Further south too, foreign investors might fare better than the sons of the soil. The worst happening of the decade, the war of the Gran Chaco between Bolivia and Paraguay which broke out in 1932, was fuelled by American as well as European arms dealers. 'During the first six months of the war the shares of the Du Pont de Nemours Company showed a substantial gain in Wall Street.'[176] Standard Oil had made finds in the disputed territory. A Committee of Neutrals meeting at Washington failed to bring about an agreement, and in 1933 the League sent a commission to investigate. At Montevideo it was warmly welcomed by the Pan-American Conference then in session, and Hull gave it his blessings.[177] But it was not until 1935 that the murderous conflict was brought to an end, by the efforts of the U.S. and five Latin American governments.

By that time South America was being ardently wooed by Germany, Italy and Japan, each of them with a multitude of settlers there. This made its political condition a cause of anxiety. Argentina was a particular nuisance, not because it was falling under military sway but because its foreign minister was a warm admirer of Franco and Mussolini.[178] He was the sort of politician who would be very acceptable to America after 1945. In 1936 Roosevelt initiated a special inter-American discussion at Buenos Aires. Shortly after this his government was obliged to exercise self-restraint over Mexico. It was helped by its envoy there,

Josephus Daniels. He had once been Wilson's Secretary of the Navy, and was blamed for the bombardment of Vera Cruz; when he first arrived the Spanish ambassador, who was mistaken for him by an angry crowd, ran some risk of being lynched.[179] He turned out to be unexpectedly liberal, and won national esteem.

Mexico was going through one of its phases of ferment and progress, and this required, as very often in countries seeking to develop, recovery of control over its natural resources. In 1938 President Cárdenas expropriated sixteen American and Anglo-Dutch oil companies. An unofficial boycott of Mexico's oil followed, most of its export trade was cut off, and large sums were spent on publicity to turn U.S. opinion against it. Hull had to demand prompt payment of compensation, with the never-failing approval of the A.F.L., though not of the new, less conservative C.I.O. Mexico may again have been saved by Washington's preoccupation with Europe. Goodwill and security in the Western hemisphere had to be put first, at the cost of some writing off of 'the somewhat dubious claims of the American oil companies'.[180]

In the wider world, through the fatal decade of the 1930s, the U.S. continued 'almost fanatically devoted to the maintenance and extension of the principles of neutrality'.[181] The fact that during these years the forces of reaction were in the ascendant suggests that many who mattered in America (as in Britain and France) were able to view them without too much repugnance. Foster Dulles, the later Cold War paladin, had a sister so overflowing with admiration for Nazism that she settled in Germany, to bask in its rays.[182] Roosevelt's ambassador Dodd there, carefully chosen by him as a liberal, noted in his diary in 1934 that his colleague Earle at Vienna was very pleased with Dolfuss's 'ruthless handling of the Socialist rebellion'.[183] Next year there was no more alacrity to stand by Abyssinia than there had been to stand by China over Manchuria. As the Italian threats grew louder, Haile Selassie was anxiously seeking American support. There was no prospect of his getting arms, even before the first Neutrality Act was pushed through in August by the isolationists. Roosevelt hoped this might benefit Abyssinia, since Italy was better able to buy arms; but he induced an oil company to abandon a concession given it by Haile Selassie in the hope of securing at least economic aid.[184]

A harsher test came with the Spanish Civil War of 1936–39. Public opinion polls disclosed a strong preponderance in favour of the Republic, though also against any direct involvement.[185] Congress tied the government's hands with neutrality resolutions, with little remonstrance from Roosevelt or Hull. Refusal of any help to the Republic was buttressed by anxiety not to offend Latin America,[186] where Mexico alone was well-disposed towards it. Most of the other Latin American states sided more or less wholeheartedly with Franco and his fascist patrons; they were swayed partly by a Catholic propaganda campaign which made a great stir in the U.S. itself and foreshadowed the hysteria of the Cold War epoch. Washington did not formally join the Non-Intervention Committee in London, but it seemed to Maisky, the Soviet representative, that 'figuratively speaking its ghost was always present at the conference table, exerting the strongest of influences on the . . . "democratic" powers'.[187] In reality White House feelings were more complicated. Sumner Welles after a visit to Europe gloomily agreed with Roosevelt that there seemed not the 'slightest possibility' of Britain or France making a stand against aggression; their 'pusillanimous role' in the Civil War testified to this. 'It must be sadly admitted', Welles adds, 'that the part of the United States was no more courageous.'[188] It was left to the Abraham Lincoln battalion of the International Brigade to strike an American blow at fascism.

Roosevelt thought a coming to power of fascism in the U.S. itself not an impossibility, even if he did not think it so imminent as Sinclair Lewis did in 1935 in his novel *It Can't Happen Here*. Neither America nor Britain would be fighting the next war in order to liberate mankind, however this might figure in wartime speeches or in the minds of their more idealistic citizens. They would go to war because, at bottom, Germany and Italy and Japan as members of the capitalist family were behaving too atavistically, making themselves impossible. Roosevelt and his advisers saw them more and more clearly as a menace to American rights in both the Atlantic and Pacific.[189] Danger was also opportunity. With their defeat, American 'rights' would be transformed into American power. Mastery of the Pacific was an old dream, and the time was at hand for dreams to turn into realities, less romantic and never complete.

Roosevelt's 'quarantine' speech at Chicago in October 1937, against aggression as something to be warded off like 'an epidemic of physical disease' – yet another exercise in the imagery of hygiene – met with no applause from either Congress or public, but instead 'a blast of furious denunciation'.[190] From then on, the government was edging its way towards a confrontation, but amid such a confusion of mixed motives, open or unavowed, that no clear comprehension of what was happening could dawn on the people. The armed forces were as much in the dark as everyone else about what they were expected to be getting ready for: they could get plenty of money from Congress, but very little guidance. It was typical of the 'general American apathy' that regular army strength in 1940 was still only 250,000, and that the War Department was scattered haphazardly over a score of buildings.[191] Lippmann wrote of the 'total absurdity' of undertaking world-wide commitments not matched by any corresponding power.[192] America's hitherto unassailable position had bred unrealism, a tacit assumption that because this country knew itself to be invincible everyone else must know it too.

When a policy at last began to be put together, it had to be done fumblingly, piecemeal, sometimes by sleight of hand; and Roosevelt was by temperament and long practice an improviser, free of fixed dogmas. In the same way the country had been forced to grapple with the equally unforeseen problems of the Depression. These two bewilderments now went together, because the economy was sagging ominously again in the later 1930s. Roosevelt was not turning to war as a way out, but he might well turn with relief from intractable difficulties at home to perils abroad that were at least more tangible, more capable of being measured and dealt with. The new strategy was to end in triumph, with America restored to prosperity and unity, but by a route which dodged internal dilemmas instead of solving them.

'It was true, I thought, that the President ... was leading the nation step by step towards war ...'.[193] This observer thought him right; others were attacking him more and more fiercely. Big business was as surly and recalcitrant about being led towards world power as about being led out of the slump; a good example of the short-sightedness of capitalism on its own, its need of political management. Roosevelt could not, of course, even had he wished, give it the simple summons to march towards the conquest of power to which it might have responded. Talk of defending democracy merely irritated it. Some of its pundits argued that the price of a successful war would be socialism in the U.S., or that a collision between one set of capitalist nations and another would destroy capitalism everywhere.[194] It has been often remarked that such conservatives, isolationist in the 1930s when fascism was rampant, were to be zealous interventionists after 1945, when it was a question of action against social or national revolt. Those who called for firmness to halt aggression might be imperialists, as Churchill was in Britain; those who stood for peace might be pro-fascist, like many British and French appeasers. The war and its outcome would fuse the two together.

Some of those appeasers in Europe felt resentfully that America, or its government, was stretching out across the Atlantic not to succour them, but to push them into a war – with no intention of taking part itself. Joseph Kennedy, the U.S. ambassador in London, was convinced that if Britain and France fought they would lose.[195] When war came, he believed that Germany would (and evidently thought *should*) have been left to fight Russia alone, if it had not been for his meddling colleague Bullitt at Paris who persuaded Roosevelt to put pressure on the British and French to make a stand over Poland. Kennedy is even said to have reported Chamberlain as complaining that 'America and the world Jews had forced England into the war'.[196]

Before war broke out Roosevelt was 'seeking desperately to persuade the Congress to amend the Neutrality Act', which had been renewed in 1937.[197] Now in November 1939, he was able to get it altered on lines highly favourable to Britain and France. It may be true, as some thought about that time, that he was still wavering between support for Britain and ideas like Wilson's in 1916 of trying to smother the war; that 'he had not abandoned the ambition of achieving historical greatness as the peacemaker of the world'.[198] Next year in his re-election campaign he was assuring American parents that their sons were not going to be sent into any foreign wars. But the exchange of destroyers for Caribbean bases, following the fall of France, was little challenged: 'the public was indifferent to legal arguments over neutrality', and Wendell Wilkie, his Republican opponent, was very restrained.[199]

Between sympathy with democracy, and a sense of what kind of world American capitalism required, the nation was coming together. Two prominent Republicans were brought into the government this year, Stimson as Secretary for War and Knox for the Navy. Hitler had always vastly underrated America's potential strength, industrial and military;[200] pliant courtiers and racialist prejudices combined to delude him. But he could not fail to realize that Britain's chances of survival rested more and more on American aid. In March 1941 this took the form of Lend-Lease. When he turned away from Britain to invade the Soviet Union, he may have expected the U.S. to look on more complacently. On the British side there were fears that the moving of British and Russian forces into Persia would raise the old cry of imperialism from America; instead American army teams of technicians were sent to join them.[201]

As in the First World War, America's actual entry came long after the start. The final challenge came from Japan instead of from Germany, which must have made it more acceptable to the nation at large, and the Pacific war was more directly America's than the Atlantic. Roosevelt himself was always sensitive to Japanese expansion as a menace. He had been for seven years Assistant Secretary of the Navy, and, as Welles writes, became 'imbued with the Navy's conviction that Japan was America's Number 1 antagonist'.[202] In 1934 Japan withdrew from the Washington Naval Treaty. Later in 1936 the Anti-Comintern Pact linked it with the European sabre-rattlers. Roosevelt embarked on a big warship-building programme. In the summer of 1937 he was meditating an Anglo-American trade embargo against Japan, but the admirals were not ready for the war they felt must ensue, and it seemed that 'public opinion would refuse to support any action that entailed even the remotest possibility of war'.[203]

For long, indeed, the man in the street had appeared indifferent to everything in the further Pacific, ready to take advantage of coming Filipino independence to abandon it and fall back on Hawaii.[204] There was a tenacious myth according to which doughty American exertions to get Japan out of Manchuria had 'left the United States to bear the brunt of a Japanese antagonism that Stimson's discreet European collaborators were altogether happy to avoid'.[205] It could go on being urged that, if Japan were stopped, the only effective barrier against communism in that part of the world would be lost.[206] Grew at Tokyo was of this persuasion. Invasion of China went on, relying very largely on oil and steel bought from America. Japan was a far better market than China, the isolationist Griswold argued in 1938, and 'attempting to preserve the territorial integrity of China was not and never had been a truly vital American interest'.[207]

All the same, a more and more distinct prospect of China overrun and its resources monopolized by a militaristic Japan was unpalatable. Grew could not help observing that, even if American trade with Manchuria had flourished since the occupation, Japanese extremists would not be content until all foreign interests were shut out of China. Foolishly ignorant of 'the practical working of economic laws', they failed to grasp their country's incapacity to exploit China without the help of foreign capital.[208] It was not, in other words, capitalist greed that was at fault, but nationalistic hysteria. Once more American economic

rationality confronted an Old World alien to it. Still, had Japan seemed willing
to be satisfied with its army and the Asian mainland, it could have been left to go
on much longer; an oceanic threat by its navy was another matter. Even those
who thought like Grew had no desire to see Japan let loose in South-east Asia.
There, instead of holding the fort against communism, it would be overturning
the old-established empires with which America had learned to get on, and
would either create chaos or grow unmanageably strong. This, more than any
impulse to rescue China, was what in the end made Washington ready to throw
down the gauntlet.

War in Europe freed Japan from any risk of interference from that side in its
war in China, and left it confident that any American protests would be no more
than sermonizing.[209] In July 1939, however, Washington had given notice of
abrogation in six months of the trade treaty, and a cutting off of essential
supplies had to be reckoned with. Rational calculation was that this would
compel Japan to knuckle under; the result was the opposite. The war party had
long been arguing that Japan was dangerously dependent on trade with the U.S.
and the British empire, and now argued all the more loudly that it must make
itself self-sufficient, by mastering all Eastern Asia.[210] Besides, guerrilla resistance
by the Chinese peasantry was endless, and Japan's ruling circles were impatient
for swifter triumphs, necessary to safeguard their own position. To pave the way,
Matsuoka, foreign minister during the twelve months from July 1940, in September signed the Tripartite Pact with Germany and Italy. This, unlike the
Anti-Comintern Pact, was clearly aimed at America, or at least at America's
client Britain; though no real harmony of purpose lay behind it, since Germany's
private aim was the conquest of the Soviet Union.

There were still Japanese anxious for an understanding with America, and they
were able to get talks initiated at Washington by Admiral Nomura, lately sent as
ambassador and respected by Grew. Matsuoka himself, with all his blustering,
had lived in the U.S. in his youth, and 'aspired to be a peacemaker in this afflicted
world'; he wanted not merely to avoid war with the U.S. but, jointly with it, to
restore peace to Europe.[211] His grand design was a new world order within which
Asia would be directed by Japan, Europe by the fascist powers, the Western
hemisphere by the U.S.[212] Some such parcelling out of the globe among governments strong enough to keep order in their own spheres had floated before
American minds often enough. But this version would leave the U.S. out-

numbered by two to one, with the U.S.S.R. an incalculable outsider; to say nothing of any such intangibles as an ideology of liberty and democracy.

Nomura found the climate at Washington much frostier than he had expected. Matsuoka fell in July 1941, after the invasion of Russia made Germany a far less useful ally. It was too late for Japan to turn back; army and navy chiefs were increasingly in control of the government. Tokyo and Washington were challenging each other more openly now, although, as an American in Japanese service writes, 'neither would believe the other side would go to an extreme'.[213] Japanese forces occupied French Indochina; Churchill met Roosevelt in August and appealed for a sharp warning. Roosevelt issued a milder one instead: it was important for him not to seem to be led by the nose by Churchill, and London was kept a good deal in the dark about American intentions.[214] But trade dealings with Japan were being frozen; by October a final choice by Tokyo was inescapable. Grew cabled repeated warnings about the psychology of 'a country so recently feudalistic', so liable therefore to draw the sword in defiance of common sense,[215] and about the hazard of trying to subdue it by 'drastic economic measures'. With characteristic Western incomprehension, he thought of the drive to 'integrate Japan's national economy' as putting an end to capitalism, instead of intensifying it. Hopes among American economists that Japan would be brought down by depletion of resources seemed to him to rest on a false assumption that the determining motive would be desire for 'retention of the capitalist system', imperilled by economic mobilization for war.[216] This was nonsense; but that the U.S. was being too rationalistic, as so often before, in counting on economic levers to do its work for it unaided, was true enough.

In the final Japanese rejoinder, on 7 December a few hours before Pearl Harbour, the U.S. was accused of 'always holding fast to theories in disregard of realities, and refusing to yield an inch on its impractical principles ...'. Japan's terms had been put forward on 20 November; they implied, as the British ambassador at Tokyo pointed out, that China should be abandoned to its fate.[217] This was no longer acceptable: the U.S. might find itself faced before long by a Japan in control of China, allied with a Germany in control of Russia as well as Europe. The reply on 26 November, whether or not it should be qualified as an ultimatum, was a firm enough rejection to decide Tokyo on war. 'That the American government was as stern as a righteous schoolmaster cannot be denied', an American historian commented; though he noted also that to the last moment it had to preserve something of an enigmatic attitude, because 'a revelation of the whole situation' would still have divided the country deeply.[218] One harsh critic of Roosevelt was to maintain, too rhetorically, that 'Japan veritably crawled on its diplomatic belly' in search of an agreement, only to be met with 'cold and hostile rebuffs'.[219] The peace party was still entrenched in the government itself. 'Hull wanted peace above everything', an associate wrote a few weeks later, 'because he had set his heart on making an adjustment with the Japanese'.[220] Pearl Harbour put an end to this, and demonstrated that the Pacific was not wide enough to hold these two formidable powers, both because they were in many ways very similar and because in other ways they were totally dissimilar.

Already before this, Hitler was impressing on Franco that U.S. aid to Britain was only a cloak for empire-building,[221] and Goebbels gave out to his henchmen the propaganda theme: '"America will fight to the last Englishman." It is perfectly obvious what Roosevelt wants; he wants to step into the British position of power in the world.'[222] Now, with a free hand to describe the president as 'a war-criminal, an enemy of the world, a hireling of Jewry',[223] German propaganda struck this note frequently. Goebbels was a master of the art of interweaving truth and fiction. Much of what he had to say was what the Third International was saying, more prematurely, after 1918. The U.S. was the citadel of capitalist wealth and greed. 'The Minister believes', it was laid down at his departmental conference on 9 June 1942, 'that a massive attack on plutocracy would again be in order in the German press'.[224] Five months later, commenting on the Anglo-American landing in French North Africa, he was bursting with virtuous indignation at this 'infamous breach of law by the gangster President ... Britain has readily given her consent to this seizure of European property by America, since America is gradually taking over Britain's colonial possessions anyway'.[225] The French must have it rubbed into them that their own folly in not joining hands with Germany was to blame: their mine-owners for instance were being ousted, and 'needless to say, the Americans will now never quit North Africa'.[226]

Even without Dr Goebbels's promptings there was an undercurrent of uneasiness among America's partners, far livelier now than after 1918, about the prospect of the U.S. supplanting them, economically at least, in the Afro-Asian territories now being defended or recaptured. Early in 1944 Churchill told Roosevelt that 'certain British quarters were apprehensive that this country wished to deprive the British of their Near Eastern oil interests'. Roosevelt retorted that 'he himself was concerned over a rumoured British desire to "horn in" on the oil reserves of Saudi Arabia'.[227] Politically, the goal of the colonial powers was to restore the situation of 1939; America wanted the war over quickly, wanted therefore to mobilize the energies of Asian nationalism on the Allied side, and, conscious of its own swelling power, was confident – over-confident – of its ability to go on guiding and directing them after the war. During 1942, with the Japanese advancing, the British empire so many Americans had admired was showing its feet of clay, along with the French and the Dutch: the spectacle must have helped to cure them of any inclination they may have felt to behave as the Nazis predicted, and go in for direct colonial rule.

India, now as earlier, was the touchstone. Roosevelt resorted to the same pushing and prodding at Delhi that he employed before 1939 in London and Paris. He sent two successive special agents to influence the British towards concessions to the Indian National Congress, whose leaders after the August rising of 1942 were in jail, in order to enlist active instead of only mercenary support for the war effort. These agents met with little success, the result of their own unawareness of local realities as well as of British obstruction. William Phillips proposed to Roosevelt in March 1943 that a conference of all Indian parties should be held, to agree about the future, under American chairman-ship.[228] Not surprisingly Lord Linlithgow, the obstinately unprogressive vice-roy, was perturbed by these machinations, and the superfluously large mission the Americans were assembling in Delhi: 'he suspected that they were making ground where they could with a view to strengthening America's post-war position in Indian markets at Britain's expense'.[229] It was a jaundiced but not altogether unfounded view. In the course of 1943 Roosevelt met Queen Wilhelmina and reminded her that Indonesia was going to be freed by U.S. arms, and got her to promise it 'dominion status with the rights of self-rule and equality'.[230] Queen as well as viceroy must have guessed at some ulterior motives.

While the old empires were strong enough to 'keep order', but not strong enough to keep out American enterprise, the U.S. had been content to trade with and invest in them. Now it was time for a change. Some further readjustment was proving necessary in the U.S.'s own sphere of influence. With the coming of war in Europe, there were intensified efforts towards 'welding America's northern and southern neighbours into an economic and military bloc'.[231] When

Argentina and Chile, at the Pan-American conference at Rio de Janeiro in early 1942, refused to break off relations with the enemy, Hull wanted to have them outlawed; Welles, the U.S. representative, got Roosevelt to veto this.[232] All the other republics agreed to break off relations or even enter the war, and Brazil, whose goodwill was important for enabling airfields to be constructed for operations across the Atlantic, and Mexico were rewarded with installations such as steel plants, or funds to build them: Washington now had to respect the wish of such big countries to have industries of their own.[233]

In Asia, Roosevelt was thinking, Welles records, of helping to build a strong China, under Chiang Kai-shek, after the war, as a fourth major power along with the Allies. (This might be put in another way by saying that China was to be America's outpost or platform in the Far East.) He found Churchill very reluctant to fall into line, because unwilling to see that 'the British Empire as it had existed at the turn of the century was long since a thing of the past'.[234] But America too was having to move forward into a new age. A sense of this came very clearly to Grew as he digested 'The Lessons of History' on the tenth anniversary of his appointment to Tokyo, where he was now interned. 'We cannot permit nations to seize and pre-empt by processes of conquest areas whose resources should be available to all.' But if a country like America shuts itself up in its own concerns, instead of helping to sort out those of its neighbours, 'just so long will the progress of civilization and the welfare of mankind be retarded through unnecessary and futile wars'. The hour had come to understand that isolationism as a practical policy was gone forever; or the chance would be lost 'to employ our limitless strength, both material and moral, towards the development of civilization . . .'.[235] Civilization and capitalism being interchangeable terms, it was an excellent statement of the American philosophy, and a programme for the epoch about to open.

References

1. A.T. Mahan, *Lessons of the War with Spain* (1899; 2nd edn., London, 1899), p.231; J.R. Dos Passos, *The Anglo-Saxon Century and the Unification of the English-Speaking People* (New York, 1903), p.155 ff.

2. H.C. Allen, *Great Britain and the United States* (London, 1954), p.608.

3. A. Malozemoff, *Russian Far Eastern Policy 1881–1904* (University of California, 1958), pp.173–4.

4. 'B.L. Putnam Weale', *The Truce in the East and its Aftermath* (London, 1907), pp.409–10.

5. D.H. Burton, *Theodore Roosevelt: Confident Imperialist* (Philadelphia, 1968), p.150.

6. W.S. Blunt, *My Diaries* (London edn., 1932), p.713 (25 April 1910); p.724 (2 June 1910).

7. Page to House, 2 November 1913, in B.J. Hendrick, *The Life and Letters of Walter H. Page* (1922–25; London edn., 1930), Vol. 1, pp.190–1.

8. General F. von Bernhardi, *Germany and the Next War* (1911; trans. A.H. Powles, London, 1912), pp.94–5.

9. Letter to H.C. Lodge, 8 December 1914, in *The Letters of Theodore Roosevelt*, ed. E.E. Morison (Harvard, 1954), Vol. 8. p.862.

10. To A.B. Roosevelt, 19 May 1915, *ibid.*, p.922.

11. Madeleine Chi, *China Diplomacy 1914–1918* (Harvard, 1970), pp.102–3.

12. See V. Rothwell, 'The British Government and Japanese Military Assistance 1914–1918', in *History* (London), Vol. LVI (1971).

13. Chi, *op. cit.*, p.31 ff.

14. O.J. Clinard, *Japan's Influence on American Naval Power 1897–1917* (University of California, 1947), p.165.

15. Chi, *op. cit.*, p.108 ff.

16. Mahan, *op. cit.*, p.45.

17. P.S. Foner, *American Labour and the Indochina War – The Growth of Union Opposition* (New York, 1971), p.9.

18. P. Dukes, *The Emergence of the Super-Powers* (London, 1970), p.91.

19. A.J. Mayer, *Politics and Diplomacy of Peacemaking – Containment and Counterrevolution at Versailles, 1918–1919* (1967; London edn., 1968), p.335.

20. J.G.K. Tengey, *The United States and the Russian Provisional Government … (the Root Mission)* (M.Litt. thesis, University of Aberdeen, 1969), pp.16–18, 42.

21. *Ibid.*, p.152.

22. *Ibid.*, pp.170–1.

23. *Ibid.*, p.186.

24. G.F. Kennan, *Soviet-American Relations, 1917–1920 – The Decision to Intervene* (London, 1958), p.407.

25. *Ibid.*, p.428.

26. *Ibid.*, p.395.

27. To G.H. Putnam, 15 November 1918, *Letters*, Vol. 8, p.1394.

28. Mayer, *op. cit.*, p.267.

29. *Ibid.*, pp.270, 272.

30. 6 December 1921, in Lenin and Gorky, *Letters, Reminiscences, Articles* (English edn., Moscow, 1973), p.203.

31. *The Memoirs of Herbert Hoover* (2nd vol.), *The Cabinet and the Presidency 1920–1933* (1951; London edn., 1952), pp.23–4.

32. Memorandum from Dept. of Information, January 1918, CAB.24/39, in Public Record Office, London. I am indebted to Mrs. T. Brotherstone for this reference.

33. *A Speech Delivered by Ghazi Mustapha Kemal, President of the Turkish Republic, October 1927* (English edn., Leipzig, 1929), pp.82, 84–5.

34. R. Lansing, *The Peace Negotiations, a Personal Narrative* (Boston, 1921), pp.83–4.

35. J.C. Smuts, *Jan Christian Smuts* (London, 1952), p.220.

36. W.R. Louis, *Great Britain and Germany's Lost Colonies 1914–1919* (Oxford, 1967), pp.109–10.

37. *Ibid.*, p.125.

38. *Ibid.*, p.77.

39. Sir A. Zimmern, *The League of Nations and the Rule of Law, 1918–1935* (London, 1936), p.212.

40. Lansing, *op. cit.*, p.85.

41. O. Spengler, *The Decline of the West* (trans. C.F. Atkinson, London, 1922), p.475.

42. See A.S. Link and W.M. Leary, *The Diplomacy of World Power: the United States, 1889–1920* (London, 1970; documents), p.163.

43. *Ibid.*, p.157.

44. *Ibid.*, p.160.

45. P. Calvert, *The Mexican Revolution, 1910–1914 – The Diplomacy of Anglo-American Conflict* (Cambridge, 1968), p.297.

46. Letter of 12 October 1890, from Samoa, in *Letters of Henry Adams, (1858–1891)*, ed. W.C. Ford (London, 1930), p.421.

47. G. Bedborough, *Arms and the Clergy (1914–1918)* (London, 1934), p.106.

48. Henry James, *The Portrait of a Lady* (1881), Preface.

49. Mark Twain, *A Yankee at the Court of King Arthur* (1889).
50. *Chips – The Diaries of Sir Henry Channon*, ed. R.R. James (London, 1967), 18 January 1936.
51. *The Forrestal Diaries – The Inner History of the Cold War*, ed. W. Millis (London, 1952), p.109.
52. 'Noname', *Denver Dan and the Renegade* (reprint, Derby, Connecticut, n.d.), Chap. 10.
53. Chap. 24.
54. J.O. Bailey, *Pilgrims through Space and Time – Trends and Patterns in Scientific and Utopian Fiction* (New York, 1947), p.128.
55. Chap. 5.
56. Chap. 6.
57. Mayer, *op. cit.*, p.334.
58. Chap. 21.
59. Chap. 9.
60. *Ibid.*
61. Chap. 18.
62. S. Moskowitz, 'Edgar Rice Burroughs', in *Science Fantasy* (London), No. 41 (1961), pp.101, 109.
63. *The Gods of Mars* (1919), Chap. 3.
64. *The Warlord of Mars* (1920), Chaps 1, 16.
65. *The Moon Maid* (1923), Chap. 4.
66. *Ibid.*, Chap. 10.
67. *Ibid.*, Chap. 11.
68. *Ibid.*, Chap. 14.
69. *The Moon Men* (1925), Chap. 1.
70. W.A. Ganoe, *The History of the United States Army* (revised edn., New York, 1943), p.479.
71. I.H. Nish, *Alliance in Decline – A Study in Anglo–Japanese Relations 1908–23* (London, 1972), p.281.
72. *Ibid.*, p.277.
73. D.H. Aldcroft, *From Versailles to Wall Street 1919–1929* (London, 1977), pp.121, 196–7, 240–1.
74. *Ibid.*, p.260.
75. A. Teichova, *An Economic Background to Munich* (Cambridge, 1974), p.4.

76. W. Lippmann, *U.S. Foreign Policy* (London, 1943), p.24.

77. S. Greenbie, *The Pacific Triangle* (London, 1921), pp.314–15.

78. English edn., London, n.d., pp.143–5.

79. J. Degras, *The Communist International 1919–1943: Documents* (London, 1956), Vol. 1, p.235.

80. *Ibid.*, pp.289–90.

81. L. Trotsky, *Europe and America – Two Speeches on Imperialism* (New York edn., 1971), p.47.

82. I owe this reference to Dr C. Davies.

83. D.H. Lawrence, *Sea and Sardinia* (1923; London edn., 1944), p.89. A work by L. Romier had the title, typical of those years: *Qui sera le maître, Europe ou Amérique?* (Paris, 1927).

84. Hoover, *op. cit.*, p.346.

85. R.W. Child, *A Diplomat Looks at Europe* (New York, 1925); see chapters on the Lausanne and Genoa conferences. He wrote also an introduction to a translation of Mussolini's autobiography, and a large quantity of fiction.

86. *Ibid.*, Preface.

87. Hoover, *op. cit.*, p.27.

88. *Ibid.*, p.331.

89. E.M. Robertson, *Mussolini as Empire-Builder – Europe and Africa 1932–36* (London, 1977), p.170. The book gives a graphic picture of international relations in the Europe of those years.

90. D.R. McCoy, *Calvin Coolidge – The Quiet President* (New York, 1967), p.336; Hoover, *op. cit.*, p.342.

91. *The Autocracy of Mr Parham* (London, 1930), pp.91–2.

92. *Ibid.*, p.208.

93. Hoover, *op. cit.*, p.182.

94. L. Corey, *The House of Morgan* (New York, 1930), p.430.

95. D. Caute, *The Fellow Travellers* (London, 1973), p.168.

96. Letter to Bryce, 26 November 1917; *Letters*, Vol. 8, p.1253.

97. E. Davies, *American Labour* (London, 1943), p.44.

98. Degras, *op. cit.*, Vol. 1, p.432.

99. Norman Angell, *The Great Illusion* (London, 1933), p.263.

100. Greenbie, *op. cit.*, p.316.

101. *Ibid.*, pp. 321–3.

102. E. May, *American Imperialism* (New York, 1968), pp.214–15.

103. McCoy, *op. cit.*, pp.346, 348.

104. Angell, *op. cit.*, p.33.

105. Hoover, *op. cit.*, p.359.

106. *Ibid.*, p.361.

107. R.F. Smith, *The United States and Cuba – Business and Diplomacy, 1917–1960* (New York, 1960), Chaps 3, 4.

108. R.F. Smith, *What Happened in Cuba? A Documentary Survey* (New York, 1963), p.162.

109. Smith, *The United States and Cuba, op. cit.*, p.102.

110. Calvert, *op. cit.*, pp.301–2.

111. D.M. Smith, *Aftermath of War – Bainbridge Colby and Wilsonian Diplomacy 1920–1921* (Philadelphia, 1970), p.119.

112. Sir R. Bullard, *The Camels Must Go – An Autobiography* (London, 1961), p.236. On the American complaint about British proceedings in Persia, see J.E. Simkin, *Anglo-Russian Relations in Persia 1914–1921* (Ph.D. thesis, University of London, 1978), pp.186–7.

113. McCoy, *op. cit.*, p.352; and see H.N. Denny, *Dollars for Bullets – The Story of American Rule in Nicaragua* (New York, 1929), Chap. 14, 'The Bogey of Bolshevism'.

114. Foner, *op. cit.*, p.10. Cf. R.de Nogales, *The Looting of Nicaragua* (New York, 1928).

115. Aldous Huxley, *Beyond the Mexique Bay – A Traveller's Journal* (1934; London edn., 1950), pp.39–40.

116. D.M. Smith, *op. cit.*, p.118.

117. *Ibid.*, p.141.

118. Hoover, *op. cit.*, p.333.

119. *Ibid.*, p.334.

120. H.F. Dobyns and P.L. Doughty, *Peru – A Cultural History* (New York, 1976), p.216.

121. *Ibid.*, p.217.

122. Lenin, *Notebooks on Imperialism* (Collected Works, Vol. 39, Moscow, 1968), p.230.

123. For detail see C. Davies, *British Foreign Policy and the Struggle for Middle*

Eastern Oil 1919–1932 (Ph.D. thesis, University of Edinburgh, 1973); B. Shwadran, *The Middle East, Oil and the Great Powers* (New York, 1955).

124. Teichova, *op. cit.*, p.3.

125. H.S. Ferns, *The Age of Mackenzie King* (London, 1955), pp.214–15.

126. M. Gilbert, *Servant of India ... Sir James Dunlop Smith, Private Secretary to the Viceroy* (London, 1966), pp.119, 163.

127. Page to E.H. House, 2 November 1913, in Hendrick, *op. cit.*, Vol. 1 p.189.

128. A.R. Colquhoun, *The Mastery of the Pacific* (London, 1902) pp.48–50.

129. T.G. Fraser, *The Intrigues of the German Government and the Ghadr Party against British Rule in India, 1914–18* (Ph.D. thesis, University of London, 1974), pp.256–7.

130. Sir E. Denison Ross, *Both Ends of the Candle* (London, 1943), p.230.

131. Letter of 10 December 1931, in the Lothian Papers, GD 40 Sec.17, Vol. 151, in Register House, Edinburgh.

132. Information from Dr R. Jeffreys-Jones, of the University of Edinburgh.

133. Sinclair Lewis, *Gideon Planish* (Cleveland, 1943), Chap. 10.

134. D. Kincaid, *British Social Life in India, 1608–1937* (2nd edn., London, 1973), p.65.

135. P. Addison, 'Churchill and the United States', in *New Edinburgh Review*, Nos. 38–39 (1977), p.69.

136. Greenbie, *op. cit.*, pp.391–2.

137. Younghill Kang, *The Grass Roof* (New York, 1931), p.342.

138. Sir J.T. Pratt, *War and Politics in China* (London, 1943), p.123.

139. Scott Nearing and J. Freeman, *Dollar Diplomacy* (1925; New York edn., 1969), p.126.

140. Akira Iriye, *Across the Pacific – An Inner History of American–East Asian Relations* (New York, 1967), p.148.

141. J.E. Baker, *Explaining China* (London, 1927), p.90.

142. J. Spence, *The China Helpers – Western Advisers in China 1620–1960* (London, 1969), p.164.

143. *Ibid.*, pp.177–82.

144. McCoy, *op. cit.*, p.344.

145. Hoover, *op. cit.*, p.180.

146. *Ibid.*, p.366. Sara R. Smith, *The Manchurian Crisis 1931–1932* (Cambridge, 1948), finds Stimson a good deal less valiant.

147. Hoover, *op. cit.*, p.369.

148. G. Kennan, *American Diplomacy 1900–1950* (1951; New York edn., 1952), pp.53–4.

149. J.C. Grew, *Ten Years in Japan* (London, 1944), p.14.

150. H. Feis, *The Road to Pearl Harbour* (Princeton, 1950), p.6.

151. J.K. Galbraith, *The Great Crash 1929* (1954; Harmondsworth edn., 1961), pp.194–5.

152. Aldcroft, *op. cit.*, p.281.

153. Hoover, *op. cit.*, p.184.

154. L. Mayo, *Bloody Buna* (1974; London edn., 1975), p.87.

155. J. Ellis, *The Social History of the Machine Gun* (London, 1975), p.160.

156. B.W. Aldiss, *The Shape of Further Things – Speculation on Change* (1970; London edn., 1974), pp.56, 60.

157. 'Claude Farrère', *Useless Hands*; see Bailey, *op. cit.*, p.156.

158. Olaf Stapledon, *Last and First Men* (London, 1937).

159. S.G. Weinbaum, *A Martian Odyssey* (1934; reprint, with introduction by Isaac Asimov, 1974; London edn., 1977), p.61.

160. T. Milne, 'The Western', in *Sunday Times* (London), 8 November 1970.

161. Huxley, *op. cit.*, pp.251–2, 265.

162. Emma F. Estabrook, *Givers of Life – The American Indians as Contributors to Civilization* (Boston, 1931).

163. L.C. Kelly, *The Navajo Indians and Federal Indian Policy 1900–1935* (University of Arizona, 1968), pp.37 ff, 99 ff.

164. *Ibid.*, Chap. 10.

165. *Ibid.*, pp.154–5.

166. W.T. Hagan, *American Indians* (University of Chicago, 1961), p.154.

167. W. H. Haas, ed., *The American Empire – A Study of the Outlying Territories of the United States* (Chicago, 1940), pp.367–8.

168. Hoover, *op. cit.*, p.359.

169. J.A. Silen, *We, the Puerto Rican People – A Story of Oppression and Resistance* (trans. C. Belfrage, New York, 1971), pp.39, 51, 60–2, 66.

170. Haas, *op. cit.*, pp.58, 76. Cf. R.G. Tugwell, the then governor, on Washington's neglect of the island about that time: *The Stricken Land – The Story of Puerto Rico* (New York, 1947), pp.130–2.

171. See R.F. Weston, *Racism in U.S. Imperialism – The Influence of Racial*

Assumptions on American Foreign Policy, 1893–1946 (University of South Carolina, 1972), p.258.

172. R.F. Smith, *What Happened in Cuba? op. cit.*, p.195.

173. R.F. Smith, *The United States and Cuba, op. cit.*, pp.149–51.

174. *Ibid.*, p.144.

175. *Ibid.*, pp.142–3.

176. J. Alvarez del Vayo, *The Last Optimist* (London, 1950), p.250.

177. *Ibid.*, pp.255–6. Del Vayo represented Spain on the Commission.

178. Sumner Welles, *Seven Major Decisions* (London, 1951), p.106 ff.

179. Del Vayo, *op. cit.*, pp.236–7; cf. E.D. Cowan, *Josephus Daniels in Mexico* (Madison, 1960), p.18 ff.

180. H.F. Cline, *The United States and Mexico* (Harvard, 1953), p.251.

181. D. Perkins, *America's Quest for Peace* (University of Indiana, 1963), p.40.

182. W.E. and M. Dodd, eds., *Ambassador Dodd's Diary 1933–1938* (London, 1945), p.311.

183. *Ibid.*, p.94 (24 February 1934).

184. Robertson, *op. cit.*, p.170.

185. S.G. Payne, *The Spanish Revolution* (London, 1970), p.275.

186. R. P. Traina, *American Diplomacy and the Spanish Civil War* (University of Indiana, 1968), pp.110–11, 144–5. Cf. R.H. Whealey, in *The Republic and the Civil War in Spain* (ed. R. Carr, London, 1971), pp.206 and 233.

187. Ivan Maisky, *Spanish Notebooks* (trans. R. Kisch, London, 1966), p.30.

188. Welles, *op. cit.*, p.30.

189. On the U.S. and Nazi Germany, see J.V. Compton, *The Swastika and the Eagle* (London, 1968), e.g. pp.258–9.

190. Welles, *op. cit.*, p.98; cf. D.F. Drummond, *The Passing of American Neutrality 1937–1941* (Ann Arbor, 1955), p.61.

191. Ganoe, *op. cit.*, pp.513, 519; cf. A. Vagts, *A History of Militarism* (revised edn., London, 1959), p.421.

192. Lippmann, *op. cit.*, pp.17, 25–6.

193. F. Moore, *With Japan's Leaders . . . Fourteen Years as Counsellor to the Japanese Government* (London, 1943), p.74.

194. W.A. Williams, 'The Large Corporation and American Foreign Policy 1890–1958', in *American Socialist*, September 1958. Cf. C.A. Beard, *American Foreign Policy in the Making 1932–1940* (Yale, 1946), Chap. 6,

which begins by contrasting rival arguments for isolation or imperialism as the best way back to prosperity.

195. Harold Nicolson, *Diaries and Letters 1930–1939*, ed. N. Nicolson (1966; London edn., 1969), p.396 (14 June 1939).

196. *The Forrestal Diaries – The Inner History of the Cold War*, ed. W. Millis (London, 1952), p.129.

197. Welles, *op. cit.*, p.88.

198. C. Sykes, *Troubled Loyalty – A Biography of Adam von Trott zu Solz* (London, 1968), pp.302–3. Trott was on a mission to the U.S. late in 1939, with conflicting aims.

199. R.W. Van Alstyne, *American Crisis Diplomacy – The Quest for Collective Security 1918–1952* (Stanford, 1952), p.57.

200. Compton, *op. cit.*, Part 1.

201. Bullard, *op. cit.*, pp.235–6.

202. Welles, *op. cit.*, p.78.

203. *Ibid.*, pp.80–1.

204. Van Alstyne, *op. cit.*, p.15.

205. A.W. Griswold, *The Far Eastern Policy of the United States* (New York, 1938), pp.437–8.

206. Feis, *op. cit.*, pp.6–7.

207. Griswold, *op. cit.*, p.466.

208. Grew, *op. cit.*, p.237.

209. Moore, *op. cit.*, p.71.

210. Sir R. Craigie, *Behind the Japanese Mask* (London, 1945), pp.100 and 104–5.

211. Moore, *op. cit.*, p.120.

212. Akira Iriye, *op. cit.*, p.209.

213. Moore, *op. cit.*, p.126.

214. P.C. Lowe, 'Great Britain and the Outbreak of War with Japan, 1941', in *War and Society*, ed. M.R. Foot (London, 1973), pp.19–20, 24.

215. Grew, *op. cit.*, p.379 (29 September 1941), etc.

216. *Ibid.*, pp.404–5 (3 November 1941).

217. Craigie, *op. cit.*, p.130.

218. Feis, *op. cit.*, pp.275, 336.

219. H.E. Barnes, ed., *Perpetual War for Perpetual Peace – A Critical Examination of*

the Foreign Policy of Franklin Delano Roosevelt and its Aftermath (Caldwell, 1953), p.642.

220. Harry Hopkins, quoted in Welles, *op. cit.*, p.97.

221. Compton, *op. cit.*, p.32.

222. W.A. Boelcke, ed., *The Secret Conferences of Dr Goebbels, October 1939–March 1943* (trans. E. Osers, London, 1967), p.149.

223. *Ibid.*, p.174.

224. *Ibid.*, p.242; cf. E.K. Bramsted, *Goebbels and National Socialist Propaganda 1925–1945* (University of Michigan, 1965), p.440.

225. Boelcke, *op. cit.*, p.296.

226. *Ibid.*, p.303.

227. *The Memoirs of Cordell Hull* (London, 1948), pp.1, 523–4.

228. A.G. Hope, *America and Swaraj* (Washington, D.C., 1968), Appendix C. Cf. Hull, *op. cit.*, Section 108: 'Independence for India'.

229. John Glendevon, *The Viceroy at Bay* (London, 1971), p.269.

230. Chester Wilmot, *The Struggle for Europe* (London, 1952), p.635.

231. Compton, *op. cit.*, p.95.

232. Welles, *op. cit.*, pp.xiv, 124 ff.

233. H.S. Ferns, *The Argentine Republic* (Newton Abbot, 1973), p.143.

234. Welles, *op. cit.*, pp.152–3.

235. Grew, *op. cit.*, p.445 (19 February 1942).

PART SIX

THE AMERICAN HEGEMONY

1

Capitalism, Militarism and the Cold War

At the end of July 1945 the Senate ratified the charter of the new U.N.O. by eighty-nine votes to two. It was a striking reversal of its rejection of the League after the First World War, and sealed America's full and permanent entry into the world and all its affairs. As to what this would or should portend, during the war very diverse ideas had been showing themselves. Wendell Wilkie's open-minded book *One World*, written after a tour in 1942 which included Siberia, received an enthusiastic welcome. On the other hand many were moving towards the assumption that American participation must mean American headship. 'The war', two Americans wrote soon after its close, 'left us in a position of world leadership. With the spirit of 1941–1945, one could be sure that the leadership would be exercised wisely and effectively.'[1] Now at last the hour was striking for that rational harmony of the developed nations, brought together by community of interest, which had floated before many minds; particularly minds with a New World distaste for the muddle and waste that Europe, still not far from its medieval past, took for granted.

But history fulfils no dreams in the shape men have dreamed them. And there were others in the air, of a less pacific cast. A historian writing of the Mexican War of a century earlier rejected the long-standing account of it as a piece of indefensible aggression on the part of the U.S., and portrayed it instead as 'an inescapable and a not inglorious step in the historical process by which the

United States of America was brought to its present place in the world'.[2] (A growing proportion of the country's illegal immigrants are Mexicans, flocking back into the provinces their ancestors were bereft of and offering cheap labour that undercuts American workers.) Expansionism, as reflected at many magnifications by science fiction, had been graduating from themes of interplanetary to interstellar, even intergalactic conflict; before panting time on earth reached the atom-bomb, Hollywood was already at *Flash Gordon Conquers the Universe*, a serial viewed by gaping wartime audiences as far away as Lahore.

Even in more prosaic attempts to visualize the U.S.'s new place in the scheme of things, there was a streak of the old mystic faith in its special destiny, the beckoning finger of Providence, combined now with the twin themes of anti-communism and defiance of a Soviet power which would take the lead if America failed to do so. Americans ought to be grateful for the Soviet challenge, according to Kennan, for compelling them to take up 'the responsibilities of moral and political leadership that history plainly intended them to bear'.[3] James Burnham, the herald of managerialism, spelled out in 1947 the message of unavoidable struggle with the U.S.S.R. in more realistic detail. With the era of a throng of states genuinely as well as formally independent at an end, the atom-bomb made it feasible for a single state to achieve primacy. 'A World Empire has become possible, and the attempt will be made to establish a World Empire.' It would be disguised under some other name, he added;[4] his own name for it, revealed later in the book, was *'the policy of democratic world order'*.[5]

All this meant that the War was being succeeded immediately by 'Cold War' and all its consequences. To capture the leadership, or dominion, of what it was soon calling the 'free world', the U.S. had not a few qualifications, but was conspicuously lacking in others. It was being suddenly, prematurely, advanced to primacy in the capitalist camp, without any adequate inner preparation, by the suicidal behaviour of the older nations. Burnham was critical of some deficiencies, such as 'provincialism and smugness', and tactless manners with foreigners.[6] American soldiers in China during the War, and in Korea after it, were taxed with arrogance and misconduct;[7] in fairness it must be added that this could not be said of American soldiers everywhere. More fundamental shortcomings lay in the structure and organization of a very exceptional state.

'America' is a loose code-word for a complex array of social *circuitry*, allowing great concentration of visible authority to go with great dispersal, or concealment, of real responsibility. This made for easy self-assertion on the part of the swollen power of capital. In the inter-war years the economy was moving further towards concentration and monopoly, and the War accelerated this process. Its dominant sections would not readily be kept under decent restraint by an administration itself riddled with wealthy businessmen. By contrast with Europe the state had less autonomy, less existence of its own. A myriad threads, seen or unseen, linked the realm of money with that of politics. A former Under-Secretary of State, A.A. Berle, said that some big corporations dealing with foreign governments kept files on U.S. diplomatic officials, 'rating them according to their probable usefulness'.[8] Diplomats posted to Cuba regularly had ties with big business interests, and worked for them as a matter of course. A flux of employees moving between public service and private, and obscuring their boundaries, was going much further than in Europe. Government has been left in a position like that of French kings in former days, who sold so many official posts that they lost control of their own bureaucracy. An American president may be the most powerful man on earth, but it is hard to think of him resisting pressure from a strong capitalist group, on any foreign issue remote from public consciousness.

Forrestal as Navy Secretary found policy-making 'hasty, disconnected and piecemeal'.[9] It is so everywhere, more or less, but in Washington more than in most capitals, because of too many converging pressures from all over the country and the world, too many things for a president to think of and too few reliable agents to inform or act for him. When the economist Galbraith undertook the embassy at Delhi, he made the discovery that the State Department had as a rule no policy. When urgent telegrams received any answer at all, it was 'to recommend evasion of issues that cannot be evaded'.[10] More multifarious than the British empire, the new hegemony was even less capable of finding any coherent programme, other than of bullheaded negation. Hence its readiness to let plans be made for it, by company directors or secret agents. State apparatus had expanded abruptly and enormously since 1941, and to hypertrophied organs like the Pentagon a great many distortions of policy may be ascribed. But there has usually been capitalist method in any political madness.

A critic has indeed asserted without too much overstatement that 'American foreign policy during the postwar era was initiated, planned, and carried out by the richest, most powerful, and most international-minded owners and managers of major corporations and financial institutions.'[11] There have however been pressures of ideological and ethnic, as well as economic, origin. The United States might be called a federal union of *lobbies*, and professional lobbyists are a species of politician who may count more than the legislators on whom they exercise the arts of persuasion. They are registered, but there is no check on how they disburse their lavish funds. In 1975, when the powerful Greek lobby secured a ban on arms for Turkey, heedless of presidential wishes, and Turkey retaliated by closing U.S. bases, there were reported to be a hundred and fifty former Congressmen working as lobbyists, well versed in the ways of Capitol Hill.

Implementing, and even designing, strategy has to a remarkable extent been left to one of the most astonishing organizations in political history, the C.I.A. This was set up in 1941 as the OSS to integrate a number of intelligence networks (fresh ones have sprouted since). Admiral King feared at the outset that this body might acquire power beyond anything which had been intended for it,[12] and he spoke with foresight. It was heir to police practices inside the U.S., third-degree methods among them, as developed by company guards and state police forces. Between America and the vast majority of inhabitants of the lands under its sceptre, the gulf of incomprehension is very wide, and it is the Metternichian instinct of any ruling class or people whose subjects are beyond its ken to seek contact with them through the medium of espionage, and try to foil – by counter-mining – the sapping and mining it always uneasily fears is being carried on against it. Napoleon's police bureaux steadily proliferated, in Tsarist Russia at the end every department had its own secret service.

Within the U.S. itself spy agencies have been multiplying; outside, immense scientific resources have been devoted to building observatories capable of listening to the thoughts, the heartbeats, of the rest of the world. But the C.I.A. has never been content to gather information, to watch history unfold; it has been making history. Judging by the glimpses into murky depths that recent years have given us, it has often functioned as a parallel government, less closely linked to its nominal superiors than to business interests. These frequently have occasion to keep their overseas dealings under a veil, and whether or not the workings of the constitutional part of the American government are truly democratic, they are exceptionally public. Moreover business corporations, huge as they may be, are engrossed in immediate objectives; the C.I.A., as their common denominator, can help to weave the aims of both government and corporations together into a pattern.[13]

At Hiroshima the U.S. displayed its terrible swift sword, chiefly − it is not hard to believe − by way of warning to Moscow. C.I.A. philosophy has always been one of force, it has constantly thought in terms of police or military action. This was one aspect of the sudden transformation of America from a country proud of its immunity from Old World militarism into the most heavily armed nation ever known; even if its accoutrements have never ceased to hang on it with a certain awkwardness, like the cumbrous suit of armour on the Yankee at King Arthur's court. For the first time a very large conscript army was being kept up in peacetime, as well as a formidable navy and air force, all three drawn together by the National Security Act of 1947 into a unified 'defense' system. There was also the atom-bomb, of which the Baruch Plan sought to keep a monopoly for the U.S. under the camouflage of a supranational authority.[14] Leading figures from the armed forces were now a prominent part of the country's 'power elite'.[15] They entered new spheres of influence during the War, when Roosevelt worked very much with his chiefs of staff directly, relegating the State Department to the background.[16]

Since then they have seemed to some observers to be attaining a level of power equivalent to that of big business. This impression is fortified by 'the irrepressible garrulousness of American military men', remarks a writer who rejects the idea of all American policies emanating from the Pentagon.[17] It has, he allows, abused its position by setting on foot propaganda and indoctrination 'of most reactionary tendency'.[18] Most of the military figures in the public eye were of course strenuously conservative. General Wedemeyer, one of the American commanders in China during and after the War, had spent some years at a Nazi military academy, and left it imbued with hatred of 'Bolshevism'. General MacArthur, son of a general who took part in the conquest of the Philippines, 'considered the Russians a greater menace than the Nazis had ever been', his admirer the British chief of staff learned.[19] He had spent most of his life in the Pacific, and acquired much of the mentality of an old China 'hand'. 'Aggressive, resolute and dynamic leadership' was his formula for handling Orientals, he announced publicly in 1950, defying President Truman's instructions over Taiwan.[20] Such talk could be sure of applause from ex-servicemen's organizations, under conservative direction as in all countries, like the American Legion or the Catholic War Veterans.

It was a saving grace of imperial America that a General MacArthur could be dismissed by a President Truman, as a President Nixon years later was to be dismissed by the public. Another was that it did not after all, for reasons creditable as well as prudential, go to war with its great rival, even while it alone had atom-bombs and the Soviet Union was recovering from war exhaustion. Yet the paradox remains of this vanguard nation, with its mission to replace the old international anarchy with something more sensible, pushing arms production forward so gigantically, and arms sales so anarchically. It is a cognate puzzle to the limitless sales of small arms inside the country, with the resulting high death-rate. America has not fallen in love with war; the army remains a second-class profession. But if it has not been converted to the cult of Mars, it may be called a besotted devotee of Vulcan.

War between the strong does not pay, but manufacture of weapons pays extremely richly. The military establishment itself is far more than in any other country an extension of the business world, even though graduation of govern-ment employees to private firms started long since with ex-generals and admirals in Europe joining the boards of arms firms. This has been happening regularly in America since 1945.[21] The arms industry grew accustomed to incalculable profits during the World War, and it has been able to convince the public that its activity is necessary to the economy as well as to defence. Long pre-war years of depression left both employers and workers half-consciously persuaded that the precarious capitalist heaven could only be propped up by endless expenditure on arms. 'Every major sector of American manufacturing has become deeply mili-tarized in the course of the Cold War.'[22]

In the decade of the 1960s Lockheed Aircraft, biggest of all the armament firms, received contracts totalling more than sixteen billion dollars.[23] Its pal-miest year was 1969, at the height of the fighting in Vietnam. For shareholders so lucrative a war scarcely needed an excuse, win or lose. Some Congressmen were complaining of being 'prodded' to vote for it by the Pentagon through the medium of arms firms in their states.[24] Even Eisenhower, who came to the White House from the army, felt constrained to warn the nation against 'this con-junction of an immense military establishment and a large arms industry ... The total influence – economic, political, even spiritual – is felt in every city, every state house, every office of the Federal Government.' But he left this famous warning against 'the military-industrial complex' to his farewell address in 1961; and he was handing over to a successor who won his election by joining in a clamour about an imaginary 'missile gap'. Some at least of America's arguments for rejecting Soviet proposals for arms limitation were 'singularly unimpressive'.[25] The arms race was too rewarding, politically as well as financially, to be allowed to flag.

Between 1957 and 1964 manufacturing output nearly doubled, while the number of workers in industry was unchanged. This was due to the country's fertility of technological invention, but it was bolstered too by the steady growth of the military budget. Similarly an American could write of the efficiency of his country's enterprise abroad as 'a major cause for apprehension among nations. This peacetime aggression … is almost impossible to combat';[26] but here too professional skill was not the sole weapon. 'The old imperialism – exploitation for foreign profit – has no place in the concepts of democratic fair dealing', Truman might declare in his inaugural address of January 1949; to many abroad, American capitalism has often seemed to be functioning on very much the lines traced by the theory of imperialism pioneered by Hobson and developed by Lenin.

American capitalism has undeniably been acquiring more and more a monopolistic structure. During the Second World War big companies got the lion's share of the contracts, while many small ones were squeezed out. This process continued, and a Senate enquiry disclosed that the hundred biggest corporations held 46% of all industrial capital in 1947, and nearly 57% in 1962.[27] A few more years, and sales of the fifty biggest amounted to nearly a quarter of the gross national product.[28] There was a democratic underpinning for all this in the very widespread habit of dabbling in shares: America was still a gambling nation, and even modest stockholders, workmen among them, could enjoy the sensation of being in the same boat with the multi-millionaires. Control on the other hand remained firmly in the hands of 'tiny, self-perpetuating oligarchies',[29] collectively making up the big-business elite, real master of the country and its empire. Hobson maintained that a top-heavy capitalism, to escape congestion at home and to make higher profits abroad, will export capital in ever-increasing volume; the case of America seems to corroborate this very fully. During 1947–55 direct investment abroad came to 6.3 billion dollars; during 1956–64, to

15.8.[30] A total stock of 32 billions of foreign investment abroad in 1960 rose to 86 in 1971.

The more U.S. capital moved forward from trade with other countries to investment in them, the more concerned it would be to ensure their having congenial governments. Of the total U.S. investment abroad in 1960, 57%, and in 1971 62%, were in areas more or less independent, Canada or Europe or Japan. Like the old British empire with its white Dominions and 'coloured' colonies, the American hegemony has covered two contrasting types of regions, on which its effect has been divergent. Among weak, economically underdeveloped, divided peoples, as in most of Latin America, it is scarcely possible for any foreign capital not to domineer; and in such settings American investments, though on a smaller scale than in the advanced countries, have reaped much higher returns. Similarly, at home, capital makes liberal wage agreements with well-organized unions, while it exploits unprotected labour: women, Blacks, Mexican seasonal workers.

As prefect over the developed industrial nations, America has undoubtedly done them much good, if not undiluted good. It was high time for capitalist Europe's senseless squabblings to be put a stop to; if the U.S. could not eliminate them, it has at any rate damped them down, and helped to divert energies into productive activity. (Moscow has rendered an analogous service to Eastern Europe.) Much of the post-war prosperity of Western Europe and Japan must be credited to this, and Washington can fairly say to them, as the Tory leader Macmillan said to the British electorate, 'You never had it so good'. For European, especially British, scientists and technicians and doctors, there was for many years the same ready access to employment in the U.S. at higher pay as in earlier times had made ordinary workers its well-wishers; though there were protests in Europe against this 'brain drain' as a new sort of imperial tribute.

Under such tutelage the major capitalist countries have actually come to show more solidarity than the socialist camp. True, the hegemony has not been able to prevent, and in some ways has undesignedly helped to precipitate, shooting-matches among the smaller fry, like Pakistan and India, Cyprus and Turkey, and of course Israel and the Arabs. But none of these have been authentic capitalist contests; and despite many dire Marxist predictions any prospect of armed conflict among the advanced nations has seemed to be vanishing. They are afraid of getting too badly hurt, and of opening the door to socialism; and they have known that any such folly would meet with an American veto. There is also in this novel harmony an element of the 'ultra-imperialism' foreseen by Kautsky, and in another way by Theodore Roosevelt when he said in a London speech that 'we ought to make common cause in our dealing with the backward races of the world'.[31]

American money has poured into Europe, both because labour was cheaper there than at home and because goods manufactured there could circumvent tariff barriers. By 1968 U.S. capital was giving employment to half a million Britons, even if this was not all new employment. Governments, especially the French, might feel nervous, like Canada much earlier, about this pacific invasion; Marxists assailed it as imperialistic; the ordinary workmen cared very little who his employers were, so long as he had a job. Besides, his employer's identity might be shrouded by the anonymity of a multinational corporation, that logical outgrowth of political *rapprochement*.

Multinational corporations disarmed many jealousies by finding comfortable berths for foreign as well as American businessmen. Thus a far-reaching control over the Australian economy has been disguised or kept out of sight, and local men given a decent share. As elsewhere, 'American management increasingly aims, not at direct dominance, but at the creation of multi-national firms.'[32] Over much of the globe today there is so complex a criss-crossing of American capital in Arabia and Japan, Arab and Japanese investment in America, Dutch syndicates buying real estate in the Scottish Highlands, British in Germany, that Lenin would be hard put to it to say which is the imperialist, who is subjugating whom. But most of the multinationals are predominantly American; and one side of their ancestry is the arms trade, which was among the first to develop inter-national ramifications. There were devious accords over patents in the inter-war years between American groups like Standard Oil and companies in Nazi Germany.[33] Like ships sailing under flags of convenience, multinationals enjoy a double dose of freedom from responsibility, moral or legal.

Towards the close of the World War and after it, America and Britain were each by turns, in spasmodic jerks, pushing the other into Cold War attitudes. Americans were not without some inkling that Britain was once more playing the part of evil genius; that the dying imperialism of the Old World was trying to lure America on, and wanted to appoint that country its heir. A cabinet memorandum of March 1945 observed that Britain would welcome a conflict between the U.S. and Russia, and that 'to follow the British programme would be to proceed towards that end'.[34] Henry Wallace as presidential candidate warned the public of this. There was no real inconsistency in his warning the British public in 1947 not to be duped by American anti-communist scares; on both sides of the Atlantic the peoples were being stampeded by their rulers.

Half a century before this, Senator Hoar, back from Europe, when asked what the British thought about America going into the Philippines, replied: 'They think we are making asses of ourselves, but are very anxious that we should continue to do so.'[35] Lately a British historian writing of British policy-makers after 1945 has spoken of 'the contempt displayed in private for American naivety, ignorance, and sheer professional incompetence'.[36] A more tactful countryman of his has congratulated Britain on being still, when the Cold War was getting under way, 'the principal support and counsellor of the United States'. He was hoping, in 1967 when Britain was shut out from Europe by De Gaulle, for 'an ever closer association with the United States', even for 'some kind of Anglo-Saxon *bloc*', with Washington as its centre.[37] Anglo-Saxonism was shedding its parting gleams. Another was the notion of a well-known American evangelist that 'Saxon' is derived from 'Isaac', and that Britain and America were joint heirs of the Chosen People, two 'Birthright nations', sadly negligent of their high calling to rule the earth.[38]

Cold War began with discords over Poland with Moscow, and conflict in Greece with the Greek left (not with Moscow which had agreed to the country being part of the Western sphere). Here especially Britain led the way and America with misgivings followed. British intervention in the Greek civil war, to ensure the setting up of a conservative regime by collaboration with Greeks many of whom had lately been collaborating with the Nazis, at first startled Washington. Before long, however, the bogy of communism conduced to 'a more understanding attitude';[39] America's own subsequent interventions in Korea and Vietnam would follow the Greek precedent. But at the time it felt that things were going too far, and there were fresh twinges of doubt when, early in 1947, Britain could bear the cost of the operation no longer, and America had to agree to take it over. Dean Acheson, then Under-Secretary of State, declared that 'the Greek government was not a satisfactory one to us; that it contained many elements that were reactionary', obvious targets for Soviet criticism.[40] Truman perceived that aid to Greece was being used 'to further partisan political, rather than national, aims', and wanted the ruling clique to broaden its base and seek popular support.[41]

For a while America did insist on ministries from the right of centre at Athens instead of from the extreme right. Liberal and progressive feeling fostered by the war years could not be stifled all at once, and the public was wiser than its mentors; Cold War hysteria had to be artificially induced, first by manoeuvres and then by the stage thunder of McCarthy. Truman's weak political position exposed him to right-wing nudges. He and his inner group of advisers were moving well ahead of opinion, exploiting the Greek conflict to rouse fears of communism.[42] They were going ahead of and manipulating opinion as they had watched Roosevelt do before 1941, though now in an opposite direction. Taft himself, the arch-Republican, acquiesced reluctantly in the Greek affair, asking awkward questions which as his biographer says were never properly discussed.[43]

No nation was to be allowed to quit the capitalist – or feudal – camp, whether it wanted to or not. (Marxism was to follow suit with a similar ban, though it was not invariably enforced.) America had fought its own civil war to prevent any member states from going their own way, and the memory had a tenacious hold; the same principle was now to be enlarged to global dimensions. In the same month of March 1947 while Washington was swallowing its doubts about Greece, Truman delivered the address to a joint session of Congress embodying what was soon called the 'Truman Doctrine'. 'I believe', he pronounced, 'that it must be the policy of the United States to support free peoples who are resisting attempted subjugation by armed minorities or by outside pressures.' At the close he received a standing ovation from all present, with the exception of one labour representative, Vito Marcantonio.[44] In effect, as Owen Lattimore wrote, this gospel 'offered support to any country claiming to be under pressure either from Russia or from its own Communists – with no reforms stipulated and no questions asked'. Lattimore noted too that 'The Truman Doctrine originated more in out-of-date British thinking than in up-to-date American thinking.'[45] In retrospect it has come to look to American as well as other historians a symptom of 'the often irrational anti-communism, which was subsequently to distort the vision of makers of American foreign policy';[46] though there is little to suggest that its axioms have been abandoned in the corridors of power today.

As a sweetener, and to make sure of America's most vital outwork, Western and Central Europe, the Truman Doctrine was promptly followed by the Marshall

Plan. 'Our policy', Marshall declared, 'is directed not against any country or doctrine but against hunger, poverty, desperation and chaos.' But he went on at once to speak of creating 'political and social conditions in which free institutions can exist',[47] and there was no need for him to labour the fact that the chief of these was free enterprise. There was genuine goodwill in the plan, and among those who footed the bill for it, but as after 1918 food and raw materials were being used to steer a hungry Europe on to the right path. In Britain the Labour government could not fail to heed the admonition against too many socialistic experiments.

There were other parts of the world where the revolutionary tide, in spite of King Canute's command to halt, went on flowing, most strongly in China where a vaster civil war was being fought. During the War with Japan some American commanders were obstreperously anti-communist; those like 'Vinegar Joe' Stilwell, who were more concerned with winning the War, knew that Chiang Kai-shek and his corrupt and repressive Kuomintang government were not fighting the Japanese, as Mao's forces were, but were saving their American arms for use against the communists later on.[48] After the Japanese surrender Truman, and Marshall whom Truman sent to China to see how things were, had enough sense to realize that they were very precarious. There could be no question of the U.S. intervening directly in a Chinese struggle, if only because after 1945 its soldiers, like British soldiers in India, were impatient to go home. Several years of indoctrination would be needed before new American armies could be sent to fight in the Far East. As to the Kuomintang, the Foreign Office expert on China Sir John Pratt once said that propping it up was like trying to pin apple-jelly on a wall. Truman was soon forming a similar opinion, and grasping the fact that, as he remarked later on, money given to it was liable to be embezzled. 'They're all thieves, every damn one of them.'[49] History was to saddle America with many allies of the same stripe.

The best that could be done was to work for a compromise, as Stalin also was doing. Unluckily for Truman, Chiang was bent on provoking a struggle, in the hope of dragging America in to do his fighting for him again. He and his regime then showed themselves totally inept, in spite of lavish stocks of equipment from the U.S. By June 1947 the Secretary of State had to tell his colleagues that the situation was collapsing, thanks to the 'Nationalist' government's 'incompetence, inefficiency and stubbornness'.[50] By the end of 1948 Mao's armies had triumphed, and what was left of the Kuomintang was in flight to Taiwan. For the

U.S. this was a painful reversal of the victory over Japan. It did much to pre-cipitate the Cold War fever. At the time, there were still Americans who understood that revolution in Asia could no longer be put down by force, as was the Boxer Rebellion in 1900. 'A few western guns,' the *New York Herald Tribune* wrote in 1949, 'or even many of them, are no longer effective instruments to cow and control millions of Asiatics.'[51] But there was a clamour for more positive action, in quarters where, as often in like circumstances later on, no account was taken of social realities difficult for America to comprehend. Any anti-commu-nist down to the most benighted feudal landlord was being hailed as a paladin of 'freedom'. 'In China', Lattimore wrote, 'the American inability to distinguish between feudalism and capitalism drove Chinese capitalists, managers and technicians frantic.'[52]

Canute was now turning into a sorcerer's apprentice. In any weighing up of U.S. foreign policies the wrestlings of political factions, however destitute of any serious meaning, must be taken into account; and instead of Truman's position being improved by his Doctrine, he was soon being outdone by Republicans who could roar against the communist menace even louder. As Taft wrote to a friend in 1951, they could not hope to win the next election on domestic issues, and therefore must hammer at the administration's 'utter failure and incapacity' abroad.[53] This would be a constant factor, since the Republican Party proved much less able than the Tory to give itself a new look in domestic policy. In spite of Taft's scepticism about Greece he was all for making the most of the 'loss' of China, the country which was to have been as important a bastion of America's world system as India had been of the British empire.

Loudest of all was the 'China lobby', that impressive example of a pressure group in action. It was financed by Kuomintang money, much of which had originally come out of the pocket of the American taxpayer, who was thus paying for his own deception. How strong it was, Truman years afterwards told an interviewer, the public had little inkling. 'They had a great many Congressmen and Senators lined up to do pretty much what they were told, and they had billions of dollars to spend, and they spent it. They even had some newspapers lined up ....'.[54] Their achievement amounted to a rewriting of history as astonishing as any of Stalin's. Books realistically depicting Kuomintang China had circulated widely; Jack Belden's description of China at the end of the World War was one of the finest things any American has ever written.[55] Now all this was being wiped off the slate, and replaced with a stereotype of a communist China dominated by Russia, where the family was being destroyed;[56] a new Yellow Peril, aggressively expansionist, which must be forcibly 'contained', partly because it was bursting with over-population, like the old China, and partly because it was communist.[57]

Treason in high places, especially in the State Department, supplied a convenient excuse for the defeat. This led on very directly to McCarthy's wild and whirling allegations against all kinds of progressives in the country. Conservatism was the beneficiary. It had deeply disliked Roosevelt's mild liberalism, and was now rendered neurotic by the prospect of something far worse. The virulence of the reaction which was being worked up, the return to the 'Red-baiting' of the 1920s, betrayed fear that forces of change at home might be much stronger than they proved to be, and that socialism might gain ground in America as everywhere else. At the same time defeat in China lent catastrophic proportions to the menace to world capitalism. An anti-socialist international must be set up in place of the Communist International now disbanded: free enterprise was to unite the human race.

All this was reviving the familiar syndrome which identified dissent with disease. In Kennan's language communism was 'a malignant parasite', an outbreak of 'pathogenic bacteria'.[58] In the same spirit Frederick William IV of Prussia, when his subjects wanted a Constitution, denounced liberalism as a disease of the spinal column, and Von Moltke in 1914 talked of the cancer of Serbian 'anarchism' having to be burned out with the hot iron of war for the sake of European order and civilization.[59] America was now to be the Great Surgeon, or sanitary cleanser of the globe, 'flushing out' communists as formerly it had flushed out equally ruthless and cunning Red Indians at home.

Every dominant group needs a dash of the mystical in its thinking, to give it confidence in its vocation. Anti-communism as an ideology was America's substitute for the 'civilizing mission' of earlier imperialism. It could be grafted on to the ostensible purpose of the Second World War, defence of democracy. Religion could be enlisted as easily as in old empire-building days. A critic discussing Henry James and *The Bostonians* has spoken of 'the puritan obstinate need to regenerate the world'.[60] We have heard much about puritanism and the rise of capitalism, but its connection with that of imperialism, especially American, calls for notice too; though in the course of its expansion American capitalism has merged with other, more primitive things, and moved far away from the puritan ethos as defined by Max Weber with its ideal of sober rationality, its 'horror of illegal, political, colonial booty', and of 'monopoly types of capitalism which depended on the favour of princes and men'.[61] But divers Churches at home and abroad threw themselves into the Cold War; in this unanimity may be seen the *fons et origo* of the ecumenical movement towards reconciliation of all Christians, a spiritual parallel to that among capitalists of all nations. Moral Rearmament was its most disreputable pacemaker. Roman Catholicism was eagerest of all to regenerate a sinful world by fire and sword, as it had done so lately with Spain after the Civil War there. Not long before his death Cardinal Spellman, who would have been in his element as chaplain to Franco or Pizarro, was in Vietnam as chaplain-general preaching a Christmas message of fire and slaughter.

Once basking in the sunshine of Marshall aid Western Europe had a transparent motive for doing all it could, with short-sighted egotism, to keep relations between the U.S. and the Soviet Union as bad as it could. They were greatly worsened by the – rash and ill-judged, perhaps – communist *coup* in Czechoslovakia in 1948, which turned U.S. policy towards the building of Western Europe into an armed coalition. Next year the NATO alliance came into being. From this achievement Washington went on to press for European unification. In 1962 Kennedy was proposing an equal alliance between the U.S. and a united Europe including Britain, a 'splendid idea' which, an English enthusiast thought, should have silenced any suspicions of the U.S. 'seeking to dominate its allies, or impose any kind of veiled hegemony'.[62] Any such aims were indeed secondary to the overriding one of hostility to the U.S.S.R. But Europe, though chastened by war, was still inveterately particularist.

In Washington's eyes, since the ultimate goal, preservation of democracy, was righteous, all means towards it were warrantable, including suppression of democracy. It was generally expected in Europe at the end of the War that the allies would liberate Spain from Franco (and Portugal from his fellow-dictator Salazar), as a collaborator with the Axis, who could be brought down by economic pressure. But this was no part of the American plan. 'Spain has nothing to fear from the United Nations', Roosevelt wrote to Franco, as a 'sincere friend', during the War,[63] and it became clear now that the Spanish government at least had nothing to fear. Excluded for the sake of appearances from Marshall aid, it got financial help in another way, by leasing bases to the U.S.; meanwhile U.S. business interests were moving in to take over Nazi and other assets, and Spanish capitalists made haste to fraternize with them.[64] Spain had to be left out of NATO, because of European prejudice, but Dulles treated it as virtually a member; in 1959 President Eisenhower set the seal on this by visiting Spain, and three years later a new agreement over bases constituted 'an alliance in all but name'.[65] Friendship with America 'remained the corner-stone of Franco's foreign policy.'[66]

Foster Dulles, Secretary of State from 1952 to 1959, was a pious lawyer well equipped to furnish both the moral fury and the dialectical ingenuity that were called for, even if his sermonizing on the wickedness of communism wearied even the willing ear of Winston Churchill. Whereas British diplomacy had been practical and empirical, because the British place in the world was old and assured, America's was always more theorizing and argumentative. But its new order was taking shape in an atmosphere far removed from the Enlightenment still lingering into early 20th-century America. Under Dulles' management the U.N.O. made a convenient scaffolding, as Wilson's League could scarcely have done, for American leadership. Economic weapons, and much private 'arm-twisting' of delegates from minor capitals anxious not to lose their comfortable posts, ensured docile majorities and kept the Soviet Union isolated and communist China excluded. Neutralism was not to be tolerated: any country, like India, choosing 'non-alignment', fell under resentful suspicion.

Instead of the former clinging to isolationism, America's non-alignment of the 1930s between democracy and fascism, it was as busy as France had been after 1918 constructing a network of alliances. NATO was enlarged in 1955 to embrace West Germany, whose rearmament was one of a good many things imposed on Europe against the grain. Greece and Turkey, not much closer to democracy than to the Atlantic, were also members. In 1954 came SEATO, the South-East Asia Treaty Organization, which bore a marked family likeness to the Anti-Comintern Pact of 1936. Next year there was the Baghdad Pact, composed of Britain, Turkey, Iran, Iraq (which withdrew in 1958 after the overthrow of the reactionary monarchy) and Pakistan. In this combination Britain provided democratic respectability, and the U.S. stage-management through military advisers. In 1959 it was reorganized as the Central Treaty Organization

(CENTO). The utility of the Baghdad Pact 'has never been apparent';[67] the same might be said of most of the others.

These tactics were not unlike Britain's 'subsidy-system' in 18th-century Europe, but with America taking a far more active, leading part. A student of the American-Australian partnership emphasizes how little say Australia has had in its proceedings. 'The alliance ties Australia to purposes defined in Washington.'[68] America has kept its own footholds, in the shape of a chain of islands, rather as the Portuguese once ruled the eastern seas, in addition to the bases provided by its allies. In 1953 some objectors published a list of these, intended 'to reveal the almost incredible extent of our military commitments throughout the world. It will stagger even most of those who are already alarmed at the trend.'[69] America has been sanguine of being able to keep control because of its crushing military, naval, and technical superiority over all its associates. Frequently action has been threatened against countries not amenable to its wishes. In 1977 a Brookings Institute report found that 'On no fewer than 215 occasions since the end of World War II, the U.S. has seriously threatened to unleash some of its military might in order to gain diplomatic leverage.' (The U.S.S.R.'s tally was 115.[70])

2

The Old Empires and Neo-Colonialism

In a pre-war newsreel Roosevelt said with unction, a Thanksgiving Day turkey in front of him, that carving a turkey was better than carving up a map, like the fascist buccaneers. At the Yalta conference he made fun of Churchill's obsession with territorial acquisitions, to be grabbed without rhyme or reason.[71] After the War there was much cutting up of frontiers to be done, and talk of an 'American empire' was current in Washington, but to outward appearance the U.S., just as in 1919, was taking nothing except some odds and ends for strategic reasons. Here was a moderation more striking than Britain's in the share-out of 1815. In 1946 the U.S. set a good example to colonialists by fulfilling its pledge of independence for the Philippines, a year ahead of the British withdrawal from India. It drove a hard enough bargain. By threatening to withhold compensation promised for war damage, it secured not only military and naval bases on long lease, but a commercial treaty guaranteeing 'parity' of opportunity, which as between strong and weak could not mean equality. The new nation retained its preferences and sugar quota in the U.S. market, but this perpetuated the old pattern of relations; there was little fresh investment, and it was always exceeded by the profits repatriated to America.

Independence was being negotiated not with the Filipino people, but with the dominant class, headed by Manuel Roxas, many of whose members had collaborated with Japan and could be relied on to collaborate with Washington. 'No colony in the world', an apologist has asserted, 'was more vigorously tutored to be a democracy, or responded more enthusiastically.'[72] But this was only on an academic plane, completely divorced from social realities. U.S. rule had further enriched the landlord, following the adage that to him that hath, more shall be given. Between 1918 and 1938 the number of farm-owners fell by half, while the big estates expanded.[73] Despite the lack of tariff protection against American dumping, low wages allowed some manufacturing to grow in the post-war period. But the country retained a heavily feudal bias. Concentration of landed property continued: more and more of the soil came to be cultivated by tenant farmers, occupying smaller and smaller plots.[74]

America could not avoid some uneasiness, early on, in view of the Hukbalahap revolt. Many peasants who had resisted the Japanese went on resisting their landlords, under communist leadership. Sent out to study the situation, the Bell Commission pressed for reform; the Filipino oligarchy remained obdurate, and since there was nothing to replace it with, there was no means of enforcing change. In such circumstances American influence has been much weaker for good than for ill. With the arms bestowed on it, the Manila government was able to defy its rebels; through it the U.S. was waging a second war of conquest. It seemed to some that Manila's mailed fist methods were fanning peasant resistance instead of quelling it.[75] In fact, by 1953, as an organized movement it was defeated; but social unrest driven underground took other, more morbid forms. 'Guerrilla warfare and banditry' continued endemic, with more resemblance to a Mafia than to a Maoist movement.[76]

Disorder of this elemental type would cause little uneasiness to Washington; nor would 'the paralysis of incentive and the sterility' which an American writer found hanging over the country.[77] The Philippines had avoided dictatorship, another reported, but 'at the price of stagnation, political corruption, and an economic system which is virtually a colony of the United States'.[78] Near-dictatorship was to come, without bringing much change, when President Marcos gave himself enlarged powers in 1972 under martial law. One of his first decrees dealt with land reform, but it left plenty of loopholes for evasion, and for eviction of tenants.[79] It had been the same with agrarian legislation in inde-pendent India, as the Filipino ruling class must have been aware. 'Meanwhile, friends and relatives of President Marcos and some top ranking military officers have joined the small group whose wealth surpasses comprehension.'[80]

Puerto Rico's political status became in 1950 that of a 'Free Associated State'. This was in part a concession to discontents which broke out in October that year in a revolt; in part it reflected the fact that American investment was giving the island some industry, though at the same time bringing its economy more completely under U.S. ascendancy and crippling small local competitors.[81] Puerto Rico was being polarized between the dispossessed masses, among whom there was some recrudescence of guerrilla activity in the late 1960s, and those attached by new ties of interest to the U.S. In this it was a microcosm of the Third World. Meanwhile the low wages which attracted American capital, along with open access to the U.S. market, brought unwelcome competition there. Trade-union protests compelled wages in Puerto Rico to be raised; but then, a further contradiction, its manufactures were undercut by still cheaper labour – some of this also employed by American capital – in the Far East. On top of this, from 1974, came recession.

In the First World War the European monarchies destroyed themselves by falling out once too often; in the Second, the European empires in Asia crippled themselves in the same way. America would have liked them to follow its lead and transfer power to reliable colonial governing classes. From the point of view of its own interests this would be a further implementing of the Open Door, though it took care to make Marshall aid conditional on full access to colonial raw materials. Along with the U.S.S.R., the U.S. endorsed the declaration of the Bandung Conference of Third World countries in 1955 in favour of freedom for all colonial territories. Colony-owning powers were reluctant. Far smaller than their empires, they could not so easily count on being able to keep the economic whip-hand after surrendering the political whip. Their aim was restoration of the old order in Asia; they appealed, like Talleyrand at the Congress of Vienna when the old order in Europe was being restored, to the sacred principle of legitimacy. Britain (which in 1815 handed over Belgium to Holland) was actively assisting the Dutch after the Japanese surrender to re-establish their authority in Indonesia; replacement of Churchill by Attlee and Bevin made no difference.

Anxious to rebuild all the colonialist nations in Europe, America must hesitate to impoverish and antagonize them by depriving them of their possessions in Asia or Africa. As a Portuguese foreign minister complacently reflected, it was in the awkward position of having to champion anti-colonialism while taking care not to alienate its colonialist allies. 'The United States does not seem to have succeeded in resolving this dilemma.'[82] It tried in the post-war years to dodge it by professing impartiality between colonial rulers and rebels, though in reality leaning to the side of the former. The Dutch had to be driven out of Indonesia, even if Washington did give some help by putting a squeeze on Holland through regulation of economic aid; and American opinion must have done something towards making the British decide against trying to hold on to their main bastion, India with Burma and Ceylon. Britain, however, successfully kept Malaya with its tin and rubber. Its people were racially divided, but to American ears a more convincing argument was that the rebels could be set down as communists.

In Asia the Cold War was being set in motion not by either superpower, or by any issue between them (apart from China), but seems to have originated from these clashes between European imperialism and left-wing nationalism. Africa was to recapitulate the same story. It was simple for the French in Indochina to profit by the same anti-communist pretext; and here embitterment over the loss of China, and fear of subversion spreading into its borderlands, ensured unqualified American agreement. The result was vastly to strengthen communism there, as Japanese invasion had done in China; America's willingness to back the French, instead of removing them, was a signal miscalculation which landed it before long in enormous trouble.

Progressive impulses flowering during the World War in America's more liberal precincts led to ideas of social reform, as well as political emancipation, for the Third World, which were to suffer from a similar ambivalence or ineffectiveness. In principle, the U.S. emerged from the War eager to befriend the common man everywhere and win his confidence. Secretary Forrestal was of one mind with General Hodges in 1946 that Russia ought not to be the sole nation with an appeal to the Korean masses. 'The U.S. must do likewise and not be satisfied with dealing with wealthy U.S.-educated Koreans.'[83] In Japan some genuine reforms were carried out, chiefly in the countryside, in the direction of making Japan less feudal and more bourgeois. Here America was in occupation, and wanted to undermine the military caste, with which landlordism could be associated. Japanese businessmen had always been regarded as more 'moderate' and sensible; it was not in any case likely that the attempts to break up their monopoly combines would be more successful than trust-busting at home.

This special case of Japan could not well be duplicated elsewhere. Taiwan was the nearest case: the island was in an extremely vulnerable position on America's strategic frontier, and its Kuomintang rulers were runagates from the mainland, not feudalists with local roots. Local landlords were bought out, partly by government compensation managed in such a way as to transform them into industrial shareholders. In 1950 the U.N.O. at American prompting advised all Third World countries to go in for agrarian reform, as essential for raising living standards and providing a platform for industry. But this wholesome idea was being overlaid by anti-communism, and its advocates pushed out of responsible positions. Social reform could seldom be had without political change, and this in turn could scarcely be had without bringing the left to the front. Joseph Conrad prefixed to his novel about corruption, muddle and tyranny in South America sixty years ago the motto: 'So foul a sky clears not without a storm.'[84] And whereas in Japan or Taiwan or the Middle East, Americans owned no agricultural land, in parts of their own continent they possessed a great deal, besides having close political ties with landowning ruling classes.

Failure to make room for social reform was a principal reason why an American contrasting Marshall aid with the 'Point Four Programme' for the Third World had to confess: 'Our policies succeeded in Europe; by and large they fell short of success, or failed, everywhere else.'[85] Thoughts of America promoting social and economic advancement for the world's poor would only revive at odd moments, as in 1965 when President Johnson was hard put to it to give his Vietnam War a decent look. We should be 'deeply mistaken', he admitted then, to fancy that communists depended on force alone. 'Here, as in other places in the world, they speak to restless people – people rising to shatter the old ways which have imprisoned hope – people fiercely and justly reaching for the material fruits from the tree of modern knowledge.' How to cope with all this, he had sent a financial expert, Eugene Black, to South-east Asia to find out.[86] There may be a touch of unconscious self-caricature in these remarks being addressed to the Association of American Editorial Cartoonists. General Westmoreland, showing an Indian journalist round his Vietnam parish, was at pains to make it clear that he did not regard the struggle as purely military, but was alive to the need for winning over the peasantry. This sounded well, but what made a more vivid impression on the visitor was a trip he had just taken with an American-trained squad of 'anti-terrorist terrorists', 'as fierce and scruffy a crew of ruffians as ever I saw anywhere'.[87]

Reform was one thing, charity another. In earlier history the benefit professedly conferred by imperial sway consisted mainly of Order; in Roman eyes it included 'civilization', in Spanish or Portuguese religion. In our age what is expected is, as Johnson saw, of a more material sort, and from many points of view America has lived up to expectations very fully. There are features of its national make-up, as Gunnar Myrdal has written, to explain 'a basic sentiment of generosity towards those who are less fortunate – a sympathy for, and solidarity with, the underdog'. He thought the U.S. was being left to meet far too high a proportion of the cost of aid to poor countries. On the other side, he noted that this same nation can be 'niggardly and selfish' in business dealings.[88] The contrast is between American people and American capitalism. It is true that the country has had large surpluses, especially agricultural, to dispose of, and they have formed the staple of its aid programmes; but they none the less have to be paid for by the taxpayer, and entitle him to a good conscience. Perhaps he has got on rather too good terms with his conscience, and so been hard of hearing when complaints have come up about what is happening in the far-off lands whose benefactor he is. And too much 'aid' has been military, useless in most cases, or positively vicious.

In 1946 the World Bank was set up, with American capital in the lead. It was a salient difference between the U.S. and the old imperialists, now grudgingly folding their tents and departing, that it was already very rich when it moved into the colonial field on a big scale. It has often seemed to be hurrying out abroad in order to get rid of its wealth, so as to be able to keep itself busy producing more. It has at all events given away immense sums. John Bull used to pull a dreadful face if his government was ever asked to donate a few thousand pounds to famine relief in his India; in February 1974 Uncle Sam wrote off claims on India of £977,000,000 for food shipped over the past twenty years.[89] All the same, the World Bank with its anti-communist orientation was not free from 'the strong element of self-interest in American global foreign policy'.[90] Aid programmes have notoriously been geared to policies of economic and political encroachment on the part of the U.S.

An American critic has censured too 'the "neo-colonial" syndrome' often associated with them, 'high-consumption foreigners bringing "wisdom" and condescension under the guise of assistance'.[91] Someone in Rome in the 1950s noticed how tourists were turning a whole area near the Pincian Gate into a little

America. 'These haters of colonialism have indeed created a barefaced colony where they feel safe and at home ... It is, in its way, imperial. *Civis Americanus sum.*'[92] Arnold Toynbee commented on how their style of living 'insulates Americans on missions abroad from the foreign people whose good will they are seeking to win ... An American ... can be identified from miles away', whereas a Russian is 'invisible'.[93] He was visiting Afghanistan, where the two were in competition. He met with Afghan technicians of whom most had studied in the U.S., some had American wives, all had a 'nostalgia for the American way of life'. 'The new world that they are conjuring up out of the desert at the Helmand River's expense is to be an America-in-Asia.'[94] These were individuals belonging to a new elite, professional instead of feudal, looking forward to a good share of the benefits of progress. Elites of any kind were very small minorities everywhere. Most of the aid received by the Philippines went into the pockets of the ruling class, a tacit arrangement winked at by Washington in the interests of the higher harmony. 'U.S. aid is a long pipe', a Vietnamese said to an American woman, 'with many holes in it. Only a few drops reach the peasants.'[95]

Kennan was lapsing into a familiar habit of projecting one's own mode of behaviour on to others when he found fault with the Soviet Union for practising 'the device of the puppet state and the set of techniques by which states can be converted into puppets with no formal violation of, or challenge to, the outward attributes of their sovereignty and their independence'.[96] No words could more accurately describe the methods that America itself was perfecting. They had precedents in the 'informal empire' widely exercised by 19th-century Britain, particularly in Latin America where annexation was ruled out; but American control has often been much more intensive. What is essential to the arrangement is a dominant local stratum capable of comprehending and harmonizing with the requirements of foreign capital. This stratum has always been present in Latin America, and in the post-colonial world which the U.S. was taking over, as it were, pre-digested from the old empires.

U.S. private investments since 1945 have belonged more generally than before to the economic sphere, since loans to governments have been partly replaced by official aid or credits. This means that American capital involves itself increasingly with local business interests, and can manipulate governments or armies through them, keeping Washington in reserve. A natural consequence has been pointed out by a former employee of the Overseas Development Corporation, that aid may nourish 'a class which is dependent on the continued existence of aid and foreign private investment and which therefore becomes an ally of imperialism'.[97] It is a new kind of comprador class, and the partnership tends to perpetuate social and political structures which badly need to be overhauled because they stand in the way of any real progress.

In practice, American influence had to rest on co-operation like this with the rich or would-be rich. Frequently, as in the Philippines, these are strata not far removed from feudal origins, which foreign rule preserved or even fortified. Reciprocally, a swarm of landlords, usurers, political racketeers quickly learned to turn to America as their new patron, and recite the standard phrases about freedom which were the Open Sesame to a cave stored with good things for them by the American taxpayer. Having started its history with (except in the South) a blessed absence of feudal groups of its own, the U.S. was acquiring a top-heavy 'external aristocracy' of hangers-on. 'Western imperialism' has often been Oriental feudalism making its final stand.

In such dubious company, the U.S. was soon coming to put its trust in dictators, strong (or strong-arm) men able to safeguard the order formerly maintained by British or other governors. Suitable candidates had to be picked up where they could be found; Pibul Songgram of Thailand for instance in the jail where he had been lodged as a creature of the Japanese. There has been a marked shift among these dictators from civilian to military. Itself increasingly militarized, America found the men of the sword attractive. In countries as raw and ramshackle as many of this era, an army can be the nearest thing to the great industrial-financial organizations which dominate American life. A modern army is an embodiment of technology, closely geared to industry by its equipment, rational like big business in its structure and routine, if not in its objectives, and with an analogous chain of command. Militarism blends with capitalism as smoothly as it did with feudalism.

To pump endless supplies of arms into developing countries can therefore be conceived of at Washington as a *nation-building* operation. But in bigger, more important countries of the Third World, where big profits could be looked for from economic growth, or in exposed border areas, the U.S. could not be content with static order, the mere inertia of the old colonial regimes. It wanted strong men of more forward-looking type; men who, in the quagmire of a decaying feudalism mixed up with beginnings of capitalism, would align themselves with the new, help to push it on, and thus not only give foreign capital fresh nourishment but multiply vested interests better able to buttress law and order than any dull-witted landowners could do. In some of these countries there really has come about, as in Taiwan, a removal of the centre of gravity from feudal towards capitalist, with the privileged sections turning from old-fashioned rack-renting to more rewarding business enterprise, and with U.S. investment shepherding them.

Rule by dictator was wanted most promptly in a country where the Second World War left U.S. troops on the spot, and where the American hegemony was to undergo its first ordeal by battle. Roosevelt during the War had in mind for Korea – and other regions – a spell of trusteeship and then independence, something like the mandate system brought up to date. It would not have been simple to manage in any case, even if the accidental factor of partition had not come about. Korea like China and Vietnam, and unlike Indonesia or the Philippines, had a long national history to look back on, before a fairly brief foreign occupation, and also a long record of class strife and peasant rebellion. It would be fatally easy for an outsider to combine against him a fierce patriotic spirit with that of social revolt. The south came at once under the rule of Syngman Rhee, who as an old nationalist long in exile in the U.S. seemed ideal for American purposes, but, like sundry other dictators employed by the hegemony, proved an awkward puppet to control.

Washington desired mild social reform, to obviate a peasant upheaval like China's; Rhee, though not embedded in the landlord class, was quite out of touch with social conditions, and in any case cared nothing about them, but was only intent on getting control of the whole country. Sumner Welles, with an incomprehension not uncommon in American officialdom, was querulous because the South Korean regime after 1945 was not given enough arms 'even for the preservation of internal order', and because it was not encouraged 'to carry out the radical and far-reaching reforms that the South Korean people demanded'.[98] These two things excluded each other: the more arms given, the fewer reforms would be conceded. It may be said with fair confidence that if Korea had been left to itself it would have come together quickly enough under northern leadership, and landlordism would have disappeared.

Arms, if not reforms, were soon plentiful. With the enthusiasm of a new-found faith, America was relying on military aid to stiffen the south. Part of the scheme was to emulate the old empires by acquiring a reservoir of reliable local troops. This was in advance of Eisenhower's dictum: 'Set Asians to fight Asians', which curiously echoed one by Commissioner Lin at the time of the first Opium War, when Peking was hoping for discords among the westerners: 'Let barbarians fight barbarians'. In June 1950, just before the outbreak of war, the chief of the American 'Military Advisory Group' was quoted as saying that he had men with every South Korean division, and that 'an intelligent and intensive investment of five hundred combat-hardened American officers and men can train 100,000 men who will do the shooting for you'.[99]

In January a fresh agreement had ranged Korea within the U.S. defence perimeter in Asia. Who started the war in June has always been debatable. Sir John Pratt lost his Foreign Office post because he was convinced (like a minority of historians since) that it was started by Syngman Rhee. He dwelt on various implausible details in the case which the U.N.O. was induced to swallow; and, as he said, the American advisers were sanguine that the south could speedily defeat the north.[100] Both Rhee and Kim Il-Sung had been rattling their sabres; and the best answer to the problem may be a recent Japanese student's conclusion, that the war was not instigated by either Russia or America – which each accused the other – but was the outcome of north-south hostility, with each leader pushed on by factions within his own camp.[101] However the fighting started, the northern army's rapid march south, little more than a military promenade, may be proof of its right as well as ability to unify the country. On the stage of world politics it looked like an invasion; and this, together with the Czech *coup* two years before, was the grand argument which enabled Cold War propagandists to convince hearers everywhere of communist aggressiveness, and the necessity of American protection.

Faced with this argument the U.N.O. gave its blessing to the U.S. intervention in the civil war, or rather walkover, and, a good deal more reluctantly, Britain and other members contributed some forces. The frontier was restored, but MacArthur's intransigence then provoked Chinese intervention. Truman, who detested him, later regretted having let himself be talked out of dismissing him six months earlier than he did: it might have shortened the war by six months, he thought, and saved America from going to the brink of another world war.[102] Generals as well as dictators may be hard to fit into rational designs. In allied eyes a defensive struggle was turning into an offensive against China, and nobody wanted to be entangled in this further adventure. Now as on other occasions, it appeared that American security required everyone else to be very insecure. Increasing resort to violence, the terror-bombing of enemy ground, were a revival of methods of the World War, for what was now virtually colonial conquest. Here, as later in Vietnam, revenge was being taken on villagers as scapegoats for Peking and Moscow. America has built much in the world since 1945, it has also destroyed very much. For an older ideal of 'civilized warfare' the U.S. was substituting that of scientific warfare, which as waged against enemy populations means mass murder. It was pioneered by fascism, and came within sight of its promised land with the invention of the hydrogen-bomb, followed by threats of 'instant and massive retaliation'. 'It would hardly be possible', wrote an observer who knew Eastern Asia well, during the Korean War, 'to exaggerate the hatred of the West that our military airplanes have sown in the hearts of Asian civilians'.[103]

3

War in Vietnam and its Repercussions

Fighting in Korea petered out in an uneasy stalemate. Before it ended, an enlightened American historian drew the moral that the peace of Asia must in the long run be left 'in the hands of the Asians, notably the Japanese and the Chinese'.[104] In 1954 on the other hand an unenlightened State Department spokesman was telling a Congressional committee that the U.S. must 'dominate Asia for an indefinite period and pose a military threat against Communist China until it breaks up internally'.[105] Between Washington and Peking there can be seen, looking back now, a gradual and reluctant move towards greater caution and realism on each side, and a rhythm of crises of diminishing intensity, while restraints were placed on Chiang Kai-shek's harassment of the mainland from Taiwan.[106] But there were many windings and turnings on this road; and America's 'colonial' policies towards smaller countries were unchanged. Aid continued to be given to the French, struggling with growing desperation to defeat the national movements in Indochina. Americans could prove to their own satisfaction that Ho Chi Minh was a puppet of either China or Russia,[107] just as they had proved that Mao was a puppet of Moscow. An empire with so many marionettes in its own cupboard was instinctively ready to suspect that any colonial leader hostile to it must be the tool of some bigger opponent.

'It is impossible to lay down arms until victory is completely won', Vice-President Nixon declared in Paris in 1953.[108] On 4 August that year Eisenhower stated that 'Indochina and the whole of South-East Asia are essential to the US both for strategic and political reasons.' He did not allude to the economic reasons that underlay both, but an American journal explained that 'One of the world's richest areas is open to the winner in Indochina ... Tin, rubber, rice, key strategic raw materials are what the war is really about.'[109] War is the continuation of business by other methods, as a modern Clausewitz might say. This note was to be struck over and over again during the Vietnam War, and had its due weight with business interests able to direct the public mind. In 1965 Secretary of State Dean Rusk impressed on the House Foreign Affairs Committee that South-east Asia had 'rich natural resources' as well as 'great strategic importance', so that its loss would be 'a serious shift in the balance of power against the interests of the free world'.[110] Even if in the end the buried treasures of Indochina were to elude the free world's clutch, incalculable profits were made out of the War itself, and other countries shared in them in a way that helped to damp down any official objections to it. Britain – for one – sold large quantities of materials, including allegedly napalm.[111]

In 1954 when the French were facing defeat, military advice, especially from General Ridgeway, convinced Eisenhower that it would be folly to plunge into Vietnam, so soon after the 'tragic error' of Korea; and the proposal to intervene was dropped.[112] In July, by the terms of the Geneva Conference, which had met in April initially to wind up the Korean War, France gave up the contest, leaving the country divided on a temporary basis between the north led by Ho Chi Minh and the south under Ngo Dinh Diem, Catholic heir to the French puppet regime. There were to be nationwide elections in 1956 which, few doubted, would unite the country behind Ho. Diem therefore refused to hold them, and the U.S., wiser counsels soon forgotten, backed him. Dulles had been busy putting together the SEATO alliance; this provided the U.S. with a figleaf of international support, but a very much smaller one than in Korea, in the renewed war soon breaking out. It began with guerrilla resistance to Ngo Dinh Diem, whose support consisted of little beyond army, landlords, and Catholics, and his programme of little beyond killing and jailing opponents *en masse*, while he antagonized the peasantry by reimposing rent payments it had shaken off for years.

Kennedy's inaugural speech in 1961 was a minatory declamation against any trifling with American wishes. His first attempt to translate it into action, by allowing an invasion of Cuba from U.S. territory, was a disastrous failure, whose effect was to compel Castro to seek Soviet aid. In the ensuing 'missile crisis', Kennedy forced Krushchev to retreat, at the cost of frightening the Western alliance and making it wonder whether U.S. protection was not too expensive a form of insurance. In domestic affairs he found big business too big for him, for instance over his 1961 tax reform proposals.[113] He needed to win another round somewhere, against some weaker opponent, and thought he could see one in Vietnam. There were many voices, of professional anti-communists and their financial friends, ready to lure him on.

All the same, it was not for want of warning that he got into the Vietnam swamp. Galbraith, trying to mend broken fences at Delhi, was writing private letters of good advice to the president. He was dismayed to hear of Johnson, the Vice-President, touring Southern Asia and being tutored. 'Johnson will hear much about the need to contain Communism, and about the effectiveness of military measures for doing so. It will sound exceedingly straightforward and simple.'[114] Galbraith had lately visited Saigon and seen Diem at work. 'It is certainly a can of snakes', he wrote. 'I am reasonably accustomed to oriental government and politics, but I was not quite prepared for Diem.'[115] His warnings were fruitless, and the flow of supplies and advisers to Saigon swelled. The hoped-for success proved elusive: if the war could be won, it would not be won by Diem's leadership. Within two years the ambassador at Saigon, Lodge, was cabling to the State Department: 'We are launched on a course from which there is no respectable turning back; the overthrow of the Diem government.'[116] Diem was duly terminated, not in order to purge the 'can of snakes' and introduce democracy, but to make room for even more iron-handed rule. A confused series of *coups* followed, settling into dictatorship by one general after another. Something like this has been more and more the standard outcome of partnership between Third World countries and the U.S.

When Kennedy followed Diem into another world, late in 1963, there were thousands of American assistants in South Vietnam, and a 'broad commitment' to it had been accepted. Johnson did not know very much about Asia, and was easily persuaded to continue this, very soon to a point where he could no longer extricate himself. From the spring of 1964 he and his advisers were planning a full-scale war, a year before the public was allowed to know what was happening.[117] A pretext for action was found in August, with a story about North

Vietnam patrol boats attacking two powerful task-forces of the Seventh Fleet – 'on the high seas in the Gulf of Tonkin', Johnson indignantly declared in an address to the nation.[118] What he would have thought of a Soviet fleet on the high seas in the Gulf of Mexico, he did not say. Bombing of North Vietnam began.

It was only much later, in April 1970, that a Senate enquiry revealed heavy U.S. participation in the fighting in Laos ever since 1964, muffled in secrecy so deep that the White House itself may not have been fully aware of it. 'This is something', a British journalist observed, 'which is likely to frighten America's friends as much as her enemies'.[119] Senator Morse of Oregon was one of those who were protesting in 1965 that the waging of an undeclared war was unconstitutional. 'In Vietnam', he argued moreover, in a debate on 23 September, 'we have totally flouted the rule of law, and we have flouted the United Nations Charter.' That year the conflict was being intensified, with a large American army gathering, and the North Vietnam army taking the field against it. Ordinary people in South Vietnam could only feel that this was an American war, and their own government a puppet.[120] They might well, for Washington was being drawn little by little into the direct colonial control it always preferred to avoid. 'The American Embassy,' a French correspondent reported, 'with its enormous staff and numerous departments, and protected by barbed wire and guards, enjoys more authority than the South Vietnam government. Mr Cabot Lodge is as powerful as any French Governor-General in the good old days.'[121]

Vietnam was becoming America's running ulcer, like Napoleon's occupation of Spain; but whereas that general's troops had faced a benighted peasantry stirred up by priests, here the invader faced an opponent far inferior to himself in weapons but infinitely superior in leadership and thinking. On America's moral credit the drain was far more severe than on its physical resources, even with half a million men in action on the other side of the world. There had been disgust in America at the barbarities of the Japanese invasion of China, but this was in many ways far worse. The *Pentagon Papers* – leaked or purloined, and published in 1971 – revealed, one of their editors commented, no sense of 'responsibility for such matters as civilian casualties or the restraints imposed by the rules of land warfare and the Geneva and Hague Conventions'.[122] Everything that ingenuity could devise and money pay for was used in this long-drawn vivisection of a nation, except atom-bombs. Some at least wanted to go to this final length.

'*Why*', cried a religious zealot, 'is the United States now discredited, despised, hated, throughout so much of the world? ... *Why* can't the United States whip little North Vietnam?' America was 'a tremendous *blessing* to the other nations of the earth', he answered, but it was feebly shrinking from using its full might against Vietnam, and incurring divine displeasure by thus failing to fulfil its destiny.[123]

As 1966 dragged on the Defense Secretary, McNamara, was losing faith in victory, partly because of the army's insatiable demands for more and more men. One of his assistants, J.T. McNaughton, revealing among other things how much the Pentagon mind was the prisoner of its own jumble of clichés and metaphors, was writing: 'We have in Vietnam the ingredients of an enormous miscalcula- tion.' 'We are in an escalating military stalemate' (*sic*). 'At each decision point we have gambled ... we have upped the ante ...'.[124] The blissful time when war could be fully automated had not yet come; and whatever the public might think about the merits of the War, there was diminishing willingness to go and take part in it. Abroad it was giving communism the best possible advertisement. A communist woman candidate in Naples in 1968 found that for many of her hearers – workers, students, party and non-party men and women – '*the* most important political fact of their lifetime is the defeat inflicted on the American Cyclops by the tiny Vietnamese nation'.[125] In Paris the Marxist philosopher Althusser could trust that this conflict was fatally undermining the ideology of capitalism, hitherto a formidable obstacle to progress.[126] Many other Europeans, who did not hope for this, feared it. Secretary of State Rusk, visiting Europe, cabled to Johnson: 'I am deeply disturbed by general international revulsion'; he wanted the bombing slowed down.[127] But by now the U.S. was, like Macbeth, 'in blood stepped in so far' that to draw back was as hard as to go on.

Nixon won the presidency in 1968 partly by renouncing a military solution. Within a year he was extending the war into Cambodia and renewing the bombing of North Vietnam; he laid all the blame on Hanoi's obstinacy, very much like Henry V besieging Harfleur and summoning its inhabitants to come to terms with blood-curdling threats. By 1971, 45,000 Americans had been killed, and estimates of the total loss of life in Vietnam since 1945 varied between one and two million.[128] For three decades the U.S. had been endea- vouring to dominate the Far East by force of arms; but after the triumph over Japan, with poor success. Nixon's eventual 'settlement' of the war satisfied all who simply wanted to forget about it, and left Saigon to carry it on with American weaponry.

This was a strategy of indirect war, the military counterpart of neo-colonialism, which the debacle in China and then the initial rout of the South Korean army had made to appear impracticable.

South Vietnam's puppet regime was another balloon very quickly punctured. It had been puffed up by corruption and terrorism, which win adherents and silence opponents but do not make men ready to risk their lives for a cause. No evidence has yet been seen that any of the Third World forces so numerous on America's payroll would be prepared for any serious fighting on their own. As *Le Monde* had written: 'The United States, which has come to defend order in this country, is itself making a powerful contribution to the general disorder. The state is corrupt, the family broken up, the social order disintegrating.'[129] By thus pulverizing the old society, the American steamroller was making it morally easier, even if very arduous in material terms, for communism to build a new one out of the wreckage.

A prominent feature of the demoralization carried by the Stars and Stripes was its sexual aspect. Most American officers in Saigon had concubines, paraded without concealment.[130] One of many haphazard consequences of this and the Korean War, and the ramifying American bases in Asia, was a vast multitude of Asian women reduced to prostitution. Women and camp-followers have been part of war and imperialism everywhere, but the spectacle must have added fuel to the enmity that the U.S. was arousing. It was a repetition in new guise of the sexual exploitation of black women which was part of the old Southern slavery. A Burmese traveller commented that if the U.S. army stayed in Asia much longer there would not be a pure-blooded race left there.[131]

The vortex of the Vietnam War was felt by other Asian lands far and near. A share in its business profits helped to bolster conservatism in various of them, including Japan. Oil-refining in Singapore gained a very strong impetus. Thailand was a ready-made auxiliary for the war, even if, as an American sceptic said, 'the typical opportunistic ally ... the most risky type of aid-and-alignment relationship for the United States' – all for America today, as yesterday all for Japan.[132] Never having been reduced to a colony, it had not been compelled to develop a nationalist movement. Monarchical rule, too anachronistic now, was pushed into the background after 1945 by the army, whose bosses were more wide awake. One dictator in uniform, Sarit Thanarat, was succeeded in 1963 by another, Thanom Kittikachorn.

Thailand was turned into a military camp from which Vietnam could be conveniently bombed. Before the end of the 1960s it was estimated that 850 million dollars had been put into the country, half of it in military aid and much of the rest for building strategic roads.[133] This, with American troops spending money, has had a big enough impact to affect the social and economic structures of this small country, pushing it towards capitalism. There has been opportunity for many Thais, though not for many on the same scale as for Sarit, who died worth 150 million dollars; hardship for far more, and a widening gap and mounting tension between the classes. Thailand was not far from being converted into 'a bona fide U.S. colony'[134] before student demonstrations late in 1973 led to the overthrow of army rule and the inauguration of democracy. America, in the person of its envoy Kentner, described as of 'military and C.I.A. background', took this in very bad part: he was an admirer of the South Korean regime, and wanted the U.S. bases in Thailand to be kept indefinitely.[135] It was not too long before the army returned to power; Wall Street doubtless heaved a sigh of relief, and presumably some C.I.A. officials won promotion.

South Korean troops were employed in Vietnam, Asians again being set to fight Asians. They seem to have made themselves useful by diligence in killing people and terrorizing civilians. With American troops still in South Korea, and lavish supplies of arms kept up, dictatorship was emboldened to establish itself still more firmly and tyrannically. It had been in military hands since 1961; in 1963 a caudillo from the army, Park (Pak Chung Hee), got himself elected president. Power was consolidated by repression, with backing from vested interests old and new, among the latter businessmen enriched by a rapid industrial growth based on cheap and well-disciplined labour.

Both Johnson and Nixon gave credit to the massive American entry into Vietnam for the army seizure of power in Indonesia in 1965[136] – another democratic domino knocked over. Here therefore the Vietnam War can be said to have achieved an important victory for capitalism. These islands' wealth of natural resources, oil above all, were a very seductive bait, and the C.I.A. was at work from 1950, its agents and those of the oil companies hand in glove as elsewhere.[137] Soekarno, the populist leader of the new nation, was objectionable because, though himself no more than a windbag, he accepted the support of a large communist party, as well as aid from the U.S.S.R. This was incompatible with the 'stability' required by big business for the tranquil digestion of profits. Its advisers, and the C.I.A., turned more and more towards the army as the only reliable force in a country desperately poor and hungry for social progress. Viewed through such eyes, the officer corps as in so many other retarded lands could seem the destined rock of order, a natural elite inspiring the same hopes of salvation as Marxism fixed on the proletariat.

Indonesia's army was not a colonial force continuing into independence, like India's and Pakistan's; but it quickly turned into a professional force under ambitious commanders, innocent of any progressive ideas and hostile to communism both as a foreign idea and as atheistic, a menace to the Islamic bigotry easily whipped up. Americans were making cordial contacts with it. One influential C.I.A. man, from 1958, Pauker, was an advocate of strengthening the army for a takeover of power by channelling economic as well as military aid through it. He credited the officers with 'above-average qualities of leadership, patriotism, and commitment to moral values', and did not conceal his hope that they would before long 'strike, sweep their house clean, and rededicate themselves to higher purposes ...'.[138] Habits of 'double-talk' were now incurably a part of the American language. Unwarlike Americans could be fascinated by the sword-bearing castes they had once despised; and secret servicemen were likely to have a poor estimate of their own politicians, and a correspondingly poorer one of any in Asia.

As in the many analogous cases, it is impossible to attribute sole responsibility for the events of 1965 to the U.S. There were plenty of inflammable materials within Indonesia. Army and communist party were manoeuvering for the succession to power, each could be suspected of meaning to take the offensive. What can be said was that U.S. influence was being thrown firmly into the scales. A large proportion of the officer corps had undergone some American training. Pentagon and C.I.A. were giving the same counsel as the witches gave Macbeth, to be bloody, bold, and resolute. 'American policy-makers knew in advance about planning for the military take-over, facilitated it, took credit for it when it occurred ...'.[139] Its pretext was an alleged communist plot; it took the form of a wholesale massacre of communists or alleged communists, most of it carried out not by the soldiery but by mobs given a free hand. At least half a million perished. White terror in the form of massacre was not altogether new to this century, or confined to Asia; it happened in Finland in 1919. But now, with religious passion to inflame it, it was on a grander scale than ever before in modern times. Whether its American sponsors would have hesitated had they known in advance what the toll would be, must unhappily be doubted. Nor has American opinion shown much inquietude over the inordinate number of people kept in prison ever since.

There was a discreet interval before the new President Suharto's visit to Washington in 1970, when close official links began to be forged, with military aid burgeoning and military advisers thronging. It can be surmised that Indonesia is one of a number of countries, like Iran and Brazil, which Washington hopes to be able not only to rely on but to utilize at need against anyone in their neighbourhood who may require to be disciplined. At the end of 1975, in the breakup of the Portuguese empire, Indonesian forces invaded East Timor. James Dunn, former Australian consul-general there, believed that between 50,000 and 100,000 people were wiped out, or 10% to 20% of the population.[140] A Congressional hearing took place, and the State Department admitted to 10,000 at least, but refused any reduction of aid to Indonesia, economic or military. Economically Indonesia is dominated by foreign capital, as in colonial days; this is now American and Japanese, with a growing Australian share, a good example of capital working in harmonious fraternity. Here as in various other regions, rich nations which may be critical of America's methods are quite ready to benefit by their results, just as in the last century the U.S., however censorious of British imperialism, was always ready to join in the good things its doings in Asia made available.

In the same year 1965 which marked the triumph of higher purposes in Indonesia, a brief war between India and Pakistan signalized one of the failures of the American hegemony to co-ordinate Asia as it had done Europe, and an alliance misfiring. With India, any alliance had been ruled out by Nehru's non-alignment, which gave deep offence to the America of Foster Dulles. There was resentment too at the enlargement of the 'public sector' of the Indian economy; the very idea of five-year plans was heretical. Washington wanted India to prosper, as a counterweight in Asia to communist China, but to point the contrast it must prosper on strictly capitalist lines; Indians must get to heaven by private transport, or not at all. Unlike Russia, West Germany, and Britain, the U.S. refused to contribute to the public sector by building a steel mill. There were endless wranglings over whether India should be allowed to produce its own fertilizers, again under national ownership, instead of importing them.

Indian businessmen, nervous of socialism, have been avid for partnership with American capital, bringing with it the technology which has been modern America's supreme asset; though they have also had to fear being relegated to the background by it. An Indian grateful for aid in food felt obliged to add that 'the United States has been clandestinely aiding the private sector into disloyal positions *vis-à-vis* the national development plans'.[141] Progressive Indians, in the Congress Party or further left, were conscious of disturbing American pressures, abetted by much of big business and its newspapers, right-wing parties like the Jan Sangh and Swatantra, and conservative Congressmen like Morarji Desai, later premier.[142] This was the more serious because by 1959 India's official foreign debts rose to 925 crores of rupees, 600 of them owing to the U.S., and the Third Plan was expected to require even more foreign aid. It is not hard to see a connection between these facts and the central government's decision in 1959 to dismiss the elected Communist ministry in Kerala State. There was a well-entrenched Catholic community there, allied at the top with the big estates threatened by land reform, and it took the lead in organizing a loud agitation against the new state government – as the Church had done in Mexico, or Spain – with generous financial assistance, it was credibly rumoured, from U.S. sources.[143]

From now on there were nagging left-wing suspicions of intrigues between Indian reaction and the C.I.A., not merely to alter Delhi's foreign policy, but to upset Indian democracy. It would be rash to deny them any substance. Like a housemaid in charge of unruly children, Washington was more and more ready to assume that any country not under bolt and bar would turn to communism. It was an unwitting tribute to the wiles, if not virtues, of this grand 'enemy of mankind'. To more realistic eyes, not fevered by the C.I.A.'s professional alarmism, it was evident that India was firmly anchored to private property, that its public sector represented not socialism but an adjunct to monopoly capitalism, and that its Congress government, whatever radical talk it might indulge in on occasion, was a right-of-centre one. In short, the state of affairs was as close to American specifications as could rationally be desired. But Washington was in many ways no longer capable of rational reckoning. When Galbraith went to Delhi in 1960, President Kennedy agreed with him that aid ought to be forthcoming for public enterprises in India, but was convinced by other advisers that this would be politically unwise at home.[144]

Pakistan from its early days wore a more attractive look, and appeared to American planners an eligible ally. 'There is an obduracy', Galbraith reflected, 'about our determination to do the wrong thing which would be admirable in any other context.'[145] British influence, during the years of the translation of the empire from London to Washington, seems to have been lamentable. American thinking about the subcontinent has been traced to Sir Olaf Caroe's counsel, in 1951, to make Pakistan an outpost of 'Western defense'.[146] Caroe was foreign policy expert of the British Raj in India in its last days, a former governor of the North-West Frontier Province, a man in short (though with redeeming literary tastes) firmly rooted in a moribund past. A more backward country in every way than India, Pakistan was quickly coming under the sway of British-trained army officers and bureaucrats; socialists were few and jails roomy enough to hold them all; foreign investments were solicited, and there were no trade unions to give sleepless nights.

A Pakistani conservative credits U.S. military and economic aid with enabling Pakistan to survive 'during her tender infancy';[147] it would be more accurate to say that it enabled the country's ruling cliques to survive without making any concessions to their subjects in the way of social, especially agrarian, reform. Like kindred groups elsewhere they knew how to recite the catch-phrases of the Cold War. Early in 1952 Mohamed Ali Bogra, ambassador in Washington and soon to become premier, expatiated on the duty of Islam, Christianity and Judaism, to stand together against the atheist monster, communism.[148] Next year Pakistan was on the brink of famine, and American food hastened its slide into the net. It was enrolled in SEATO and CENTO, and its peasant army loaded with weapons. In 1957 the prime minister Suhrawardy made the ritual pilgrimage to Washington and regaled both Houses with talk about how 'peace is safe' in America's hands, and how proud his country was to be its partner in the 'great adventure' of protecting individual rights (such as feudal estates, he refrained from adding) from expansionist communism.[149]

A year later a long era of full dictatorship, under General Ayub Khan, started. It met with a good reception from American opinion, summed up by a *Time Magazine* aphorism that the politicians had been turned out by 'the most stable and uncorrupted institution in the country'.[150] In point of fact an officer corps in a country like Pakistan, permeated with corruption in every sphere of public life, was very quickly infected by the temptations of civil power and its openings for self-enrichment. Some of its failures against India may be traced to this.[151] Meanwhile it was no disadvantage to the American business interests which were piling up. Ayub's Pakistan was given a high credit-worthiness rating, investments flowed in, and industry, with a much narrower independent base than India's, flourished, though only in the favoured western wing of the country. This link between industrialization and military rule, as a guarantee of labour docility, has been a familiar feature of the American world, at the opposite pole from the *laissez-faire* environment of the original industrial revolution in Europe. In Pakistan as in Taiwan, though here there was no land reform, it had the effect of shifting the centre of gravity some distance away from feudal towards capitalist. Ayub's son was a prosperous car manufacturer.

It was an ill-starred alliance from the first, an object-lesson in the sort of confusions Washington was apt to land itself in by failing to perceive that its clients' aims might be far removed from its own. Pakistan could play on fears that India was sliding towards subversion. But it was against China that Washington was combing South and East Asia for allies. Pakistan's rulers, on the other hand, though brutally anti-socialist at home, had none of the world-wide perspectives and sense of responsibility of Wall Street and the White House, and were liable to behave with as little heed for the higher interests of free enterprise as inter-war Europe had done. They valued the alliance as a means of securing diplomatic backing and arms for use against India. Their goal was Kashmir, the Muslim province fought over between the two after independence, most of it still in Indian hands; the cry for Kashmir had an appeal to both popular nationalism and (not much distinct from it) Muslim fanaticism, which could do something to remedy the unpopularity of the regime. When in 1962 India and China, with equal obtuseness, bungled themselves into a fight over some patches of Himalayan ice and rock, Pakistan was angry with America and Britain for hastening to give India weapons, which did not save it from defeat. Pakistan then, while continuing to receive American supplies, struck up a partnership against India with China, which had no scruples about encouraging a right-wing dictatorship.

It seemed safe in 1965 to Ayub, steered by his power-hungry foreign minister Bhutto, to risk an effort to seize Kashmir by an under-cover invasion. India retaliated by attacking Pakistan itself, which had to accept a profitless peace through Soviet mediation. All this was a ridiculous enough outcome of Washington's schemings. It was alienating India without earning any gratitude from Pakistan, as some Americans shrewder than their government came to see. One of them recommended in 1969 'a scrupulous detachment from local power rivalries in South Asia'.[152] As usual, wise advice went unheeded. But the continuing *entente* between Pakistan and China may have had an important consequence in that dramatic turn in American policy, the reconciliation with Peking sealed by Nixon's visit in 1972, by convincing Washington that Maoist foreign policy, despite its clamorous revolutionism, was at bottom as self-regarding and opportunist as anyone else's.

In 1971 all three countries were in the same camp against India. East Pakistan had at last revolted against exploitation by the western half of the country, which American advisers, too late and too mildly, had begun to try to moderate. Nixon and Kissinger showed themselves determined to hold the country together by force, and went on delivering arms to the West Pakistan troops engaged in indiscriminate butchery in Bengal. It seemed as if the cult of the bayonet, determination to uphold right-wing army regimes anywhere and everywhere, through thick and thin, had taken a pathological hold on the decision-makers; a grotesque parody of the law-abiding, demilitarized earth which was once the American dream. When India was at length compelled to intervene, under the shield of a defence treaty with the U.S.S.R., Pakistan suffered swift defeat. American aid to India was cut off; as a last clumsy resort, the Seventh Fleet steamed into the Bay of Bengal, and a landing was threatened. While the contest ran its course Congress and press were roused to an unwonted pitch of protest, which went some way towards soothing Indian feelings. 'We did not mistrust the Americans – that is the American people', a cabinet minister at Delhi wrote to an old English friend. 'They have been extremely friendly throughout this crisis. But so far as the American Government is concerned it is a different matter.'[153]

4

The Middle East and Africa

From the Second World War the U.S. emerged 'an oil-hungry power',[154] with a predictably keen appetite for the Middle East. By 1950 its investments in oil-fields there amounted to 596 million dollars, and it controlled about 40% of production; Britain was still in the lead with nearly 50%.[155] In 1951 British insistence on clinging to old 'rights' in Iran led to the government headed by Mosaddeq nationalizing the oil industry. He was of course accused by the British, largely with the aim of inciting America against him, of acting under communist tutoring. An American had been nearer the truth when he wrote, not long before these events: 'Britain's fear of the Soviets is making progress synonymous with Communism, and making Communism attractive to the exploited peoples of the Middle East.'[156] But by this time his words were equally true of America; a transmigration of soul was taking place, of Toryism from its old carcass into a vigorous young body. General Zahedi was plotting against his government, with the Shah's sanction, and the army had close ties with America, its purveyor of advisers and equipment. In August 1953 it struck: Mosaddeq was arrested, massive repression launched, the Shah installed in full power. Economic aid from Washington was suspiciously ready; a year later a new settlement was made with the foreign oil interests, giving 40% of shares in a new controlling corporation to five big American companies.[157]

Because of the proximity of Russia to the Middle East, especially to Iran, a frontier province, and the necessity therefore of humouring the oil countries, they have had to be permitted by stages to raise their prices, with ominous repercussions on Western economies. In this sense they have been 'decolonized', though with little matching political progress. Iran, the most westernized of them, has used part of its wealth, under a parvenu monarchy fond of proclaiming itself leader in a national 'revolution', to go further than Pakistan in modernizing and industrializing, and has carried out a land reform as well. This, combined with firmly autocratic and anti-socialist methods, has fitted in very well with American views. The Shah won esteem also by spending a vast part of his money on buying armaments from the U.S. American arms sales (followed latterly by Russian) have spread a feverish craving for them, often with no rational motive detectable. The Shah has vaulting ambitions, however, and for Washington seems to have become one of the satellites it feels able to trust as informal guardians of law and order in its neighbourhood.

In the Arab countries European imperialism left other festering legacies. With the biggest population and intelligentsia and a well-rooted nationalism, Egypt was the most sensitive point. Britain after 1945 was still bent on clinging to as much as it could. 'The question of arrangement between America and ourselves is a delicate one', the British representative at Cairo told the Egyptians in 1950, when negotiations were going on about the Suez Canal Zone, still in British hands. 'I understand however that in general the Americans are leaving this part of the world to Britain and her allies.'[158] He was trying to frighten the Egyptians with the bogy of a Soviet attack; they disregarded it, and the overthrow of the disreputable monarchy in 1952 was a blow to British hopes. With Washington, on the contrary, the army officer with whom power came to rest, Nasser, got on initially quite well, and it was ready with grants of aid. Friendly to foreign investment, he could be viewed as 'the most effective anti-Communist in the Arab world and the Middle East', and possessed 'an extremely tough apparatus of repression'.[159]

But Egypt's relations with the U.S. have been a story of chronic fallings-out and *rapprochements*. Washington wanted to draft Nasser into a regional combination against the U.S.S.R.; he wanted to be free to go his own way, as leader of Pan-Arabism, offering guidance also to Africa. In 1956 he recognized Peking; Dulles withdrew an offer of money to build an Aswan dam; Nasser nationalized the Canal; Tory Britain and France, in a galvanic spasm of the old imperialism now dying, set upon Egypt in collusion with Israel. This swift sequence of events took Dulles aback; he did not blame his own maladroit bullying, but was very angry with the reckless Europeans and greedy Israelis. After the abrupt and undignified disappearance of the British and French from the Middle Eastern scene, the U.S. had to take over their role. Early in 1957 Congress approved an 'Eisenhower Doctrine' which authorized use of force against 'any country controlled by international communism'. This was a very elastic conception, as was speedily underlined by a landing of marines next year in the Lebanon in support of its government against a quite un-communist rising. There was much Arab discontent at this arbitrary assumption of suzerainty; and, coming on top of the Suez adventure, it opened the way for Russia to make an appearance – surprisingly late in the day – in the Middle East, with the aim of preventing it from being turned into an anti-Soviet *place d'armes*.

Russia too has floundered in the sands or quicksands of the Middle East, and America's ascendancy has been hampered less by any Soviet machinations than by its own ally, or heel of Achilles, Israel; by the self-imposed obligation to underwrite Zionism, when its own interests prescribed alliance with the Arabs. Most of them economically under-developed, conservative, pious, the Arabs were tailor-made clients for America; by arming Israel against them Washington allowed Moscow to gain ground instead. Here was another blatant irrationality in its effort at rationalizing the world. To think of Israel as an instrument of American imperialism is very wide of the mark. There is, unquestionably, an Israeli expansionism; and while the original mischief was done as usual by Europe, American Zionism has added its contribution. It led the way in demanding all Palestine, a claim which Weizmann felt obliged to censure in 1946 as too extreme; later on as well, there is an observable association between American Zionism and 'right-wing and chauvinistic tendencies within Israel'.[160] Instead of exercising the restraint which both American national interests and Israel's long-term prospects dictated, official American Zionism has seemed to encourage its excesses. These have been accompanied by a steady erosion of the socialist ideals with which many of the pioneers set out, but which had to be abandoned if a flow of American arms on the necessary scale was to be maintained. Non-Jewish American capital has been invested in Israel in large quantities,[161] and close links have been forged between it and the apartheid regime of South Africa. Washington has been gratified by this shift to capitalist normality;

but power for the right wing means a foreign policy more firmly wedded to religious zeal and its annexationist impulses, very much as in the case of Pakistan and Kashmir. No nation in history has had a more expensive and more disobliging ally.

Its ability to demand everything and give nothing has been the supreme triumph of the lobby system. In the first post-war year, Truman's memoirs[162] show him being manoeuvred inch by inch into support of Zionism, against his better judgement and that of the State Department, by pushing and prodding from influential quarters. Forrestal was another who deplored the way things were going; as Navy spokesman he recognized the importance of Saudi oil, and the unwisdom of antagonizing the Arabs.[163] America found itself landed with the contradictory task of safeguarding both Israel's holy places and its own, the oil-wells. Every occupant of the White House in turn must sometimes have felt like Sinbad with the Old Man of the Sea on his shoulders. It is noteworthy all the same that among ordinary Americans there has been all along a great deal of generous sympathy with Jewish wartime sufferings in Europe; even if it may seem strange logic to compensate A. for the crimes of B. at the expense of C. They have sincerely thought of themselves as protecting the weak against the strong, a small man against a ring of bullies.

Inevitably this admirable feeling has come in the course of time and conflict to be mixed with other ingredients. As with every foreign call on his pocket, the taxpayer has been assured that he is preserving a useful outpost of American power, a citadel against communism and Russia. The truth is the precise opposite: very little communism would have been heard of in the Middle East if there were no Israel. To this obvious fact public opinion was blind, having been conditioned to react automatically to the red rag. It must be supposed, also, to have found some consolation for failures against better-organized opponents further east, by savouring Israeli victories, which have certainly been remarkable. This vicarious relish may explain why since the 1967 War 'American public opinion has been overwhelmingly sympathetic to Israel and its policy of *de facto* annexation'.[164] Meanwhile there has been a parallel drift of American Jewry, as well as of Israel, away from progressive ideals towards support of, for instance, the Vietnam War, another required sacrifice on the Zionist altar. This diversion of Jewish radical energy and idealism must be regarded as a valuable prize for conservatism.

None the less, in the Middle East Israeli intransigence has cost the U.S. dear.

This was prominently displayed in 1967, when Israel refused to see that America, unlike Russia, had to aim at good relations with both sides.[165] Just as the Vietnam War alienated well-wishers of America all over the world, this situation alienated not only Arabs, but many people in Muslim countries further away which Washington was anxious to keep on its leading-strings – Turkey, Iran, Pakistan, Malaya, Indonesia. One consequence of a general churning up of feeling can be seen in the fall of the Libyan monarchy in 1969; a shock for the West, which had found in the Middle East's royal dynasties its firmest props. Yet in 1973 it was still the case that 'It would be a rash presidential candidate indeed who would dare openly to oppose Zionism or Israeli government policies'.[166] Next year there was the extraordinary spectacle of the U.S. subjecting its primary alliance with Western Europe to a heavy strain, in a fit of anger at Europe's unwillingness to imperil its oil supplies by helping America to back Israel in yet another war. American 'leadership' had often enough before appeared dictatorial; but this was a revelation. President Ford began 1975 by endorsing Kissinger's threat to resort to armed force in the Middle East in case of emergency, if for instance lack of oil portended economic strangulation. (Troops had been rehearsing desert warfare in Arizona, it was rumoured.) Enormous Saudi investments or holdings in the U.S., and their growing significance for its financial balances, accentuate the contradiction between enlightened self-interest and ideological commitment.

Many threads connected Middle Eastern affairs with Africa. In most of that continent, however, by comparison with Asia, American concern was restricted for long to its rich storehouse of minerals. About 1930 there had been apprehension in London when U.S. capital seemed to be trying to move into Northern Rhodesia and get control of its copper.[167] Now such minerals were increasingly wanted by U.S. industry because not available at home or less cheaply produced there. At the end of the Second World War only about 2% of U.S. private investment abroad was in Africa, and the African share remained relatively slight.[168] Yet it was growing, from 104 million dollars in 1943 to 834 million in 1959,[169] while between 1957 and 1970 it was growing more rapidly than the total of American foreign investment. Before 1957 it included virtual control of Libya's very profitable oilfields. There was even some investment in manufacture, limited in scale and mostly confined to South Africa, yet of significance in a continent which still had so little.

As in Asia with the Philippines, the U.S. had its own model of neo-colonial relations here, in Liberia. American rubber companies had got a firm footing in the inter-war years; during 1942–45 the country was a valuable American base; subsequently, under President Tubman – not quite a dictator, and with a fund of popularity – both American and European investments expanded, with free entry and freedom to remit their profits, after tax, to the metropolis. 'Liberia is the only country in Africa which permits the complete domination of the economy by foreign interests.'[170] But nationalism in Africa was only incipient after 1945, and, even more than in Asia, Washington began with a readiness to accept and work with the European empires which covered nearly the whole continent. When Algeria rebelled, Eisenhower remonstrated mildly with the French, but he could scarcely take a firm line with them after backing them so unquestioningly in Indochina. Indirectly at least, by enabling France to get loans, America was in fact helping it to carry on this colonial war too.[171] There was a penalty to be paid when France joined in the attack on Egypt in 1956 because Nasser was taking sides with Algeria.

In Tunisia in its early years of independence after 1956 American aid helped to establish the autocratic rule of Bourguiba, who proved willing to subscribe to the Eisenhower doctrine. But Chester Bowles, one of America's more sober diplomats, gave a salutary warning in 1956 about the failure to get on sensible terms with emerging Afro-Asia countries, due to policies remaining 'narrowly focussed on the military aspects of the Cold War'.[172] Morocco, unlike Tunisia, moved towards non-alignment when it received its independence in that year, and was provoked by the U.S. action in Lebanon into calling for the gradual removal of American bases.[173]

A Senate study in 1959 recognized the need to take account of anti-colonial feeling in Africa. Next year the government offered special concessions to promote investment there, which would enable it to exert more influence, with the general aim of helping to mould a respectable African copy of Western society, and a business elite to take the lead. This degree of sympathy with black Africa was enough to elicit heated reactions from white settlerdom. 'I hate America's guts', one of its headmen bellowed drunkenly at a race relations conference at Lusaka.[174] From Africans there might be other hostile reactions, sometimes aroused by the army of missionaries, America's auxiliary in its civilizing task, hoping for better success in less sophisticated Africa than they had met with in

China. A group of youngsters brought to Pittsburgh for a YMCA meeting reproached their hosts with their 'narrow, selfish and colonialist attitudes towards the Congo whose sons you have invited to this country primarily for political and ideological indoctrination'.[175]

This followed the chaotic events in the Congo resulting from Belgium's sudden abandonment of power in 1960. Neither Belgians nor any other foreigners had any intention of withdrawing economically; this colony contained some of Africa's richest minerals, and the U.S. did not mean to forego its right to a cut. It could take an anti-colonialist pose, but it seems to have shared European dislike of Lumumba, the only Congolese of anything like national stature, as a man who might make the country too independent. In obscure circumstances, Lumumba was got rid of by being handed over to the secessionist leader of the mining province of Katanga, and murdered. This man, Tshombe, had been educated in an American mission school, and there was loud support for him in the U.S., where many conservatives regarded him as the best bulwark against socialism. Washington's decision was to back U.N.O. intervention against him instead; it helped also to prevent secession by another region, round Stanleyville, under left-wing leadership.[176]

A confused, long-drawn conflict was compounded by sharp rivalries among foreign interests, with American capital challenging Belgian and British, and French and German pushing in. Washington's declarations were sometimes inconsistent, and its aims opaque. It may be entitled to some credit for the country being kept together instead of disintegrating. But the outcome was a 'national' government at Kinshasa (Leopoldville) propped up by foreign support. The man who eventually got to the top, a soldier named Mobutu, and who was to prove a good survivor (unlike many of his opponents), presided over an elitist, right-wing regime, cordial to foreign investors. The country has changed its name, to Zaire, but not its structure, which remains colonial, and still closely linked with Belgium and Europe, but with America's place far from negligible.

In 1955 Angolans dissatisfied with Portuguese rule appealed for a U.S. trusteeship under the U.N.O. 'If God has given those people power, wealth, and intelligence, it is for the good of humanity, or oppressed peoples.'[177] This simple faith in the great Democracy, reminiscent of the desire of some Turks in 1919 to be taken under the American wing, shows the reputation it still had in the postwar years. But by the time serious unrest showed itself in Angola, richest of the three Portuguese territories, its early post-war reforming impulses had evaporated. At the outset of the Kennedy era they had a fresh flicker, to the extent of some thought being given to the advisability of compelling the Portuguese to go over to indirect rule, or showing them the door and replacing them with trustworthy nationalists.[178] To Cabral, the highly talented guerrilla leader in Portuguese Guinea, it appeared in 1961 that 'the American Imperialists are emerging from the shadows and, astonished by the weakness of their partners, are seeking to replace them everywhere, with varying degrees of subtlety'.[179]

An eligible candidate for Angola was at hand in Roberto Holden, who made several trips to America that year to angle for support. Even the C.I.A., with its exacting standards, was believed to have vouched for his reliability. There were said to be American advisers with him, one an officer who had served in Vietnam. He had his headquarters at Kinshasa, where he lived comfortably, on friendly terms with Mobutu, who assisted his movement against the far more militant and more left-wing MPLA. In spite of all these credentials, Washington reverted to the easier line of leaving Portuguese misrule to go on. Events in the Congo had a happy ending, but they showed the dangers which might arise from any big upheaval. Lisbon had a persuasive card to play in the value of the Azores for American strategic planning. It also made a shrewd move in the early 1960s by scrapping the old restrictive policy and throwing the colonies open to foreign investment. Much capital poured in, chiefly into Angola, and vested interests desirous of seeing resistance crushed multiplied. American investment probably overtook British, hitherto in the lead. Portugal was fighting largely with American or NATO weapons; West Germany and South Africa were also liberal contributors. Cabral spoke in 1968 of the 'international character of the Portuguese colonial war against Africa'.[180]

In the later 1960s Washington was preoccupied with Vietnam, and inclined to feel that 'Europe had primary responsibility for the security of Africa'.[181] Appropriations for aid to African countries were reduced. Any memory of Kennedy's more enterprising approach was erased. The longer the resistance movements were compelled to go on fighting, the more they were obliged to turn to communist sources for ideas and arms. Portugal could then paint its rebels red, and Washington's reflexes functioned automatically. Others could play the same game. France had led the way, justifying its Algerian War, more absurdly than in Indochina, by pretending to be shielding the West from communism. 'We must persuade the West', Admiral Biermann of South Africa wrote, 'that Communist penetration into the southern hemisphere is a direct threat to Western Europe and the rest of the free world.'[182] Some Americans joined in raising the hue and cry. In 1967 Attwood, another magazine-writer turned diplomat, evoked a protest from Kenya, where he had been ambassador, by boasting of having helped to eject the left wing from the governing KANU party. His memoirs were called *The Reds and the Blacks;* he found Reds under every bush.

In this mood Washington hailed with relief the fall in 1966 in Ghana of Nkrumah, who in marked contrast with that other West African, Tubman, indulged in socialist talk and sharp strictures on America. There were ready credits for those who ejected him. In another area the U.S. was collaborating as unhesitatingly with the unregenerate feudal monarchy of Ethiopia as with Portuguese imperialism. Here, strategic location was the prime attraction. By the early 1950s British influence was supplanted, and a large military mission established. In 1963 there were reported to be some ten thousand Americans in the country, nearly half of them in uniform, playing a big part in the running of things.[183] A Senate report of 1970 disclosed that under a 1960 agreement secret commitments had been made to subsidize the army, in return for permission to set up a vast monitoring station; and that this led to involvement in army operations, and an indirect role in suppression of Eritrean insurgents.[184] It was very plain after the collapse of the monarchy that during two decades of predominance at Addis Ababa, America did very little by way of recommending reforms, while a revolutionary movement was coming on the scene. As a result, the fall of the monarchy meant the elimination of American influence, and its replacement by Soviet.

In Portuguese Africa it underwent another defeat. In 1971 the Azores agreement was extended, and Lisbon got fresh loans and 'anti-partisan' training in America for officers. In 1973 Portuguese pilots were still being trained in the U.S., and helicopters and light aircraft supplied for use in Mozambique.[185] Nemesis was at hand: next year the army, tired at last of being doomed to endless warfare, overthrew a dictatorship which had lasted fifty years. In the new Portugal the Communist Party was a force to be reckoned with. In the colonies Marxist parties took power, in Angola after a brief civil war. Unable to launch a direct intervention so soon after Vietnam, Washington gave secret aid to anti-MPLA forces by financing an incursion into the north of the territory from Zaire.

This was organized by the C.I.A., whose local director, Stockwell, has since resigned, a sadder and wiser man.[186] It was countered by Cuban troops bringing far more effectual succour to the MPLA. America's chickens were coming home to roost.

From then on white rule in Rhodesia was in jeopardy, while its protector, South Africa, was isolated and condemned by world opinion. It had been giving a warm welcome to foreign capital, partly in order to secure foreign friends, and with considerable success: American as well as European investors saw tempting pickings out of the cheap labour provided by the racialist police state. In 1968 nearly a third of all American trade and investment in Africa was in this southern corner. To topple a weak government is simpler for Washington than to bridle the conduct of a big American corporation abroad. But off and on in the past few years it has been compelled to put a distance, real or imaginary, between itself and white supremacy, and even to try to push South Africa towards solid concessions, over Namibia and Rhodesia in particular. The Portuguese lesson has shown that the alternative may, before very long, be far worse. So far, most of Africa has been kept safely within the 'free world'; but this unsolved racial issue in the deep south is a disturbing factor for conservatism all over the continent, as Zionism remains for the whole Arab and Muslim expanse.

5

Latin America

Writing in 1951, Sumner Welles took pleasure in eulogizing the Good Neighbour policy and its happy results for the New World. 'The just resentment aroused by our armed interventions had been ended by our willingness to join in a convention forbidding all interference by one American republic in the affairs of another.'[187] In reality it is in Latin America, its primary sphere of action, that America's hegemony has displayed its worst qualities most saliently. U.S. investments have mounted less rapidly than in Canada or Europe; during the 1960s there was actually a decline, from 26 to 18 billion dollars; but profits on them have been exceptionally high, swiftly replacing the capital exported. Though there has been a gradual turn towards industrial investment, U.S. enterprise has been largely parasitic, concerned with removal of raw materials or foodstuffs at the cheapest rates, and denuding the continent of more wealth than it brings into it. Talk of mutual benefits, at Inter-American conferences, has often sounded like Japan's wartime publicity about its Co-Prosperity Sphere in Eastern Asia. 'Latin American economies have too often been controlled from the United States much as colonial empires were controlled from the metropolitan countries.'[188]

Control has been maintained through a blend of charity and coercion. Aid has sometimes been beneficial; but it has not seldom suffered from the defect noted in programmes in Peru in the 1960s, that the direct gains from jungle highway-building, and so on, went to American contractors and their Peruvian associates, while not much good percolated to the common people who had been taught to expect a lot from them.[189] Too much 'aid' has consisted of weaponry supplied to the local elites through whom coercion is ordinarily exercised. All imperialism has practised divide-and-rule in some form. There would be a plethora of class conflict in Latin America (often worsened by racial tensions) if no U.S. existed; but it would have been less extreme, and less regressive in its political outcome, in the absence of this interference from outside.

When Vice-President Nixon visited Latin America in 1958 he talked, for the record, of the U.S. making a stand against dictatorship – 'but Secretary Dulles insisted that non-interventionist principles forbade this'.[190] Men like him could scarcely feel secure with any other species of government in their vicinity. In a curious way the U.S. was adopting the same creed as Marxists had held in the inter-war years, but were now leaving behind, that there could be nothing between communism and some equivalent of fascism; Marxists' belief in revolution by force was likewise being succeeded by an American faith in counter-revolution by force. This, increasingly ferocious, has been carrying to a logical extreme the maxim current in the U.S. of the 19th century, that sentimentality could not be allowed to hold up 'the march of empire'. Burnham in 1947 considered it a minimum requisite that communism, which had got footholds in the Americas from the 1920s, should be contained and 'progressively weakened'; also that in time of war the resources of the hemisphere must be at the U.S.'s disposal.[191] Setbacks in Asia and Africa only made Washington more brutally determined to crush any dissidence in its own continent. The upshot has been to leave Latin America, in spite of economic growth here and there, politically as benighted as any part of the 'free world', and to subject large areas of it to barbarities which a hundred years ago would have been thought inconceivable.

Cold war was not long in leading to interventions in Central America, with the partly genuine, partly pretended aim of forestalling communism, as formerly of halting 'anarchy', but with dollar appetites playing their part now as earlier. Guatemala was the first victim. Since the fall of a villainous boss in 1954 it had made enough progress for its liberal government to be stigmatized as 'communist', though even a communist party did not exist before 1951. In 1953 Spruille Braden, formerly in the Latin America section of the State Department and now earning better money from the United Fruit Company, denounced 'international communism' there and argued that the use of force against it would not be intervention. The government was taking over a large tract of uncultivated land from the company, offering what it thought, as corporations always think, inadequate compensation.[192] It was a signal instance of the growing integration of power in the U.S. that Dulles and his brother Allen, head of the C.I.A., and an Assistant Secretary of State, all had close links with United Fruit. Such facts must inspire puzzlement as to whether Dulles was really a victim of self-induced paranoia, brought on by continual trumpeting of the communist menace, or had a shrewd eye all the time to the main chance. Shamans have been observed, however, to alternate quickly between rhapsodic flights and attention to prosaic detail.

Washington did not wish to seem to be acting alone, or directly. Dulles harangued a docile Inter-American Conference in March 1954 and got it to pass a resolution condemning communism. The right man to get rid of President Arbenz was found in his opponent Castillo Armas; he and his followers, encamped in Honduras and Nicaragua, were generously furnished with U.S. arms. In June Guatemala was invaded, and 'order' restored with a heavy hand. Dulles thanked Eden for British help in preventing the matter from being taken up by the U.N.O.[193] But what had happened 'was public knowledge, and its brazenness shocked many US allies', in the British Labour Party for example.[194] Castillo Armas was not indeed a U.S. agent pure and simple: as in every such case the country was divided, and a minority was ready to utilize foreign assistance.

Dictatorial rule, behind a thin constitutional screen, has gone on, holding in check the land-hunger of the mostly Indian peasantry. It has always depended on supplies from the U.S. of what may in such countries be called the machinery of government, including helicopters, so useful in Vietnam, and 'counter-insurgency' experts. Between 1954 and 1966 Guatemala was receiving about two million dollars a year in military aid, plus a total of 170 millions in economic.[195] Guerrilla resistance broke out, and in August 1968 scored a success by shooting the American ambassador, but it was stifled by a resort to unlimited official terrorism.[196] One administrative refinement, which has been copied elsewhere, most recently in Uruguay, has been a 'death squad' to dispose of suspects quickly and informally. It had a parallel in Vietnam in 'Operation Phoenix'. In the two years before August 1968 the total of murders, executions, private or guerrilla killings was variously estimated at between 2,000 and 4,500. 'The papers', it was reported in 1971, 'carry daily the pictures of those who have disappeared and the descriptions of unidentified and mutilated bodies found here and there.'[197] On 22 February 1978, Amnesty International gave details of 113 'death squad killings and disappearances' in the last quarter of 1977. One dividend on all this was a lucrative nickel concession to an American-Canadian company.

In 1957 U.S. investments in Cuba had passed a billion dollars. They were well protected by the dictator Batista, back in office since 1952, 'the symbol of stability to many Americans ... The United States Government fully realized that military aid to Batista was essentially for the purpose of keeping order.'[198] 'Order' meant a stagnant economy distorted by its colonial relationship with the U.S. In 1958 this tyranny was ended by the Castro revolution, and Cuba alone, thanks to a long history of struggle against slavery and foreign rule, and to a new social philosophy and practical assistance from the U.S.S.R., was able to shake off American over-lordship. In 1961 Washington sought to repeat its masked intervention on Guatemalan lines. The fiasco of the Bay of Pigs invasion, by right-wing exiles with U.S. equipment, was a damaging one. 'American prestige in all Latin America fell disastrously', a Canadian wrote, 'as people saw in this episode proof of American "dollar imperialism"'.[199] Americans felt a 'pathological hatred' of Cuba as a ward which had dared to throw off their tutelage,[200] the same hatred as China had earned. An economic blockade was organized; how much further Washington was prepared to go was only revealed much later. A C.I.A. base was set up, illegally, in Miami, to direct commando raids on the island by the Cuban emigrés; serious thought was given to methods of assassinating Castro.[201]

Partly in retaliation, Cuba was seeking to spread revolution to neighbouring Caribbean countries, which it could suspect of being otherwise hostile bases; Washington then had an additional argument for condemning it as a menace to the region's tranquillity, or that of its ruling classes. Next time there was a danger signal – a quite faint one – action was even prompter. In the Dominican Republic the long and brutal despotism of Trujillo was rounded off in 1961 by his murder; by that time he and his family had stacked away abroad an enormous fortune. His heir Balaguer was quickly ousted; an exiled liberal, Juan Bosch, was brought back and elected president, but faced enmity from the Trujillo faction, army, and Church, and was speedily overturned by a military *coup*. In April 1965 another *coup*, assured in advance of U.S. approbation, was mounted to prevent his return.

Its success hung in doubt, because the army was split, part of it taking the popular side, so that this time direct intervention became indispensable. There was little hesitation in Washington, where the House of Representatives had carried this same year by 312 votes to 52 a resolution – very much in the spirit of the Holy Alliance – that 'The U.S. or any other American country has the right of unilateral intervention in order to keep communism outside the Western Hemisphere.'[202] Johnson despatched troops, ostensibly at first to protect U.S. citizens, and then to avert a fictitious communist takeover. Bosch's adherents were being manipulated, it was alleged, by 'a small band of conspirators who receive their directions from abroad'. Support was drummed up from the Organization of American States (O.A.S.), several of its members contributed soldiers, and they and the U.S. force were placed, by way of disguise, under the command of a Brazilian general. These states were joining what amounted to a league of mutual insurance against their own subjects, and in this guise the Pan-Americanism preached for so long by the U.S. was at last acquiring reality. As for the Dominican Republic, in 1974 when the restored Balaguer was re-electing himself for a third term as president, a journalist reported that 'Dr. Balaguer's exceedingly discreet and lethally efficient formula for repression has become something of a hemispheric legend.'[203] Not surprisingly, U.S. interests have been in command of the economy. Of the people, some have fared well under the regime, thanks in part to a sugar boom in the early 1970s, but class division has deepened, and social discontent spread to a formerly quiescent peasantry.

Theodore Roosevelt once said that the Monroe Doctrine must not be the means of allowing Latin American countries to degenerate into 'small bandit nests of a wicked and inefficient type'.[204] It is precisely regimes of this type, efficient only in repression, that Washington has been fostering in Central America in the past three decades. It would even seem to have come to regard hereditary dictatorship as a stabilizing force. In these small countries with little industry and economies largely pre-capitalist, and with political evolution arrested by blockage from outside, there has been a marked tendency to personal rule by families, bastard monarchies only imperfectly coinciding with any corporate class interests.

In Nicaragua, the Somoza family took power in 1936, a son stepping into a murdered father's shoes in 1956. Local business circles, America's natural allies, become irritated by the family's determination to monopolize profit; it ran its own bank, mines, ranches, plantations. If a state did this, private enterprise philosophy would be outraged. Yet the privileged National Guard on which the regime depended was under officers many of whom had been at U.S. centres for training, chiefly in counter-insurgency. Guerrilla warfare had been smouldering in the countryside, and the rebel 'Sandinista' movement inevitably took on a Marxist orientation: here too American tactics help to engender the peril they are supposed to exorcize. Early in 1978 there was a two-week general strike in protest at the murder of the opposition editor P.J. Chamorro. 'Many Nicaraguans believe', it was reported half a century ago, 'that under the present system Nicaragua has the disadvantages of vassalage without the advantages of a pro-tection', and would rather be annexed outright.[205] They might well feel the same now.

Most notorious, and most senseless from any point of view but its own, was the long reign starting in 1957 of the Duvalier family in Haiti, propped up by the sinister 'ton-ton macoute' organization. Year by year thousands of refugees from persecution or starvation have been arriving clandestinely in that pleasure-haunt of the American tourist, the Bahamas; many others are known to perish on the way in unseaworthy craft. As an American historian wrote in 1968, in Central America all non-communist governments are acceptable, 'and all, including the outrageously tyrannical and corrupt regime of President Duvalier in Haiti, receive aid to bolster their armed forces and their economies'.[206] The insane excesses of the regime embarrassed the State Department at times; aid was suspended for a time after a U.S. citizen was beaten to death by the Haitian police in 1957. But when the patriarch died in 1971 Washington gave its blessing to his son's succession; the ambassador, Knox, was forthright in his approval of the dynasty.[207] Yet there are no big economic stakes in Haiti, and the purpose of such a course can be little more than the blindly negative one of preventing Haiti from emulating Cuba. For several decades, American statesmanship seemed incapable of thinking of any other alternative. Possibly it felt apprehensive of what might come to light if such a government were allowed to fall. There are too many skeletons in the cupboard. Also, of course, the more tyrannical and unpopular a ruler, the more closely he is tied by loyalty to Washington.

Habits formed in Central America could not but affect U.S. strategy further south, among bigger countries and more complex problems. Over the years, since 1945, speculations about whether the Latin American region was on the whole

turning away from U.S. suzerainty, or falling more deeply under it, have fluctuated widely and frequently; and it would be rash to suppose that any final stage
has yet been reached. As late as 1973 army leaderships, headed by the Peruvian
and Argentinian, seemed to be in a mood for confrontation with Washington.[208]
Clearly, however, reaction had strong native roots from the first, and governments needed little warning after 1945 against radical tendencies which had been
gathering, especially where industry was sprouting, as in Chile, and to which the
World War gave an impetus. In 1945 Vargas, the mildly progressive leader in
office in Brazil since 1934, fell foul of his businessmen. 'The prompting of the US
embassy was scarcely necessary, and Vargas was overthrown by the generals.'[209]
In the 1946 elections the Brazilian Communist Party got 800,000 votes, in 1947
it was outlawed; the same thing happened in Chile, where the party had had
members in a popular front government.

With political advance impeded, and feudal ascendancy still only in the
process of giving way to capitalist, progress was largely confined to forms of
populist leadership. This might give it a very lopsided character, but could pave
the way, somewhat as in India with its analogous economic structure, towards
forms of mixed economy, with industrial growth and some agrarian reform. Of
such populism Vargas was a pioneer. Though allowed back into office in 1950, he
had to keep one eye on the army and walk warily. Juan Perón, elected in 1946 in
Argentina, had a more secure position because he himself came from the army.
On brotherly terms with Franco, and viewed by the European left as a fascist, he
belonged rather to a novel, hybrid category, and relied a good deal on trade-
union backing. Washington disliked him (and his economic policies were
sometimes hair-brained), but was prepared for a while to humour him. For one
reason, communism was not America's only target in Latin America; it was
anxious after 1945 to prevent Britain from regaining a competitive place in
countries like Argentina or Mexico.[210]

In the meantime the U.S., government as well as businessmen, was working
up useful connections. They were often with military circles. In a Latin America
drifting away from static feudal-clerical moorings, with bourgeoisies not yet
mature, armies could provide something like equivalents of the fascist movements of inter-war Europe. But their officer corps could not be counted on
automatically as friends of 'order'. They were drawn from the inchoate middle
classes, shared their heterogeneous outlook, and might have a nationalist streak of

anti-U.S. feeling. It required therefore steady cultivation and inducements to mould them into corporations which could be relied on to see eye to eye with Washington, and enable it, like a matchmaker, to bring them and the leading business quarters together. Consignments of arms were an acceptable bribe. The more elaborate weapons were only toys to feed the vanity of generals who were no more in fact than gendarmes; though the possibility might arise of some of them being utilized one day against neighbours who might get out of step.

The Second World War gave Washington an opportunity to get military missions of its own employed in Latin American capitals, some of which had previously employed European advisers. Peruvian officers were among those who began to attend U.S. academies, where suitable ideas were imparted to them. Ordinary Peruvians might be resentful of the place the Yankees, with their military and economic aid to dole out, were taking; 'the embassy became known as "The House of the Viceroy".'[211] Vargas resisted some pressures, but submitted to an arrangement which 'opened wide the Brazilian army to U.S. political penetration'.[212] In Bolivia a government at first very anti-imperialist was won round in the early 1950s, 'permitting the Pentagon to take extensive control of the country and to build up a massive military apparatus on Bolivian territory'.[213] An hour soon came for some of these traps to be sprung. Vargas offered no open defiance, but committed suicide with dignity when about to be deposed again in 1954. Perón was banished by his army in 1955.

With social discontents glaring, and Cuban example having an obvious appeal, the ever present risk of nationalist feeling turning against the U.S. made it desirable to put a better face on its paramountcy. In 1961 it called the conference, in Uruguay, which led to the 'Alliance for Progress', with a fund available for loans and development to sterilize revolutionary germs. But as in most of the Third World, it was towards far more drastic methods that U.S. policies, or the initiatives taken by its protégés, were in reality tending. In July 1962 the army struck in Peru: the attack on the presidential palace was led by a colonel trained in the U.S., and the gates were burst open by a Sherman tank.[214] In Bolivia the ministry of Paz Estenssoro, which had carried out an agrarian reform, was ousted by the army late in 1964, with Washington's approval because of the value of the country's tinmines, and fear of the regime moving too far to the left. 'The moment had come when only the armed forces could defend interests and privileges favoured by the USA.'[215] Old reactionaries flocked back from abroad, and were consoled with the 'Condor of the Andes' ribbon. The condor is more vulture than eagle, and lives on carrion.

Most important of all, in the same year President Goulart, accused of wanting to smuggle communism into Brazil, was ejected by the army. Documents released late in 1976 show that Washington's contribution was not confined to goodwill. A naval task force was stationed off the coast; the military attaché was in close touch with the army chiefs; the C.I.A. (needless to say) was active.[216] Subsequently a former U.S. diplomat provided further detail, incriminating among others the then Deputy Secretary of Defense, later Secretary of State Vance.[217] U.S. influence and interests were making sure of their hold on a very large and promising territory. A frail facade of constitutional rule was preserved, as was sometimes done in Latin America in deference to U.S. wishes, to obviate criticism abroad. But there was friction between the State Department, whose sense of propriety made it prefer an appearance of civilian rule, and the Pentagon, which cared nothing for foreign opinion.[218] Because there were few if any political parties that Washington could depend on with nearly as much confidence as on the soldiers, it was the Pentagon that was getting the upper hand, and right-wing politics were to shift still more towards naked rule by the sword. The C.I.A. was not lagging behind; in Bolivia after guerrilla resistance started in 1967 it took over a great part of the official intelligence services.[219]

In spite of all these warnings, progressive impulses were not damped down everywhere, but were sometimes pushed further to the left by the behaviour of the American hegemony in both New World and Old. In Peru a very different army *coup* took place in 1968, chiefly nationalist in inspiration: officers felt that their government had been surrendering to U.S. oil interests, and the biggest of the foreign corporations which had long dominated Peru were nationalized; while in order to broaden its following the army went in for extensive land reforms. In Bolivia left-wing officers held sway from 1970 to 1973, and some American properties were expropriated. If it was alarming to find these armies biting the hand that fed them, it was still more so to see a politician sympathetic to Marxism elected to the presidency in 1970 in Chile, at the head of a broad front of democratic parties. Here was a menace like the election of a communist government in Kerala, but nearer home. Action was clearly called for, and was soon being prepared. Revolutionary movements cannot be artificially conjured up by foreign intriguers, as Americans accustomed to thinking in terms of the

mechanics of lever and cog-wheel have found it easy to believe. Counter-revo-
lutions on the other hand can very well be arranged by agents like the C.I.A.'s,
working hand in hand with local reactionaries.

This has come to be known in their jargon as *'destabilizing'* a foreign government. There was scarcely any concealment of the fact that it took place in
Chile. President Ford himself informed the world of it in September 1974 with
brutal frankness; part of the purpose of such operations is to strike fear into other
possible offenders. A programme of 'economic strangulation' against the Allende
government was not hard to organize; there was 'no important sector of the
Chilean economy that was not penetrated and in some cases dominated by
American enterprises'.[220] For the final stroke, the bloodthirsty army *coup* in 1973,
the U.S. had, as in Brazil or Indonesia, no monopoly of responsibility. Once the
army took action an intense class hatred displayed itself, the vindictive revengefulness of a middle class against a working class encroaching on its privileges.
Feudal rule had turned into or been supplanted by that of a bourgeoisie, and
industry made room for a growing number of professional or white-collar
employees. They as well as their employers welcomed the seizure of power and
the reign of terror. Still, American interference did much at least to hasten the
one and, it must be supposed, to lend to the other a pitch of brutality quite new
to Chilean history.

There was warm American approval for another murderous *coup* in 1973,
carried out in Bolivia by Colonel Hugo Banzer, a soldier ideally suited to
Washington tastes: 'impeccably conservative and anti-Communist', and with
American training.[221] In Argentina, after the final spasms of Peronismo, the
army took full power in March 1976 and set up what before long became the
most terroristic regime of all. By 1974, seventy thousand Latin American officers
had attended U.S. training schools, notably the one set up (illegally) at Ford
Gulick in the Canal Zone, specializing in counter-insurgency. 'More than 150 of
Latin America's leading figures from Cabinet Ministers to Commanders-in-Chief,
have passed through this unique establishment.'[222] The ferocity brought into
public life by the spread of military rule has been conspicuous in Brazil, a
country which prided itself on its mildness by contrast with its Spanish-speaking
neighbours. Now it seemed to be marked out as Washington's second-in-
command for the whole region. Brazilian police came promptly to the help of the
military regime in Chile. This was followed by pressure by these two and Bolivia

on Peru, where, with the implied U.S. threat behind it, it helped to bring the spell of reforming rule to an end.

In 1965 Brazil had signed an agreement giving extraordinarily favourable terms to American investors. European and Japanese investments were flowing in as well, capital here too displaying its new international amity. A vast economic boom got going, with headlong exploitation of Brazil's resources, and lavish profits for the foreigner, but rewards also for the Brazilian commercial and professional classes. This was one of the new-style dictatorships, like Iran's; it was imbibing the Yankee creed of economic expansion, and understood that it must broaden its base by creating fresh vested interests and satisfying the better-off middle classes. These could fare better because the workers' share was held down; in time a stratum of skilled workers would also get some benefit. Economic history was to be speeded up by military fiat. The same mood seized the Banzer regime in Bolivia, where Brazilian influence and enterprise, already overflowing national boundaries, have been active.

Governments like these must have new industries, more jobs, to take credit for. Foreign investors are willing to take advantage of local materials and a controlled labour force. U.S. capital has been moving fairly extensively from extraction into production, of consumer goods, machine parts, automobiles. Capitalism in the U.S., with all its sins, has always had a constructive instinct; and sheer volume of investment must help as time goes on to bring a shift of emphasis. During the 1960s U.S. capital in Argentina grew to about 1,300 million dollars, expanding more rapidly than in any other Latin American country except Panama, despite the prevalent notion that Mexico, Brazil and Venezuela were 'the darlings of American businessmen'.[223] With these mutually reinforcing impulses, indigenous and foreign, there had been hopes that parts of South America might be on their way to genuine industrialization. A good deal of violence and coercion was required to get capitalism going anywhere in the world; to launch it in fresh areas now, when socialist ideas have spread everywhere, often intertwining with nationalism, must require a higher degree of compulsion than ever. In this direction too, force is the midwife of history.

In these developing regions a dictator today is a very different creature from the Latin American general in O'Henry's story, with his bottle of brandy under his pillow for breakfast. He is imbued with a stern sense of duty to free enterprise and high dividends, well prepared for his police work, and absolutely ruthless.

With techniques of repression brought to such perfection, dictatorships under U.S. patronage are safe so long as they can keep their economies functioning. Some of them have given hostages to fortune by undertaking 'economic miracles', before the onset of world-wide recession could be foreseen. But in mid-1976, when the O.A.S. held its conference, in conquered Chile, an observer could find it 'difficult to recall a time when the continent has caused Washington so few headaches'. The tide of reaction was running strongly, the right wing everywhere was in good heart, for instance in the old British Caribbean colonies where *destabilizers* from the U.S. were believed to be at work.[224] Over the need for the Chile *coup*, as in East Asia, the 'domino theory' had been invoked, and the determination to allow no more breakaways was unmistakable.

In terms of what used to be thought of as civilized government, the cost was heavy. The new infrastructure of power represented a whole modern technology of despotism, with torture elevated from an art into a science. Those early post-1945 days have been left far behind when Truman could lament so innocently that Chiang Kai-shek and his police were persecuting 'liberal elements of the population', or murdering professors connected with the Democratic League.[225] What else are policemen for, a C.I.A. expert might wonderingly exclaim! Torture, above all, which Americans of old were so repelled by among redskins, has become dreadfully common, though not in this continent alone. 'It has long been known that torture is common practice in Haiti', wrote an Amnesty International report of the late 1970s,[226] but in Argentina 'systematic torture has increased rapidly during the military governments of the past decade'; likewise in Brazil, and in Chile since the counter-revolution.[227]

These procedures, undeniably effective, have raised up new and sometimes very unexpected enemies. They have provoked protests from the best elements in the Catholic churches, and even achieved what would have seemed the impossible task of driving some of them into sympathy with Marxism and rebellion. A priest in Argentina protested on behalf of his group against Paul VI's visit to Colombia in 1968, and 'the disgraceful political manoeuvre of bringing together so many Heads of State in honour of the Pope's arrival in America ... led by their boss Johnson'.[228] Except in Africa, the significance of churches as an adjunct to the hegemony has been diminishing; with up-to-date machinery of repression Order stands less in need of help from religion. In June 1977 the Nicaraguan bishops declared that two hundred peasants had been killed in a 'reign of terror'

in the northern jungles; Catholic priests from the U.S. said that twenty-eight
rural chapels in their district had been turned by the National Guard into
barracks and places of torture.[229] In nearby Salvador, the military dictator Carlos
Humberto Romero abused Archbishop Oscar Romero as a communist for protesting at hundreds of arrests and disappearances under a state of siege.

On the secular plane too the hegemony has been divisive. Its Midas touch,
which for some turns everything to gold, for others turns everything to ashes.
Despite flurries of nationalism, the upper classes have been easier to bring under
outside tutelage because of the social, and often racial, gulf separating them from
the masses. 'The Latin American *elites* are the most alienated in the world', full of
regrets for not being born European or North American.[230] A French investi-
gator found much acculturation among professional and technical people, taught
in the U.S. or on American lines, and borrowing the American outlook. But he
also found many intellectuals and artists turning to Marxism, under the
oppressive sense of their countries' condition and 'l'omniprésence tutélaire du
colosse yankee'.[231]

One country's recent history is proof that Europe also has no assured immunity
from the fate of so many in the New World. In 1967 a junta of officers imposed a
harsh military rule on Greece. Most Greeks took for granted that the long arm of
the C.I.A., which by this time had an established reputation, had been at work.
This seems likely to have been a mistaken idea; Washington's favourites were the
king and senior generals, not these upstart colonels. But it accepted the new
regime without demur; 'a more or less mechanical application of a world-wide
line' was the kind of diplomacy that came naturally to it.[232] Greek harbours were
required by the Sixth Fleet, and in Pentagon philosophy what happened to Greek
men and women was a trifle in the balance. 'Best damn government since
Pericles', an American general is reported to have said.

Washington went on providing arms, U.S. financiers contributed dollar loans
– on stiff terms – which kept the economy afloat. U.S. firms trooped into this
new well-policed Eden, and officialdom and businessmen gave a classic display of
how harmoniously they could work together. Many representatives of private
enterprise were former State Department officials connected with Greece.[233] In
1970 Nixon's brother was in Athens picking up contracts for a company he had
been made vice-president of. Next year the Secretary of Commerce was there,
expressing the happiness of U.S. businessmen over 'the sense of security that the

Government of Greece is imparting to them'.[234] The Junta's obvious dependence on the Pentagon stimulated anti-American feeling; and more than half the members of NATO wanted Greece expelled, but were overborne by a U.S. refusal. When torture in Greek prisons was heard of, the American response was 'to deny it where possible and minimise it, where denial was not possible'.[235] The Senate got the best of both worlds, temporal and spiritual, by rejecting a proposal at the end of 1969 to cut off aid, and then passing a unanimous, and meaningless, motion in favour of a return to constitutional government. In 1971 the House of Representatives voted against aid; this was circumvented, but at any rate, for the first time since 1945, one House of Congress 'had taken action against a right-wing dictatorship'.[236]

The junta's evil reign was not ended by any American concern for democracy, but by its own folly in trying to grab Cyprus in 1974, thus provoking a Turkish intervention in the island. True, the C.I.A. seems unwittingly to have served as its gravedigger by encouraging the gamble. The easily foreseeable consequences, two NATO partners close to war and the American position in Turkey jeopardized, were testimony to the scanty wisdom and the muddle and confusion which have beset the hegemony. When Turkey proved defiant there could be no simple solution like installing a right-wing military dictatorship, for Turkey was under one already. This too, it seems, Washington had itself to thank for. According to the Turkish foreign minister in 1976, who held the same post in 1971, the army *coup* of that year which unseated the Demirel ministry was plotted by the ubiquitous C.I.A.[237]

6

Retrospect and Prospect

In 1829 Thomas Peacock lauded Jefferson for vindicating, in the New World, principles of liberty which in Europe during the war against the French Revolution were condemned as doctrines of anarchy: 'doctrines against which, under the watchword of "social order" and shouts "for God and the King", we fired away in thirty years nearly three thousand millions of money in gun-powder'.[238] In the past thirty years the United States has fired away a great deal more gunpowder in an attempt to suffocate similar principles, and has resorted to far worse violence. It was arriving at a position of world power when national and social revolt were rampant, and these movements had to be chastised not with Solomon's whips but with Rehoboam's scorpions.

This is far from having reached any end. But to the most ambitious aims of the hegemony, limits have had to be recognized. Military parity between America and Russia, along with the schism between Russia and China, brought Washington in the early 1970s to a readiness to come to terms. Hence in May 1972 the declaration of the superpowers on coexistence, with the SALT agreement for basis. In a curiously roundabout fashion the U.S. was reverting to its old dream of an orderly planet regulated by an understanding among all great powers – both red and yellow now included; but with no relaxing of America's grip on any of the realms still under its control. *Détente* however could not mean a static equilibrium. Some shortening of lines was necessary; a process of 'decommitment

... described as a long overdue withdrawal from an exposed position, a realistic adjustment to a new situation'.[239] Kissinger's conception of *détente* implied conversely that the U.S.S.R. should be content to stand still, forego any of the expansion of world influence it felt was now its due. There could be no facile adjustment of these views, after so many years of tension, and with so many interests, not all on one side, desirous of torpedoing agreement.

Having failed to become sole master of the globe, the U.S. was losing some of its pre-eminence even within the 'free world', through sins of omission or commission but also because of shifts in economic strength. Already in 1966 an American could warn that the U.S., perhaps the West altogether, was 'doomed to a spectacular repetition' of Britain's decline from supremacy.[240] Until 1972 the U.S. maintained a surplus on exchange of goods and services; but the gigantic overhead costs of empire have more than exceeded this. It would otherwise be incomprehensible that, in spite of a huge foreign investment income, America's balance of payments has repeatedly been under a strain which now seems to have become chronic. It might have been expected that its difficulty would rather be to find ways of absorbing such an income into an economy still for the most part self-sufficient and resistant to manufactured imports. How to remit profits from dependencies to metropolis has been a problem in one shape or other of all empires.

America it is true has been having to rely more and more on imported raw materials, among them more than half the metals used by industry with the exception of iron. One thing which impressed on Washington 'the degree of the United States dependence on less developed areas for strategic raw materials' was the Korean War.[241] Oil has come very much to the fore. But neither this nor, it would seem, continuing export of capital is enough to account for the downward drift of the dollar. Foreign investment more than pays for itself from year to year,[242] though a good deal of the profit is reinvested abroad. Outflow of money to meet imperial costs reached its extremest point with the climax of the Vietnam War. Many believed in the spring of 1968 that Johnson's chief incentive to think of winding up the war was the bankers serving notice that it was putting too heavy a load on the economy.

Besides the expenses of the hegemony (including a hundred varieties of graft and palm-greasing at home and abroad), some of its other economic results have to be reckoned with. When it began, America was still reluctant to open its enormous market to imports other than industrial raw materials. With the rising wealth of the Common Market and Japan, it has had to modify this attitude in their favour, for fear of retaliation. Both have been gaining ground as against their patron; especially Japan, ardently selling and grudgingly buying as the U.S. itself used to do. Other continents have been wanting to develop, and to use their own materials or get better prices for them than the U.S., by virtue of military as well as economic strength, has been in the habit of paying.[243] Here again, America at the outset was disinclined to see industry springing up in new countries. But some concessions have had to be made to developing regions too. Moreover, although the bulk of its capital engaged in manufacture abroad was in already developed countries,[244] its inclination to take part in industry-building in new territories, as in parts of South America, has been spreading. This helps to restrain such countries from going in for state-owned industry; but it is also an expression of the semi-autonomous life which capital invested abroad may take on, not identical with its parent. Increasingly colonial industrialization, exploiting cheap labour, may compete with production at home, thus generating a fresh contradiction within the hegemony.

All these factors working together, and a prolonged net outflow of money, have been reflected in the sagging dollar exchange. By the beginning of the 1970s an end was in sight to the long epoch of monetary stability in a world of rapidly expanding trade, based on gold and the dollar, which gave the American hegemony its bloom of prosperity. Instead 'a general crisis of over-production' seemed to be looming up, and internecine rivalries within the capitalist world beyond the U.S.'s capacity to hold in check.[245] Need of fresh trade outlets furnished another motive for *détente*. In terms of political relations, this situation could not but carry further a loosening process already under way. By 1960 the demand for every country to be a faithful disciple, or be counted an outlaw, was having to be moderated; Secretary of State Herter told the National Press Club that America must seek to reinforce 'uncommitted' but non-socialist countries as well as allies.[246] Since then some of these allies (and likewise Russia's) have in turn had to be allowed more latitude.

This has not been an orderly process of rearrangement, in line with changing realities. The U.S. has been reluctant to see its foster-children growing up and growing away from it. In April 1973 Kissinger, wanting to strengthen its most important citadel in face of the necessity of withdrawal from some others, made his 'Year of Europe' speech, designed to fortify the Atlantic alliance and get Europe to bear more of its costs. The response was poor; with some justification, a European commented, for 'America had virtually stopped consulting its European allies'.[247] Indeed that same year with the Middle East War it tried to ride rough-shod over them. It appeared to many that the whole concept of permanent confrontation between two armed camps, each dominated by a superpower, was out of date. On the outskirts of empire too there has come in sight the prospect of some countries becoming strong enough to feel no need to pay attention to their guardian's wishes. An example has been the coolness caused by Washington's attempts – well justified, in this case – to veto an atomic-power contract made by Brazil with West Germany.

Such an issue may not matter to the multinationals, as it does to Washington; and the same applies to some of the consequences of manufacturing growth stimulated by U.S. investment. Production in underdeveloped countries soon runs into a need of more customers than can be found in them; and vehicles produced by U.S. subsidiaries in South America have been seeking buyers in Cuba, in breach of the boycott Washington still wants kept up. Both Argentina and Brazil have made commercial contacts with Russia or China. All this as time goes on may tend to destabilize the hegemony, though not, by itself, to soften repression within these countries. Marcos in the Philippines must have had similar reasons for seeking contacts with communist countries as a set-off to his dependence on the U.S. In 1975 he opened relations with Peking. It may be possible in some of these cases to foresee local capitalism gaining energy and reaching equality with foreign investors, and the whole process paving the way towards real 'decolonization'. This is what classical Marxism from Marx to Rosa Luxemburg seems to have expected to come of European capital export to colonies; and compared with Europe's, American capital came on the colonial scene already highly evolved.

During all this period the American public has seemed to view the outside world through a glass, darkly. As W.A. Williams wrote in his study of opinion and empire in 19th-century America, new realities call for a new social consciousness, 'but this new vision does not come automatically': it failed to evolve adequately then, and has failed again since 1945.[248] No doubt there has been a considerable cooling down since the first fine raptures released in 1945 by victory, when Representative J.D. Lodge exclaimed that 'The American point of view should be presented with dynamic enthusiasm, passionate conviction, and a burning faith in the American way of life.'[249] But the image of America in the world as an altruistic protector of the weak against the strong, of the virtuous against the rapacious, was to have a long lease of life. 'Americans think of themselves collectively', Eldridge Cleaver wrote with irony, 'as a huge rescue squad on twenty-four-hour call to any spot on the globe where dispute and conflict may erupt.'[250] An Irish writer has pointed out that in American 'comics' the rest of mankind is only 'innocent bystander, helpless and panic-stricken', waiting to be saved by Superman, just as in the ever-popular 'Western' film a town is 'cowed and terrorized by badmen' until the hero rides up and liberates it.[251]

Even amid the McCarthy hurricane America did not silence all dissent at home, as it has helped to do in so many of its tributaries. There were always some faithful socialists, and other sturdily independent critics, who saw how pursuit of a mirage was leading the country into the mire and threatening to wreck the planet. 'A small, outspoken, courageous and clear-headed minority is unsparingly denouncing the hypocrisies and iniquities of American foreign policy', a British radical recorded in 1949.[252] One member of it was T.A. Bailey, who had just been writing about 'The Miasma of Manifest Destiny'.[253] Among journalists, I.F. Stone's remonstrances took on a sharper edge as the Vietnam War got into its stride. 'The Kennedy Administration', he wrote in 1963, 'like Eisenhower's and Truman's before it, has carried on its Indochina policies behind a thick smokescreen of official falsification.'[254] Another reporter was Seymour Hersh, who exposed the concealment of the My Lai massacre. 'He did not hesitate to call Henry Kissinger a war criminal in public.'[255]

During the 1960s doubts were redoubling. In 1963 a writer on Cuba, no friend to Castro, trusted that events there would shock the U.S. into seeing the folly of being content with 'ignorance about conditions in Latin America, complacent support for the crumbling status quo, slogans about "Good Neighbours", and military aid alone ... The old order cannot be reimposed on Cuba.'[256] Next year Senator Fulbright, Chairman of the Foreign Affairs Committee, said it was high time for some rethinking of the Cuban problem, 'heavily burdened with the dead weight of old myths and prohibitions against "unthinkable" thoughts'.[257] A little later he observed that the American view of revolutions suffered from 'a simple but so far insuperable dilemma: we are simultaneously hostile to communism and sympathetic to nationalism'.[258] He might have added that nationalism with any tinge of enmity to U.S. interests was classed as *ipso facto* communist.

In 1969 misgivings found their way into a report on South-east Asia by so orthodox a pillar of banking as E.R. Black, sent out by President Johnson to take soundings; even if he sometimes still appeared to want the U.S. to maintain an indirect control or invigilation over the whole region, much as over Latin America.[259] In the same year an experienced enquirer came closer to a realistic picture of South-east Asia. Americans were very conscious of communism there, he said, but not of how much they themselves were doing to foster it; they recognized imperialist behaviour in others, 'but not the near-imperialistic character of their own actions'.[260] 'In the name of preserving peace', Senator Church declared in a debate on 29 October 1971, 'we have waged an endless war; in the guise of serving as sentinels of the "free world" we have stood watch while free Governments gave way to military dictatorships in country after country from one end of our vast hegemony to the other.'

Lichtheim could speak in that year of a 'current controversy over the problems and prospects of the American Empire'.[261] In 1972 a judicious study of American relations with India and Pakistan referred to a spreading scepticism about the utility of arms subsidies, and to a desire for 'a more just and less dangerous world community'.[262] Another book of that year, by B.P. Kiernan, went beyond this by admitting that the country was not really fighting communism in order to defend its freedom: 'we are defending our enormous wealth and power from the challenge posed by the revolutionary transformation of the emergent nations, which America ought instead to be accepting and furthering'.[263] Kiernan derided the phobia about communist plotters, and the delusion that 'political events are determined by the machinations of spies and agents', as only proper to 'the imaginary world of movie and television drama'.[264]

Newspaper readers, Stone noticed, quite enjoyed what leaked out about cloak-and-dagger exploits like the raids on Cuba.[265] Critical approaches were by and large confined to individuals and groups, and were not taken up by big enough numbers to give them practical weight. For this various reasons can be found. The country's long-standing pride in itself as a new civilization, with numberless lessons to teach the Old World, was valid enough, but lent itself perilously to perversion by demagogues; and from the time when victory in the Second World

War seemed so dramatically to vindicate it, it was taking on too much of the flavour of Bismarckian Germany's pride in *Kultur*, with 'culture' hardening into technological 'know-how'. Like Britain's former sense of superiority, that of Americans was buttressed by a high degree of insulation from and ignorance of the rest of the world. Strangely, millions were of families recently come from Europe; it was as if they had come from Venus or Mars, places too distant to remember. 'America was isolated in its safety', as Martha Gellhorn, the distinguished war correspondent, said '... a gulf as wide as the Grand Canyon separates America from all the people who have known war in their own countries.'[266]

This remoteness has helped to give the American intelligentsia in modern times an analogous remoteness from life, or historical reality. It was not easy for dissidents to break the barrier. There was a certain shallowness, a failure to rise much above the level of journalism, in the literature of protest in the inter-war years, progressive and sincere though this often was. It was a deficiency which struck Gramsci, reading the novels of Sinclair Lewis and Upton Sinclair in his prison.[267] It lacked the imaginative depth or resonance which can only be derived from a responsive environment. (Steinbeck's *The Grapes of Wrath*, written under the spur of the Slump, was an exception.) From the World War onward, intellectuals were drawn increasingly into public activities whose ultimate dynamo was the military-industrial complex. They took part in strategic planning, and the development of scientific warfare and counter-insurgency, were flatteringly invited to the White House, and rewarded presidents with the incense due to royalty.[268] For much of the Cold War, scholars engaged in Latin American studies underwrote the ideology of 'good neighbourship', of the harmony of interests between the U.S. and the rest of the continent.[269] Chomsky had good reason to speak of the 'overwhelming urgency' of the need to counteract 'the effects of a generation of indoctrination and a long history of self-adulation'; he appealed to intellectuals to open their eyes to the 'tradition of naivete and self-righteousness that disfigures our intellectual history'.[270] It will be long before all these effects of an era of deception and self-deception, as pernicious as those of Stalinism in the U.S.S.R., wear off.

Political degeneracy in the labour movement similarly hindered any broad opposition to policies pursued abroad. Its leaders actively, the rank and file at least passively, gave the system their endorsement with far less questioning than

European working-class parties in the days of the empires. America's empire had little of the old romantic colour or glamour; on the other hand it was so anonymous that anyone who chose to ignore its existence could do so. Still, world power had its excitements, amid which labour was being welded into the national life, receiving full citizen status in return for accepting its rulers' outlook on the world. In December 1965 the A.F.L.-C.I.O. convention had no fault to find with Johnson's escalation of the Vietnam War, or with his intervention in the Dominican Republic.[271] To the rank and file the war could be recommended for its economic benefits, its speeding the wheels of industry. Criticism grew, but it could only be really vocal, as it was in 1967–68 in spite of the leaders' efforts to damp it down, when rising prices and taxes began to counteract the gains from fuller employment.[272]

Ordinary people in any country find it hard to understand accusations by foreigners, because they are not conscious of the gulf between their well-meaning selves and what their government is doing in their name. America's abstraction from the rest of the world has made this gulf exceptionally wide. In all complex modern societies, too, people feel unequal to grappling with problems outside their ken, and abdicate responsibility to 'experts'. In Britain public and parliament left their colonies to be run by 'the men on the spot'; the same disposition had a basic part in ensuring support for so many years for the war in Vietnam. Serious protest against it developed with painful sluggishness – by comparison, for instance, with the anti-war protest in Britain during the American Revolution, when many felt at the capture of Cornwallis's army as Horace Walpole did: 'I cannot put on the face of the day, and act grief.'[273]

But no country will easily be brought to dislike a war it thinks it is doing well out of. Johnson could boast in 1965 that few Americans were feeling ill effects from this one. 'Prosperity rises, abundance increases, the nation flourishes.'[274] He expressed regret at having to send young men to fight; and this really was a grave drawback. A movement against the war began with students, in 1965, inspired by ideals, but also swayed by the prospect of being sent to the Far East to kill or be killed. Early in 1970 the retiring chairman of the joint chiefs of staff confessed that he saw danger in a deepening public hostility to the military-industrial complex. 'On Vietnam itself, General Wheeler said that the military situation had never been better'[275] – which may in one sense have been true. Yet as soon as the risk of having to serve at the front was removed, agitation and concern over

Vietnamese sufferings died down abruptly; a year or two more, and Vietnam was forgotten. So was the promise at the end of the War to make some kind of restitution by giving aid to Vietnam for reconstruction. The Chilean bloodbath, which made a profound and lasting impression on Europe, appeared to disturb America very little.

Limited, and on the whole ineffectual, opposition to all these things recapitulated 19th-century protest against the treatment of Black Americans and Amerindians at home. Since 1945 both of these peoples have been taking their fate more into their own hands, and organizing movements in their own defence which have at times been oblique challenges to the external hegemony as well. One cause of scepticism among foreigners listening to the 'Voice of America' was the condition of Black Americans, brought by degrees to light; although the appreciable, if halting, progress towards remedying it was not overlooked. The record has been much better than anywhere in white-ruled Southern Africa. This of course owed much to the U.S.'s need to show a better face to the world, particularly to the coloured nations of Afro-Asia with their growing representation in the U.N.O. As late as 1958, celebration in India of Paul Robeson's sixtieth birthday alarmed Americans, and Indians 'more American than Americans themselves', as 'one more evidence that India was heading for Communism'.[276] Measures to improve Black status and opportunity were, as a Dutch observer noted, 'closely related to the moral leadership which the United States has taken upon itself since the war'.[277]

Black American militants often wanted their movement to align itself with peoples still not free in Africa, and with colonial struggles in general. This has been confusedly mixed up with the continuing and growing part played by Black American army recruits. They were allowed to become first-class soldiers before they ceased to be second-class citizens, though not until after the Second World War. In 1942 the Secretary of State for India commented wryly to the Viceroy on the 'intense friendliness for Indians' displayed by American servicemen, and added: 'Here, [in England], while as you know we have been working hard to make our own people free from colour prejudices, we have had complaints from the Americans that our people are too friendly to their coloured troops!'[278] Segregation was abandoned by the army after this and the Korean Wars, because it was found to cause too much animosity; and service came to be attractive to Blacks as a livelihood.[279] But this helped to bring a disproportionate number of

Black soldiers into combat units in Vietnam, and a sense that they were being treated as cannon-fodder intensified their campaign for civil rights. There were similar reactions among Puerto Ricans, who contributed 43,000 men to the Korean War, many of them volunteers seeking an escape from poverty.[280] Some Black American champions, like Martin Luther King, condemned the Vietnam War outright. They were conscious that prominent opponents of Black American rights were often prominent supporters of the War; also that the presence of Black troops in Indochina could set colonial feeling against them as well as the white man.[281]

Areas in Vietnam harbouring guerrillas were sometimes dubbed 'Indian country'. In 1940 a sympathetic writer on Red Indian history observed, retrospectively but also prophetically, that 'even loyal Americans should occasionally be told some of the unbelievable things their government does'.[282] In 1975 another wrote that 'Even today, it is a shock to visit Navajoland and realize how intense is the Indian's hatred of the white man.'[283] After 1945 there had been a reversion to the trouble-saving idea of getting rid of the Indian problem by assimilation. Twenty or thirty years later nearly half the Indian population of some three-quarters of a million was urban, and it was these Indians living in towns who were 'the cutting edge of the new Indian nationalism'.[284] Many had been pushed out of the reservations by overcrowding and poverty, most found adaptation to urban life painful. Nations, or national movements, have been made out of more unpromising materials.

In 1969 one group asserted its claim to land under dusty old treaties by occupying Alcatraz island. In 1971 tribesmen in Washington State were attacked and arrested for trying to reassert their right to catch salmon, the fish which held 'a position of absolute centrality in their daily lives, in their culture, their religion, and their art'.[285] An 'American Indians Association' was set up to protect this right of fishing, and it was after this that a committee drew up a fifteen-point programme for an all-Indian movement. Next year spokesmen of a number of tribes went to Stockholm to put their grievances before a United Nations conference. In November the Bureau of Indian Affairs was occupied by a body of Indians who marched to Washington on a 'trail of broken treaties'. More dramatically still, in 1973 the American Indian Movement defied the government for months at the South Dakota hamlet of Wounded Knee, scene of the bloodshed of 1890. There was some fighting again now, and the episode grew into a symbol of all Amerindian grievances. It may have been a sign of greater readiness to take them seriously when the Senate, on 9 September 1975, opened its session with a prayer in the Sioux language.

These protesters were groping towards a way to keep alive their own traditional qualities. As one of those at Stockholm said, 'we are no longer attracted by the white man's values'.[286] Many in the towns felt that industrial life was 'turning human beings into unthinking robots', and they brooded over vanished forests, polluted rivers, 'things which most non-Indians took for granted as a natural part of life but which the Indians viewed as signs of perverted value systems and meaningless waste'.[287] Some Americans at least have begun to recognize afresh an element better than merely picturesque in a life founded on respect for Nature, and on mutual aid instead of cut-throat competition. No doubt there was substance in the standard charge of the civilized white man that the red men of old were always fighting. But some 25,000 red men were enrolled by white men to fight in the Second World War, and more than one of those arrested for salmon-fishing had served in Vietnam, where one leader was wounded. 'Alaska became a full American State just in time for its young Eskimos to be drafted to Vietnam.'[288]

Whatever impulses towards a new outlook on the world these multiple forces of change and criticism may have stirred, a new president like Carter with no hampering political past might be thought the leader most likely to be responsive. He did not fail to let the public at home and abroad know that his desire was to inaugurate a more flexible, more realistic foreign policy. Some positive efforts to frame one were soon visible. A Canal Zone treaty was taken in hand to meet Panama's national feeling. This was of long standing, and the U.S. had appeared in an invidious light early in 1964 when it had to use its veto, after rioting in the Zone and an appeal by Panama to the Security Council. But any serious new departures would be faced, like all reforms at all times, with a dead weight of inertia, and often with active obstruction. One early good resolution of the new administration was to curb the sale of arms with which America (imitated by others) has been flooding the globe; but this soon seemed to drop out of sight, under cover of esoteric diplomatic reasonings, in reality it must be suspected because the arms dealers, or 'merchants of death', objected to it.

Liberals have long been asking how policy-making, for Latin America in particular, can be extricated from the control of the big corporations. In recent years a great deal has come to light about the misdeeds of the C.I.A., so habitually the confederate of these same companies. An American today might say with Coleridge in 1806, after his spell of official employment at Malta: 'I have learnt the *inside* character of many eminent living men and know by heart the awkward and wicked machinery, by which all our affairs *abroad* are carried on.'[289] In 1976 the White House undertook to review the C.I.A.'s practice of gathering information through missionaries.[290] Release of a mass of C.I.A. documents, even though 'heavily edited', late in November 1977, was part of an unfolding revelation which has prompted demands for amendment. New devices like spy satellites were reducing the need for human spies, and this made it easier for a new director, Admiral Turner, to carry out a partial purge. Early in 1978 he let it be known that political intrigue and interference abroad were to be scaled down, as less useful than they used to be deemed, but not ruled out.[291]

It has been admitted that after the fall of the Portuguese dictatorship in 1974 funds were channelled through the C.I.A. to anti-communist parties. (One of the discoveries of November 1977 was that in the early 1960s the C.I.A. was outdone in Mexico by the FBI, which, with no legal title to operate abroad, carried out manoeuvres to disrupt the communist party.) There has been similar C.I.A. generosity to parties or politicians in Italy. It must have worsened the corruptness of the governing class, which Washington, so heavily tarred with the same brush, cannot curb, and which has done as much as anything to bring into being a mass communist party, now within reach of a place in the government. To this prospect Carter has reacted angrily and publicly, thereby putting a fresh strain on NATO. Not only communists or Italians disliked his meddling; in France indignation was widespread. It is only too evident that destabilizing tactics like those employed in South America could be brought to bear on Europe too.

Carter's brightest promise of change was his taking up the cause of 'human rights'. It is impossible to know how far any politician is sincere in any humanitarian pledge. Ambition should be made of sterner stuff, and usually is. A moralizing style has always been forced on public men of all types in America. 'We are a nation under God', said President Ford solemnly, announcing his pardon of ex-President Nixon. Listeners to American statesmen must often have been reminded of Joseph Surface and his *sentiments*. 'Earth is sick, and Heaven is weary', wrote Wordsworth, of the sound of governments talking of truth and justice. The call for human rights must be welcomed; but it can hardly be overlooked that it has served to give America, after Vietnam and Watergate, a quick moral rehabilitation, and allow it to turn the tables on the U.S.S.R., even at a grave risk to *détente*. From this point of view it has too much resemblance to the Cold War talk of defence of democracy.

The test will be how much real effort is made to resurrect freedom in the 'free world' where it has been so widely suppressed. American insistence was being tempered before long by due regard to strategic and other considerations. No burial was proposed of what came to be known in 1964 as the 'Schwartz Doctrine', but has really been Washington orthodoxy ever since 1945, of no interference with regimes unconstitutional but anti-communist. Human rights, in other words, are essential for Poles or Russians, but not for Iranians or Indonesians. On 9 February 1978, the State Department let it be known that military aid would not be cut off from their governments, or from Taiwan, South Korea, and other unsavoury regimes, because security had to come first. It thought there were only about 2,200 political prisoners in Iran; it hoped that in the Philippines police torture had declined, though it had not ended.[292] President Park of South Korea had taken absolute powers in 1972, and was persecuting dissidents of every complexion through his own C.I.A. There were many calls for withdrawal of the American troops on whom his power largely depended. But during 1976 disclosures were seeping out of elaborate South Korean bribery on Capitol Hill; they brought back memories of the China lobby of former days. Other dictators have their own means of making themselves felt at Washington through corporations which do well out of their countries. Here is a dimension of the hegemony which European empires were as a rule free from, and a limit on the nominal authority of president or nation.

In Latin America the U.S. bears a special responsibility, and strategic pleas are not easily invoked. Military aid to Nicaragua for 1977 was cut off; a promising start, but Somoza's friends in Congress soon got it restored. Andrew Young, energetic U.S. envoy to the U.N.O., visited Haiti and the Dominican Republic and obtained some promises, whose worth remained to be seen. In Chile the Pinochet government went through the motions of abolishing its terroristic secret police, DINA, but the consensus of opinion was that nothing was happening except a change of name; and at the beginning of 1978 the Exxon Company was able to announce a huge investment in Chile without remonstrance from the State Department. At the O.A.S. meeting in June 1977 Chile, Uruguay and Argentina were all angry at Secretary of State Vance's talk of human rights; as they said, Washington had seen nothing wrong with their methods until lately, and had often been their instructor. Argentina and Uruguay renounced aid, rather than allow such heresy to be bruited within their borders; General Geisel of Brazil terminated his military pacts with the U.S.

Such regimes could feel comfortably sure that they had no reprisals to fear. For diverse reasons neither the petty brigand bosses of Central America nor the bigger sharks of the south could be cashiered as easily as a liberal government. Ngo Dinh Diem was not a helpful precedent; his removal was planned in the heat of war, and he was a civilian killed to make room for an army dictator. On a brief Latin American tour at the end of March 1978, Carter gave the impression that human rights were still in his mind, but very much at the back of his mind. The worst monthly trade deficit in U.S. history was about to be announced.

Every empire has been both Jekyll and Hyde, but the American, with an almost boundless capacity for good and evil, far more than any forerunner. If the 20th century has taken note of some elements of culture in barbarian societies, it has been compelled also to see how much of barbarism lurks within civilization. These two things, regarded by the last century as antithetical, have been converging. In the moods of suspicion and ferocity to which it has been roused by the Iagos of the C.I.A., America has looked very different from the country Tom Paine thought of, the fulcrum whence reason and liberty, like Archimedes' lever moving the earth, would reclaim Europe;[293] far more like the one depicted by Lenin when he wrote in 1917 that 'Both England and America, the greatest and last representatives – in the whole world – of Anglo-Saxon "liberty" in the sense of absence of militarism and bureaucracy, have completely sunk into the all-European filthy, bloody morass.'[294]

Lenin's own new-made country was to sink as low in some ways, and it, as well as the U.S., was to go far astray in the management of countries within its sphere. It would have liked to see more genuine socialism there but was content in the meantime with left-wing dictatorships. America would have liked to preside over the true 'capitalistic-democratic' societies which Forrestal wanted it to foster,[295] but where these two terms proved mutually exclusive it made do with right-wing dictatorships. And this happened the more readily in the two cases because the U.S.S.R. was far from perfectly socialist, the U.S. far from perfectly democratic, at home. America, the richer and stronger, has been far more violent and destructive abroad; neither can be said to have stood in any consistent way for human emancipation, and, as in the age when Catholic and Protestant were at strife, freedom has had its partial survival through the collision between them. In retrospect neither looks black or white: each has accomplished much, each has much to learn from the other, and the world from both.

Soviet shortcomings made anti-communist propaganda all too easy. It was waged so obsessively and stridently by the 'Campaign of Truth' that as early as 1953 it was being criticized as too noisy, quarrelsome, and patronizing to have the desired effect.[296] World events too often contradicted the message of the 'Voice of America', broadcasting by the early 1960s in 38 languages, 700 hours a week. In a less directly political way a bigger impression was made through channels which could be described as giving 'an entirely new dimension to the notion of "cultural imperialism"'.[297] Among the educated in the Third World a sophisticated journal like *Encounter*, and invitations to write for it, could be very persuasive. On the mass level, now as before, American popular culture was a potent force. It could be adapted to propagandist purposes, as Disney cartoons were, among them crude comic-strips portraying the Vietcong as evil, sub-human creatures. When Vietnam was nearing final liberation in 1975 its leaders showed some nervousness about contagion from the glossy magazines, full of sex appeal, with which the southern towns had long been regaled. The hegemony has not built an American world, but it has furthered the advent of an Americanized world.

Most of the criticism levelled at the U.S. is really criticism of capitalism, in the form it has taken on there; it has had long enough to colour the national disposition, but need not be thought identical with it. Theodore Roosevelt and the Progressivists and Wilson admonished their countrymen of the need for capitalism at home to be placed under watch and restriction; since 1945 it has been high time for it to be subjected to discipline abroad. This will be a more difficult task. The fact that at home it has had to submit to a good deal of regulation and put up with checks from organized labour must have been one of its incentives for turning to fields outside where it can still behave in the high-handed fashion for which it has a nostalgic hankering, and reap unrestricted profits. How far any reforms like respect for human rights can go will depend, first, on how strong a public opinion can be mobilized in favour of controls on American capitalists operating abroad; secondly, on whether the nature of capitalism makes it possible for it to submit to them.

On the second question, it may be a hopeful consideration that some of the darker doings of all societies have been dictated by requirements of fantasy, or ideology, rather than utility however base. Aztecs sacrificed prisoners to keep the sun shining over Mexico, Inquisitors burned heretics to avert divine wrath from Spain. Napalm dropped on a village in Asia may belong to the same realm. There is perhaps an element of tautology in the dictum that 'The US economy as it is now constituted *needs* its empire.'[298] Various corporations, it is clear, are able to make abundant extra profits out of 'colonial' products like tin or copper or bananas. But the overhead costs of the system as a whole are so staggering as to throw doubt on whether such spoils should be regarded as vital and intrinsic to U.S. capitalism as a whole, or only marginal and optional. When the balance of payments is upset by government spending overseas, mainly to safeguard conditions in which private enterprise can continue to harvest them, the process must appear a circular one, irrelevant to any organic requirements of the national economy.

Whether or not American capitalism as a whole has done well out of the policies of the hegemony, and could not have done so well without them, it can scarcely be disputed that the *nation* has gained little or nothing from them, except on the hypothesis that without them a good part of the nation would have been unemployed. As Chomsky has reminded us, 'The costs of empire are in general distributed over the society as a whole, while its profits revert to a few within.'[299] Here is the same truth that the experiment in direct colonial rule demonstrated on a smaller scale. It has come to be generally agreed that 'the Philippine colony was not a paying proposition', and meant a small sector of American capitalism being subsidized by the taxpayer.[300] It can, indeed, be conjectured that without these policies the massive unemployment of the 1930s would have returned, and even that the hidden, half-conscious purpose of the whole gigantic effort was to avert this, and a consequent crisis of the social order. Both domestic prosperity and the huge military and imperial machine can be accounted for by the simple fact that the millions idle in the 1930s were brought back to work, or put into uniform, and induced to accept all the accompaniments of their well-being by fear of it collapsing as before, a fear which could be turned outward against the menace of enemies abroad.

A fresh pitfall may be opening with world over-production, deepened by cheap mass production in more and more of American's satellite countries. One result might be to convince American labour, belatedly, that it has been short-sighted in leaving its employers free, on the plea of countering communism, to undercut it by exploiting 'colonial' workers. In the long run there can scarcely be a way out except to expand consumption by cutting the social and political bonds which keep the majority of inhabitants of the Third World poor. This would only be a repetition of what capitalism, far more adaptable than some of its opponents have understood, was obliged to learn at home in industrial countries. That something like it would happen after the Second World War was the optimistic prediction of the then American communist leader Earl Browder. He was speedily proved wrong, but the causes may have had more to do with social psychology than with economic science. It will not happen now except under compulsion of a strong movement of public opinion. Given this, the question argued during the First World War between Lenin and Kautsky, whether capitalism was doomed by its nature to perpetual aggression abroad, or could be brought under restraint, is still an open one. It is America's version of the grand problem, facing mankind in many forms in many epochs, of necessity or free will.

References

1.   K.D. and E.P. Miller, *The People and the City – 150 Years of Social and Religious Concern in New York City* (New York, 1962), p.187.

2.   R.S. Henry, *The Story of the Mexican War* (1950; New York edn., 1961), p.37.

3.   G. Kennan, *American Diplomacy 1900–1950* (1951; New York edn., 1952), p.62.

4.   J. Burnham, *The Struggle for the World* (London, 1947), pp.58–61.

5.   *Ibid.*, pp.226–7.

6.   *Ibid.*, p.194.

7.   See e.g. Jerome Ch'en, *Mao and the Chinese Revolution* (London, 1965), p.264; J. and G. Kolko, *The Limits of Power – The World and United States Foreign Policy, 1945–1954* (New York, 1972), p. 282.

8.   Cited by E. Mandel, *Marxist Economic Theory* (trans. B. Pearce, London, 1968), pp.471–2.

9.   *The Forrestal Diaries – The Inner History of the Cold War*, ed. W. Millis (London, 1952), pp.121–2.

10. J.K. Galbraith, *Ambassador's Journal – A Personal Account of the Kennedy Years* (London, 1969), p.187.

11. G.W. Domhoff, 'Who Made American Foreign Policy, 1945–1963?' in D. Horowitz, ed., *Corporations and the Cold War* (New York, 1969), p.25.

12. *Forrestal Diaries, op. cit.*, p.53.

13. See V.G. Kiernan, 'American Hegemony under Revision', in *The Socialist Register 1974*, ed. R. Miliband and J. Saville (London, 1974).

14. See P.M. Blackett, *The Military Consequences of Atomic Energy* (London, 1956).

15. C. Wright Mills, *The Power Elite* (New York, 1959), p.202.

16. A. Vagts, *A History of Militarism* (revised edn., London, 1959), p.479.

17. S.E. Finer, *The Man on Horseback – The Role of the Military in Politics* (London, 1962), pp.74, 141. A similar view is taken by R. Miliband, *The State in Capitalist Society* (1969; London edn., 1973), p.122.

18. Finer, *op. cit.*, p.142.

19. *The Alanbrooke War Diaries 1943–46*, ed. A. Bryant (1959; London edn., 1965), 18 November 1945, pp.395–6.

20. Harry S. Truman, *1946–1952 – Years of Trial and Hope* (1956; New York edn., 1965), p.404.

21. Miliband, *op. cit.*, p.117.

22. C.E. Nathanson, 'The Militarization of the American Economy', in Horowitz, ed., *op. cit.*, p.232.

23. R.A. Faramazyan, *USA: Militarism and the Economy* (1970; English edn., Moscow, 1974), pp.216–17.

24. *Ibid.*, p.33.

25. P.J. Noel-Baker, *The Arms Race* (New York, 1958), p.217. Cf. R. E. Osgood, *Ideals and Self-Interest in America's Foreign Relations* (Chicago, 1953), Chap. 16; 'The New Realism'.

26. W.H. Haas, ed., *The American Empire* (Chicago, 1940), p.vii.

27. H. Magdoff, 'Problems of United States Capitalism', in *The Socialist Register 1965*, p.65; cf. Miliband, *op. cit.*, p.13.

28. Clair Wilcox *et al., Economics of the World Today* (3rd edn., New York, 1976), p.159.

29. A.A. Berle, cited by Miliband, *op. cit.*, pp.29–30.

30. Magdoff, *loc. cit.*, p.65.

31. N. Angell, *The Great Illusion* (1933 edn., London), p.290.

32. H.G. Gelber, *The Australian–American Alliance – Costs and Benefits* (Harmondsworth, 1968), p.79.

33. See G. Reimann, *Patents for Hitler* (London, 1945).

34. *Forrestal Diaries, op. cit.*, p.53.

35. *The Scotsman* (Edinburgh), 2 October 1899, p.5.

36. D.C. Watt, 'Britain and the Cold War in the Far East, 1945–58', in Yonosuke Nagai and Akira Iriye, eds, *The Origins of the Cold War in Asia* (New York and Tokyo, 1977), p.101.

37. Lord Gladwyn, *The European Idea* (1966; revised edn., Harmondsworth, 1967), pp.47, 90, 104–5.

38. H.W. Armstrong, *The United States and British Commonwealth in Prophecy* (Pasadena, 1967), p.150, etc.

39. R.W. Van Alstyne, *American Crisis Diplomacy – The Quest for Collective Security 1918–1952* (Stanford, 1952), p.114.

40. *Forrestal Diaries, op. cit.*, 7 March 1947, pp.247–8.

41. Truman, *op. cit.*, p.132; cf. pp.127–8.

42. W. LaFeber, 'American Policy-Makers, Public Opinion, and the Outbreak of the Cold War, 1945–50', in *The Origins of the Cold War in Asia, op. cit.*, p.63, etc.

43. J.T. Patterson, *Mr. Republican, a biography of Robert A. Taft* (Boston, 1972), p.370.

44. Truman, *op. cit.*, pp.128–9.

45. Owen Lattimore, *The Situation in Asia* (Boston, 1949), pp.148, 248.

46. Patterson, *op. cit.*, pp.370–1.

47. Speech of June 1947, in R.D. Heffner, *A Documentary History of the United States* (new edn., New York, 1965), p.302.

48. See generally H. Feis, *The China Tangle – The American Effort in China from Pearl Harbour to the Marshall Mission* (Princeton, 1953); and J. Spence, *The China Helpers* (London, 1969), Chaps 8–10.

49. M. Miller, *Plain Speaking – An Oral Biography of Harry S. Truman* (1973; London edn., 1976), p.309.

50. *Forrestal Diaries, op. cit.*, p.278.

51. Cited by I. Epstein, *From Opium War to Liberation* (Peking, 1956), p.127.

52. Lattimore, *op cit.*, p.73.

53. Patterson, *op. cit.*, p.491.

54. Miller, *op. cit.*, p.308.

55. J. Belden, *China Shakes the World* (London, 1951). On American misconceptions see for example p.71.

56. See Felix Greene, *A Curtain of Ignorance* (1964; London edn., 1965).

57. J. Rowland, *A History of Sino–Indian Relations: Hostile Co-existence* (Princeton, 1967), p.176 ff.

58. Yonosuke Nagai, 'The Roots of the Cold War Doctrine', in *The Origins of the Cold War in Asia, op. cit.*, pp.20–1.

59. I. Geiss, *July 1914 . . . selected documents* (London, 1965), p.282.

60. G. Markow-Totevy, *Henry James* (trans. J. Griffiths, London, 1969), p.42.

61. Max Weber, *The Religion of China* (English edn., ed. H.H. Garth, New York, 1951), p.247.

62. Gladwyn, *op. cit.*, p.119.

63. Sir S. Hoare (Viscount Templewood), *Ambassador on Special Mission* (London, 1946), pp.178–9.

64. See V. Uribe, *Yankee Imperialism in Spain* (New York, 1949).

65. B. Crozier, *Franco – A Biographical History* (London, 1967), p.482.

66. *Ibid.*, p.478.

67. S.C. Easton, *World History Since 1945* (San Francisco, 1968), p.784.

68. Gelber, *op. cit.*, p.80; cf. p.101 ff.

69. G.A. Lundberg, in H.E. Barnes, ed., *Perpetual War for Perpetual Peace* (Caldwell, Idaho, 1953), p.615. Cf. H. and M. Sprout, *Foundations of International Politics* (New York, 1954), Chap. 21.

70. *Time Magazine*, 17 January 1977, p.25.

71. C. Wilmot, *The Struggle for Europe* (London, 1952), p.652.

72. R. Butwell, *Southeast Asia Today and Tomorrow* (2nd edn., London, 1969), p.27.

73. W.M. Ball, *Nationalism and Communism in East Asia* (Melbourne, 1952), pp.91–2.

74. I. Palmer, *The New Rice in the Philippines* (Geneva, 1975), pp.46, 48; cf. *World Marxist Review* (Prague), April 1972, p.34 ff.

75. On the fighting see Ball, *op. cit.*, p.103 ff.

76. Easton, *op. cit.*, p.863.

77. R. Shaplen, *Time Out of Hand – Revolution and Reaction in Southeast Asia* (London, 1969), pp.234–5.

78. B.P. Kiernan, *The United States, Communism, and the Emergent World* (Bloomington, 1972), p.145.

79. Palmer, *op. cit.*, pp.56–7.

80. R. Whymant, in *Guardian* (London), 14 March 1978.

81. J.A. Silen, *We, the Puerto Rican People – A Story of Oppression and Resistance* (trans. C. Belfrage, New York, 1971), pp.69–77, 116–18.

82. Franco Nogueira, *The United Nations and Portugal, a study of anticolonialism* (English edn., London, 1963), p.49.

83. *Forrestal Diaries, op. cit.*, 15 February 1946.

84. Joseph Conrad, *Nostromo* (1904).

85. D.F. Dowd, ed., *America's Role in the World Economy: The Challenge to Orthodoxy* (Boston, 1966), p.x.

86. Speech of 13 May 1965; U.S. Information Service, London, *Why Vietnam?* (collected documents, 1965), pp.42–3.

87. F. Moraes, *Witness to an Era* (Bombay, 1973), pp.209–10.

88. Dowd, *op. cit.*, pp.115, 120.

89. On U.S. food and India cf. W.J. Barnds, *India, Pakistan, and the Great Powers* (London, 1972), p.228.

90. P.S. Gupta, *Imperialism and the British Labour Movement 1914–1964* (Cambridge, 1975), p.357.

91. W. Wilcox, *The Emergence of Bangladesh – Problems and Opportunities of a Redefined American Policy in South Asia* (Washington, D.C., 1973), p.70.

92. H.V. Morton, *A Traveller in Rome* (London, 1957), p.76.

93. A.J. Toynbee, *Between Oxus and Jumna* (London, 1963), p.188.

94. *Ibid.*, p.68.

95. Martha Gellhorn, *The Face of War, from Spain (1937) to Vietnam (1966)* (London, 1967), p.249.

96. Kennan, *op. cit.*, p.96.

97. Teresa Hayter, *Aid as Imperialism* (London, 1971), p.9.

98. Sumner Welles, *Seven Major Decisions* (London, 1951), p.165; on peasant misery in South Korea cf. Lattimore, *op. cit.*, pp.92–7.

99. *A Chronicle of Principal Events relating to the Korean Question 1945–1954* (Peking, 1954), p.25.

100. See his pamphlet *Korea, the Lie that Led to War* (London, 1951).

101. Okonogi Masao, 'The Domestic Roots of the Korean War', in *The Origins of the Cold War in Asia, op. cit.*

102. Miller, *op. cit.*, p.313.

103. Ball, *op. cit.*, p.196.

104. Van Alstyne, *op. cit.*, p.140.

105. D.R. Sardesai, *Indian Foreign Policy in Cambodia, Laos, and Vietnam, 1947–1964* (Berkeley, 1968), p.34.

106. See J.H. Kalicki, *The Pattern of Sino-American Crises ... in the 1950s* (Cambridge, 1950).

107. Noam Chomsky, 'The Pentagon Papers and U.S. Imperialism in South East Asia' (*The Spokesman*, Nottingham, Winter 1972–73), p.22.

108. Sardesai, *op. cit.*, p.32.

109. *US News and World Report*, 16 April 1954, cited by Hilda Vernon, *Vietnam, United States 'Special War'* (London, n.d.), p.4.

110. *Why Vietnam? op. cit.*, p.17.

111. Vietnam Solidarity Campaign, *Vietnam and Trade Unionists* (London, 1967), pp. 9–10.

112. Kalicki, *op. cit.*, pp.109–10.

113. Miliband, *op. cit.*, pp.135–6, 152.

114. Galbraith, *op. cit.*, p.118 (May 1961).

115. *Ibid.*, p.266 (28 November 1961).

116. *The Pentagon Papers (New York Times*, 1971), p.197 (29 August 1963).

117. *Ibid.*, p. xi.

118. Nguyen Nghe, *Facing the Skyhawks* (Hanoi, 1964), pp.29–30.

119. R. Scott, *Guardian* (London), 20 April 1970.

120. Senate speech, 23 September 1965.

121. M. Bernal, *Vietnam, Signposts* (London, 1966), p.5.

122. *Vietnam, the dirty war* (articles of May 1966 from *Le Monde*; London, 1966), p.9.

123. Armstrong, *op. cit.*, pp.173, 187, 195.

124. *Pentagon Papers, op. cit.*, p.472.

125. M.A. Macciocchi, *Letters from inside the Italian Communist Party to Louis Althusser* (trans. S.M. Hellman, London, 1973), p.269; cf. pp.12, 18.

126. *Ibid.*, p.313.

127. *Pentagon Papers, op. cit.*, p.478.

128. *Ibid.*, p. ix.

129. *Vietnam, the dirty war, op. cit.*, p.4.

130. *Ibid.*, p.8.

131. Dr Shwei Tin, of Rangoon, to the writer.

132. G. Liska, *The New Statecraft – Foreign Aid in American Foreign Policy* (Chicago, 1960), p.85.

133. Easton, *op. cit.*, p.813.

134. B. Garrett, 'The Dominoization of Thailand', in *Ramparts* (Berkeley), November 1970. See also D.L. Elliott, *Thailand: Origins of Military Rule* (London, 1978).

135. T.D. Allman, *Guardian* (London), 7 January 1974.

136. P.D. Scott, 'America and the Overthrow of Soekarno, 1965–67', in M. Caldwell, ed., *Ten Years' Military Terror in Indonesia* (Nottingham, 1975), p.216.

137. *Ibid.*, p.212, 226.

138. *Ibid.*, pp.228, 230.

139. *Ibid.*, p.209.

140. *Guardian*, (London), 12 April 1977.

141. D. Latifi, *India and U.S. Aid* (Bombay, 1960), p.110.

142. A.K. Ghosh, *Articles and Speeches* (Moscow, 1962), pp.167, 287; E.M.S. Namboodiripad, *Economics and Politics of India's Socialist Pattern* (Delhi, 1966), pp.267–9.

143. Ghosh, *op. cit.*, p.144.

144. Galbraith, *op. cit.*, pp.80–1; For another well-balanced view see J.P. Lewis, *Quiet Crisis in India – Economic Development and American Policy* (Brooking Institute, 1962).

145. *Ibid.*, p.175.

146. Selig Harrison, cited by Barnds, *op. cit.*, p.91.

147. S.M. Burke, *Pakistan's Foreign Policy – An Historical Analysis* (London, 1973), p.393.

148. *Ibid.*, pp.94–5.

149. Anwar Hussain Syed, *China and Pakistan* (Amherst, 1974), pp.72–3.

150. *Time Magazine*, 20 October 1958, cited by Ghosh, *op. cit.*, p.119.

151. This impression is confirmed by a remarkable study of the 1971 war: Pran Chopra, *India's Second Liberation* (Delhi, 1973).

152. S.S. Harrison, 'Troubled India and her Neighbours', in K.P. Misra, ed., *Studies in Indian Foreign Policy* (Delhi, 1969), p.213. For a typical Pakistani view see Mohammed Ahsen Chaudhri, *Pakistan and the Great Powers* (Karachi, 1970), Chap. 2.

153. S.M. Kumaramangalam to A. Gillett, who showed me this letter of 21 February 1972 after the writer's death. On the threatened U.S. intervention see Chopra, *op. cit.*, p.196 ff.; V.B. Kulkarni, *India and Pakistan* (Bombay, 1973), p.504 ff.

154. Van Alstyne, *op. cit.*, p.121.

155. U.N.O., *Review of Economic Conditions in the Middle East 1951–52*, pp.93, 101–5.

156. B.C. Crum, *Behind the Silken Curtain* (London, 1947), p.213.

157. See L.P. Elwell-Sutton, *Persian Oil – A Study in Power Politics* (London, 1955), p.306 ff.; S. Aaronovitch, *Monopoly* (London, 1955), p.68; Kolko, *op. cit.*, pp.419–20.

158. Ministry of Foreign Affairs, Cairo, *Records of Conversations ... between the Royal Egyptian Government and the U.K. Government ...* (1951), p.38.

159. Anouar Abdel-Malek, *Egypt: Military Society* (New York, 1968), pp.103, 244.

160. Noam Chomsky, *Peace in the Middle East?* (1969; London edn., 1974), pp.48, 159.

161. H. Lumer, *Zionism – Its Role in World Politics* (New York, 1973), p.79.

162. Truman, *op. cit.*, Chaps 10–12. On Zionist organizations in America see Lumer, *op. cit.*, p.58 ff.; *Free Palestine* (London), December 1977.

163. *Forrestal Diaries, op. cit.*, p.93.

164. Chomsky, *op. cit.*, p.34.

165. W. Laqueur, *Confrontation – The Middle-East War and World Politics* (London, 1974), p.32.

166. Lumer, *op. cit.*, p.62.

167. Gupta, *op. cit.*, p.147.

168. See R. Emerson, *Africa and United States Policy* (Englewood Cliffs, 1967), 'Conclusion'; S. Smith, *US Neocolonialism in Africa* (Moscow, 1974), p.22.

169. S. Smith, *op. cit.*, p.53; V. McKay, *Africa and World Politics* (New York, 1963), p.249.

170. Easton, *op. cit.*, p.170.

171. S. Smith, *op. cit.*, p.26.

172. Chester Bowles, *Africa's Challenge to America* (Berkeley, 1956), p.55.

173. See C.F. Gallagher, *The United States and North Africa – Morocco, Algeria and Tunisia* (Harvard, 1963) pp.240–1.

174. J. Mendelsohn, *God, Allah, and Ju Ju* (New York, 1962), p.136.

175. *Ibid.*, pp.210–11.

176. McKay, *op. cit.*, p.356 ff.; J. Woddis, *Introduction to Neo-Colonialism* (London, 1967), p.69.

177. Basil Davidson, *In the Eye of the Storm – Angola's People* (London, 1972), pp.149–50.

178. D.M. Abshire and M.A. Samuels, eds, *Portuguese Africa – A Handbook* (London, 1969), pp.392, 395; J. Saul, 'Neo-Colonialism vs Liberation Struggle', in *The Socialist Register 1973*, p.314.

179. Amilcar Cabral, *Revolution in Guinea – An African People's Struggle* (anthology; English edn., London, 1969), p.14.

180. *Ibid.*, p.101.

181. Abshire and Samuels, *op. cit.*, p.434.

182. Saul, *loc. cit.*, p.313.

183. *Guardian* (London), 15 February 1978.

184. *Ibid.*, 11 March 1975.

185. *Observer* (London), 12 August 1973.

186. *Guardian* (London), 11 April 1977; cf. 15 February 1978.

187. Welles, *op. cit.*, p.104.

188. C.A. Thomson and W.H.C. Laves, *Cultural Relations and U.S. Foreign Policy* (Bloomington, 1963), p.178.

189. H.F. Dobyns and P.L. Doughty, *Peru – A Cultural History* (New York, 1976), pp.246–7.

190. L. Gelber, *America in Britain's Place* (London, 1961), pp.115–16.

191. Burnham, *op. cit.*, p.195.

192. See D. Horowitz, *From Yalta to Vietnam – American Foreign Policy in the Cold War* (1965; London edn., 1967), Chap. 10; and the protest against American pressure by J.J. Arévalo, Arbenz's predecessor as president: *The Shark and the Sardine* (New York, 1961), especially Chaps 13, 14, 17.

193. *Movement for Colonial Freedom* leaflet, 'Guatemala' (London, 1954).

194. T. & M. Melville, *Guatemala – Another Vietnam?* (Harmondsworth, 1971), p.102. The authors were Catholic missionaries in Guatemala.

195. I.F. Stone, *In a Time of Torment* (London edn., 1968), p.427.

196. R. Gott, *Guardian* (London), 3 April 1974.

197. Melville, *op. cit.*, p.267.

198. R.F. Smith, *The United States and Cuba – Business and Diplomacy, 1917–1960* (New York, 1960), pp.170–1.

199. D.W. Robinson, ed., *As Others See Us – International Views of American History* (Boston, 1969), p.170.

200. B.P. Kiernan, *op. cit.*, pp.125–6.

201. *The Times* (London), 18 June 1977.

202. Melville, *op. cit.*, pp.199–200.

203. B. Lexton, *Guardian* (London), 14 May 1974.

204. D.H. Burton, *Theodore Roosevelt: Confident Imperialist* (Philadelphia, 1968), p.112.

205. H.N. Denny, *Dollars for Bullets* (New York, 1929), p.392.

206. Easton, *op. cit.*, p.639.

207. *Guardian* (London), 30 April 1973.

208. R. Gott, *Guardian* (London), 4 September 1973.

209. J. Quartim, *Dictatorship and Armed Struggle in Brazil* (trans. D. Fernbach, London, 1971), p.30.

210. Kolko, *op. cit.*, pp.76–8.

211. Dobyns and Doughty, *op. cit.*, p.217.

212. Quartim, *op. cit.*, p.35.

213. G. Lora, *A history of the Bolivian labour movement 1848–1971* (trans. C. Whitehead, Cambridge, 1977), p.299.

214. Felix Greene, *The Enemy – Notes on Imperialism and Revolution* (London, 1970), p.126.

215. Lora, *op. cit.*, p.334.

216. *Guardian* (London), 30 December 1976.

217. *Ibid.*, 10 February 1978.

218. Lora, *op. cit.*, p.335.

219. *Ibid.*, p.349.

220. R. Miliband, 'The Coup in Chile', in *The Socialist Register 1973*, pp.458–9.

On C.I.A. intrigue against the Allende government, see a two-page article in *Sunday Times* (London), 27 October 1974.

221. R. Gott, *Guardian* (London), 30 March 1973.

222. R. Gott, *Guardian* (London), 16 April 1974.

223. H.S. Ferns, *The Argentine Republic 1516–1971* (Newton Abbot, 1973), p.183.

224. *Latin America* (London), 28 May 1976.

225. Truman, *op. cit.*, p.102.

226. Amnesty International, *Report on Torture* (1973; 2nd edn., London, 1975), p.223.

227. *Ibid.*, pp.195, 198 ff., 203 ff.

228. A. Gheerbrant, *The Rebel Church in Latin America* (1969; trans. R. Sheed, Harmondsworth, 1974), p.31.

229. *Guardian* (London), 15 June 1977.

230. Fr. Combrin, in Gheerbrant, *op. cit.*, p.225.

231. F. Chevalier, *L'Amerique Latine de l'independance a nos jours* (Paris, 1977), p.509.

232. M. Goldbloom, 'United States Policy in Post-War Greece', in R. Clogg and G. Yannopoulos, eds., *Greece under Military Rule* (London, 1972), p.228.

233. A.G. Xydis, 'The Military Regime's Foreign Policy', *ibid.*, pp.200–1.

234. Goldbloom, *loc. cit.*, pp.249–50, 252.

235. *Report on Torture*, p.81 ff.

236. Goldbloom, *loc. cit.*, p.253.

237. *Guardian* (London), 13 March 1976.

238. Review of Jefferson's Memoirs, in T.L. Peacock, *Essays and Reviews*, ed. H. Mills (London, 1970), pp.169–70.

239. Laqueur, *op. cit.*, p.140.

240. Dowd, *op. cit.*, p.32.

241. D.A. Baldwin, *Economic Development and American Foreign Policy 1943–62* (Chicago, 1966), p.86. Cf. Greene, *The Enemy, op. cit.*, p.138; H. Magdoff, *The Age of Imperialism – The Economics of U.S. Foreign Policy* (New York, 1969), p.195 ff.

242. Magdoff, in *The Socialist Register 1965*, pp.65–6.

243. Wilcox, *op. cit.*, p.179.

244. For detail see K. Buchanan, 'The Geography of Empire', Part 3, in *The Spokesman* (Nottingham), December 1971–January 1972, p.50.

245. H.L. Robinson, 'The Downfall of the Dollar', in *The Socialist Register 1973*, pp.415, 442.

246. B.L. Sharma, *The Pakistan–China Axis* (London, 1968), p.128.

247. Laqueur, *op. cit.*, p.130.

248. W.A. Williams, *The Roots of the Modern American Empire* (1969; London edn., 1970), p.445.

249. Thomson and Laves, *op. cit.*, p.64.

250. Eldridge Cleaver, *Soul on Ice* (1968; London edn., 1970), p.112.

251. P. O'Flinn, *Them and Us in Literature* (London, 1975), pp.89–90.

252. K. Zilliacus, *I Choose Peace* (London, 1949), p.341; cf. pp.308–13, on America's world status and outlook.

253. T.A. Bailey, *The Man in the Street – The Impact of American Public Opinion on Foreign Policy* (Gloucester, Mass., 1948), Chap. 23.

254. Stone, *op. cit.*, p.183.

255. C. Bernstein and B. Woodward, *All the President's Men* (New York, 1974), p.282.

256. R.F. Smith, *What Happened in Cuba? A Documentary History* (New York, 1963), p.247.

257. J.W. Fulbright, *Old Myths and New Realities* (1964; London edn., 1965), p.24.

258. J.W. Fulbright, *The Arrogance of Power* (1966; London edn., 1967), p.77.

259. E.R. Black, *Alternatives in Southeast Asia* (London, 1969), e.g. p.121.

260. Butwell, *op. cit.*, p.216.

261. G. Lichtheim, *Imperialism* (London, 1971), p.143.

262. Barnds, *op. cit.*, pp.222–3, 268.

263. B.P. Kiernan, *op. cit.*, pp.216–17.

264. *Ibid.*, p.182.

265. I.F. Stone, *The Haunted Fifties* (New York, 1963), pp.336–9 (article of 16 January 1961).

266. Gellhorn, *op. cit.*, p.180.

267. Antonio Gramsci, *Lettere del Carcere* (Turin, 1965), p.778 (8 May 1933).

268. On this there is much of interest in R. Nisbet, *Twilight of Authority* (London, 1976), Chap. 3: 'The Lure of Military Society'.

269. R. Petras, 'The "Harmony of Interest"', *International Socialist Journal* (Rome), November 1966.

270. Noam Chomsky, *American Power and the New Mandarins* (London, 1968), pp.196, 262.

271. P.S. Foner, *American Labor and the Indochina War* (New York, 1971), pp.27, 30–1.

272. *Ibid.*, pp.22, 77.

273. Horace Walpole to Sir Horace Mann, 26 November 1781.

274. *Why Vietnam? op. cit.*, p.46.

275. *Guardian* (London), 15 April 1970.

276. M.C. Chagla, *The Individual and the State* (Bombay, 1958), p.104.

277. D.W. Robinson, *op. cit.*, p.210.

278. L. Amery to Lord Linlithgow, 8 August 1942, in N. Mansergh, ed., *The Transfer of Power, 1942–7; Constitutional Relations between Britain and India*, Vol. 2 (London, 1971), p.682.

279. M. Janowitz and Lt. Col. R. Little, *Sociology and the Military Establishment* (revised edn., New York, 1965), pp.51–2, 78–9.

280. Silen, *op.cit.*, pp.125–7.

281. Cleaver, *op. cit.*, pp.111–12, 119.

282. C. Wissler, *Indians of the United States* (New York, 1940), p.204.

283. J.M. White, *The Great American Desert* (1975; London edn., 1977), p.160. For another sympathetic account see Ruth M. Underhill, *Red Man's America* (Chicago, 1953).

284. V. Deloria, *Custer Died for Your Sins – An Indian Manifesto* (London, 1969), p.248.

285. P. Collier, 'Salmon Fishing in America', *Ramparts*, April 1971, p.39.

286. M. Stuart, *Guardian* (London), 6 June 1972.

287. Mary Patrick, 'Indian Urbanisation in Dallas', *Oral History Review* (New York), 1973, p.59.

288. *Observer* (London), 6 May 1973.

289. Letter to D. Stuart, 22 August 1806.

290. *Guardian* (London), 20 January 1976.

291. *Ibid.*, 29 January 1978.

292. *Ibid.*, 8 February 1978.

293. Tom Paine, *The Rights of Man (1791–92)*, Introd. to Part 2.

294. Lenin, *Collected Works*, Vol. 25 (Moscow, 1964), pp.415–16.

295. *Forrestal Diaries, op. cit.*, p.134.

296. Thomson and Laves, *op. cit.*, p.96.

297. Miliband, *The State in Capitalist Society, op. cit.*, p.208.

298. H. L. Robinson, *loc. cit.*, p.405.

299. Chomsky, 'The Pentagon Papers', *op. cit.*, p.18.

300. W.J. Pomeroy, *American Neo-Colonialism—Its Emergence in the Philippines and Asia* (New York, 1970), p.222.

Epilogue
The American Imperium: From the Cold War to the Age of Bin Laden
John Trumpbour

The Empire Strikes Back: Using Holy War to Fight Cold War

In *Between Two Ages: America's Role in the Technetronic Era* (1970), Zbigniew Brzezinski acknowledged:

> in the aftermath of World War II ... the United States in matters of security, politics, and economics created a system that in many respects including that of scale, superficially resembled the British, Roman, and Chinese empires of the past ... The 'empire' was at most an informal system marked by the pretense of equality and non-interference ... [1]

Rather than rely solely on coercive institutions, the American imperium for Brzezinski 'works through the interpenetration of economic institutions, the sympathetic harmony of political leaders and parties, the shared concepts of sophisticated intellectuals, the mating of bureaucratic interests ... '.[2]

During the Second World War, *Fortune* magazine (May 1942) included a pamphlet on 'The U.S. in a New World: Relations with Britain', which anticipated Brzezinski's later vision of U.S. Empire:

> Thus, a new American 'imperialism', if it is to be called that, will – or rather can – be quite different from the British type. It can also be different from the

premature American type that followed our expansion in the Spanish war. American imperialism can afford to complete the work the British started; instead of salesmen and planters, its representatives can be brains and bulldozers, technicians and machine tools. American imperialism does not need extra-territoriality; it can get along better in Asia if the tuans and sahibs stay home.[3]

There is a distinctive emphasis that the new American Empire will rely more than its predecessors on what Joseph Nye (former U.S. Assistant Secretary of Defense for International Security Affairs and chairman of the National Intelligence Council) calls 'soft power' – the diffusion of political ideas, educational know-how, and a sometimes omnipresent popular culture. Yet even the most exuberant advocates of 'soft power' concede that the velvet glove of persuasion requires the iron fist of coercion. As three-time Pulitzer Prize-winning journalist Thomas Friedman of the *New York Times* urges in his celebration of globalization, *The Lexus and the Olive Tree* (1999):

> The hidden hand of the market can never work without the hidden fist – McDonald's cannot flourish without McDonnell Douglas, the designer of the U.S. Air Force F-15. And the hidden fist that keeps the world safe for Silicon Valley's technologies to flourish is called the United States Army, Air Force, Navy, and Marine Corps.[4]

In the 21st century, the Pentagon openly admits that worldwide there are 725 U.S. military bases outside the country.[5] In the late 1970s, Zbigniew Brzezinski as National Security Advisor to Jimmy Carter found himself at one of those fateful crossroads for U.S. liberalism in which 'The hidden hand of the market will never work without the hidden fist . . . '. Between 1974 and 1980, there developed an astonishing wave of Third World revolutions and upheavals, as noted in a chart by the scholar of international relations Fred Halliday:

Revolutionary Upheavals in the Third World 1974–1980

Country	*Event*	*Date*
1. Ethiopia	Deposition Haile Selassie	12 September 1974
2. Cambodia	Khmer Rouges take Phnom Penh	17 April 1975
3. Vietnam	NLF take Saigon	30 April 1975
4. Laos	Pathet Lao take over state	9 May 1975
5. Guinea-Bissau	Independence from Portugal	9 September 1974
6. Mozambique	Independence from Portugal	25 June 1975
7. Cape Verde	Independence from Portugal	5 July 1975
8. São Tome	Independence from Portugal	12 July 1975
9. Angola	Independence from Portugal	11 November 1975
10. Afghanistan	PDPA military coup	27 April 1978
11. Iran	Khomeini's government installed	11 February 1979
12. Grenada	New Jewel Movement to power	13 March 1979
13. Nicaragua	FSLN take Managua	19 July 1979
14. Zimbabwe	Independence from Britain	17 April 1980

Chart reproduced from *The Making of the Second Cold War* (London, 1986, 2nd ed.) by permission of F. Halliday.

Looking back at this revolutionary ferment and alleged U.S. trepidation at deploying armed might after the defeat in Vietnam, the neo-conservative critic Norman Podhoretz railed in 1983 against 'the sickly inhibitions against the use of military force', echoing Richard Nixon's earlier fear that a United States averse to intervening would deteriorate into 'a pitiful, helpless giant'.[6] Nixon had warned in a presidential address of 30 April 1970 that abject timidity 'will threaten free nations and free institutions throughout the world', thereby emboldening 'the forces of totalitarianism and anarchy'. Condemning the 'age of anarchy both abroad and at home', the president spoke of 'mindless attacks on all the great institutions which have been created by free civilizations in the last 500 years'. Stressing that the anarchic breakdown transcended the hot spots of the

Third World, Nixon emphasized: 'Even here in the United States, great universities are being systematically destroyed.'[7]

The New Right would in due course demand stepped-up forms of *Kulturkampf* at home; but abroad their efforts received a boost from the foreign-policy team of Jimmy Carter, whom they otherwise so passionately loathed for vacillating when Dominoes tumbled. Seeking to break the paralysis, Brzezinski hatched a plan to support counter-revolutionary war against the pro-Soviet regime of Afghanistan. In an interview with France's *Le Nouvel Observateur* (15–21 January 1998), Brzezinski explained how this came about:

> Q: The former director of the C.I.A., Robert Gates, stated in his memoirs that American intelligence services began to aid the Mujahidin in Afghanistan six months before the Soviet intervention. In this period, you were the national security advisor to President Carter. You therefore played a role in this affair. Is that correct?
>
> **Brzezinski**: Yes. According to the official version of history, C.I.A. aid to the Mujahidin began during 1980, that is to say, after the Soviet army invaded Afghanistan, 24 December 1979. But the reality, secretly guarded until now, is completely otherwise: indeed, it was on 3 July 1979 that President Carter signed the first directive for secret aid to the opponents of the pro-Soviet regime in Kabul. And that very day, I wrote a note to the president in which I explained to him that in my opinion this aid was going to induce a Soviet military intervention.[8]

Joyful that the Russian bear had subsequently stepped into his trap and invaded, Brzezinski at the time spoke of inflicting on the Soviets a defeat of Vietnam-style proportions. Pretending to be shocked at the U.S.S.R.'s pouring troops into Afghanistan, President Carter issued an immediate statement: 'Such gross interference in the internal affairs of Afghanistan is in blatant violation of accepted international rules of behavior.'[9] The C.I.A. soon assembled more forces from some of the most reactionary elements of contemporary Islam, not only in Afghanistan but also from distant reaches of the Arabian peninsula.

When in the election of 1980 Ronald Reagan had crushed the no longer beloved Georgian peanut-farmer, partly on the grounds that Carter had coddled communists and hostage-taking Iranians, the Republican administration kept the Brzezinski project on track. Special help came from Texas congressman Charlie Wilson, who rammed through Congress massive appropriations for the Afghan counterinsurgency. A legendary booze-hound surrounded by a staff and entourage of luscious women known as 'Charlie's Angels', Wilson worked with 'a blue-collar James Bond' at the C.I.A., the Greek-American Gust Avrakotos, to convert the shepherds, tribesmen and global Muslim recruits into an effective fighting force.[10] In March 1985, with National Security Directive 166, Reagan escalated administration backing to the resistance, solidifying its standing as a global movement of Islam, an international *jihad*.

In the House of Islam, by strict definition, there had not been a global armed *jihad* since the late 19th century and perhaps only four during the past nine centuries. In the 1880s, the Mahdi had called for a *jihad* mobilizing anti-colonial forces against General Gordon of Britain and the Ottomans and Egyptians entrenched in the Sudan. The three previous armed *jihads* included the campaigns of Saladin (1138–93) to expel the Christian Crusaders from the Holy Land; the Sufi effort to smash aristocratic elements trafficking in slavery and mayhem in West Africa during the 17th century; and finally the surge of Wahhabi movements to seize control of the Arabian peninsula from what they regarded as decadent Ottoman occupiers. The political scientist and anthropologist Mahmood Mamdani has given special attention to these four sustained episodes of armed jihads, and he shows that, with the exception of Saladin's resistance to the Crusaders, the *jihads* had been largely directed against fellow Muslim believers. Even the Mahdi's confrontations with British imperialism included major forays against Ottoman and Egyptian Muslims who dared to question his prophetic claims of invincibility.[11]

The C.I.A. poured billions into the *jihad* international, making it one of the largest operations in the institution's history. Working closely with Pakistan's I.S.I. (Inter Services Intelligence), the C.I.A. turned to *mujahideen* recruited throughout the Arab world, including the Palestinian Sheikh Abdullah Azzam, an instructor at King Abdul-Aziz University in Saudi Arabia who expressed a certain boredom with the conference-laden world of academe. Instead he lived by a formula alluring to the C.I.A.–I.S.I. operatives: '*Jihad* and the rifle alone: no negotiations, no conferences, and no dialogues.'[12] Azzam then successfully brought one of his prize pupils, Osama bin Laden, into the struggle in Afghanistan. A student of management and administration, bin Laden used his organizational training to build a database on the volunteer network against Soviet tyranny. Initially bin Laden had recognized that many mothers and siblings made inquiries about long-missing family members still fighting in the Hindu Kush, and so he began work on methodical record-keeping and rosters. The knowledge probably paid off when it came to building his future resistance network al-Qaeda.[13] *The 9/11 Commission Report* gave further indication of the value of the business administration curriculum for the Saudi rebel's maturation as an entrepreneur of terror. While based in the Sudan in the early 1990s, bin Laden would create, according to the report, 'a large and complex set of intertwined business and terrorist enterprises'. While his construction company built a highway from Khartoum to Port Sudan, he allowed al-Qaeda operatives to exploit 'their positions in bin Laden's businesses to acquire weapons, explosives, and technical equipment for terrorist purposes'.[14]

Though he was closer to the Pakistani I.S.I. than the U.S. C.I.A., bin Laden gave U.S. operatives a share of credit for the success of his earliest Afghanistan operation: 'I set up my first camp where the volunteers were trained by Pakistani and American officers. The weapons were supplied by the Americans, the money by the Saudis.'[15] Saudi Arabia's ambassador to the United States, Prince Bandar, recalled meeting Osama in the mid-1980s: 'He came to thank me for my efforts to bring the Americans, our friends, to help us against the atheists, he said the communists.'[16] According to Ahmed Rashid, who for decades has studied the fortunes of extreme Islam in Central Asia: 'Before the Taliban, Islamic extremism had never flourished in Afghanistan.'[17]

Bin Laden made two fateful decisions. First, in the late 1980s, he broke with his mentor in extreme Islam, Abdullah Azzam. Bin Laden decided it was time to intensify violent resistance to decadent Muslim regimes in the Arab world, but Azzam opposed him on the ground that the movement should not take action that would end by slaughtering fellow Muslims. In 1989, Azzam and two of his sons were killed in a car-bombing while en route to Peshawar, an act generally thought to be a warning to those in the movement lacking audacity when it comes to punishing the corrupt princes and politicians polluting Islam.[18] The second fateful moment came with Iraq's invasion of Kuwait. Regarding Saddam Hussein as hopelessly reprobate, bin Laden planned to repel the Iraqi occupation of Kuwait with a well-assembled array of warriors derived from the recently triumphant resistance against the Soviets in Afghanistan.[19] When the House of

Saud spurned his strategy and instead agreed to install U.S. forces in Saudi Arabia, bin Laden erupted into fury and promised revenge against both the Saudi regime and the now well-embedded American Infidels.

During the Nixon years, U.S. Secretary of Defense Melvin Laird had explained that U.S. hegemony in the Middle East was predicated on 'cops on the beat', by which he meant three U.S. allies who culturally seemed destined to be odd bedfellows: Saudi Arabia, Israel and the Shah-led regime of Iran.[20] While the Defence Ministry in Tel Aviv made sure that Tehran's secret police received training in the most sophisticated arts of torture, the Wahhabi Sunnis in Saudi Arabia resisted co-operative enterprises with both Israelis and the Shiite but decidedly secular Shah. With the triumph of the Iranian Revolution in 1979, the U.S. had desperately to seek a new cop on the beat. Toying with the idea that Saddam Hussein might serve as one of the regional gendarmes, the Reagan team followed through with vital intelligence assistance to the Iraqi despot. Breaking with the stingy levels of foreign aid granted to the rest of the Third World, Washington also delivered billions of dollars to Egypt in hopes of promoting de-Nasserization, appeasement toward Zionism, and possible future status as a cop on the beat.

Still, arrangements with Iraq and Egypt remained unsatisfactory, and some hawkish elements longed for a more direct U.S. military presence in the region. Even liberal dissidents such as George Ball condemned the Nixon–Laird legacy of 'cops on the beat' by calling for enhanced U.S. capabilities for direct intervention: 'If the debacle of Iran proves anything, it is that we cannot assure – as the Nixon Doctrine assumed – the security of a strategic region by stuffing a backward state with massive quantities of arms.'[21] Urging the U.S. to improve its capability to strike from its own military bases in the Indian Ocean, Ball demanded that Washington find avenues to bulk up surveillance equipment to the Saudis, which came to fruition in the sale of AWACs radar war planes. The fall of the Soviet Union at the end of the 1980s finally opened opportunities to plant military bases in the new nations of Central Asia, and also removed the constraints of superpower rivalry as an obstacle to military expansion in the Middle East.

In the second half of the 1980s, Kuwait had resisted U.S. overtures for military bases, while Washington was busy encouraging the massive bloodletting of the Iran–Iraq war, with approximately a million deaths by its close. In September 1991, following the first Gulf War, the U.S. secured a joint defence agreement with Kuwait that now recognized the Arab kingdom as essentially a U.S. protectorate. Standing as 'military midgets dependent on U.S. might', wrote Leon Hadar in *Current History* (January 1996), the Gulf states via Bahrain shelter the U.S. Gulf naval force, the Fifth Fleet – a major irritant to the al-Qaeda movement under bin Laden's leadership. In Aden harbor during October 2000, al-Qaeda operatives used a rubber speedboat rigged with heavy explosives to blow a giant hole in the Fifth Fleet's U.S.S. Cole, resulting in the deaths of seventeen sailors. According to reporter Lara Marlowe in the *Irish Times* (19 November 2001), F.B.I. agent John O'Neill had 'complained bitterly that the U.S. State Department – and behind it the oil lobby who make up President Bush's entourage – blocked attempts to prove bin Laden's guilt. The U.S. ambassador to Yemen, Ms. Barbara Bodine, forbade O'Neill and his team of so-called Rambos (as the Yemeni authorities called them) from entering Yemen.' Angry at the Yemeni rebuffs and Bush complacency, O'Neill resigned his post in August 2001 and became head of security at the World Trade Center, where he perished on September 11. Throughout the 1990s, the U.S. continued to craft a policy of 'dual containment' toward Iraq and Iran, as fears developed that the Ayatollahs might become more assertive with the weakening after the first Gulf War of the dictator regarded by George H.W. Bush as a Hitler-on-the-Tigris.

As the decade progressed, with U.S. forces still in Saudi Arabia and near the holiest sites of Islam, bin Laden issued a *fatwa* in 1998 calling for the killing of Americans, and his inner circle allegedly teemed with ideas of carrying out 'a Hiroshima' on U.S. soil.[22] One of bin Laden's closest lieutenants in al-Qaeda, Abu 'Ubeid Al-Qureshi, explained the network's growing confidence in its methods of warfare:

> ... [T]he Islamic nation has chalked up the most victories in a short time, in a way it has not known since the rise of the Ottoman Empire. These victories were achieved during the past twenty years against the best armed, best trained, and most experienced armies in the world (the U.S.S.R. in Afghanistan, the U.S. in Somalia, Russia in Chechnya, and the Zionist entity in southern Lebanon) ... In Afghanistan, the Mujahideen triumphed over the world's second most qualitative power at that time ... Similarly, a single Somali tribe humiliated America and compelled it to remove its forces from Somalia. A short time later, the Chechen Mujahideen humiliated and defeated

the Russian bear. After that, the Lebanese resistance [Hizbullah] expelled the Zionist army from southern Lebanon.[23]

In the midst of this *mujahideen* crowing about Islamic invincibility through what some military experts called 'fourth-generation warfare', the United States had throughout the 1980s and 1990s expanded its own use of 'low-intensity conflict' (LIC), a strategy designed to prevent any repeat of the spectacular run of revolutions that had occurred between 1974 and 1980. Funding the Nicaraguan Contras, who killed thousands of *campesinos*, blew up medical clinics, and engaged in genital-slitting atrocities, the Reagan foreign-policy team made sure that the Sandinista revolutionaries had slim chances of providing an alternative model for a region otherwise impoverished under the suzerainty of banana-republic-style capitalism. (Despite much liberal-left admonishment, Reagan himself saluted the Contras as 'the moral equivalent of our Founding Fathers'. Some Founding Fathers with an ardour for massacring Shawnee and Iroquois might have heartily approved.)[24] In Angola, the Reagan team relied on the forces of Jonas Savimbi to wage warfare against a Marxist regime whose leadership oddly had found itself since the Carter years turning to Cuban forces to help protect the petroleum installations of Chevron Oil and other transnational corporate goliaths. There were few revolutionary breakthroughs during the 1980s and 1990s, a reversal for the generation of 1968 whose forecasts of a transformed world order on the horizon turned out ashen and empty. Meanwhile, in the House of Islam, the children of the pious professionals and middle classes who had supported the Ayatollahs and their overthrow of the Shah grew increasingly disenchanted as the new order delivered massive unemployment and forms of bazaar cronyism that rewarded connections to theocrats over technical competence.

When bin Laden made his reverse *Hegira* from Mecca to Sudan and back to the hills of Afghanistan in 1996, it could be argued that extreme Islam as a model for a political and economic order had suffered huge setbacks not only in Iran, but also in Egypt and Algeria where Islamist insurgents had shown that their alternative to the sclerotic ruling order was what France's Gilles Kepel calls 'a blood-drenched nightmare'. He adds that 'Algeria's paroxysms of violence' had been 'fanned by the *jihadists* from Afghanistan'.[25] After September 11, the Taliban and bin Laden's Afghanistan-based warriors found themselves initially thrashed, though remnants are resprouting and growing bolder as the ham-fisted occupation of Iraq in particular inspires mounting global resistance to the newest version of Pax Americana.

The U.S. construction of a *jihad* international in Afghanistan has been called a textbook case of 'blowback', though few of the Vulcans who brought neo-conservative statecraft to fruition in the aftermath of September 11 will admit any connection between the Carter–Reagan policy on Afghanistan and the later al-Qaeda terror.[26] In the folklore of conservatism, their forerunners had often blamed the Germans for supposedly bankrolling Lenin and the triumph of Bolshevism in Russia toward the end of the First World War. European fascism had expanded the charge to international bankers with 'Judeo-Bolshevik' proclivities. Yet the right, who are so quick to find foreign complicity and outside agitators in explaining Marxist triumph, cannot admit their role in building the *jihad* international, which received a scale of funding that dwarfed any sums that may have fallen into the hands of the Russian revolutionaries. (It has been estimated that Germany spent 1/10th as much on propaganda and sabotage activities in Russia compared to what it expended on disrupting other individual Allies such as France and Britain.)[27] Much as with the constant charges that Lenin was 'a German agent', it might be preposterous to classify bin Laden as 'an American agent'. Neither Lenin nor bin Laden were prone to take orders from aspiring capitalist or Infidel paymasters, though Ayatollah Khomeini liked to rail against Osama's Taliban allies as a form of 'islam-i-imirikai' (American Islam).[28] But the decision of the Enlightenment United States to turn to Holy War as a means of winning Cold War continues to have reverberations into the 21st century.

The End of the Cold War and the Neo-conservative Offensive

The collapse of the Soviet Union and the end of the Cold War became the occasion for great self-celebration of the superiority of the capitalist West, but it also produced undercurrents of anxiety in elite circles.

In the first place, some of the most dogged neo-conservatives had not anticipated 'victory', even though they would later employ historical re-write teams to congratulate themselves on their combination of clairvoyance and resolve. Four weeks before the fall of the Berlin Wall, Reagan's top Soviet expert Richard Pipes published a commentary in the *New York Times* (9 October 1989) entitled 'The Russians Are Still Coming', which proclaimed that Gorbachev's *perestroika* was a ruse designed to put the West asleep so that Soviet communism could pursue a new wave of global expansion. '[P]rojected with all the propaganda means at its disposal' and with 'the desired effect of blurring the Soviet Union as a hostile power', wrote Pipes, Gorbachev's *perestroika* had allowed the U.S.S.R. and 'its clients in Cambodia, Angola, Nicaragua, and Afghanistan' to grow 'stronger at the expense of U.S. allies'. George Will and others regularly lauded Pipes for his genius and prescience in the Cold War, and Pipes himself at his Harvard University campus rarely missed an opportunity to take credit for having been stunningly accurate throughout, in contrast to the liberal-left mendacity that he attributed to the dominant currents of academic Kremlinology.

In January 1989, the flagship organ of neo-conservatism, *Commentary*, had published Jean-François Revel's essay 'Is Communism Reversible?', a work that blithely extinguished hopes of any democratic transition in the communist world: 'Despite what so many in the West appear to regard as an extremely easy process, we cannot name a single *completed* instance of Communist reversibility.' A decade earlier, Jeane Kirkpatrick wrote for *Commentary* (November 1979) what was widely regarded as the most influential intellectual tract for the Reagan Administration's foreign policy, entitled 'Dictatorships and Double Standards'. In it, she justified support for even blood-soaked dictatorships of the right because in her view they could evolve toward democracy, whereas communist regimes would remain frozen in their totalitarian ways. Reagan thought so highly of her arguments that he appointed her U.S. Ambassador to the United Nations, where she regularly defended U.S. allies in Central America and elsewhere who had presided over wholesale torture and butchery of peasants and political rebels. Not even the rape and murder of nuns or the mass slaughter of Jesuit priests could bring Kirkpatrick and the Reagan team to break with their right-authoritarian allies.

Forgetting this intellectual and policy backdrop, a variety of political currents simply declared victory in the Cold War, while a determined minority feared that the United States without an enemy might sink into a prolonged decadence and loss of national purpose. In the early decades of the twentieth century, H.L. Mencken had noted that the United States seemed to thrive on a propensity for finding enemies, some real but many spurious:

The whole history of the country has been a history of melodramatic pursuits of tremendous monsters, some of them imaginary: the Red Coats, the Bank, the Catholics, Simon Legree, the Slave Power, Jeff Davis, Mormonism, Wall Street, the Rum Demon, John Bull, the hell hounds of plutocracy, the trusts, General Weyler, Pancho Villa, German spies, hyphenates, the Kaiser, Bolshevism. The list might be lengthened indefinitely; a complete chronicle of The Republic could be written in terms of it, and without omitting a single important episode.[29]

Richard Condon, the spy-thriller novelist best known for *The Manchurian Candidate*, explained that 'now that the Communists have been put to sleep, we are going to have to invent another terrible threat'.[30] Harvard political scientist and former director of national security planning under Jimmy Carter, Samuel P. Huntington, decried 'the decay of Western liberalism in the absence of a cohesive ideological challenge by a competing ideology, such as Marxism-Leninism. Fragmentation and multiculturalism are now eating away at the whole set of ideas and philosophies which have been the binding cement of American society.'[31] For the neo-conservative Irving Kristol, 'Multiculturalism is as much a "war against the West" as Nazism and Stalinism ever were.'[32] Immigration reform in the U.S. after 1965 had led to waves of immigration from Asia and Latin America. Ideologies of multiculturalism had suggested that these cultures deserved relative equality in the curriculum, while in some versions holding the West responsible for historic crimes: slavery, imperialism and fascist barbarism.

For Kristol, liberalism was abetting multiculturalism, and he gallantly proposed that it should be the new enemy. U.S. capitalism may have won the ideological and economic war against communism only to see the fruits of victory squandered by the ravenous excesses of U.S. liberalism. At a conference celebrating the end of the Cold War, Kristol explained that he found opposition to communism to be obvious and too easy, and that the dissident liberal Lionel Trilling had opened his eyes to a deeper reality: 'to Liberalism's dirty little secret — that there was something basically rotten about its progressive metaphysics that led to an impoverishment of the imagination and a desiccation of the spirit'. Indeed, he admits, 'what began to concern me more and more was the clear signs of rot and decadence germinating within American society — a rot and decadence that was no longer the consequence of liberalism but was the actual agenda of contemporary liberalism'. The real enemy was always liberalism, Kristol affirms, and he relished the opportunity to return to this more permanent battlefield: 'So far from having ended, my Cold War has increased in intensity, as sector after sector of American life has been corrupted by the liberal ethos.'[33] Noting that U.S. capitalism is prone to promoting narcissistic materialism, and only the Cold War had restrained this appetite, Peregrine Worsthorne of the *Daily Telegraph* (UK) admitted that 'worrying about communism intellectually – as against militarily – was a gigantic red herring, deflecting intellectual attention from liberalism, which was a much more dangerous enemy of civilization'.[34]

During the Reagan years, the term 'liberal' acquired a foul odor, and Massachusetts Governor Michael Dukakis in running against George H.W. Bush for President in 1988 sought to distance himself from the tradition, to little avail. In the 1990s, a network of rightist 'talk radio' stations kept up the warfare on liberalism '24/7', heaping the sort of opprobrium on it that characterized the anti-communist Jeremiads of the 1950s. Norman Podhoretz of *Commentary* pledged a life mission of 'challenging the regnant leftist culture that pollutes the spiritual and cultural air we all breathe, and to do so with all my heart and all my soul and all my might'.[35]

For the spiritual regeneration of the United States to occur, leading lights of neo-conservatism argued that the United States had to rededicate itself to a global project of historic destiny. In the late 1990s, the Project for the New American Century (P.N.A.C.) called for the removal of Saddam Hussein from the reins of power in Iraq, an intervention that would provide the platform for the democratization of the Middle East. P.N.A.C. asserted in a document entitled *Rebuilding America's Defenses: Strategy, Forces, and Resources for a New Century* (September 2000) that the U.S. had taken a 'procurement holiday' since the Age of Reagan, and it might possibly take 'some catastrophic and catalyzing event – like a new Pearl Harbor' to wake the nation from the slumber induced by liberal treachery and Clintonian complacency. As 767 and 757 jets plunged into the Twin Towers and the Pentagon, the PNAC faithful, who shortly before assuming power treated this 'catalyzing event' as an unlikely scenario, had their 'new Pearl Harbor'.

Economic Retrenchment and the Fall of the House of Labour

In the early post-war years, the Truman administration took fright at the possibility that rapid cuts in military spending could plunge the U.S. back into the economic funk of the Great Depression. With NSC-68 and the Korean War, the U.S. embarked on the permanent war economy, introducing measures that would allow the U.S. to project power on a world scale as well as give a stimulus to the domestic economy.

The end of the Cold War had brought much talk about a Peace Dividend. Making frequent claims during the presidential campaign of 1992 that he would upgrade the nation's 'infrastructure' and also find avenues to provide health insurance to the over 38 million Americans then lacking it, William Jefferson Clinton soon lost determination to use the Peace Dividend for social reconstruction. Perhaps intimidated by an insurgent Republican right in the U.S. Congress, Clinton grew enamoured of the Wall Street-crafted economic nostrums of U.S. Secretary of the Treasury Robert Rubin, who fastened the president's attention on deficit reduction. Buoyed by a stock market soaring to stratospheric levels, Clinton took the U.S. out of the deficit morass of the Reagan–Bush years. By the end of the 20th century, Democratic Party activists had replaced the earlier decade's talk of 'The Peace Dividend' with 'The Surplus', which would be harnessed to shore up Social Security and perhaps pursue some projects of national grandeur.

Earlier in the 1980s, the director of the Office of Management and Budget (O.M.B.), David Stockman, had confessed to a journalist that the Reagan administration's support of deficits was predicated on a strategy to strangle social spending. By simultaneously pushing through defence spending increases and tax cuts for the affluent, the Reagan men could build up deficits that then would be used to justify the pruning of budgets for health and human services. When George W. Bush was declared the winner of the 2000 presidential election by the U.S. Supreme Court, he returned to the Reagan programme and eliminated the lurking surplus with a massive tax cut heavily weighted toward the wealthiest two per cent. With the crisis of September 11, he had a freer hand to ladle otherwise dwindling budget resources to the Pentagon. Yet Bush's inability to pare down health and human services spending more aggressively brought cries of betrayal from some of his base, who waxed nostalgic about Reagan.

Lost in all of the focus on federal spending during the past two decades was the deteriorating economic situation for substantial portions of the middle and working classes. A significant factor in all of this has been the decline of labour unions, which represented 29.6 per cent of the total U.S. workforce in 1970 and tumbled to 12.9 per cent by the end of 2003.[36] The average unionized member of the U.S. workforce earned 27 per cent more in median weekly earnings than non-union counterparts in 2003, and the differential exceeds 51 per cent for Latinos, who find themselves pushed heavily into 'sweated' labour environments.[37]

In the late 1960s and early 1970s, labour exhibited a militancy that had shaken both corporate executives and even many union leaders, who lost control of a wildcat-striking rank and file. In 1970, there had been 381 work stoppages involving 1000 or more workers, which resulted in 52,761,000 days of idleness. In 1974, the numbers remained acute: 424 work stoppages of 1000 or more workers leading to 31,809,000 days idle. But by 2002, the U.S. labour movement could muster only 19 work stoppages of 1000 or more workers totaling only 660,000 days idle, and in 2003 this dropped to only 14 large-scale work stoppages.[38] The strike as a weapon of U.S. labour appears to be on a voyage to virtual extinction. Confronted with little strategic power on the part of labour, corporations continue to push wages and benefits downward.

How this cleavage of union density and blunting of the strike weapon came about would require a separate treatise. But several strikes of the late 1960s and early 1970s had inspired calls for a state and corporate counterattack on recalcitrant workers: the New York sanitation strike of February 1968 that left the city abounding in freeze-dried, vermin-occupied silos of rubbish; the General Electric job action of twelve allied unions during 1969–70 that paralyzed the nation's fourth largest employer; and the postal strike of 1970 that Nixon sought to overcome by calling out National Guard, Army, and Air Force reservists, many of whom instead opted to shirk their duty as olive-clad scabs. G.E. executives moaned that strikers had not only been tapping union strike funds, but they were also helping themselves to state welfare benefits. G.E. executive Thomas Litwiler expressed the employer's horror: 'It's a mind-boggling situation. The strikers are living reasonably well on welfare ... '. [39]

Lasting 101 days, the national walkout at G.E. built momentum from an estimated $30 million of public aid including food stamps, unemployment benefits, and welfare assistance, representing ten times the aid that the A.F.L.-C.I.O. could deliver from a special strike fund. In the state of Massachusetts alone, over 5,000 of the 20,000 strikers had tapped welfare assistance to outlast management.[40] When strikes later convulsed the construction industry, the U.S. Secretary of Labor George Shultz proclaimed, as wages for workers continued to go higher: 'This is a formula for disaster.'[41] Richard Nixon, 'America's last liberal president', had tried to quell some of the worker and activist ferment with a variety of regulatory reforms: the Occupational Safety and Health Act, the Environmental Protection Agency, the Consumer Product Safety Commission, and the Mine Enforcement and Safety Administration. Conservative ultras were appalled at Nixon's apostasy; as center-left Republican Senator Hugh Scott chuckled: 'We [Liberals] get the action, and the Conservatives get the rhetoric.'[42]

The formation of the Business Roundtable in 1972 was an important step in developing a more unified corporate response to labour and the expanding regulatory tentacles of the welfare state. Some Establishment intellectuals suggested that throttling had to be delivered to more than just the labour movement. The Democrat Samuel P. Huntington, from his Harvard professorial perch, diagnosed 'a democratic distemper' and 'a crisis of democracy' caused by 'previously passive or unorganized groups in the population', including ' blacks, Chicanos, white ethnic groups, students, and women', who have 'now embarked on concerted efforts to establish their claims to opportunities, positions, rewards, and privileges, which they had not considered themselves entitled to before'. Decrying the public's willingness to challenge 'the legitimacy of hierarchy, coercion, discipline, secrecy, and deception – all of which are, in some measure, inescapable attributes of the process of government', he concluded that 'the effective operation of a democratic political system usually requires some measure of apathy and noninvolvement on the part of some individuals and groups.'[43] Delivered in a report for the Trilateral Commission, a body founded by David Rockefeller in 1972 that would later supply the heart of the leadership of the Carter administration, the Huntington diagnosis met vitriolic denunciations in marginalized organs of the far right and far left.

With deindustrialisation gaining momentum, progressive labour activists held out hope for passage of the Humphrey-Hawkins Full Employment Act, which labour historian Jefferson Cowie argues could have 'knit together white and black working-class interests'. But, in his view, the Act 'had the guts torn out of it by Jimmy Carter and Congress'.[44] Resigning in 1978 from John Dunlop's Labor-Management Group, a body founded under the Nixon administration to encourage consensus between workers and business, Douglas Fraser of the United Auto Workers (U.A.W.) observed about the new corporate counteroffensive beginning to gain momentum: 'I believe leaders of the business community, with few exceptions, have chosen to wage a one-sided class war today in this country – a war against working people, the unemployed, the poor, the minorities, the very young and the very old, and even many in the middle class of our society.' Fraser's rage had been provoked by the business community's successful obstruction of the Labor Law Reform bill, which he called:

> an extremely moderate, fair piece of legislation that only corporate outlaws would have had need to fear. Labor law reform itself would not have organized a single worker. Rather, it would have begun to limit the ability of rogue employers to keep workers from choosing democratically to be represented by unions through employer delay and outright violation of existing labor law.[45]

The opening hammer blows to workers would be delivered by Jimmy Carter's new chairman of the Federal Reserve Board, Paul Volcker. Imposing massive leaps in interest rates, Volcker hinted that spoiled workers now needed a bracing recession, soon to be the worst downturn since the 1930s. 'The standard of living of the average American has to decline', asserted Volcker in testimony before the Joint Economic Committee of the U.S. Congress on 17 October 1979. 'I don't think you can escape that . . . '.[46]

Swallowing Volcker's medicine with gusto, the former actors' union leader Ronald Reagan soon filled judgeships and the National Labor Relations Board with armies of anti-union activists who would deliver the *coup de grâce* to much of organized labour. Reagan's most dramatic salvo was, of course, his firing of striking air traffic controllers in 1981; but the greatest damage came from routine failure to enforce labour law and the regulatory frameworks that had expanded under Nixon.

Vaguely reminiscent of the pattern in the Afghanistan *jihad*, which was hatched by the Carter Democrats and then finished off by the so-called Reagan cowboys, Washington extinguished labour's hopes in a similar bipartisan, tag-team type of enterprise. Essentially the Carter regime began to beaver away at some of the foundations of working-class power, and then the Reagan men and women came in wielding power chain-saws to complete the job. The U.S. labour leadership's faith that the Democrats would somehow rescue their fortunes proved especially debilitating, though Doug Fraser in his blast against the 'one-sided class war' now underway hinted that F.D.R.'s party could no longer be relied upon. Observing that 'No democratic country in the world has lower rates of voter participation than the U.S., except Botswana', Fraser pointed out that 'The Republican Party remains controlled by and the Democratic Party heavily influenced by business interests. The reality is that both are weak and ineffective as parties, with no visible, clear-cut ideological differences between them because of business domination.' Referring to 'class-skewed' voting participation, he added that 'about 50 percent more of the affluent vote than workers and 90 to 300 percent more of the rich vote than the poor, the black, the young, and the Hispanic'.[47]

Even if obstacles to voting could be removed, Fraser harbored doubts that it would make a huge difference in outcomes because of the peculiar apathy and ideological casting of contemporary U.S. politics. In the 2000 presidential election, for instance, the poorest county in the nation voted close to 80 per cent for the union-averse George W. Bush, whose rawhide Texas campaign stylings attracted impoverished rural whites by mobilizing moral and cultural resentments against the effete snobs and Hollywood star-studded hanger-ons in the Democratic Party.[48] In the election of 2004, Carl Rove, known as 'Bush's brain' and the president's chief campaign strategist, mobilized additional millions of God-fearing Christian evangelicals to deny the White House to the French-speaking, pseudo-sophisticate John Kerry, whose attempts to show that he served as an altar boy and regularly attended Catholic mass failed to impress the surging Moral Majority. A foreshadowing of the types of resentments that would be tapped to defeat Kerry emerged during the Iowa primary in a notorious right-wing advertisement which condemned liberal Vermont Governor Howard Dean as 'a tax-hiking, government-expanding, latté-drinking, sushi-eating, Volvo-driving, *New York Times*-reading, body-piercing, Hollywood-loving, left-wing freak show'.[49]

During the Clinton reign of the 1990s, the Democrats may have contributed to the erosion and 'civic death' of part of their electoral base by pursuing draconian policies of imprisonment. By largely enforcing strict drug sentencing laws against African-Americans, Latinos and the urban poor, the Clinton team catapulted the U.S. into the world lead in per capita imprisonment, as the nation went from 1,351,000 prisoners in 1993 to 2,019,234 by mid-2002.[50] With 5 per cent of the world's population, the U.S. now holds 25 per cent of the global prison population.[51] In 1991, 3,437,000 U.S. adults had served time in a state or federal prison; by 2001, the total had reached 5,618,000, and this does not include the millions who have done time in a local jail.[52] Republicans recognized that in many U.S. states felons can be stripped of voting rights, and they adopted this crucial strategy of enforcing 'civic death' in Florida to help secure Bush victory. The otherwise affable Clinton has been known to explode in rage at those who challenged him to soften drug enforcement or to legalize marijuana.

Meanwhile, the one-sided class war at home has its counterpart in the economic policies pursued abroad. Since the early 1980s, trade liberalization and privatization of public enterprise have carried the day under a banner known as the Washington Consensus. Formulated in the 1990s, the North American Free Trade Agreement (N.A.F.T.A.), the World Trade Organization (W.T.O.), and later the Free Trade Area of the Americas (F.T.A.A.) are among the institutions and frameworks designed to enshrine the Washington Consensus. Harold McGraw III, the chair of the Business Roundtable's international trade and investment task force, cites World Bank estimates that the removal of trade barriers 'could add $2,800 billion to the world economy by 2015, of which $1,500 billion would accrue to developing countries, lifting 320 million people out of extreme poverty'.[53]

Yet, what has happened during the two decades since the widespread expansion of the Washington Consensus? In 1980, the richest 10 per cent of nations had 77 times higher median income than the poorest 10 per cent; by 1999, it had grown to 122 times.[54] Prior to the victory of the Washington Consensus, Latin America and the Caribbean experienced a 75 per cent growth in per capita GDP from 1960 to 1980; but since then this has stagnated with total growth of 7 per cent in the following two decades. Sub-Saharan Africa has actually tumbled 15 per cent during this period, after experiencing a 34 per cent total growth from 1960 to 1980 – an era supposedly stifled by onerous tariffs and over-regulation.[55]

Now it would appear that the rich countries have done quite well by this unleashing of free markets. But, alas, most of the benefits have gone to the wealthiest sectors of society. According to *Business Week*, the C.E.O.s of major corporations made 42 times the average U.S. worker in 1980, 85 times more in

1990, and 531 times in 2000.[56] A significant proportion of the erosion occurred when the Democrats controlled the U.S. presidency. Under Bill Clinton, who engineered the passage of N.A.F.T.A. as well as new legislation favoring executive stock options, the ratio of C.E.O. wages to those of the average U.S. worker skyrocketed from 113 to 1 in 1991 to 449 to 1 at the end of his presidency.[57] Scholars Lucian Bebchuk and Jesse Fried explain that between 1992 and 2000 'the average real (inflation-adjusted) pay of chief executive officers (C.E.O.s) of S&P 500 firms more than quadrupled, climbing from $3.5 million to $14.7 million. Increases in options-based compensation accounted for the lion's share of the gains, with the value of stock options granted to C.E.O.s jumping ninefold during this period'.[58] Meanwhile, the Congressional Budget Office reports that from 1979 to 1997 the average household in the lowest quintile declined from $9,300 of income to $8,700, while the average household in the top 1 per cent soared from $256,400 to $644,300. Households in the middle quintile barely rose from $31,700 to $33,200.[59] Yes, someone is prospering from the Washington Consensus, and it is clearly not Joe and Josephine Six-Pack.

The opulence of the new billionaires in this epoch has led to such developments as yacht wars, with U.S. software aristocrats and Russian oligarchs competing for the largest private ships in world history. Paul Allen of Microsoft owns *Octopus*, a 413-foot yacht equated to 'an aircraft carrier' by a rival executive. With an estimated cost of $200 million and a mere $250,000 charge to fill the gas tank, his mega-yacht has a pair of landing pads for two helicopters, a state-of-the-art music studio, and a screening room for the latest movies. Oracle's Larry Ellison reportedly sold his 244-foot yacht *Katana* (since renamed *Enigma*) for an asking price of $68 million, so that he could make room for delivery of a new 452-foot yacht called *Rising Sun* that has since dethroned *Octopus* as the world's largest. Silicon Valley venture capitalist Jim Clark ordered a more modest 300-foot yacht, while Russian capitalist Roman Abramovich bought a boat previously owned by Paul Allen as he awaits delivery of his new ship, *Ecstasea*. German shipyard owner Michael Breman explained in 2004 that 'Ten years ago a 50-metre boat was big. Now it is kind of run-of-the-mill.'[60]

The W.T.O., N.A.F.T.A. and F.T.A.A. provoked an efflorescence of social movements and resistance to the Washington Consensus, as Turtles and Teamsters converged on cities such as Seattle, Quebec, Washington and Miami. Media mogul Conrad Black labelled activists resisting trade liberalization as 'the political equivalent of football hooligans', and maintained that 'They are incapable of coherent articulation and they should be dispelled with as little force as necessary whenever they become disorderly. They should not be accorded any credence in discussions of serious issues.'[61] Foreign-affairs commentator Thomas Friedman speaks for most of the North American elite when he condemns 'these anti-W.T.O. protesters – who are a Noah's ark of flat-earth advocates, protectionist trade unions and yuppies looking for their 1960s fix.'[62] Yet, even within the World Bank and the International Monetary Fund, there are some voices admitting that the Milton and Thomas Friedman range of policy prescriptions has led to misery for much of the world.

Caught up in the enthusiasm for the Washington Consensus, the I.M.F. had sought to dismantle capital controls, a break from its founding principle in 1944 that an individual nation should retain some mechanisms for charting its economic destiny. Article VI of the I.M.F.'s Articles of Agreement gave permission for capital controls, which ratified John Maynard Keynes's argument at the time that financial markets could not be trusted to be rational. Speaking at a Trilateral Commission convocation of the late 1990s which focused on economic turbulence in East Asia, Martin Wolf of the *Financial Times* virtually repeated Keynes's wisdom: 'The capital markets, when they were euphoric, simply ignored bad news. And when depressed, they have simply ignored the good news. *Either way, they have overshot wildly, and have destabilized the host countries in the process.*'[63] Even Henry Kissinger at the same Trilateral gathering in Berlin worried that market fundamentalism could be cooking the political goose for many U.S. allies:

> I believe the attempt to solve a currency problem with a huge program of economic reform has created a massive political program that makes the economic problem insoluble. It means that every economic proposal is seen through the prism of an attempted political revolution by the outside world. Must every last economic institution of the West be transported to other countries? ... Even in those countries where it looks as if we are solving them, like Korea, we are creating a nationalist backlash that in the second round will create a problem between Asia and the United States. That is an issue Europe and America should discuss.[64]

Kissinger's mild dissent from the Washington Consensus may have been a portent of a deeper rift in U.S. ruling circles. With the neo-conservative ascen-

dancy in the administration of George W. Bush, there emerged greater emphasis
on unilateral U.S. action and bilateral treaty arrangements, rather than reliance
on the political, military and financial architecture established after the Second
World War. An alarmed Kissinger joined Harvard University president
Lawrence Summers for a series of conclaves on preserving U.S.–European coop-
eration, thought to be threatened by Bush actions taken brusquely and with an
air of disdain toward N.A.T.O. and the U.N. At the very least, it would be
pointed out by the enlightened wing of the American Imperium, the first Gulf
War cost $61 billion, with $54 billion of that paid by the other nations
including Japan, which chipped in $13 billion.[65] Gulf War II required an
appropriation of $87 billion, with total costs expected to escalate to $200 billion.
This time other nations have declined to subsidize Bush and Blair's big adventure, with the U.S. picking up over 90 per cent of the cost.

In the early 20th century, Karl Kautsky had opposed Lenin by proposing that
capitalism might develop what he called ultra-imperialism – forms of co-
operation that would help share the fruits of Empire without resort to inter-
imperialist warfare. In the early post-war period, the U.S. and Atlanticist ruling
classes of Europe created an array of institutions (N.A.T.O., I.M.F., World Bank,
U.N.) to reinforce such thinking. The Bush men and women began to regard this
as constraining and 'old thinking'. With annual military spending six times the
next largest power in the world, the U.S. should not feel the need to achieve
consensus with what Bush–Cheney regarded as European candy-asses and Third
World demagogues.[66]

In occupying Iraq, Bush's foreign-policy team liked to point to Japan's and
Germany's transition from fascist militarism to parliamentary democracy after
the Second World War. Yet they conveniently neglected to mention some
important differences. Historian John Dower of M.I.T. notes that Japan 'was
spared the presence of carpetbaggers who might have tried to manipulate
occupation policy to serve their private interests. In oil-rich Iraq, foreign capital
is poised to play a major political as well as economic role.'[67] In Germany, the
U.S. Occupation authorities warned many U.S. corporations that they would not
be permitted to take over German industry. If certain U.S. industries proved too
overwhelming to a war-damaged European bourgeoisie, this class would be
hampered in seeing prospects for recovery. In a worst-case scenario, certain
capitalist sectors could tumble into terminal decay, rendering Western Europe

susceptible to radical contagion. As Eugene Anderson of the State Department's Occupied Areas Division explained in a secret memorandum of 7 February 1946 rejecting Paramount Pictures' proposal to take over the German film industry: 'Paramount's proposal amounts to economic imperialism under the guise of wishing to assist in the re-education of Germany.' He then added:

> The utilization of the German defeat to acquire control of their movies by borrowing Reichmarks might be imitated in every other line, so that in the end Germany might have provided the money through loans of its blocked currency for the sale of all of its property to foreigners. This kind of policy might well destroy the possibility of Germany ever reviving as a prosperous and independent nation. It would undermine the basis of our re-education policy and would supply an excellent foundation for the revival of some kind of Nazism.[68]

Two and a half years earlier, John McCloy, the future High Commissioner of Germany, told F.D.R. adviser and former Secretary of Commerce Harry Hopkins that 'The Zanuck proposal to abolish the German industry ... would also be a concern to the State Department ... The logical outcome of this almost amounts to continuous Allied control of their industry and culture, and I think that approaches nonsense.'[69]

In contrast, what happened in Iraq? U.S. companies received giant no-bid reconstruction contracts or else arrangements with severe constraints on competitive bidding. In response to those disturbed by the extravagant costs of the intervention and reconstruction, administration apologists reassured them that Iraqi oil wealth would soon begin reflowing and could defray the costs of a Saddam-free polity. 'We are dealing with a country that can really finance its own reconstruction, and relatively soon', pledged neo-con darling Paul Wolfowitz in testimony to the U.S. Congress during the war's opening phases.[70] Unlike what happened in Germany, the Bush apparatchiks had no worry about establishing U.S. domination over the commanding heights of the Iraqi economy. The Coalition Provisional Authority (C.P.A.) in 2003 imposed Order 39 allowing for complete foreign ownership of Iraqi companies and assets, though it excluded natural resources. The C.P.A. also took special steps to enforce a law of 1987 banning labor unions in public enterprises, and they used this Saddam Hussein-era contrivance to detain key members of the Iraqi Federation of Trade Unions and the Iraqi Union of the Unemployed. Referring to U.S. sub-contractors importing large amounts of low-wage workers from South Asia, despite massive unemployment in Iraq, an Iraqi construction manager wonders: 'U.S. contractors are importing labor and expatriating the benefits – where is the benefit for Iraq?'[71]

Vice-president Cheney overtly denied that the second Gulf intervention was motivated by desires to control Iraqi petroleum reserves, estimated to be the second largest in the world. Neo-conservative ideologue William Kristol told an audience at the Kennedy School of Government that for all he cared French and Russian firms could dominate the future Iraqi oil industry. While neo-conservatism probably took less interest in petroleum politics than other sections of the U.S. right, the Bush regime had trouble selling to the rest of the world the line that this intervention was solely about eliminating Weapons of Mass Destruction and spreading democracy.

After all, the U.S. government under Bush of 'Harken Energy' and Cheney of 'Halliburton' has been well described as a 'petroarchy', with eight Cabinet members and the National Security Advisor herself having held executive posts in the oil industry.[72] Again, though, the Republican Party's special service to petroleum interests should not be regarded as unique in U.S. political history. In contrast to Michael Moore's Saudi-centric documentary about Bush-style Republicanism, the Democratic Party has a long history of affection for the House of Saud, starting with F.D.R.'s great meeting on the U.S.S. Quincy with King Ibn Saud in which the U.S. president pledged long-term military support to the Kingdom in exchange for guaranteed flows of the nation's copious fuel supplies. President Jimmy Carter later enunciated what became known as the Carter Doctrine, the assertion that any blockage of Middle East oil supplies would provoke U.S. military intervention in the region.

Environmental journalist Jeffrey St Clair also points out: 'The three biggest oil and gas bonanzas attributed to the rapacity of the Bush regime – the Alaska petroleum reserve, the Gulf of Mexico, and the Powder river – were all initiated by the Clinton Administration.' Bush is excoriated for desiring drilling in the Arctic National Wildlife Reserve (A.N.W.R.), but Clinton had already delivered to the oil executives the National Petroleum Reserve – Alaska (N.P.R.-A), which St Clair calls 'the largest undeveloped tract of land in North America', virtually 'indistinguishable from the hallowed grounds of A.N.W.R.'. While Nixon, Ford,

Reagan and Bush I had been, in St. Clair's words, 'unwilling or unable to deliver' the 24-million acre prize to the petrol barons, Clinton had no hesitation in bringing smiles to the eight oil executives who visited the vacationing Democratic president in 1994 in Jackson Hole, Wyoming with this specific demand on their wish list.[73] The previous year at the White House, Clinton had presented the former C.E.O. of A.R.C.O. Lodwrick Cook with a gargantuan artery-clogging birthday cake and wished him many happy returns.[74] The United States was well on its way to becoming S.U.V. nation, and Clinton–Gore made sure that the petroleum would keep on flowing.

With all the chaos in the Middle East after the Bush invasion of Iraq, liberal commentator Chris Matthews asked in tones emitting first calm and then anguish: 'what happens to *our* oil?'.[75] Even liberal Democrats will slip and admit that 'our oil' must never be threatened, and they maintain that their multilateral policies would secure the precious black gold better than the unilateralist policy manoeuvres of certain Republicans.

In the 21st century, one of the deeper contradictions at the heart of U.S. civilization is coming to the fore. America's civilizing mission has projected its universalizing aspirations on to the rest of the globe; that is to say, the belief that all the world would be better off if only they would embrace the American way of life. 'We wage a war to save civilization', proclaims George W. Bush.[76] Yet, as Perry Anderson has so sharply observed about the predatory over-consumptionism of the economic model underlying this project: 'If all the peoples of the earth possessed the same number of refrigerators and automobiles as those of North America and Western Europe, the planet would become uninhabitable. In the global ecology of capital today, the privilege of the few requires the misery of the many, to be sustainable.' He adds:

> If all human beings simply had an equal share of food, at a diet with less than half the American consumption of animal-based calories, without altering any other distribution of goods whatever – scarcely a radical demand – the globe could not sustain its present population; were U.S. food consumption to be generalized, half the human race would have to become extinct – the Earth could support no more than 2.5 billion inhabitants.[77]

Confronted with the ecological limits of this model, even George W. Bush admits that in the end the U.S. may require rescue, though he sees salvation through Yank technological ingenuity. Both political parties are trumpeting the emancipatory powers of the coming N.B.I.C. revolutions (nanotechnology, bio-technology, information technology, and cognitive science). While remarkable strides are being made in these fields and it would be a mistake to dismiss them all as 'techno-hucksterism', the dawning of a 21st-century Golden Age needs to be seen as a common motif when Americans are confronted with limits. In 1953, the *Ladies Home Journal* forecast that nuclear energy would soon deliver a planet where 'there is no disease.... Where hunger is unknown.... Where food never rots.... Where 'dirt' is an old-fashioned word.... Where the air is everywhere as fresh as on a mountain top and the breeze from a factory as sweet as from a rose.'[78]

For all the flaws in American techno-optimism, the United States is regarded as the pacesetter in so many fields of endeavour from music to medicine, from athletics to astrophysics, that its social life remains a pole of attraction for millions of immigrants. Despite significant pockets of poverty, it has also gen-erated spectacular levels of wealth that remain a challenge to any movements proposing an alternative social order. Citing data on Germany, Canada, and the Scandinavian lands which indicate that these nations may have greater upward social mobility than the United States, the Century Foundation raises scepticism about the 'rags to riches' aura of 'The American Dream'.[79] Still, compared to the rest of the advanced industrial world, including almost all of Western Europe and Japan, the United States is demographically a much younger society than its potential rivals, and this will be a source of continued vitality throughout the 21st century.[80] In the decades ahead, there are forecasts that China will be producing three times as many science and engineering PhDs as the United States; but China is an aging society which will be under heavy stress due to social safety nets for the elderly far inferior to those in place for the major nations of the advanced industrial world.

Meanwhile, China's own mounting thirst for oil is pushing global petroleum prices to record levels, and this raises the stakes for the botched occupation of Iraq which had once promised abundant flows of the world economy's lifeblood. While looting convulsed the museums and government ministries of Iraq, the U.S. left one of the war's most enduring memories by making sure that the petroleum ministry stood amply guarded, snug and secure. Even so, it bears repeating that U.S. foreign policy is driven by more than petroleum politics; otherwise the hardened realists in the Establishment who have called for a tougher line toward Israel would likely receive more of a hearing in Washington. Neo-conservatism regards frequent military intervention as a necessity just to fortify U.S. hegemony and to make sure that potentially recalcitrant nations practise fealty to the Washington Consensus. A more accurate label for it might be 'militarized neo-liberalism'. As Michael Ledeen, one of the movement's most admired figures, expressed it in a public lecture in the early 1990s: 'Every ten years or so, the United States needs to pick up some crappy little country and throw it against the wall, just to show the world we mean business.'[81] Partisans of neo-conservatism had denounced George H.W. Bush for pusillanimous behavior in Gulf War I and rejected Bush the Elder's spontaneous proclamation: 'By God, we've kicked the Vietnam syndrome once and for all.'[82] Neo-con defence expert Eliot Cohen lamented in his treatise *Supreme Command: Soldiers, Statesmen, and Leadership in Wartime* (2002) that 'the Gulf War did not end the Vietnam syndrome, but, if anything, strengthened it'.[83] U.S. power over the world is regarded in these circles as all good and an end in itself. Failure to flex military muscle early and often is a prelude to national atrophy and decadence, and for them it imperils what they proudly call 'The Project for the New American Century'.

An Empire Means Never Having to Say You're Sorry

The electoral triumphs of the Bush dynasty continue to frustrate critics of U.S. Empire throughout the world. Much liberal-left analysis has fixated on the belief that Bush is an intellectual featherweight, a leader more suited for the nation of Moronica (the fascist utopia in the Three Stooges film *You Nazty Spy*) than a modern democratic polity. In the radical *Z Magazine* (February 2001), Chicago-based social policy researcher Paul Street calls Bush 'one of the meanest and certainly one of the dumbest Presidents in the history of the United States'. This widespread view of post-war Republican presidents as simpletons may be comforting, but it does little to explain why this formula is so appealing to many U.S. voters. The Bushes and other Republicans (Eisenhower, Reagan, Ford, and perhaps even the bumbling Dan Quayle) may have stumbled upon the truth of film mogul Harry Cohn: 'If you don't learn anything else from me, learn this: Always let the other fellow think he's smarter than you.'[84] The head of Columbia Pictures, the studio that produced the Three Stooges for two and a half decades, Cohn was thought to be illiterate; but his biographers show that it was a total act. The know-it-all liberalism of Kerry, Gore, Dukakis, Mondale or Adlai Stevenson has proven vulnerable to the Republican posture of downplaying signs of overt cleverness. 'They misunderestimated me', said George W. Bush, whose gift for mangling the English language then supplies future occasion for self-deprecation and general merriment.[85]

Revulsion towards Bush can be acute in some circles – Hollywood actor Alec Baldwin and director Robert Altman threatened to leave the country in 2000 should he be elected. In 2004, many European allies gave Bush less support in polls than they might deliver to their own parties of the extreme right: Norway – 74 per cent for Kerry, 7 per cent for Bush; Germany – 74 per cent to 10 per cent; France – 64 to 5 per cent; Netherlands – 63 per cent to 6 per cent, and on and on.[86] If he 'possessed a single virtue it has eluded the conscientious research of the writer of these pages', said Motley of Philip II; a condemnation that liberal ultras and European publics might fasten upon Bush II. 'If there are vices – as possibly there are – from which he was exempt, it is because it is not permitted to human nature to attain perfection even in evil.'[87] Just as Motley elsewhere admitted that Philip II 'distributed alms to the poor of Brussels with an open hand', Bush too has exhibited moments of compassion, for example in his opposition to rightist efforts to ban the children of immigrants from Texas schools.[88] There are those who remain sceptical that the Bushes exhibit an unusual degree of meanness compared to the rest of the U.S. political class. As the novelist Henry Miller reflected:

> Once I saw in a store window a framed photo of all the Vice-Presidents we have had. It might have served as a rogues' gallery. Some of them looked like criminals, some looked feeble-minded, some like plain idiots. The Presidents haven't been much better, to tell the truth. To be sure, politicians and statesmen the world over have a dull or foxy look about them. Churchill was no exception.[89]

A significant portion of the U.S. public has come to regard maintenance of Empire as a great sacrifice, involving humanitarian devotion to the spread of democracy and global well-being. Midge Decter, the author of a fawning biography of the U.S. Secretary of Defense entitled *Rumsfeld: A Personal Portrait*, expresses it this way: 'After all, Americans in general are nice people, probably the nicest in the world, afraid of mean-spiritedness in others, and perhaps even more afraid of the accusation of being mean-spirited themselves.'[90] The average American believes that the U.S. devotes 15 per cent of the national budget to foreign aid, rather than the true figure of 0.1 per cent, making the U.S. government the least generous of the twenty-two nations in the Organisation for Economic Co-operation and Development.[91] (It is fair to say, however, that Americans are more altruistic and willing to volunteer than many other O.E.C.D. nations when it comes to church and private charitable forms of aid.)

Few Americans seemed aware of the scope of devastation wrought by frequent cycles of 'surgical strikes', aerial bombardments and death-squad counter-insurgencies sponsored in their name. In the Vietnam War alone, estimates of the numbers of Vietnamese perished range from a low of 1,300,000 to highs exceeding 3,000,000. Yet a survey indicates that the average American has no idea of the numbers of deaths of Vietnamese, with the most common guess being 100,000. As a team of social scientists concluded: 'The median estimate of Vietnamese casualties by respondents in our survey was around 100 thousand – a figure nearly twenty times too small. This is a little like estimating the number of victims of the Nazi holocaust at 300 thousand rather than 6 million.'[92] Many know that 58,000 U.S. troops died, a number seared in memory by constant references from media, movies and politicians. Justifying America's refusal to apologize, let alone pay any reparations for the devastation in Vietnam, President Jimmy Carter flatly said: 'The destruction was mutual.'[93]

Representing the apogee of human rights and humanitarian sentiments among post-war U.S. presidents, Carter also rebuffed Iranian demands for an apology from the U.S. for installing the Shah in power since 1953 and the subsequent decades of S.A.V.A.K. torture that continued well into this 'soft' Democrat's administration. 'I don't think we have anything to apologize for', assured Henry Kissinger.[94] Ruminating about the United States of Amnesia, Carter's principal White House aide for Iran throughout the hostage crisis, Mr. Gary Sick, admitted that from the standpoint of U.S. policy-makers 'anything that happened more than a quarter century before – even an event of singular importance – assumes the pale and distant appearance of ancient history. In Washington, by 1978, the events of 1953 had all the relevance of a pressed flower.'[95] Barely over a year before the Iranian people toppled this modernizing despot, Carter toasted the Shah's Iran as 'an island of stability', which he called a 'great tribute to the respect, admiration and love of your people for you'.[96] A defiant George H.W.

Bush announced, after the U.S. shot down a large Iranian airliner filled with 290 civilians, 'I will never apologize for the United States of America. I don't care what the facts are'.[97]

When Bill Clinton finally issued a reparations-free apology to African-Americans for their enslavement for 250 years of colonial and U.S. history, he faced severe rebuke from outspoken elements of the American right who demanded in articles and advertisements that African-Americans should instead thank white America for abolishing the Peculiar Institution. Accused in these same quarters of pursuing a foreign policy soft as a kitten, Clinton retained strict sanctions on Iraq that routinely refused equipment to repair the nation's heavily bombed water, water-purification and sewerage systems. Saddam Hussein, it was alleged, would use new pipes for missiles and weapons of mass destruction. Facing C.B.S. journalist Lesley Stahl on *Sixty Minutes* (12 May 1996), who cited U.N. data on Iraq indicating that 'half a million children have died ... more children than died in Hiroshima', U.S. Secretary of State Madeleine Albright coldly replied: 'I think this is a very hard choice, but the price – we think the price is worth it.' Beloved in Western Europe as much more humane than the savage Bush clan, Clinton denied U.S. responsibility for the excess child mortality, as he reassured the media, on the rare occasions they raised the issue, that Saddam Hussein alone was at fault for diverting funds which would have ameliorated his people's suffering. Medicines were routinely blocked to the suffering people, including by the British government which alleged that exporting vaccines for tetanus, diptheria and yellow fever might be diverted to mad scientists in Saddam Hussein's entourage looking to make bio-weapons for use against Israel and the West. From 1989 to 1996, the infant mortality rate in Iraq soared from 47 per 1000 to 108 per 1000, with as many as 5000 children per month losing their lives.[98] Though he may have inflated the already controversial U.N. statistics, Osama bin Laden in his opening speech justifying September 11 cited U.S. complacency about the horrendous death toll of Iraqi children. Arab media continued to show footage of a comfortable Albright saying the U.S. thinks the price of several hundred thousand Iraqi lives is 'worth it'.

For most of U.S. history, the American public has resisted the very idea that the nation is an Empire, an entity that would represent a stark repudiation of the nation's colonial revolutionary heritage and founding as a republic. Nevertheless,

Walter Lippmann in *Men of Destiny* (1927) saw that the reality looks very different in the court of world public opinion:

> All the world thinks of the United States today as an empire, except the people of the United States. We shrink from the word 'empire' and insist that it should not be used to describe the dominion we exercise from Alaska to the Philippines, from Cuba to Panama, and beyond. We feel there ought to be some other name for the civilizing work which we do so reluctantly in these backward countries.[99]

For those apt to regard imperialism as a dead or moribund monstrosity, it is one with zombie-like recuperative powers. In the 1990s, the Anglo-conservative ideologue Paul Johnson spoke for Westerners disenchanted with post-colonial regimes and thus eager for a more interventionist Pax Americana. His views were enunciated in an article in the *New York Times Magazine* (18 April 1993) entitled 'Colonialism's Back and Not a Moment Too Soon'. According to retired U.S. foreign service officer Robert A. Lincoln, 'Paul Johnson's article dignifies what some of us in foreign service . . . increasingly felt but seldom dared to say for fear of banishment from our profession' (*New York Times Magazine*, 9 May 1993). In 'Why the Empire Must Strike Back' (*Observer*, 18 August 1996), Oxford historian Norman Stone praises France in particular for practising throughout Africa 'a sort of enlightened re-imperialism, with the consent of a local elite'.

Though no longer able to summon the gallant lancers of Gary Cooper and the charging light brigade of Errol Flynn, the new imperialists still have much at their disposal. There is a mass media prone to portray the Third World as the heart of darkness and a global culture industry designed to create the Rambos, the Indiana Joneses, and echoing Stone, the intergalactic warriors who grace *The Empire Strikes Back*. The commander-in-chief of the U.S. Central Command, General Anthony Zinni, expressed the view to journalist Dana Priest that indeed 'he had become a modern-day proconsul, descendant of the Warrior statesmen who ruled the Roman Empire's outlying territory, bringing order and ideals from a legalistic Rome'.[100] Americans had finally won the victory over themselves, thought the neo-conservative movement; they now loved Empire. The colossal failure of the Iraq Occupation has reopened an historic space for resistance.

References

1. Zbigniew Brzezinski, *Between Two Ages: America's Role in the Technetronic Era* (New York: Penguin Books, 1978 [1970]), p.32.

2. *Ibid.*, p. 33.

3. The *Fortune* supplement is quoted and discussed at much greater length by Leo Panitch and Sam Ginden, 'Global Capitalism and American Empire', in Leo Panitch and Colin Leys, eds., *Socialist Register 2004: The New Imperial Challenge* (London and New York: Merlin Press and Monthly Review Press, 2003), pp.14 and 15.

4. Thomas L. Friedman, *The Lexus and the Olive Tree* (New York: Farrar, Straus, Giroux, 1999), p.373.

5. Chalmers Johnson, *The Sorrows of Empire: Militarism, Secrecy, and the End of the Republic* (New York: Henry Holt/Metropolitan Books, 2004), p.4. It might be noted that when Brzezinski published *Between Two Ages* in 1970 he estimated the number of U.S. military bases as 'some four hundred major and almost three thousand minor United States military bases scattered all over the globe' (p.32).

6. Norman Podhoretz, 'Proper Uses of Power', *New York Times*, 30 October 1983, p.E19. Nixon's words come from his presidential address of 30 April 1970.

7. The text to the presidential address of 30 April 1970 can be accessed at www.nixonlibrary.org.

8. This interview is quoted by Mahmood Mamdani, *Good Muslim, Bad Muslim: America, the Cold War, and the Roots of Terror* (New York: Pantheon, 2004), pp.123–4. The interview circulates widely on the Internet in both French and translated versions.

9. 'Carter's Statement on Iran and Afghan Situations', *New York Times*, 29 December 1979, p. 5.

10. See George Crile, *Charlie Wilson's War: The Extraordinary Story of the Largest Covert Operation in History* (New York: Atlantic Monthly Press, 2003).

11. See Mamdani, *op. cit.*, pp.127–8.

12. Azzam quoted by Mamdani, *op. cit.*, p.127.

13. As'ad AbuKhalil, *Bin Laden, Islam, and America's New "War on Terrorism"* (New York: Seven Stories Press, 2002), p.72.

14. *The 9/11 Commission Report* (2004) available at www.9-11commission.gov/
report/911report.pdf took note of this development, p.57.

15. Bin Laden quoted by Ahmed Rashid, *Taliban: Militant Islam, Oil, and Fundamentalism in Central Asia* (New Haven: Yale Nota Bene/Yale University Press, 2000), p. 132.

16. Prince Bandar interviewed on 'Larry King Live', CNN, 1 October 2001.

17. Rashid, *op. cit.*, p.85.

18. Mamdani, *op cit.,* p.133. Many accounts accuse Egyptians of carrying out this assassination.

19. *The 9/11 Commission Report*, p.57.

20. Melvin Laird quoted by Thomas A. Bailey, *A Diplomatic History of the American People* (Englewood Cliffs, NJ: Prentice-Hall, 1980, tenth edn.), p.923. 'America will no longer try to play policeman to the world', the Secretary of Defense remarked on what became regarded as the Nixon Doctrine. 'Instead, we will expect other nations to provide more cops on the beat in their own neighborhood.' Though its advocates regarded the Nixon Doctrine as proof that the United States was not behaving in imperialist ways, they neglected to note that most empires depend on colonized nations to provide what Bailey called 'the bulk of the cannon fodder'. As a British music-hall song of the late 19th century would have it, 'We don't want to fight/ But, by jingo, if we do/ We won't go to the front ourselves/ We'll send the mild Hindoo.'

21. George Ball, 'The Lessons from Iran', *Boston Globe*, 2 April 1979, quoted and discussed by Naseer Aruri, *The Obstruction of Peace: The U.S., Israel, and the Palestinians* (Monroe, Maine: Common Courage Press, 1995), p.49.

22. *The 9/11 Commission Report* makes two very brief mentions of the Hiroshima-level ambitions of Bin Laden on pp.116 and 380. In the report's words, he thought that a successful 'Hiroshima' meant 'at least 10,000 casualties'.

23. Abu 'Ubeid Al-Qurashi, 'Fourth Generation Wars', excerpted in *MEMRI: The Middle East Media Research Institute*, Special Dispatch Series–No. 344, 10 February 2002.

24. Alexander Cockburn makes a similar point in the special issue of *Counter-Punch* following the death of Ronald Reagan in 2004.

25. Gilles Kepel, *Jihad: The Trail of Political Islam* (Cambridge: Harvard University Press, 2002), p.366.

26. Jim Mann, in *Rise of the Vulcans: The History of Bush's War Cabinet* (New York: Viking, 2004), explains how the Bush team became known as Vulcans. Founding member Condoleezza Rice hails from the steel city of Birmingham, Alabama, which has as its symbol a statue of the Roman god of metal and fire. Cf. another word probably derived from the same Latin root: 'Volcano'.

27. 'The February Regime', *Times Literary Supplement*, 30 June 1966, especially p.566. See also the exchanges on this topic in the *TLS* of 14 July and 28 July 1966. Though anonymous at the time, Isaac Deutscher wrote the review essay exploring the question of German support for the Russian Revolution. Z.A.B. Zeman and others wrote tart replies.

28. Fred Halliday, 'Kabul's Patriarchy with Guns: Fighters Armed by Pakistan Have Turned the Afghan Capital into a No-Woman's Land', *The Nation*, 11 November 1996, p.20.

29. H.L. Mencken, *Notes on Democracy* (New York: Knopf, 1926), pp.22–3.

30. Condon quoted by Daniel Pipes, 'The Muslims are coming, the Muslims are coming ... '. *National Review*, 19 November 1990, p.28.

31. 'The Islamic–Confucian Connection', interview with Samuel P. Huntington, *New Perspectives Quarterly*, 10.3, 22 June 1993.

32. Irving Kristol, 'The Tragedy of Multiculturalism', *Wall Street Journal*, 31 July 1991, p.15.

33. Irving Kristol, 'My Cold War', *The National Interest*, Spring 1993, pp.143–144.

34. Peregrine Worsthorne, 'Liberalism Is the Real Enemy', *Sunday Telegraph*, 18 October 1992, p.28.

35. Norman Podhoretz, *Ex-Friends* (New York: Free Press, 1999), p.21.

36. Data on U.S. union membership from the *Union Sourcebook, 1947–1983* and the Bureau of Labor Statistics prepared by the Labor Research Association at www.laborresearch.org. For some alternative numbers, see Richard B. Freeman, 'Spurts in Union Growth: Defining Moments and Social Processes', in Michael D. Bordo, Claudia Goldin and Eugene N. White, eds, *The Defining Moment: The Great Depression and the American Economy in the*

Twentieth Century (Chicago: NBER and University of Chicago Press, 1998), pp.291–3.

37. See U.S. Department of Labor, Employment and Earnings, January 2004, cited in 'The Union Difference' at www.aflcio.org.

38. The Bureau of Labor Statistics in the U.S. regularly updates annual strike statistics of 1,000 or more workers at www.bls.gov.

39. Litwiler quoted by Christian Parenti, 'Us Against Them in the Me Decade', in Thomas Frank and Dave Mulcahey, eds., *Boob Jubilee: The Cultural Politics of the New Economy* (New York: W.W. Norton & Company, 2003), p.332. The examples in my essay on labour unrest are drawn from Parenti's incisive commentary.

40. James P. Gannon, 'Strikers on Welfare: Workers on Public Aid During Walkouts Draw Increasing Criticism', *Wall Street Journal*, 14 July 1971, pp.1 and 29.

41. Shultz quoted by Parenti, *op. cit.*, p.335.

42. Senator Hugh Scott quoted in American Conservative Union publication *Battle Line*, February 1970, as cited by Gary Allen, *Richard Nixon: The Man Behind the Mask* (Belmont: Western Islands, 1971), Chap.1. The sobriquet for Nixon ('America's last liberal president') is delivered in the campus lectures of Harvard Law School professor Paul C. Weiler.

43. Samuel P. Huntington, 'The United States', in Michel J. Crozier, Samuel P. Huntington and Joji Watanuki, *The Crisis of Democracy: Report on the Governability of Democracies to the Trilateral Commission* (New York: NYU Press, 1975), pp.61–2, 93, 113–14.

44. Jefferson Cowie, 'From Hard Hats to NASCAR Dads', *New Labor Forum*, Vol. 13, Issue 3, Fall 2004, p.13. Cowie's essay was part of a larger forum on 'The Enigma of Working-Class Conservatism'.

45. Fraser letter published and discussed in Jefferson Cowie, '"A One-Sided Class War": Rethinking Doug Fraser's 1978 Resignation Letter from the Labor-Management Group', *Labor History* 44, 2003, pp.307–14. See also the rejoinder by Victor G. Deminatz, 'Doug Fraser's 1978 Resignation Letter from the Labor-Management Group and the Limits of Liberalism', *Labor History*, Vol. 45, No. 3, August 2004, pp.323–31.

46. 'Volcker: "Standard of Living Has to Decline"', *Wall Street Journal*, 29 October 1979, p.26. The *WSJ* published the transcript of Volcker's remarks

and argued that seen in its context the call for a 'decline' was far less heartless than commonly portrayed. Volcker in particular hailed 'the American people' for 'restraining themselves from a big further increase in wage gains', and he applauded them for their 'sacrifice'.

47. Fraser letter and discussion in Jefferson Cowie, *op. cit.*, pp.307–14.

48. Thomas Frank, *What's the Matter with Kansas?* (New York: Metropolitan Books, 2004), which has an opening paragraph discussing impoverished McPherson county in Nebraska, part of the Great Plains region of 'struggling ranchers and dying farm towns'. Frank, in an article called 'Lie Down for America: How the Republican Party Sows Ruin on the Great Plains' for *Harper's Magazine* (April 2004), beckons readers: 'Welcome to the Great Backlash, a style of conservatism that is anything but complacent. Whereas earlier forms of conservatism emphasized fiscal sobriety, the backlash mobilizes voters with explosive social issues – summoning public outrage over everything from busing to un-Christian art – which it then marries to pro-business economic policies.... It makes possible the policy pushers' fantasies of 'globalization' and a free-trade empire that are foisted upon the rest of the world with such self-assurance. Because some artist decides to shock the hicks by dunking Jesus in urine, the entire planet must remake itself along the lines preferred by the Republican Party, U.S.A.'

49. Advertisement discussed by Jefferson Cowie, 'From Hard Hats to NASCAR Dads', *New Labor Forum*, Vol. 13, Issue 3, Fall 2004, p.9.

50. Tracy L. Snell, BJS Statistician, 'Correctional Populations in the United States, 1993: Executive Summary', *Bureau of Justice Statistics*, October 1995, NCJ-156675, and Paige M. Harrison and Jennifer C. Karberg, BJS Statisticians, 'Prison and Jail Inmates at Midyear 2002', *Bureau of Justice Statistics Bulletin*, April 2003, NCJ-198877.

51. L. Randall Wray, 'A New Economic Reality: Penal Keynesianism', *Challenge*, Vol. 43, No. 5, September 2000.

52. Thomas P. Bonczar, B.J.S. Statistician, 'Prevalence of Imprisonment in the U.S. Population, 1974–2001', *Bureau of Justice Statistics Special Report*, August 2003, NCJ-197976.

53. Harold McGraw, 'Stop the Bickering Over World Trade Talks', *Financial Times*, 20 November 2003, p.21.

54. Christian E. Weller and Adam Hersh, 'Free Markets and Poverty', *The American Prospect*, Winter 2002 supplement, p.A13.

55. Mark Weisbrot, 'The Mirage of Progress', *The American Prospect*, Winter 2002 supplement, p.A10.

56. This data comes from the *BusinessWeek* executive compensation scoreboard, cited by Christopher Farrell, 'Stock Options for All!', *BusinessWeek* Online, 20 September 2002.

57. Data from Robert Pollin, *Contours of Descent: U.S. Economic Fractures and the Landscape of Global Austerity* (London and New York: Verso, 2003), p.9. His data on workers came from the U.S. Bureau of Labor Statistics, and his C.E.O. wages from *BusinessWeek* (30 March 1992 and 15 April 2002).

58. Lucian Bebchuk and Jesse Fried, *Pay Without Performance: The Unfulfilled Promise of Executive Compensation* (Cambridge: Harvard University Press, 2004), p.1.

59. CBO data cited by Kevin Phillips, 'How Wealth Defines Power: The Politics of the New Gilded Age', *The American Prospect*, May 2003 supplement.

60. Breman quoted by Peter Thal Larsen, 'Gulf Widens Between the Haves and the Have-Yachts', *Financial Times*, 13 May 2004. *Power & Motoryacht* magazine (August 2004) has listings and details on the world's largest yachts, while the issue of November 2004 covers 'America's 100 Largest Yachts' including Ellison's new craft costing $200 million.

61. Conrad Black, 'Counsel to Britain: U.S. Power, the "Special Relationship" and the Global Order,' *The National Interest*, Fall 2003.

62. Thomas L. Friedman, 'Senseless in Seattle', *New York Times*, 1 December 1999, p.A23.

63. Martin Wolf, 'Lessons of the Asia Crisis', in 'Berlin 1998: The Annual Meeting of the Trilateral Commission', *Trialogue* 52, 1998, p.11. For a more developed discussion of the commentaries of Wolf and Kissinger, see William K. Tabb, *The Amoral Elephant: Globalization and the Struggle for Social Justice in the Twenty-first Century* (New York: Monthly Review Press, 2001), Chap.5.

64. Henry Kissinger, 'The United States and Europe: What Are We Trying to Do?', in 'Berlin 1998: The Annual Meeting of the Trilateral Commission', *Trialogue* 52, 1998, p.49.

65. Johnson, *op.cit.,* p.307.

66. See Lawrence J. Korb, former Assistant Secretary of Defense under Reagan, '10 Myths About the Defense Budget', *In These Times*, 2 April 2001, p.10. Korb notes: 'the U.S. share of the world's military spending stands at 35 percent, substantially higher than during the cold war'. By 2002, prior to the invasion of Iraq, the Bush military resurgence pushed the figure up to 43 per cent, according to the *SIPRI Yearbook 2003* (Oxford: Oxford University Press, 2003), p.304. S.I.P.R.I. (Stockholm International Peace Research Institute) argues that under market exchanges rates the U.S. exceeds the next biggest military spender by over seven times; but in PPP dollar terms (Purchasing Power Parity) the U.S. tops China by less than triple. Those who reject P.P.P. approaches for military equipment point out, writes S.I.P.R.I. on pp.304–5, that these types of 'overall price comparisons do not account for the level of technology that may be purchased with Western, and especially U.S. military expenditure, which is well beyond the capacity of countries such as China and India'. In the *SIPRI Yearbook 2004* the U.S. share of world military expenditures jumped in 2003 to 47 per cent, 9 times greater than the next biggest military spender.

67. John Dower, 'Lessons from Japan About War's Aftermath', *New York Times,* 27 October 2002, Section 4, p.13.

68. Eugene Anderson memorandum to John Begg, 7 February 1946, 'Acquisition of Movie Theatres in Germany by Paramount Pictures', U.S. National Archives, Record Group 59, 862.4061, 1945–9 Motion Pictures.

69. Letter of J.J. McCloy to Harry Hopkins, 8 January 1944, re 'Motion Picture Production in Post-war Germany', U.S. National Archives, Record Group 59, 862.4061, 1945–9 Motion Pictures, MP1-1145 (This document from 1944 is filed in a box covering film policy in Germany, 1945–49).

70. Wolfowitz quoted by Stefan Halper and Jonathan Clarke, *America Alone: The Neo-Conservatives and the Global Order* (New York: Cambridge University Press, 2004), p.222.

71. Iraqi construction manager quoted by Khalid Mustafa Medani, 'State Building in Reverse: The Neo-Liberal "Reconstruction" of Iraq', *Middle East Report* 232, Fall 2004, p.29. This essay is notably insightful.

72. Jeffrey St. Clair, 'Big Oil and the Two Party System', *CounterPunch*, Vol. 11, No. 15, 7–15 September 2004, p.1.

73. *ibid.*, p.2.

74. Kathy Lewis, 'Exchange of Ideas on Menu at White House CEO Lunches: President Reaches Out to Array of Business Leasers', *Dallas Morning News*, 7 December 1993. It is sometimes reported that the beaming Cook, a Bush supporter in 1992, received the presidential birthday cake in 1994, but Lewis indicates this occurred in 1993.

75. See interviews on 'The Chris Matthews Show', 19–20 September 2004.

76. 'A Nation Challenged: Excerpts from President's Speech', *New York Times*, 9 November 2001.

77. Perry Anderson, 'The Ends of History', in P. Anderson, *A Zone of Engagement* (London: Verso, 1992), pp.352–53.

78. *Ladies Home Journal* quoted by Vincent Mosco, *The Digital Sublime: Myth, Power, and Cyberspace* (Cambridge: MIT Press, 2004), p.186, n.4.

79. See Bernard Wasow, Century Foundation Senior Fellow, 'Rags to Riches? The American Dream is Less Common in the United States than Elsewhere', (New York and Washington, D.C.: The Century Foundation, 2004), accessed at www.tcf.org on 5 November 2004, and Gary Solon, 'Cross-Country Differences in Intergenerational Earnings Mobility', *Journal of Economic Perspectives* 16, No. 3, Summer 2002, pp.59–66.

80. The youth of U.S. society probably gives the U.S. sustained advantages in fields such as the high-tech and the culture industries. Still, some Europeans are sceptical about the U.S. edge in the long term. As Geof Rayner, chair of the U.K. Public Health Association, retorts in a letter to the *Financial Times* (7 July 2003): 'The U.S. population may be younger than Europe's but it is unhealthier. Owing to successful marketing of snack foods, alongside declining physical activity, the proportion of children who are overweight in the U.S. has risen from 6 per cent to 14 per cent over the past twenty years. Obesity costs were estimated at $117bn in 2000 – almost catching up with the $140bn cost of smoking. Most obese people today are elderly, but in fat-of-the-land America, where already more than 60 per cent are over-weight and almost one in five is obese, diet-related illnesses will strike earlier, with massive lifetime cost.' Rayner adds that high incarceration rates in the U.S., typically over five times higher than in Western Europe, will lead to huge costs and prevent broader forms of social investment.

81. Ledeen quoted by Jonah Goldberg, 'Baghdad Delenda Est, Part Two',

National Review Online, 23 April 2002. Ledeen later confirmed the accuracy of the quotation, though he said that some of the context was missing. Incidentally Goldberg wrote the article to express his sincere admiration for his 'friend' Ledeen and what he called the 'Ledeen Doctrine'.

82. Bush speech to state legislators at the White House quoted by Maureen Dowd, 'War Introduces a Tougher Bush to Nation', *New York Times*, 2 March 1991, p.1. His Vietnam syndrome comment was also named 'Quotation of the Day' by the *NYT*.

83. Cohen quoted by Halper and Clarke *op. cit.*, p.30. Cohen's anger that the Vietnam syndrome lives on can be contrasted with the euphoria in such circles in the early days of triumph after Gulf War I. See Dov S. Zakheim, Deputy Under-Secretary of Defense in the Reagan Administration, 'Is the Vietnam Syndrome Dead? Happily, It's Buried in the Gulf', *New York Times*, 4 March 1991, p.A17.

84. Bernard F. Dick, *The Merchant Prince of Poverty Row: Harry Cohn of Columbia Pictures* (Lexington: University Press of Kentucky, 1993), p.8.

85. Bush quoted by Jake Tapper, 'One Last Group Hug', *Salon*, 7 November 2000, at salon.com. Bush was actually speaking at a political rally in Bentonville, Arkansas on 6 November 2000 when he made the comment about his determination to reform Social Security.

86. See Steven Kull and Doug Miller, principal investigators, 'Global Public Opinion on the U.S. Presidential Election and U.S. Foreign Policy', a report by the Program on International Policy Attitudes (P.I.P.A.) and Globescan Incorporated, 8 September 2004. Bush did command huge majorities in polls of the Philippines and Israel, though U.S. Jews remained staunch supporters of John Kerry. According to a worldwide survey published in the *Guardian* (UK, international edition, 15 October 2004), 50 per cent of Israelis backed Bush and 24 per cent supported Kerry.

87. John Lothrop Motley, *History of the United Netherlands*, Vol. III (New York: Harper and Brothers, 1868), p.535. For a discussion of this famous indictment, see J.H. Elliott, 'The Enigma of Philip II', *New York Review of Books*, 25 September 1997, p.45.

88. John Lothrop Motley, *The Rise of the Dutch Republic: A History*, Vol. I (New York: Harper and Brothers, 1864), p.146. Though Motley believed that Philip's 'talents were, in truth, very much below mediocrity' and his 'mind

was incredibly small', he at least 'had a taste for sculpture, painting, and architecture. Certainly, if he had not possessed a feeling for art, he would have been a monster' (pp.142 and 145).

89. Henry Miller, 'A Nation of Lunatics', in Erica Jong, Thomas Sanchez, Kay Boyle and Henry Miller, *Four Visions of America* (Santa Barbara: Capra Press, 1977), p.114.

90. Midge Decter, 'An Amazing Pass', *National Review*, Vol. LVI, No. 21, 8 November 2004, p.30.

91. See the research by the FrameWorks Institute on U.S. perceptions of foreign aid, cited by David Morrison, president of NetAid, 'What U.S. Needs is Some Straight Talk', *Financial Times*, 20 October 2003. Arguing that 'Private giving from Americans to the poor abroad is now three times that of its government's official assistance account', Jeremiah Norris, Adjunct Fellow at the Hudson Institute, sharply rebukes critics of stingy U.S. government foreign aid in a separate letter to the *FT* in that same issue.

92. Justin Lewis, Sut Jhally and Michael Morgan, 'The Gulf War: A Study of the Media, Public Opinion, and Public Knowledge', a paper of The Center for the Study of Communication, Department of Communication, University of Massachusetts/Amherst, February 1991. This paper can be accessed at www.sutjhally.com. I am aware that some may challenge the figure of 6 million cited by the researchers for not including the several million Slavs and the hundreds of thousands of Roma (Gypsies), homosexuals and the 'physically unfit' liquidated by Nazi Germany.

93. For the Carter quotation, see the transcript of the press conference of 24 March 1977 in 'Carter: "Nothing but Sympathy for Families" of MIAs', *Washington Post*, 25 March 1977, p.A12.

94. Youssef M. Ibrahim, 'Kissinger Opposes a U.S. Apology as a Way to Free Hostages', *New York Times*, 20 June 1980, p.A7.

95. Gary Sick, *All Fall Down: America's Tragic Encounter with Iran* (New York: Random House, 1985), p.7.

96. Carter quoted by Flora Lewis, 'Itinerary is Shifted: Presidents' Parley Designed to Find Ways to Broaden Mideast Peace Talks', *New York Times*, 1 January 1978, pp.1 and 10.

97. Bush quoted by R.W. Apple, 'Political Memo; Bush Appears in Trouble Despite 2 Big Advantages', *New York Times*, 4 August 1988.

98. For a more detailed look at this data and the devastation of sanctions on Iraq, see the special double issue of *CounterPunch* (April 2003) featuring Alexander Cockburn and Jeffrey St. Clair, 'The Thirteen Years War'.

99. Walter Lippmann, *Men of Destiny* (New York: Macmillan, 1927), pp.215–16.

100. See Dana Priest, *The Mission: Waging War and Keeping the Peace with America's Military* (New York: W.W. Norton, 2003), p.70. Zinni's remark is a paraphrase by the journalist.

BIBLIOGRAPHY

(Any bibliography of this inexhaustible subject can only be very selective. The following list is limited to works drawn on in the text).

Abshire, D.M., and Samuels, M.A., eds, *Portuguese Africa – A Handbook* (London, 1969)

Adams, B., *The Law of Civilization and Decay* (1895; New York edn., 1943, ed. C.A. Beard)

Adams, John Quincy, *Memoirs*, ed. C.F. Adams (Vol. II, Philadelphia, 1874)

Addison, P., 'Churchill and the United States', in *New Edinburgh Review*, Nos. 38–39 (1977)

Alanbrooke War Diaries 1943–46, The, ed. A. Bryant (1959; London edn., 1965)

Aldcroft, D.H., *From Versailles to Wall Street 1919–1929* (London, 1977)

Allen, H.C., *Great Britain and the United States – A History of Anglo-American Relations (1783–1952)* (London, 1954)

Alstyne, R.W. Van, *American Crisis Diplomacy – The Quest for Collective Security 1918–1952* (Stanford, 1952)

Alstyne, R.W. Van, *The Rising American Empire* (Oxford, 1960)

Amnesty International, *Report on Torture* (2nd edn., London, 1975)

Angell, N., *The Great Illusion 1933* (London, 1933)

Anon. ('A Citizen of the United States'), *America: or a General Survey ... of the Western Continent* (London, 1828)

Anon., *The Great Naval War of 1887* (London, 1887)

Arevalo, J.J., *The Shark and the Sardine* (New York, 1961).

Armstrong, H.W., *The United States and the British Commonwealth in Prophecy* (Pasadena, 1967)

Bailey, J.O., *Pilgrims through Space and Time – trends and patterns in scientific and utopian fiction* (New York, 1947)

Bailey, T.A., *The Man in the Street – The Impact of American Public Opinion on Foreign Policy* (Gloucester, Mass., 1948)

Baker, J.E., *Explaining China* (London, 1927)

Baldwin, D.A., *Economic Development and American Foreign Policy 1943–62* (Chicago, 1966)

Ball, W.M., *Nationalism and Communism in East Asia* (Melbourne, 1952)

Barnds, W.J., *India, Pakistan, and the Great Powers* (London, 1972)

Barnes, H.E., ed., *Perpetual War for Perpetual Peace* (Caldwell, Idaho, 1953)

Bauer Paiz, A., 'Imperialism in Guatemala', in *Science and Society* (New York), Vol. XXXIV, No. 2 (1970)

Beard, C.A., *American Foreign Policy in the Making 1932–1940* (Yale, 1946)

Belden, J., *China Shakes the World* (London, 1951)

Bellamy, E., *Looking Backward 2000–1887* (1888)

Belmont, P., *An American Democrat* (2nd edn., New York, 1941)

Bingham, H., *The Monroe Doctrine – an obsolete shibboleth* (New Haven, 1913)

Black, E.R., *Alternatives in Southeast Asia* (London, 1969)

Blackett, P.M., *The Military Consequences of Atomic Energy* (London, 1956)

Blunt, W.S., *My Diaries* (London edn., 1932)

Boelcke, W.A., ed., *The Secret Conferences of Dr Goebbels Oct. 1939–March 1943* (London, 1967?)

Bowers, C.G., *Beveridge and the Progressive Era* (New York, 1932)

Bowles, C., *Africa's Challenge to America* (Berkeley, 1956)

Bramstead, E.K., *Goebbels and National Socialist Propaganda 1925–1945* (Michigan State Univ., 1965)

Buchanan, J., *Sketches of the History, Manners, and Customs of the North American Indians* (London, 1824)

Buchanan, K., 'The Geography of Empire', in *The Spokesman* (Nottingham, December 1971–January 1972)

Burke, S.M., *Pakistan's Foreign Policy – An Historical Analysis* (London, 1972)

Burnham, J., *The Struggle for the World* (London, 1947)

Burroughs, E.R., *A Princess of Mars* (1912)

Burroughs, E.R., *Tarzan of the Apes* (1914)

Burroughs, E.R., *The Gods of Mars* (1919)

Burroughs, E.R., *The Warlord of Mars* (1920)

Burroughs, E.R., *The Moon Maid* (1923)

Burroughs, E.R., *The Moon Men* (1925)

Burton, D.H., *Theodore Roosevelt: Confident Imperialist* (Philadelphia, 1968)

Butwell, R., *Southeast Asia Today and Tomorrow* (2nd edn., London, 1969)

Cabral, A., *Revolution in Guinea – An African People's Struggle* (English edn., London, 1969)

Cady, J.F., *Foreign Intervention in the Rio de la Plata, 1835–1850* (Philadelphia, 1929)

Cairnes, J.E., *The Slave Power* (London, 1863)

Caldwell, M., ed., *Ten Years' Military Terror in Indonesia* (Nottingham, 1975)

Callcott, W.H., *The Caribbean Policy of the United States, 1890–1920* (New York, 1966)

Calvert, P., *The Mexican Revolution, 1910–1914 – The Diplomacy of Anglo-American Conflict* (Cambridge, 1968)

Campbell, P., *Chinese Coolie Emigration to Countries within the British Empire* (London, 1923)

Cather, T., *Journal of a Voyage to America in 1836* (London, 1955)

Chamberlain, S.E., *Recollections of a Rogue*, ed. R. Butterfield (London, 1957)

Chamberlin, J.E., *The Harrowing of Eden – White Attitudes towards Native Americans* (New York, 1975)

Chaudhri, M.A., *Pakistan and the Great Powers* (Karachi, 1970)

Chevalier, F., *L'Amérique Latine de l'indépendance à nos jours* (Paris, 1977)

Chevalier, M., *Society Manners and Politics in the United States* (1839; New York edn., 1966)

Chi, M., *China Diplomacy 1914–1918* (Harvard, 1970)

Child, R.W., *A Diplomat Looks at Europe* (New York, 1925)

Chips – The Diaries of Sir Henry Channon, ed. R.R. James (London, 1967)

Chomsky, N., *American Power and the New Mandarins* (London, 1968)

Chomsky, N., *Peace in the Middle East?* (1969; London edn., 1974)

Chopra, P., *India's Second Liberation* (Delhi, 1973)

Chronicles of the Pilgrim Fathers (Everyman edn., London, 1910)

Clay, The Papers of Henry, ed. J.F. Hopkins (Univ. of Kentucky Press, 1959)

Cleaver, E., *Soul on Ice* (1968; London edn., 1970)

Clinard, O.J., *Japan's Influence on American Naval Power 1897–1917* (Univ. of California, 1947).

Cline, H.F., *The United States and Mexico* (Harvard, 1953)

Clogg, R., and Yannopoulos, G., eds., *Greece under Military Rule* (London, 1972)

Collier, J., *The Indians of the Americas* (New York, 1947)

Collier, P., 'Salmon Fishing in America', in *Ramparts* (Berkeley, April 1971)

Colquhoun, A.R., *The Mastery of the Pacific* (London, 1902)

Commager, H.S., *Documents of American History* (3rd edn., New York, 1946)

Compton, J.V., *The Swastika and the Eagle* (London, 1968)

Conger, S.P., *Letters from China* (Chicago, 1909)

Conrad, J., *Nostromo* (1904)

Cooper, J.F., *The Pathfinder* (1840)

Corey, L., *The House of Morgan* (New York, 1930)

Corwin, A.F., *Spain and the Abolition of Slavery in Cuba 1817–1886* (Univ. of Texas, 1967)

Cosenza, M.E., ed., *The Complete Journal of Townsend Harris* (revised edn., Rutland, Vermont, 1959)

Cowan, E.D., *Josephus Daniels in Mexico* (Madison, 1960)

Craigie, Sir R., *Behind the Japanese Mask* (London, 1945)

Crow, C., *Harris of Japan* (London, 1939)

Crum, B.C., *Behind the Silken Curtain* (London, 1947)

Davies, C., *British Oil Policy in the Middle East 1919–1932* (Ph.D. thesis, Univ. of Edinburgh, 1973)

Davies, E., *American Labour – The Story of the American Trade Union Movement* (London, 1943)

Davis, H.B., *Nationalism and Socialism – Marxist and Labour Theories of Nationalism to 1917* (New York, 1967)

Dawson, W.H., *Richard Cobden and Foreign Policy* (London, 1926)

Degras, J., *The Communist International 1919–1943 – Documents* (London, 1956)

Deloria, V., *Custer Died for Your Sins – An Indian Manifesto* (London, 1969)

Dennett, T., *Americans in Eastern Asia* (New York, 1922)

Denny, H.N., *Dollars for Bullets – The Story of American Rule in Nicaragua* (New York, 1929)

De Novo, J.A., *American Interests and Policies in the Middle East 1900–1929* (Minneapolis, 1963)

Depew, C.M., *My Memories of Eighty Years* (New York, 1922)

Dermigny, L., *La Chine et l'Occident – Le commerce à Canton au XVIIIe siècle 1719–1833* (Paris, 1964)

Dictionary of American Biography

Dobyns, H.F. and Doughty, P.L., *Peru – A Cultural History* (New York, 1976)

Dodd, M.E. and M., eds, *Ambassador Dodd's Diary 1933–1938* (London, 1945)

Dowd, D.F., ed., *America's Role in the World Economy: The Challenge to Orthodoxy* (Boston, 1966)

Downey, F., *The Cruise of the Portsmouth, 1845–1847*, ed. H. Lamar (New Haven, 1963)

Dos Passos, J.R., *The Anglo-Saxon Century and the Unification of the English-Speaking People* (New York, 1903)

Doyle, C., *The Valley of Fear* (1915)

Drummond, D.F., *The Passing of American Neutrality 1937–1941* (Ann Arbor, 1955)

Dukes, P., *The Emergence of the Super-Powers* (London, 1970)

Dunn, J.P., *Massacres of the Mountains* (1886; London edn., 1963)

Easton, S.C., *World History since 1945* (San Francisco, 1968)

Edwards, O.D., 'The American Image of Ireland: a Study of its Early Phases', in *Perspectives in American History*, Vol. IV (1970)

Edwards, O.D., 'American Diplomats and Irish Coercion, 1880–1883', in *Journal of American Studies*, Vol. 1, No. 2.

Ellis, J., *The Social History of the Machine Gun* (London, 1975)

Emerson, R., *Africa and United States Policy* (Englewood Cliffs, 1967)

Estabrook, E.F., *Givers of Life – The American Indians as Contributors to Civilization* (Boston, 1931)

Ettinger, A.A., *The Mission to Spain of Pierre Soulé (1853–1855)* (Yale, 1932)

Evans, R.D., *A Sailor's Log* (New York, 1901)

Faramazyan, R.A., *USA: Militarism and the Economy* (1970; English edn., Moscow, 1974)

Fast, H., *The Last Frontier* (1948; Harmondsworth edn., 1953)

Fast, J., *Monopoly Capital and Empire: the Sugar Trust and American Imperialism, 1883–1909* (Ph.D. thesis, Univ. of London, 1976)

Feis, H., *The Road to Pearl Harbour* (Princeton, 1950)

Feis, H., *The China Tangle – The American Effort in China from Pearl Harbour to the Marshall Mission* (Princeton, 1953)

Ferguson, J.H., *American Diplomacy and the Boer War* (Philadelphia, 1939)

Ferns, H.S., *The Age of Mackenzie King* (London, 1955)

Ferns, H.S., *The Argentine Republic* (Newton Abbot, 1973)

Finer, S.E., *The Man on Horseback – The Role of the Military in Politics* (London, 1962)

Flint, C.R., *Memories of an Active Life* (New York, 1928)

Foner, P.S., *American Labor and the Indochina War* (New York, 1971)

Ford, W.C., ed., *Letters of Henry Adams (1858–1891)* (London, 1930)

Forrestal Diaries (The) – The Inner History of the Cold War, ed. W. Millis (London, 1952)

Foulke, W.D., *Slav or Saxon* (1887; 2nd edn., New York, 1899)

Franco Nogueira, *The United Nations and Portugal, a study of anti-colonialism* (English edn., London, 1963)

Fraser, T.G., *The Intrigues of the German Government and the Ghadr Party against British Rule in India, 1914–1918* (Ph.D., thesis, Univ. of London, 1974)

Freeman, J., *Herman Melville* (London, 1926)

Freidel, F., ed., *Union Pamphlets of the Civil War* (Harvard, 1967)

Fritz, H.E., *The Movement for Indian Assimilation, 1860–1890* (Philadelphia, 1963)

Fulbright, J.W., *Old Myths and New Realities* (1964; London edn., 1965)

Fulbright, J.W., *The Arrogance of Power* (1966; London edn., 1967)

Fuller, J.D.P., *The Movement for the Acquisition of all Mexico 1846–1848* (Baltimore, 1936)

Galbraith, J.K., *Ambassador's Journal – A Personal Account of the Kennedy Years* (London, 1969)

Gallagher, C.F., *The United States and North Africa – Morocco, Algeria, and Tunisia* (Harvard, 1963)

Ganoe, W.A., *The History of the United States Army* (revised edn., New York, 1943)

Gantenbein, J.W., *The Evolution of our Latin-American Policy – A Documentary Record* (New York, 1950)

Garland, A., *South American Conflicts and the United States* (Lima, 1900)

Garrett, B., 'The Dominoization of Thailand', in *Ramparts* (November 1970)

Gelber, H.G., *The Australian–American Alliance – Costs and Benefits* (Harmondsworth, 1968)

Gellhorn, M., *The Face of War, from Spain (1937) to Vietnam (1966)* (London, 1967)

Gheerbrant, A., *The Rebel Church in Latin America* (1969; trans. R. Sheed, Harmondsworth, 1974)

Gladwyn, Lord, *The European Idea* (revised edn., Harmondsworth, 1967)

Gooch, G.P., and Temperley, H., eds, *British Documents on the Origins of the War 1898–1914*, Vol. 1 (London, 1927)

Greenbie, S., *The Pacific Triangle* (London, 1921)

Greene, F., *A Curtain of Ignorance* (1964; London edn., 1965)

Greene, F., *The Enemy – Notes on Imperialism and Revolution* (London, 1970)

Grew, J.C., *Ten Years in Japan* (London, 1944)

Griffis, W.E., *Corea the Hermit Nation* (New York, 1882)

Griswold, A.W., *The Far Eastern Policy of the United States* (New York, 1938)

Haas, W.W., ed., *The American Empire – A Study of the Outlying Territories of the United States* (Chicago, 1940)

Hagan, W.T., *American Indians* (Chicago, 1961)

Hall, F., *Travels in Canada and the United States in 1816 and 1817* (London, 1818)

Hamilton, A., *Korea* (London, 1904)

Handlin, O., ed., *Readings in American History* (New York, 1957)

Hardy, J., *The First American Revolution* (London, 1937)

Hart, A.B., *The Monroe Doctrine* (Boston, 1916)

Hawthorne, N., *Passages from the American Notebooks (Collected Works, Vol. IX, London, 1883)*

Hayes, Diary and Letters of Rutherford Birchard, ed. C.R. Williams, Vol. III (Columbus, Ohio, 1924)

Hayter, T., *Aid as Imperialism* (London, 1971)

Heffner, R.D., *A Documentary History of the United States* (new edn., New York, 1965)

Heindel, R.H., *The American Impact on Great Britain 1898–1914* (Univ. of Pennsylvania, 1940)

Hendrick, B.J., *The Life and Letters of Walter H. Page* (1922–25; London, edn., 1930)

Henry, R.S., *The Story of the Mexican War* (new edn., New York, 1961)

Hofstadter, R., *Social Darwinism in American Thought* (revised edn., New York, 1955)

Hollon, W.E., *Frontier Violence – Another Look* (New York, 1974)

Holmes, O.W., *The Professor at the Breakfast-table* (1859)

Hoover, The Memoirs of Herbert (1951; London edn., 1952)

Hope, A.G., *America and Swaraj* (Washington, D.C., 1968)

Horowitz, D., *From Yalta to Vietnam – American Foreign Policy in the Cold War* (1965; London edn., 1967)

Horowitz, D., *Corporations and the Cold War* (New York, 1969)

Horsman, R., *Expansion and American Indian Policy 1783–1812* (Michigan Univ. Press, 1967)

Hull, The Memoirs of Cordell (London, 1948)

Huxley, A., *Beyond the Mexique Bay – A Traveller's Journal* (1934; London edn., 1950)

Hyman, H., ed., *Heard Round the World – The Impact Abroad of the Civil War* (New York, 1969)

Impact of the American Revolution Abroad, The (Library of Congress, Washington D.C., 1976)

Ireland, A., *The Far Eastern Tropics – Studies in the Administration of Tropical Dependencies* (London, 1905)

Iriye, Akira, *Across the Pacific – An Inner History of American–East Asian Relations* (New York, 1967)

Irving, W., *Astoria* (London, 1836)

Israel, J., *Progressivism and the Open Door – America and China, 1905–1921* (Pittsburg, 1971)

Jacobs, W.R., *Dispossessing the American Indian – Indians and Whites on the Colonial Frontier* (New York, 1972)

Jacoby, E.H., *Agrarian Unrest in Southeast Asia* (New York, 1949)

Janowitz, M., and Little, R., *Sociology and the Military Establishment* (revised edn., New York, 1965)

Jefferson, The Papers of Thomas, Vols. 8, 10 (Princeton, 1953–54)

Jeffreys-Jones, R., 'Violence in American History: Plug Uglies in the Progressive Era', in *Perspectives in American History*, Vol. VIII (1974)

Jeffreys-Jones, R., *American Espionage: from Secret Service to C.I.A.* (London, 1978)

Jernigan, T.R., *China's Business Methods and Policy* (Shanghai and London, 1904)

Johnson, W.F., *America's Foreign Relations* (New York, 1916)

Joseph, P., *Foreign Diplomacy in China* (London, 1928)

Josephy, A.M., *The Indian Heritage of America* (1968; Harmondsworth edn., 1975)

Kalicki, J.H., *The Pattern of Sino–American Crises ... in the 1950s* (Cambridge, 1950)

Kang, Y., *The Grass Roof* (New York, 1931)

Kawakami, K.K., *American–Japanese Relations* (New York, 1912)

Kelly, L.C., *The Navajo Indians and Federal Indian Policy 1900–1935* (Univ. of Arizona, 1968)

Kennan, G.F., *American Diplomacy 1900–1950* (1951; New York edn., 1952)

Kennan, G.F., *Soviet–American Relations, 1917–1920 – The Decision to Intervene* (London, 1958)

Kent, P.H., *Railway Enterprise in China* (London, 1907)

Kiernan, B.P., *The United States, Communism, and the Emergent World* (Bloomington, 1972)

Kiernan, V.G., *British Diplomacy in China 1880 to 1885* (1938; new edn., New York, 1970)

Kiernan, V.G., 'Foreign Interests in the War of the Pacific', in *Hispanic American Historical Review* (1955)

Kiernan, V.G., 'American Hegemony under Revision', in *The Socialist Register 1974*, ed. R. Miliband and J. Saville (London, 1974)

Kohn, H., *American Nationalism* (New York, 1957)

Kolko, G., *The Triumph of Conservatism – A Reinterpretation of American History, 1900–1916* (1963; Chicago edn., 1967)

Kolko, J. and G., *The Limits of Power – The World and United States Foreign Policy, 1945–1954* (New York, 1972)

Kulkarni, V.B., *India and Pakistan* (Bombay, 1973)

Lane-Poole, S., and Dickens, F. V., *The Life of Sir Harry Parkes* (London, 1894)

Lansing, R., *The Peace Negotiations, a Personal Narrative* (Boston, 1921)

Laqueur, W., *Confrontation – The Middle-East War and World Politics* (London, 1974)

Lasker, B., *Human Bondage in Southeast Asia* (Univ. of North Carolina, 1950)

Latane, J.H., *The Diplomatic Relations of the United States and Spanish America* (Baltimore, 1900)

Latane, J.H., *America as a World Power 1897–1907* (New York, 1907)

Latifi, D., *India and U.S. Aid* (Bombay, 1960)

Lattimore, O., *The Situation in Asia* (Boston, 1949)

Leopold, R.W. and Link, A.S., eds, *Problems of American History* (2nd edn., Englewood Cliffs, 1957)

Lewis, S., *Gideon Planish* (Cleveland, 1943)

Lichtheim, G., *Imperialism* (New York and London, 1971)

Liebknecht, K., *Militarism and Anti-Militarism* (1907; English edn., Cambridge, 1973)

Link, A.S. and Leary, W.M., eds, *The Diplomacy of World Power: the United States, 1889–1920* (London, 1970)

Lippmann, W., *U.S. Foreign Policy* (London, 1943)

Liska, G., *The New Statecraft – Foreign Aid in American Foreign Policy* (Chicago, 1960)

London, J., *The Iron Heel* (1907)

Lora, G., *A History of the Bolivian Labour Movement 1848–1971* (trans. C. Whitehead, Cambridge, 1977)

Lowe, P.C., 'Great Britain and the Outbreak of War with Japan, 1941', in *War and Society*, ed. M.R. Foot (London, 1973)

Lumer, H., *Zionism – Its Role in World Politics* (New York, 1973)

Macleod, W.C., *The American Indian Frontier* (London, 1928)

Magdoff, H., 'Problems of United States Capitalism', in *The Socialist Register 1965.*

Magdoff, H., *The Age of Imperialism – The Economics of U.S. Foreign Policy* (New York, 1969)

Mahan, A. T., *Lessons of the War with Spain* (1899; 2nd edn., London, 1899)

Maisky, L, *Spanish Notebooks* (trans. R. Kisch, London, 1966)

Malmesbury, Lord, *Memoirs of an ex-Minister* (Leipzig edn., 1885)

Martin, R.G., *Lady Randolph Churchill – A Biography 1854–1895* (London, 1969)

May, E., *American Imperialism – A Speculative Essay* (New York, 1968)

Mayer, A.J., *Politics and Diplomacy of Peacemaking – Containment and Counter-revolution at Versailles, 1918–1919* (1967; London edn., 1968)

McCoy, D.R., *Calvin Coolidge – The Quiet President* (New York, 1967)

McKay, V., *Africa and World Politics* (New York, 1963)

McLeod, J.D., *Slavery, Race and the American Revolution* (Cambridge, 1974)

Melville, H., *Whitejacket* (1850)

Melville, H., *Moby Dick* (1851)

Melville, T. and M., *Guatemala – Another Vietnam?* (Harmondsworth, 1971)

Miliband, R., *The State in Capitalist Society* (1969; London edn., 1973)

Miliband, R., 'The Coup in Chile', in *The Socialist Register 1973*.

Miller, D.H., *Custer's Fall – The Indian Side of the Story* (1957; London edn., 1965)

Miller, M., *Plain Speaking – An Oral Biography of Harry S. Truman* (1973; London edn., 1976)

Mills, C.W., *The Power Elite* (New York, 1959)

Misra, K.P., ed., *Studies in Indian Foreign Policy* (Delhi, 1969)

Moore, F., *With Japan's Leaders ... Fourteen Years as Counsellor to the Japanese Government* (London, 1943)

Morgan, L.H., *Ancient Society* (1877)

Morison, S.E., *'Old Bruin' – Commodore Matthew C. Perry 1794–1858* (London, 1968)

Motte, J.R., *Journey into Wilderness – An Army Surgeon's Account of ... the Creek and Seminole Wars 1836–1838*, ed. J.F. Sunderman (Univ. of Florida, 1953)

Munroe, D.G., *Intervention and Dollar Diplomacy in the Caribbean 1900–1921* (Princeton, 1964)

Nagai, Y. and Iriye, A., eds, *The Origins of the Cold War in Asia* (New York and Tokyo, 1977)

Nearing, S. and Freeman, J., *Dollar Diplomacy* (1925; New York edn., 1969)

Nelson, M.F., *Korea and the Old Orders in Eastern Asia* (Univ. of Louisiana, 1946)

Newton, Lord, *Lord Lyons – A Record of British Diplomacy* (London, 1913)

Nguyen Nghe, *Facing the Skyhawks* (Hanoi, 1964)

Nisbet, R., *Twilight of Authority* (London, 1976)

Nish, I.H., *Alliance in Decline – A Study in Anglo-Japanese Relations 1908–23* (London, 1972)

Noel-Baker, P.J., *The Arms Race* (New York, 1958)

Osgood, R.E., *Ideals and Self-Interest in America's Foreign Relations* (Chicago, 1953)

Palmer, I., *The New Rice in the Philippines* (Geneva, 1975)

Papers Relating to the Foreign Relations of the United States, 1915 (Washington D.C., 1924)

Patrick, M., 'Indian Urbanisation in Dallas', in *Oral History Review* (New York, 1973)

Patterson, J.T., *Mr. Republican, a biography of Robert A. Taft* (Boston, 1972)

Penn, W., *Description of Pennsylvania* (1683)

Pentagon Papers, The (New York Times edn., 1971)

Perkins, D., *The Monroe Doctrine 1866–1907* (Baltimore, 1937)

Perkins, D., *America's Quest for Peace* (Bloomington, 1963)

Perkins, J.B., *France in the American Revolution* (London, 1911)

Peterson, H.F., 'Edward A. Hopkins: a Pioneer Promoter in Paraguay', in *Hispanic American Historical Review* (1942)

Pike, F.B., *Chile and the United States 1880–1962* (Notre Dame, 1962)

Polk – The Diary of a President 1845–1849, ed. A. Nevin, (London, 1952)

Pomeroy, W.J., *American Neo-Colonialism* (New York, 1970)

Potter, W., *The War in Florida* (1836; Ann Arbor edn., 1966)

Pratt, Sir J., *War and Politics in China* (London, 1943)

Pratt, J.W., *Expansionists of 1812* (New York, 1949)

Pratt, J.W., *Expansionists of 1898; the acquisition of Hawaii and the Spanish islands* (1936; Gloucester, Mass., edn., 1959)

Prucha, F.P., *American Indian Policy in the Formative Years ... 1790–1834* (Harvard, 1962).

Purcell, V.W., *The Boxer Uprising* (Cambridge, 1963)

Putnam Weale, L., *The Truce in the East and its Afternath* (London, 1907)

Quartim, J., *Dictatorship and Armed Struggle in Brazil* (trans. D. Fernbach, London, 1971)

Reimann, G., *Patents for Hitler* (London, 1945)

Reinsch, P.S., *Colonial Administration* (New York, 1905)

Robinson, D.W., ed., *As Others See Us – International Views of American History* (Boston, 1969)

Robinson, H.L., 'The Downfall of the Dollar', in *The Socialist Register 1973*.

Roehm, M.C., *The Letters of George Catlin and his Family* (Berkeley, 1966)

Rolfe, F., *Hadrian the Seventh* (London, 1904)

Roosevelt, T., *An Autobiography* (1913; New York edn., 1946)

Roosevelt, T., *The Letters of Theodore Roosevelt*, ed. E.E. Morrison (Harvard, 1954), Vol. 8.

Roosevelt, T., *Selection from the Correspondence of Theodore Roosevelt and Henry Cabot Lodge 1884–1918* (New York, 1929)

Rosenthal, E., *Stars and Stripes in Africa* (London, 1938)

Rowland, J., *A History of Sino–Indian Relations: Hostile Co-existence* (Princeton, 1967)

Sachse, W.L., *The Colonial American in Britain* (Madison, 1956)

Sakolski, A.M., *The Great American Land Bubble* (New York, 1932)

Sands, W.F., *Undiplomatic Memories* (New York, 1930)

Sardesai, D.R., *Indian Foreign Policy in Cambodia, Laos, and Vietnam, 1947–1964* (Berkeley, 1968)

Savelle, M., *The Origins of American Diplomacy* (New York, 1967)

Schurz, C., *Speeches, Correspondence and Political Papers*, ed. F. Bancroft, Vol. V (New York, 1913)

Sears, L.M., *A History of American Foreign Relations* (3rd edn., London, 1936)

Seymour, C., ed., *The Intimate Papers of Colonel House* (London, 1926)

Shaplen, R., *Time Out of Hand – Revolution and Reaction in Southeast Asia* (London, 1969)

Sharma, B.L., *The Pakistan–China Axis* (London, 1968)

Sheridan, R.B., *The Filipino Martyrs* (London, 1900)

Shuster, W.M., *The Strangling of Persia* (London, 1912)

Shwadran, B., *The Middle East, Oil and the Great Powers* (New York, 1955)

Silen, J.A., *We, the Puerto Rican People – A Story of Oppression and Resistance* (trans. by C. Belsrage, New York, 1971)

Singletary, O.A., *The Mexican War* (Chicago, 1960)

Slezkin, L.Y., *Ispano-Amerikanskaya Voina 1898 goda* (Moscow, 1956)

Smith, A., *The Wealth of Nations* (1776)

Smith, D.M., *Aftermath of War – Bainbridge Colby and Wilsonian Diplomacy 1920– 1921* (Philadelphia, 1970)

Smith, R.F., *The United States and Cuba – Business and Diplomacy 1917–1960* (New York, 1960).

Smith, R.F., *What Happened in Cuba? A Documentary Survey* (New York, 1963)

Smith, S., *U.S. Neo-Colonialism in Africa* (Moscow, 1974)

Smith, S.R., *The Manchurian Crisis 1931–1932* (Cambridge, 1948)

Solomon, B.M., *Ancestors and Immigrants – A Changing New England Tradition* (New York, 1956)

Spence, J., *The China Helpers – Western Advisers in China 1620–1960* (London, 1969)

Sprout, H. and M., *The Rise of American Naval Power 1776–1918* (Princeton, 1946)

Stapledon, O., *Last and First Men* (London, 1937)

Stevenson, R.L., *Across the Plains, with other Memories and Essays* (London edn., 1913)

Stewart, W., *Henry Meiggs – Yankee Pizarro* (Duke Univ., 1946)

Stewart, W., *Chinese Bondage in Peru* (Duke Univ., 1951)

Stone, I.F., *The Haunted Fifties* (New York, 1963)

Stone, I.F., *In a Time of Torment* (London, edn., 1968)

Syed, A.H., *China and Pakistan* (Amherst, 1974)

Teng, S.Y., *The Taiping Rebellion and the Western Powers* (London, 1971)

Tengey, J.G.K., *The United States and the Russian Provisional Government ... (the Root Mission)* (M.Litt. thesis, Univ. of Aberdeen, 1969)

Thomson, C.A. and Laves, W.H.C., *Cultural Relations and U.S. Foreign Policy* (Bloomington, 1963)

Thorpe, W., *et al.*, eds, *American Issues*, Vol. 1, *The Social Record* (2nd edn., Chicago, 1944)

Tocqueville, A. de, *Democracy in America* (English edn., London, 1946)

Traina, R.P., *American Diplomacy and the Spanish Civil War* (Bloomington, 1968)

Treat, P.J., *Diplomatic Relations between the United States and Japan* (Stanford, 1932)

Trotsky, L., *Europe and America – Two Speeches on Imperialism* (New York edn., 1971)

Truman, H.S., *1946–1952 – Years of Trial and Hope* (1956; New York edn., 1965)

Tugwell, G., *The Stricken Land – The Story of Puerto Rico* (New York, 1947)

Tung, W.L., *China and the Foreign Powers* (New York, 1970)

Turner, *The Early Writings of Frederick Jackson*, ed. F. Mood (Univ. of Wisconsin, 1938)

Underhill, R.M., *Red Man's America – A History of Indians in the United States* (Chicago, 1953)

Uribe, V., *Yankee Imperialism in Spain* (New York, 1949)

Vagts, A., *A History of Militarism* (revised edn., London, 1959)

Varg, P.A., *Missionaries, Chinese, and Diplomats – The American Protestant Movement in China, 1890–1952* (Princeton, 1958)

Veblen, T., *Absentee Ownership and Business Enterprise in Recent Times – The Case of America* (1923; London edn., 1924)

Vevier, C., *The United States and China 1906–1913 – A Study of Finance and Diplomacy* (New Brunswick, 1955)

Wagenknecht, E., *Longfellow: a Full-length Portrait* (New York, 1955)

Ware, E.F., *The Indian War of 1864* (1911; New York edn., 1960)

Weinbaum, S.G., *A Martian Odyssey* (1934; London edn., 1977)

Weinberg, A., *John Elliot Cairnes and the American Civil War* (London, 1968)

Weinberg, A.K., *Manifest Destiny – A Study of Nationalist Expansionism in American History* (Gloucester, Mass., 1958)

Welles, S., *Seven Major Decisions* (London, 1951)

Wells, H.G., *The Autocracy of Mr. Parham* (London, 1930)

Weston, R.F., *Racism in U.S. Imperialism . . . 1893–1946* (Univ. of South Carolina, 1972)

White, J.M., *The Great American Desert* (1975; London edn., 1977)

Whitman, W., *Specimen Days in America* (revised edn., London, 1871)

Wilcox, C., *et al.*, *Economics of the World Today* (3rd edn., New York, 1976)

Wilcox, W., *The Emergence of Bangladesh – Problems and Opportunities of a Redefined American Policy in South Asia* (Washington, D.C., 1973)

Williams, W.A., *The Tragedy of American Diplomacy* (new edn., New York, 1962)

Williams, W.A., *The Roots of the Modern American Empire* (1969; London edn., 1970)

Wilmot, C., *The Struggle for Europe* (London, 1952)

Wilson, W., *A History of the American People* (New York, 1901–02)

Winslow, E.M., *The Pattern of Imperialism – A Study in the Theories of Power* (New York, 1948)

Wissler, C., *Indians of the United States – Four Centuries of their History and Culture* (New York, 1940)

Woddis, J., *Introduction to Neo-Colonialism* (London, 1967)

Yeselson, A., *United States–Persian Diplomatic Relations 1883–1921* (New Brunswick, 1956)

Young, J.R., *Around the World with General Grant* (New York, 1890)

Young, M.B., *The Rhetoric of Empire – American China Policy 1895–1901* (Harvard, 1968)

Zilliacus, K., *I Choose Peace* (London, 1949)

Index

9/11 (World Trade Center attack, 11 September 2001) *ix*, *xi*, *xii*, 368, 370, 371–2, 375, 376, 392

Abramovich, Roman 382
Abyssinia 185, 242 – *see also* Ethiopia
Acheson, Dean 274
Adams, Brooks 110–1
Adams, Henry 209
Adams, Jane 184
Adams, John Quincy 8, 11, 67
Afghanistan 32, 289, 365, 366–7, 368, 370, 371–2, 373, 379
A.F.L. (American Federation of Labour) 148, 160, 201–2, 225, 242, 340, 378
Africa 9, 18, 28, 32, 66, 87, 102, 111, 128, 135, 149, 173, 206, 212, 234, 249, 285, 286, 313–8, 320, 330, 341, 381, 393 – *see also* South Africa
African-Americans 60, 88–100, 111–2, 148–9, 155, 159, 235, 272, 341–2, 378, 380, 392
Aguinaldo, President 153
aid programmes 121, 288–90, 319–20, 300, 332, 346
al-Qaeda 368, 370
Al-Qureshi, Abu 'Ubeid 370
Alaska 75, 151, 343
Albright, Madeleine 392
Alexander I, Tsar 17
Algeciras Conference (1906) 184
Algeria 87, 102, 150, 159, 160, 161, 314, 316, 371
Allen, H.N. 179
Allen, Paul 382
Allende, Salvadore 328
Alliance for Progress 326

Althusser, Louis 299
Altman, Robert 390
America
  Central 11, 26, 58, 60–1, 111, 119, 121, 149, 160, 162–3, 165–76, 171, 179, 181, 205, 208, 222, 224–5, 228, 320, 324, 346
  Latin 12, 32, 75–6, 77, 100, 117–22, 126, 158, 162–3, 166, 221, 224–7, 241, 243, 272, 289, 319–332, 335, 337, 339, 343–4, 345–6, 381
  North – see Canada; United States
  South 11, 60, 111, 119–122, 171, 184, 222, 224, 241, 250–1, 287, 336
  – see also individual countries
American Indian Association 342–3
American Revolution (1776) xi, 33, 37, 60
Amerindians – see Native Americans
Amnesty International 322, 330
Anderson, Eugene 385
Anderson, Perry 387
Angell, Norman 133, 185, 222, 223
Anglo-French partnership 73, 187, 197
Anglo-Japanese alliance 198, 217, 219
Anglo-Saxonism 12, 77, 111, 129–30, 185, 212, 215, 219, 229–30, 274, 346
Angola 159, 315–6, 317–8, 365, 371, 373

Anti-Imperialist League 132
anti-Semitism 245
Apache 79, 85, 98
Arabia 206, 272, 273
Arbenz, J. 321
Argentina 83, 111, 171, 241, 251, 325, 328, 329, 330, 335, 346
Arizona 85
armaments 112, 132, 181, 217, 241, 243–5, 268, 273, 290–2, 310, 326, 345, 376
Armas, Castillo 321
Armenia 206
arms spending/trade – see armaments
Army, U.S. 9, 10, 16, 25–6, 28, 35, 40, 74–5, 98, 105, 109, 154, 181–3, 217, 244, 266, 270, 292, 299, 341–2, 364, 377
Army Bill (1813) 9–10
Ashburton-Webster Treaty (1842) 20
Asia 10, 17, 28, 30, 38, 60, 61–2, 65–7, 75, 102, 121, 123–6, 135, 150, 158, 166, 177, 186, 205, 230, 251, 285, 292, 295–6, 300, 303, 320, 338
Astor, John Jacob 8, 18
Atatürk – see Kemal, Ghazi Mustapha
atom-bomb 266, 269–70
Attlee, Clement 285
Attwood, W. 317
Australia 7, 83, 184, 273, 280–1, 303
Austria 63
Avrakotos, Gust 367
Ayub Khan, General 305–6

Aztec 25
Azzam, Abdullah 367–8

Baden-Powell, R. 135
Baghdad Pact (1955) 280
Bailey, T.A. 337
Baldwin, Alec 390
balkanization 207
Ball, George 369
Balmaceda, J. 121
Bancroft, George 23, 50
Bandar, Prince 368
Bandung Conference (1955) 285
Banzer, Hugo 328, 329
Barbados 5
Baring 36
Baruch Plan 269
Batista, Fulgencio 241, 322
Bebchuk, Lucian 382
beef 171
Beer, G.L. 206
Beirut 115
Belden, Jack 277
Belgium 315
Bell Commission 284
Bellamy, Edward 109, 149, 184
Bengal 36, 307
Beresford, Admiral Lord Charles 125
Berle, A.A. 257
Bermuda 220
Bernhardi, General von 199
Bernstein, Eduard 110
Beveridge, Senator A.J. 13, 108,
    110–1, 129–30, 135, 150, 158,
    160

Bevin, Ernest 285
Bhagwan Singh 229
Bhutto, Z.A. 306
Bingham, John Armor 124
Bismarck, Otto von 186–8
Black Americans – *see* African-
    Americans
Black, Conrad 382–3
Black, Eugene R. 287, 338
Blaine, State Secretary J.G. 105, 119,
    120–2, 171
Blunt, Wilfrid Scawen 134, 155, 198
Bocock, T.S. 61
Bodine, Barbara 370
Boer Wars (1880–1; 1899–1902)
    133–6
Bogra, Mohamed Ali 305
Bolivia 120, 241, 326–7, 328–9
Borah, Senator W.E. 204, 225
Bosch, Juan 322–3
Bourboulon, Alphonse de 69
Bowles, Chester 314
Bowring, Sir John 67
Boxer Rebellion 114, 151, 178, 186,
    276
Braden, Spruille 320–1
brain drain 272
Brazil 121, 167, 251, 303, 325, 327,
    328–9, 330, 335, 336, 346
Bremen, Michael 382
Bright, John 105
Britain 9, 10–1, 21–3, 25, 32, 35,
    58, 64, 66, 68–9, 71, 72, 73, 75–
    7, 110, 119, 120, 124, 125, 127–
    30, 134–5, 162–3, 166, 169,

174, 177, 178, 184, 186, 187, 197–200, 217–20, 221, 228–9, 243, 245, 273–4, 280, 286, 296, 309, 334, 339
British Empire 5, 6, 11, 17, 18, 66, 197, 199, 251, 367
Brooke, Rupert 132
Brookings Institute 281
Browder, Earl 349
Brown, George 73
Brownson, Orestes August 60
Bryan, W.J. 131, 159, 162, 172, 173, 185, 201
Brzezinski, Zbigniew *xii*, 363, 364, 366–7
Buchanan, President James 23, 61, 64
Buffalo Bill – *see* Cody, W.F.
Bukharin, Nikolai 219
Burgevine, Henry A. 70
Burlingame Treaty (1868) 76
Burlingame, Anson 123
Burma 67, 87, 128, 286
Burnham, James 266, 320
Burr, Aaron 221
Burroughs, Edgar Rice 211–5
Bush, George W. 370, 376, 380, 384, 387–8
Bush Senior, George H.W. 370, 375, 389–90, 391–2
Business Roundtable 378
Busoni, Ferruccio 103
Butler, Major General Smedley D. 172

Cabral, Amilcar 316

caciquismo 156, 169–70
Cairnes, J.E. 72, 173
California 20, 22–3, 25, 26, 57–8, 59, 79, 100
Cambodia 299, 365, 373
Canada 6, 7, 8, 9–11, 19–20, 22, 32, 36, 37, 72–3, 74, 77, 107, 112, 127, 149, 198, 228, 272, 273
Canning, G. 17
Cape Verde 365
capitalism *xiii*, 5, 15–6, 110, 115, 117–8, 120, 125, 131, 147–8, 150, 157, 173, 180–1, 206, 223, 232, 244, 248, 251, 267, 271–2, 277, 288, 289–90, 329, 347, 348–9, 374
Cardenas, President L. 242
Caribbean 58–9, 61, 66, 70, 77, 117, 120, 130, 167, 168, 170, 173, 177, 182, 223–4, 225, 245, 322, 330, 381
Carlyle, Thomas 129
Carnegie, A. 127, 183, 227
Caroe, Sir Olaf 305
Carranza, V. 175
Carter, President Jimmy 343, 346, 364, 366, 372, 378–9, 386, 391
Cass, L. 70
Castro, Fidel 297, 322
Catholicism 15–6, 88, 100, 113–4, 166, 175, 243, 269, 279, 298, 304, 330–1, 347
Catlin, George 82
CENTO (Central Treaty Organization) 280, 305

Central America – *see* America, Central

Ceylon 286

Chafee, General 151

Chamberlain, Joseph 134

Chamberlain, Neville 245

Chamorro, P.J. 324

Chechnya 370

Cheney, Richard 386

Cherokee 21, 40–1, 103

Chester, Admiral 177

Chevalier, M. 19

Chevron Oil 371

Cheyenne 86, 87

Chiang Kai-shek 231, 251, 276, 295

Chickasaw 35

Chief Joseph 35

Child, R.W. 220, 221

Chile 74, 105–6, 119–21, 166, 251, 325, 327, 328, 330, 341, 345

China 6, 18, 22, 65, 65, 68–70, 68–70, 73, 76, 88, 110, 111, 114–5, 123–5, 124–5, 131, 134, 135, 151, 153, 161, 166, 169, 178–81, 182, 186, 200, 203, 230–1, 246–7, 248, 251, 266, 276–7, 291, 292, 295, 306–7, 310, 335, 336, 388

Chinook 98

Choctaw 103

Chomsky, Noam 339, 348

Church, Senator 338

Churchill, Randolph 128, 129

Churchill, Winston 181, 229–30, 244, 248, 249, 251, 280, 285

C.I.A. (Central Intelligence Agency) 109, 268–9, 301–2, 304, 316, 318, 321, 322, 327–8, 330, 331–2, 344, 345, 346, 366–8

cinema 234, 385

C.I.O. (Congress of Industrial Organizations) 242, 340, 378

Civil War (1861–5) 17, 59, 71–88
  Native Americans and 79–82
  slavery and 72

Clark, Jim 382

Clarke, Sir Andrew 228–9

Clay, Henry 9–10, 11

Clayton-Bulwer Agreement (1850) 58

Cleaver, Eldridge 337

Cleveland 119, 130

Clinton, (Bill) William Jefferson 376, 381, 382, 386–7, 392

Cobbett, William 36

Cobden, Richard 11

Cody, W.F. (Buffalo Bill) 98–9, 128–9, 210

Cohen, Eliot 389

Cold War (1945–89) *viii–ix, xii*, 266, 270, 273–9, 286, 292, 305, 320, 345, 372–5, 376

Coleridge, Samuel Taylor 344

Collier, John 237

Colombia 171, 330

Comanche 79, 86

comics 234–5, 337

Common Market (European Economic Community) 160, 335

Communist Party *vii–viii*

Condon, Richard 374

Confederates 72, 74, 80, 173

Conger, Mrs Sarah 151, 178, 180

Congo 314–6 – *see also* Zaire

Conrad, Joseph 163, 287

conscription 22, 182, 201

Contras 371

Cook, Lodwrick 387

Coolidge, Calvin 226, 231

Cooper, Fenimore 37, 97, 98

copper 313

Costa Rica 58, 171

cotton 20, 59, 223

Cowdray, Lord 171

Cowie, Jefferson 378–9

Crimean War (1853–6) 61, 64–5

Cromwell, Oliver 31, 209

Crowder, General E. 224

Crusades 367

Cuba 12, 58–61, 63–4, 75–7, 112,
    113, 117–8, 130–2, 135, 150,
    160–2, 165–6, 169–71, 175,
    187, 223, 224, 240–1, 267, 297,
    318, 322, 335, 337–8, 371

Curzon, Lord 198

Cushing, Caleb 68

Custer, General G.A. 54, 86–7, 99

Cyprus 272, 332

Dakota 84

Dallas, Vice-President G.M. 12

Daniels, Josephus 242

Davis, Jefferson 39

Dawes Act (1887) 103, 236

De Gaulle, Charles 274

Dean, Howard 380

death squads 321–2 – *see also* Contras

Debs, Eugene 147, 173–4, 201–2

debt cancellation 288

Decter, Midge 390–1

Democrat Party *xiii*, 20, 58, 60, 64,
    84, 119, 125, 173, 376, 380–1,
    382, 387, 390

Denby, Charles 125

Denmark 168, 173

Derby, Elias 6

Desai, Morarji 304

Dewey, Admiral G. 131

Diaz, Porfirio 170, 173–4

Diem, Ngo Dinh – *see* Ngo Dinh
    Diem

Disney, Walt 347

Disraeli, Benjamin 76

Dodd, W.E. 242

Dollar Diplomacy 20–1, 75, 169,
    173, 201, 210, 226

Dominican Republic 225, 240, 303,
    322–3, 340, 345

domino theory 330

Dower, John 384

Doyle, Conan 136

Dukakis, Michael 375, 389

Dulles, John Foster 242, 279–80,
    296, 303, 310–1, 319–1, 320–1

Duncan, James H. 202

Dunlop, John 379

Dunn, J.P. 38, 84–5, 102, 303

East India Company 18

East Timor 303

ecology 387
Ecuador 120, 171
Eden, Sir Anthony 321
Edib, Halid 205
E.E.C. – see Common Market
Egypt 198, 206, 310, 314, 369, 371
Eisenhower, President D. 270–1, 279, 295–6, 337
Eisenhower Doctrine 311, 314
Elgin, Lord 69
Eliot, George 107
Ellison, Larry 382
Encounter 347
Engels, Friedrich 107, 108
England – see Britain
Eritrea 317
Estrada Cabrera, Manuel 170
Ethiopia 317, 365 – see also Abyssinia
Europe 4, 6, 12, 17, 24, 34, 38, 61–2, 65–6, 105, 134, 149, 151, 184, 207, 218, 220–1, 265, 272, 329
European Economic Community – see Common Market
Evarts, Secretary W.M. 121, 129
expansionism x, 12, 15–6, 20, 25, 57–8, 60, 76, 108, 114–5, 149–50, 157, 278–9
exports 107–8, 178, 218
Exxon 345

Fabians 185
fascism 110, 112, 175, 186, 221–2, 227, 241, 243, 247
fatwa 370

Faulkner, William 54
F.B.I. (Federal Bureau of Investigation) 344
Federalist Party 6
Fiji 18
Finland 303
Fiske, John 129
Flash Gordon 266
Flint, C.R. 121
Florida 9, 11, 21, 22, 37, 40, 132
Ford, Patrick 127
Ford, President Gerry 313, 328, 344, 370, 386
forests 106, 157
Formosa 57, 67 – see also Taiwan
Forrestal, J.V. 210, 267, 286, 312, 346
France 5, 9, 17, 23, 25, 32, 64, 68–9, 72–4, 120, 122, 124, 150, 154, 178, 179, 186, 194, 199, 217, 224, 243, 245, 250, 273, 286, 295, 296, 314, 316, 344, 386, 393
Francis, David R. 202
Franco, General Francisco 249, 279, 325
Franklin, Benjamin 4, 5
Fraser, Douglas 379–80
Fried, Jesse 382
Friedman, Milton 383
Friedman, Thomas 364, 383
Frelinghuysen, F.T. 118
French Revolution (1789) 150, 333
Fukuyama, Francis xii
Fulbright, Senator J.W. 337–8

fur 6, 8, 18, 31–2, 38

Galbraith, J.K. 233, 267, 297, 304–5
Gandhi, Mahatma 229
Gates, Robert 366
Gellhorn, Martha 339
General Allotment Act (1887) – *see*
    Dawes Act
General Electric 377
Genoa conference (1922) 220
George V, King 34
Georgia 34, 36, 40
Germany 6, 19, 88, 113, 115, 122,
    127, 133–4, 153, 158, 167–8,
    177, 178, 182, 184, 185, 186–8,
    197, 200–1, 205, 218, 222, 248,
    249, 273, 280, 316, 384
Geronimo 87
Ghana 317
Gissing, George 39
Gladstone, William Ewart 7
Goebbels, Josef 249
gold rush 57, 79–80
Gompers, Samuel 160, 201–2
Gorbachev, Mikhail 373
Gore, Al 389
Gorky, Maxim 204
Goulart, President 327
Gramsci, Antonio 148, 339
Grant, President Ulysses S. 75, 82,
    123
Great Britain – *see* Britain
Greece 62, 112, 205, 268, 274–5,
    277, 280, 331–2
Greenland 168

Grenada 365
Grew, J.C. 246–8, 232, 251
Griffith, D.W. 235
Griswold, A.W. 246
Guam 132
Guarani 119
Guatemala *xii*, 170–1, 225, 320–2
Guiana 121–2
Guinea 316, 365

Hadar, Leon 370
Haiti 173, 225–6, 240, 324, 330,
    345
Halliday, Fred 364
Hamilton, Alexander 4–5
Hamilton, Lord G. 136
Harlan, Josiah 70
Harris, Frank 84
Harris, Townsend 67
Harrison, Governor W.H. 35
Harte, Bret 50, 76
Havemeyer, Henry 118
Hawaii 18, 58, 60, 105, 114, 118–9,
    127, 130, 131, 132, 134, 158,
    246
Hawthorne, Nathaniel 49–50, 51, 54
Hay, John 111, 129, 135, 151, 162
Hay-Pauncefote Agreement (1904)
    197
Hayes, Pres R.B. 117
Heber, Bishop 5
Hemingway, Ernest 236
hemp 161
Herbert, Sir Michael 167
Hersh, Seymour 337

Herter, C.A. 335
Higginson, T.W. 132
Hiroshima 269
Hitler, Adolf 186, 245, 249
Ho Chi Minh 154, 295
Hoar, Senator 274
Hobson, J.A. 271
Hodges, General 286
Holden, Roberto 316
Holland 4, 6, 30, 250, 273, 286
Holmes, Oliver Wendell 50
Homestead Act (1863) 81
Honduras 168–9, 220
Hoover, Herbert 204, 220, 221, 223,
    226, 231, 233, 238
Hopkins, E.A. 119
Hopkins, Harry 385
House, E.N. 186–7, 198, 228
Houston, Sam 21, 22–3
Huerta, V. 174
Hukbalahap 284
Hull, Cordell 240, 241, 243, 249,
    251
Hume, Edward 231
Hung Jen-kan 69
Hungary 65
Huntington, Samuel P. 374, 378
Hussein, Sadam 368, 369, 392
Huxley, Aldous 225

Ickes, H.L. 237
Illinois 39
immigration 34, 76, 108, 112, 128,
    148, 159–60, 182, 202, 208,
    218–9, 230, 266

imprisonment 380–1
India *viii*, 5, 6, 13, 17, 18, 20, 23,
    33, 38, 58, 70, 101, 102, 127–8,
    149, 228–9, 230, 239, 250, 272,
    276, 286, 288, 302, 303–7, 338
Indian Defence Association 102
Indian National Congress 250
Indian Reorganization Act (1934)
    237
Indian Rights Association 85
Indochina 161, 248, 295–6, 342
Indonesia 161, 228, 250, 285–6,
    291, 301–3, 345
industrial revolution 4
International Brigade 243
International Monetary Fund (I.M.F.)
    383
International Workingmen's
    Association 73, 77 – *see also* Third
    International
investments abroad (U.S.) 75, 120,
    149, 165–6, 170–1, 174, 180–1,
    207, 218, 222, 226, 227, 271–3,
    283, 289–90, 319, 322, 329, 345
Iran 280, 303, 309, 345, 365, 366,
    369, 370, 371, 372, 391–2 – *see
    also* Persia
Iraq *x*, *xiii*, 206, 227, 280, 368, 369–
    70, 372, 384–7, 388, 392
Ireland/Irish 5, 15, 30, 31, 108, 127–
    8, 157, 205, 229
Ireland, Alleyne 149, 157
Iroquois 31–2, 371
Irving, Washington 50

I.S.I. (Inter Services Intelligence) 367, 368

Islam *xi*, 205, 302, 305, 313, 366–8, 371

Israel 272, 311–3, 369, 370–1, 389, 392

Italy 59, 63, 66, 221–2, 344

Jackson, President Andrew 10, 16, 21, 36–7, 39, 40, 51

Jackson, Helen 85, 102

James, Henry 210, 278

Japan 65, 66–8, 73, 76, 105, 121, 123–4, 135, 151, 153, 162, 178–80, 182, 183, 184–6, 198, 199–200, 203, 217, 223, 230, 231–2, 246–8, 272, 273, 283, 286, 295, 300, 303, 329, 335, 384

Jay Treaty (1794) 6

Jay, John 33

jazz 234

Jefferson, Thomas 7, 8, 9, 19, 21, 33, 34, 35, 333

Jerome, Leonard 128

jihad 367, 371–2, 379

Johnson, Paul 393

Johnson, President Lyndon B. 287, 297–8, 301, 323, 334, 338, 340

Jones Act (1916) 223

Juarez, B. 73, 82

Kashmir 306

Kautsky, Karl 187, 272, 349, 384

Kellogg, F.B. 225

Kemal, Ghazi Mustapha (Atatürk) 205

Kennan, G.F. 172, 203, 232, 266, 278, 289

Kennedy, J.F. 279, 296–7, 304, 337

Kennedy, Joseph 245

Kentner, W. 301

Kepel, Gilles 371

Kerry, John 380, 389

Keynes, John Maynard 383

Kiernan, B.P. 338

Kiernan, Victor *vii–ix, xi*

Kim Il-Sung 292

King Philip 31

King, Admiral 268

King, Mackenzie 107, 228

King, Martin Luther 342

Kipling, Rudyard 136, 210, 212

Kirkpatrick, Jeane 373

Kissinger, Henry *xii*, 307, 313, 334, 335–6, 337, 383–4, 391

Knox, Henry 33

Knox, Frank (W.F.) 245, 324

Knox, P.C. 180

Kohn, H. 54

Korea 29, 124–5, 154, 179, 230, 266, 274, 286, 291–3, 295, 296, 301, 334, 341, 342, 345, 376, 383

Kossuth, L. 63, 65

Kristol, Irving 374–5

Kristol, William 386

Krushchev, Nikita 297

Kuomintang 230–1, 276–7, 287

Kuwait 368, 369–70

labour movement 201–2, 222, 285, 339–40, 348–9 – *see also* strikes
Laden, Osama bin 367–9, 370, 371–2, 392
Lafollette, R.M. 204
Laird, Melvin 369
Lansing, R. 201, 203, 206, 207
Laos 297, 365
Latin America – *see* America, Latin
Latinos 374, 377, 378, 380
Lattimore, Owen 154, 275, 277
Lausanne conference (1923) 220
Lawrence, D.H. 220
Layard, Austen Henry 117, 122, 206–9, 228, 240
League of Nations 122, 206–9, 228, 240, 280
Lebanon 115, 311, 314
Ledeen, Michael 389
Leeward Islands 6
Lenin, Vladimir Ilych 203, 204, 219, 222, 271, 273, 346, 349, 372, 384
Leopold II (Belgium) 212
Lesseps, F. de 117
Lewis, Sinclair 229, 243, 339
Liberia 173, 314
liberalism 374–5
Libya 313
Lichtheim, G. 338
Liebknecht, Karl 109
Liliokalani, Queen 119
Lincoln, Abraham 39, 73
Lincoln, Robert A. 393
Linlithgow, Lord 250

Lippmann, Walter 218, 244, 393
Livingstone, Charles 113
Lloyd George, D. 206
lobby system 16, 268, 277, 343–5
Lockheed Aircraft 270
Lodge, Henry 297
Lodge, Henry Cabot 111, 127, 147, 160, 168, 207, 212
Lodge, J.D. 336–7
London, Jack 109, 149
Longfellow, H.W. 51, 55, 63, 82
Lopez, C.A. 119
Louisiana 7, 9, 35, 63, 118
Lowell, J.R. 50
Loyalists 5
Lumumba, Patrice 315
Luxemburg, Rosa 336
lynching 100, 155–6, 235
Lyons, Lord 71, 72, 74

Macabebe 155
MacArthur, General Douglas 269–70, 292
Macdonald, Ramsey 220
Machado, G. 240–1
Macmillan, Harold 272
MacPhail, N.P. 225
Mahan, Captain T. 106, 111, 129, 130, 133, 156–7, 158, 166, 167, 184, 185, 197, 201
Malaya 286
Malmesbury, Lord 20
Mamdani, Mahmood 367
Manchuria 180, 198, 231–2, 246
Mao Tse-tung 276, 307

Marcantonio, Vito 275
Marcos, President F.E. 284, 336
Marcy, W.L. 64, 67
Marlowe, Lara 370
Mars 212–5, 235
Marshall Plan 275–6, 279, 285, 287
Martin, W.A.P. 69
Marx, Karl *vii–ix*, 57, 63, 73, 77, 336
Mason, J.Y. 63, 64
Mathews, Brigadier General George 9
Matsuoka, Y. 247–8
Matthews, Chris 387
Maximilian, Emperor 74, 82
Maya *xii*
Mayo, Katherine 229
Mazzini, G. 63
McCarthy, Senator Joseph 275, 278, 337
McCloy, John 385
McGraw III, Harold 381
McKay, Donald 38
McKinley, W. 130–1, 147, 151, 153
McNamara, R. 299
McNaughton, J.T. 299
Mediterranean 7, 18, 62–3, 84,
Meiggs, H. 119–20
Melville, Herman 49, 51–4, 60, 65, 222
Mencken, H.L. 373–4
Meriam Report (1928) 236
metals 334
Mexico *xi*, 9, 11, 12, 20, 21–7, 58, 59, 60, 63, 66, 68, 72–3, 74, 75, 76, 73, 79, 82, 111, 120, 151, 161, 170–1, 173–6, 182, 184,

186, 199, 201, 203, 222, 224, 225–6, 236, 241–2, 243, 251, 265–6, 272, 329, 344
Microsoft 382
militarism 133, 182–3, 188, 290
military-industrial complex 269–71, 339–40
Miller, Henry 390
Mine Owners' Association 147
missionaries 18, 38, 88, 100, 102, 113–5, 128, 178–9, 234, 314, 344
Missouri 21
Mitchell, General 81
Mobutu, J. 315, 316
Modoc 82
Mohican 37
Monroe, President J. 5, 9, 10–1, 17, 39, 62
Monroe Doctrine 11, 118, 120, 168, 169, 171, 226, 323
Montana 84
Moore, Michael 386
Moral Rearmament 279
Morgan, J.P. 120, 128, 147–8, 181, 221
Morgan, L.H. 31, 37–8
Mormon 79
Morocco 161, 184, 314
Morse, General W.L. 298
Mosaddeq, Mohamed 309
Motley, J.L. 50, 390
Mozambique 159, 317, 365
multiculturalism 374
multinationals 273, 335

Mulvaney, John 54, 86
Mussolini, Benito 221–2
My Lai 337
Myrdal, Gunnar 288

N.A.F.T.A. (North American Free Trade Agreement) 381–2
Namibia 319
napalm 296, 348
Napoleon I 7, 9
Napoleon III 73–4, 82
Narraganset 31
Nasser, Gamal Abdel 310, 314
National Defence Act (1920) 217
National Guard 109, 377
National Security Act (1947) 269
Native Americans 15, 21, 24, 28–41, 72, 79–88, 97–104, 111, 135, 159, 236–7, 341, 342–3
    cinema and 235–6
    Civil War and 79–82
N.A.T.O. (North Atlantic Treaty Organization) 279, 280, 316, 332, 344
Navajo 81, 99, 236, 342
Navy, U.S. xi, 11, 17–8, 24, 25, 60–1, 75, 106, 121, 151, 153, 183–4, 198, 200, 217, 219, 230, 246, 267, 281, 364
Nazism 233, 242, 273, 274, 279, 385
Negroes – see African-Americans
Nelson, Admiral Horatio 6
Neutrality Act (1934) 242

New England 6, 10, 19, 25, 65, 83, 130
New York 6, 19, 25, 37, 108
New Zealand 228
Nez Perce 87
Ngo Dinh Diem 296, 297, 346
Nicaragua 58, 117–8, 151, 170, 173, 225–6, 231, 323–4, 330–1, 345, 365, 371, 373
Nicholas I, Tsar 53, 222
Nixon, President Richard 270, 295, 299–300, 301, 307, 320, 344, 365–6, 369, 377, 378, 386
Nkrumah, Kwame 317
Nomura, Admiral K. 247–8
North Carolina 25
nuclear power 335
nuclear weapons 269–70 – see also atom-bomb
Nye, Joseph 364

Ochterlony, Sir David 5
O.E.C.D. (Organization for Economic Co-operation and Development) 391
Ohio 34
oil 171, 175, 177, 206, 223, 227, 236, 242, 249–50, 300, 301, 309–10, 312, 313, 334, 384, 388
Oklahoma 40–1, 81, 86, 103, 105, 106
Olney, Secretary R. 127
O'Neill, John 370

Open Door policy 151, 161–2, 179, 184, 186, 200, 219, 227, 230, 285
Opium Wars (1839–42; 1856–60) 18, 68–70, 292
Oracle 382
Oregon 19, 20, 22, 23, 38, 58, 62, 75, 80, 82, 83, 87, 88
Ostend Conference (1854) 64
O'Sullivan, J.L. 20, 63
over-consumption 387
over-production 348
Overseas Development Corporation 290

Pacific Ocean 19, 20, 23, 27, 58, 67, 75, 120, 200
Page, W.H. 175–6, 186–7, 198–9, 228
Pak Chung Hee – *see* Park, President
Pakistan *viii*, 272, 280, 302, 303, 305–7, 338, 367
Palestine 206, 311
Palmerston, Lord 23, 73, 77
Panama 23, 117–9, 127, 167, 168, 197, 328, 329, 343
Panama Congress (1826) 60
Pan-American Congress (1889) 122
Pan-American Congress (1933) 241
Pan-American Congress (1942) 251
Paraguay 119, 241
Paramount 385
Park, President (Pak Chung Hee) 301, 345
Parker, Peter 68–9, 114

Parkes, Sir Harry 124
Parkman, Francis 98
Pasha, Kemal 205
Paul VI, Pope 330
Peacock, Thomas 333
Pearl Harbour 248–9
Pearson, Charles 110
Penn, William 29–30, 79
Pennsylvania 6
Pequod 31
Peron, Juan 325
Perry, Commodore M.C. 25, 26, 64–7, 77
Pershing, General J.J. 175, 226
Persia 177, 187, 225, 227, 246 – *see also* Iran
Peru 65, 105, 111, 119–20, 226, 319–20, 325, 326, 327, 328
Philippines 22, 131–2, 151, 153–63, 166, 171, 172, 175, 187, 205, 222–4, 228–9, 246, 274, 283–4, 289–90, 291, 336, 345, 348
Philippines Independence Act (1934) 239
Phillips, William 250
Pibul Songgram 290
Piegan 101
Pierce, President F. 58, 61, 64
Pilgrim Fathers 30, 371
Pinkerton detectives 109, 147
Pinochet, Augusto 345
Pipes, Richard 372–3
plantocracy 5–6, 60, 76, 118–9
Platt Amendment 165

P.N.A.C. (Project for a New American Century) 375, 389
Podhoretz, Norman 365, 375
Poe, Edgar Allan 54
Poland 64, 245, 274, 345
Polk, President J.K. 16, 21, 23–7, 58
Pontiac 32, 35
popular culture 347
Portugal 17, 221, 279, 285, 315–6, 317, 244
Pratt, Sir John 276, 292
pre-emptive strikes 35
press 20
Priest, Dana 393
Priestley, Joseph 4
privatization 106, 157
Progressivism 147–9, 172, 181, 222, 347
property relations 38, 102–3
prostitution 100, 101, 300
Protestantism 5, 15–6, 113–4, 347
Pueblo 79
Puerto Rico 132, 154, 159, 168, 230, 237–8, 239–40, 285, 342
puritanism 278

Quaker 29–30, 65, 82, 85, 105

racism 29–30, 37, 38–9, 65, 82, 85, 110, 111–2, 135, 150–1, 155–6, 159–60, 172, 185, 187, 198, 199–200, 211–2, 219, 272 – *see also* Anglo-Saxonism; anti-Semitism

railways 73, 75–6, 77, 84, 120, 123, 125, 177, 201
rape 26, 80
Rashid, Ahmed 368
Reagan, Ronald 366–7, 369, 371, 372, 373, 375, 376, 379, 387
reconstruction 84
Red Indians – *see* Native Americans
Reed, W.B. 69
Reinsch 200
Reinsch, P.S. 150, 159, 200
religion 12, 15–6, 114–5, 278–9
Removal Bill (1830) 113
Republican Party *xiii*, 7, 118, 130, 173, 199, 233, 245, 275, 277, 376, 380, 381, 386, 387, 389
Revel, Jean-François 373
Rhodes, Cecil 36
Rhodesia 313, 318
Ridgeway, General 296
riots 109, 121, 231
Rivera, Primo de 221
Robeson, Paul 341
Rockefeller, J.D. 109–10, 125, 378
Rockefeller, J.D. Jr. 228
Rolfe, F. 185–6
Romero, Archbishop Oscar 331
Romero, Carlos Humberto 331
Roosevelt, Franklin Delano 233, 237, 240–1, 243–5, 246, 248–51, 269, 278, 279, 283, 291, 385
Roosevelt, Theodore 5, 87, 105, 147, 150, 110–1, 131, 150, 160, 162, 167, 168, 180, 183–5, 199, 201,

203–4, 222, 223, 226, 272, 323, 347

Root, Elihu 156, 184, 202, 203, 223

Root-Takahira Agreement (1908) 180

Ross, Sir Denison 229

Rove, Carl 380

Roxas, Manuel 283

rubber 286, 296

Rubin, Robert 376

Rumsfeld, Donald 390

Rusk, Dean 296, 299

Russell, Charles 202

Russell, Lord John (Earl Russell) 61, 71

Russia 7, 11, 17, 32, 58, 64, 67, 68, 73, 75, 77, 129, 133–4, 135, 150, 177, 178, 179, 186, 187, 200–1, 202, 219, 245, 248, 273, 286, 302, 309–10, 333–4, 335, 345, 386 – *see also* U.S.S.R.

Russian Revolution (1917) 202–4, 222

Russo-Japanese War (1904–5) 179–80, 199

Salazar, A. 221, 279

Salvador 331

Samoa 127, 134, 153, 158, 209

San Domingo 64, 75, 76, 123, 168–9, 170, 173

Sanders, Colonel 63

Santa Anna, President 21

Sarit Thanarat 301

Sarmiento, D.F. 111

Saudi Arabia 250, 313, 368–9, 370

Schenk, General R.C. 126

Schufeldt, Commodore 124

Schurz, Carl 100, 112–3, 118, 119, 150, 163

Schwartz Doctrine 345

Scotland 30, 37, 273

Scott, General W. 26

Scott, Senator Hugh 378

S.E.A.T.O. (South-East Asia Treaty Organization) 280, 296, 305

Selassie, Haile 242

Seminole 36–7, 39–40, 88

September 11 – *see* 9/11

Seven Years War (1756–63) 32

Sevier, John 34

Seward, William H. *xi*, 71, 72, 75, 76, 112

Shaw, George Bernard 185, 204, 220

Shawnee 35, 371

Shelley, Percy Bysshe 62

Sheridan, General P.H. 74

Shiite Muslim 369

Shultz, George 378

Shuster, W.M. 177

Siam 67, 123 – *see also* Thailand

Siberia 203, 265

Sick, Gary 391

Sinclair, Upton 339

Singapore 300

Singh, Maharaja Ranjit 70

Sino-Japanese War (1894–5) 133

Sioux 41, 80–2, 86, 98–9, 101, 343

Sitting Bull 86, 99

slavery 5, 8, 20–1, 24–5, 31–33, 37,
    58–61, 65, 68, 71–2, 77, 80, 83–
    4, 113, 117, 130, 166, 172
  Civil War and 72
  religion and 113
slump (1930s) 233–4
Smith, Adam 4, 16
Smith, Governor 59
Smuts, J.C. 206–7
Smyth, Alexander 62
Social Darwinism 38–9, 85, 109–11,
    112
socialism 109, 110, 119, 147–9, 168,
    182, 201, 234, 244, 272
Socialist Party 148
Soekarno, Doctor 301
Somalia 370
Somoza, General Anastasio 345
Soulé, Pierre 63–4
South Africa 21, 32, 65, 99, 103,
    128, 113, 134–5, 167, 197, 228,
    311, 313, 316–8, 341 – see also
    Boer War
South America – see America, South
Southern States – see United States,
    South
South Carolina 5
Spain 8–9, 17, 20–1, 33, 37, 38, 58,
    63–4, 71–2, 73, 74, 77, 120,
    130, 132, 134, 158, 166, 221,
    279–80
Spanish Civil War (1936–9) 242–3
Spanish Empire 4
Spanish War (1898) 105–15, 130–5,
    153, 166–7

Spellman, Cardinal 114, 279
Spengler, Oswald 104, 110, 208, 215
Spreckels, Claus 118
St Clair, A. 35
St Clair, Jeffrey 386–7
Stahl, Lesley 392
Stalin, Josef 103, 276, 339
Standard Oil 174, 241, 273
Steel Corporation 148
Steffens, Lincoln 222
Steinbeck, John 339
Stevenson, Adlai 389
Stevenson, Robert Louis 57, 65, 76,
    99
Stimson, H. 226, 231, 245, 246
Stockman, David 376
Stone, I.F. 337, 338
Stone, Norman 393
Stowe, Harriet Beecher 107
Straight, William 180
Street, Paul 389
strikes 108, 147, 171, 201, 224, 234,
    240, 324, 377–8, 379
students 378
Strong, Rev. Josiah 111
Sudan 367, 368
Suez Canal 58, 310–1
Sufi 367
sugar 117–8, 131, 132, 160, 161,
    223, 224, 237–8, 239–40, 283,
    323
Sugar Trust 118, 131, 156, 165
Suharto, President 302
Suhrawardy, H.S. 305
Summers, Lawrence 384

Sun Yat-sen 180, 230

Sunni Muslim – *see* Wahhabi Sunni

Syngman Rhee 291–2

Taft, R.A. 275, 277

Taft, W.H. 156, 160, 169, 170, 177, 180–1

Taft-Katsura Agreement (1905) 180

Taiping 68–70

Taiwan 112, 114, 269, 276, 286–7, 291, 295, 306, 345 – *see also* Formosa

Taliban 368, 371, 372

Tariff Bill (1894) 118

Taro Katsura 178–9, 180

Tarzan 211–2

Tecumseh 35, 86, 99

Tennessee 25, 34

Tennessee Company 34

Texas 12, 21–2, 24, 25, 59, 62, 72, 119, 167

Thailand 67, 290, 300–1 – *see also* Siam

Thanom Kittikachorn 301

Third Internatioanl 222, 227–8, 249

Thoreau, H.D. 51

Three Stooges 389

timber 8

tin 286, 296, 348

Timor, East 303

Tirpitz, Admiral 133

Tocqueville, Alexis de 4, 15, 17, 20, 21, 37

torture 330, 332

Toynbee, Arnold 289

Trilling, Lionel 374

Trinidad 220

Trotsky, Leon 203, 219

Truman, President H.S. 269–70, 271, 274–7, 292, 312, 330, 337, 376

Truman Doctrine 275

Tshombe, M.K. 315

Tubman, President W. 314, 317

Tunisia 314

Turkestan 150

Turkey 62, 205, 268, 272, 280, 332

Turner, Admiral S. 344

Turner, F.J. 19

Turner, Jackson 106–7

Twain, Mark 114, 128–9, 177, 210, 213

Twin Towers attack – *see* 9/11

Tyler, President John 21–2, 173

Tyndale-Biscoe, Canon 115

U.A.W. (United Auto Workers) 379

Ugarte, Manuel 171–2

unions 377–9, 385–6

United Fruit Company 165, 171, 225, 320–1

United Kingdom – *see* Britain

United States

Constitution *x–xi*, 19, 24, 61, 112–3, 159–60, 266–7

diplomacy 61, 100, 127–8, 179, 265 – *see also* Dollar Diplomacy

economy *ix–x*, 388

independence 3–5, 16, 32, 339

literature 49–55, 97, 210–5, 234–6, 266, 339

religion and expansionism 15–6, 30–1, 39, 55, 110–1, 130, 185, 209–10, 265–6, 274

South 20, 36, 38, 59–60, 61, 64, 73–6, 80–1, 84, 107, 111, 117, 135, 159, 173, 199, 213, 300

see also Army, U.S.; capitalism; immigration; investments abroad (U.S.); lobby system; Navy, U.S.

U.N.O. (United Nations Organization) 265, 279, 280, 287, 292, 298, 315, 321, 341, 345

Upshur, A.P. 61

Uraguay 321, 326, 345–6

U.S.S.R. (Union of Soviet Socialist Republics) *xi–xii*, 221, 245, 248, 266, 279, 285, 289, 307, 322, 333–4, 345, 346, 366, 370, 372–3 – *see also* Russia

Utah 98

Ute 81

Veblen, Thorstein 65, 106, 147, 165

Venezuela 121–2, 127, 128, 167, 198, 329

Vergennes 17

Verne, Jules 211

Victoria, Queen 73

Vietnam 7, 22, 31, 114, 124, 154, 176, 270, 274, 279, 287, 291, 293, 296–301, 312–3, 321, 334, 337, 340–1, 342, 343, 345, 347, 365, 389, 391

Virgin Islands 168, 173

Virginia 31–2, 34, 59, 130

Voice of America 347

Volcker, Paul 379

Wagner, Richard 4

Wahhabi Sunni 367, 369

Wake Island 132

Wallace, Henry 273

Walpole, Horace 264, 340

War of Independence (1775–83) 4, 6, 32

War of the Pacific (1879) 105, 120, 122, 125–6

Ward, F.T. 70

Ward, J.E. 69

Washington, George 32–3, 62

Washington Consensus 381–3

Watergate 344–5

Weber, Max 278

Webster, Daniel 19, 22, 62

Wedemeyer, General A.C. 269

Weinbaum, S.G. 235

Welles, Sumner 240, 243, 251, 291, 319

Wells, H.G. 16, 204, 211, 221

West Indies 5, 6, 17, 18, 57, 60, 150, 228

Westmoreland, General 287

whaling 65

wheat 107

Whipple, Bishop H.B. 82

Whitman, Walt 49, 54–5, 74, 86
Wickliffe, Robert 62
Wild West myth 97–9, 210–1, 337
Wilhelmina, Queen 250
Wilkie, Wendell 245, 265
Will, George 373
Williams, W.A. 336
Wilson, Charlie 367
Wilson, President Woodrow *xi–xii*, 16, 21, 39, 109, 122, 172–5, 181, 186, 199–209, 225, 228, 230, 280, 347
Winslow, J. 29
Wisconsin 39
Wolf, Martin 383
Wolfowitz, Paul 385
women 378
Wordsworth, William *vii*, 344
World Bank 288, 383
World Trade Center attack – *see* 9/11

World War I (1914–8) *xi*, 182–3, 199, 200–1, 222
World War II (1939–45) 72, 244–51, 271, 326, 384
Worsthorne, Peregrine 375
Wounded Knee Creek 99–100, 342
Wright, L.E. 132
W.T.O. (World Trade Organization) 381, 383

Yalta conference (1945) 283
Young, Andrew 345
Young, J.R. 124
Yüan Shih-k'ai 180, 230

Zahedi, General 309
Zaire 315, 317 – *see also* Congo
Zayas, Presodent 224
Zimbabwe 365
Zinni, Anthony 393
Zionism 311–3, 319